Authors
& Artists
for Young
Adults

ISSN 1040-5682

Authors & Artists for Young Adults

VOLUME 80

GALE
CENGAGE Learning™

Detroit • New York • San Francisco • New Haven, Conn • Waterville, Maine • London

Authors and Artists for Young Adults, Volume 80

Project Editor: Dana Ferguson

Editorial: Amy Elisabeth Fuller, Michelle Kazensky, Lisa Kumar, Mary Ruby

Permissions: Aja Perales, Kelly Quin, Robyn Young

Imaging and Multimedia: John Watkins

Composition and Electronic Capture: Amy Darga

Manufacturing: Rita Wimberley

Product Manager: Meggin Condino

Gale
27500 Drake Rd.
Farmington Hills, MI, 48331-3535

LIBRARY OF CONGRESS CATALOG CARD NUMBER 89-641100

ISBN-13: 978-0-7876-7799-2
ISBN-10: 0-7876-7799-X

ISSN 1040-5682

Printed in the United States of America
1 2 3 4 5 6 7 13 12 11 10 09

Contents

Introduction vii

AAYA Advisory Board ix

Chimamanda Ngozi Adichie 1
Nigerian writer who received the prestigious
Orange Broadband Prize for Fiction for her
second novel, *Half of a Yellow Sun.*

Gutzon Borglum 7
This sculptor and engineer spent more than a
decade designing and carving the Mount
Rushmore National Memorial in South Dakota.

Colin Dexter 15
Award-winning creator of the best-selling
"Inspector Morse" series of crime novels.

Ted Elliott 21
Screenwriter and producer whose credits include
the wildly popular animated films *Aladdin* and
Shrek, as well as the "Pirates of the Caribbean"
trilogy.

Richard Estes 29
Regarded as one of the founders of the
photo-realist movement of the late 1960s, this
American artist frequently depicts urban scenes
in his paintings.

Terence Fisher 37
British director best known for the lurid horror
films he created at Hammer Studios, including
*The Curse of Frankenstein, Dracula: Prince of
Darkness,* and *The Two Faces of Dr. Jekyll.*

Jeff Foxworthy 45
This comedian has parlayed his
southern-flavored routines into a lucrative career
that includes platinum-selling albums,
bestselling books, and numerous appearances on
television series and specials.

Elizabeth Gaskell 53
Nineteenth-century British author who examined
social change in such works as *Cranford* and
North and South.

Elizabeth George 61
American writer best known for her mystery
novels, including *A Great Deliverance* and *In the
Presence of the Enemy,* which star a team of
Scotland Yard sleuths.

Mel Gibson 69
One of the world's most popular movie stars,
this actor and director has appeared in such
well-known films as *Mad Max beyond
Thunderdome, Lethal Weapon,* and *Braveheart.*

Tyree Guyton 79
African-American painter and sculptor who
created the *Heidelberg Project,* a work of urban
environmental art in Detroit, Michigan.

Ellen Hopkins 87
Acclaimed young adult novelist who tackles
difficult subject matter in such titles as *Crank,
Burned,* and *Tricked.*

Robert E. Howard 93
Prominent and prolific writer of
sword-and-sorcery fiction who is widely known
as the creator of the heroic barbarian character
Conan.

Philip Johnson 101
American architect whose designs earned him a
major place in the history of the
twentieth-century modernist and postmodernist
movements.

Gwyneth A. Jones 111
Often writing as Ann Halam, this British
novelist garnered the James Tiptree, Jr. Award,
among other honors, for her critically acclaimed
fantasy fiction.

Elizabeth Knox 117
In works like *Dreamhunter* and *Dreamquake*, this
New Zealand writer incorporates elements of
mystery and the supernatural.

Jaclyn Moriarty 123
Australian author who writes humorous and
often poignant books for young adults,
including *Feeling Sorry for Celia* and *The Murder
of Bindy Mackenzie*.

Naomi Novik 129
Former computer game designer whose
"Temeraire" series of fantasy tales has been
widely praised by critics and readers.

David Poyer 133
Creator of the acclaimed "Tales of the Modern
Navy" series of thrillers, as well as the works of
historical fiction in the "Civil War at Sea" series.

Rick Riordan 141
Edgar Allan Poe Award-winning author of *The
Widower's Two-step* and other works in the "Tres
Navarre" mystery series.

Jennifer Roberson 149
Fantasy writer noted for her strong female
characters in both the "Cheysuli" series and
"Sword-Dancer" books.

Sax Rohmer 155
This profilic English author wrote numerous
short stories and novels featuring the clever and
manical Dr. Fu Manchu, a Chinese
super-criminal.

Elaine Viets 165
Novelist, journalist, and columnist best known
as the author of the "Dead-End Job" mystery
series.

Lynd Ward 171
Winner of the Caldecott Medal, this celebrated
artist and author was the first person to create
an entire adult novel solely from woodcuts.

Scott Westerfeld 181
Science fiction novelist who explores a dystopian
future in works like *Uglies* and *Specials.*

Author/Artist Index 189

Introduction

Authors and Artists for Young Adults is a reference series designed to serve the needs of middle school, junior high, and high school students interested in creative artists. Originally inspired by the need to bridge the gap between Gale's *Something about the Author,* created for children, and *Contemporary Authors,* intended for older students and adults, *Authors and Artists for Young Adults* has been expanded to cover not only an international scope of authors, but also a wide variety of other artists.

Although the emphasis of the series remains on the writer for young adults, we recognize that these readers have diverse interests covering a wide range of reading levels. The series therefore contains not only those creative artists who are of high interest to young adults, including cartoonists, graphic naovelists, photographers, music composers, bestselling authors of adult novels, media directors, producers, and performers, but also literary and artistic figures studied in academic curricula, such as influential novelists, playwrights, poets, and painters. The goal of *Authors and Artists for Young Adults* is to present this great diversity of creative artists in a format that is entertaining, informative, and understandable to the young adult reader.

Entry Format

Each volume of *Authors and Artists for Young Adults* will furnish in-depth coverage of approximately twenty-five authors and artists. The typical entry consists of:

—A detailed biographical section that includes date of birth, marriage, children, education, and addresses.

—A comprehensive bibliography or filmography including publishers, producers, and years.

—Adaptations into other media forms.

—Works in progress.

—A distinctive essay featuring comments on an artist's life, career, artistic intentions, world views, and controversies.

—References for further reading.

—Extensive illustrations, photographs, movie stills, cartoons, book covers, and other relevant visual material.

A cumulative index to featured authors and artists appears in each volume.

Compilation Methods

The editors of *Authors and Artists for Young Adults* make every effort to secure information directly from the authors and artists through personal correspondence and interviews. Sketches on living to roll easily off the tongue of English speakers, but Gorglum's accomplishments were, quite literally, huge. He is primarily known for the collection for four immense presidents' heads at the Mount Rushmore National Memorial in South Dakota. Borglum and his crew of over four hundred labored on these sixty-foot carvings between 1927 and 1941, blasting them out of the granite with dynamite and then chiseling the features with jackhammers. The presidents there depicted—George Washington, Thomas Jefferson, Abraham Lincoln, and Theodore Roosevelt—were all chosen by Borglum personally to represent the formation and expansion of the nation.

In his day, Borglum maintained a high profile as an artist and a one-man public relations bureau for his art, raising money from many sources, and always providing the newspapers with good copy because of his strong and strongly worded opinions on everything from art to race. Borglum also produced a number of smaller sculptures and statues in the United States and Europe, and he warmed up for the Mount Rushmore project on a memorial to Confederate heroes at Stone Mountain, Georgia, a work that was never realized and ended in a series of contentious litigations from both sponsors and artist. However, it is Mount Rushmore with which Borglum's name is inextricably linked. Opinions on that mammoth piece of artwork cum nationalistic propaganda vary. "If you hang around Rushmore a few days and keep looking, as you can't help doing, your mind . . . eventually falls prey to irreverent musings," wrote Donald Dale Jackson in a *Smithsonian* profile of the artist and his major work. "Isn't this whole thing a little well, preposterous?" continued Jackson. "Is the word 'bizarre' too much here? We're talking about a 14-year project to hack four 60-foot-high heads out of a wilderness mountain 174 miles from everywhere." Jackson went on to remark: "Is this American hyperbole in stone? Yes. The exemplification of excess? Yes, again. Definition: Rushmoritis, n. a condition of inherent outrageousness." Indeed, outrageousness might very well be the best description of Borglum himself and his career.

A Peripatetic Youth

Born on March 25, 1867, John Gutzon de la Mothe Borglum was the first child of James de la Mothe Borglum and wife Cristine, Danish immigrants who were also Mormon converts. Borlglum was born in the village of St. Charles in the county of Bear Lake in what was then the Idaho Territory. James Borglum worked as a woodcarver in his native Denmark, and he had also come close to completing his

medical studies before immigrating to the United States in the 1860s. The family moved from the Idaho Territory shortly after the birth of Gutzon, living in Ogden, Utah, where a second son, Solon Hannibal, was born in 1868. As Mormons, the Borglums practiced polygamy; James was also married to Cristine's older sister Ida. When James left the Mormon faith in 1873, he lost Cristine, but Ida stayed with him and the couple had seven more children, three girls and four boys. However, for the five-year-old Gutzon this was a turning point. Borglum biographers Howard Shaff and Audrey Karl Shaff contended in their *Six Wars at a Time: The Life of Gutzon Borglum, Sculptor of Mount Rushmore* that the loss of his biological mother turned the young Borglum into a quarrelsome and rebellious personality, a way of being that stuck with him for the rest of his life. Meanwhile, by 1874 he and his evergrowing family had moved to St. Louis, Missouri, where father James completed his medical education and thereafter set up practice as a physician in Omaha, Nebraska.

Because his father had converted to Catholicism by the time Borglum completed primary school, the boy attended St. Mary's Academy, a Catholic boarding school in Kansas, to gain a high school education. At St. Mary's Borglum first demonstrated a knack for drawing and painting. Inspired by his teachers, who steered his art toward religious themes, as well as by a fellow student, the young Borglum determined to become an artist. Upon his graduation, his family once again moved, this time to Los Angeles, California, and he accompanied them. There he worked for a time as a lithographer and engraver, then left for San Francisco, where he enrolled in the San Francisco School of Design (now the San Francisco Art Institute). There Borglum worked under the direction of landscape painter Virgil Macey Williams and was also influenced by another landscape painter, William Keith. These early influences instilled in the student a passion for dramatic motifs and for romanticism in painting.

As a young painter making his way in northern California, Borglum had the good fortune to associate with Jessie Benton Frémont, wife of the famous explorer General John C. Frémont, whose portrait he painted in 1888. The following year he married divorced art teacher Elizabeth Putnam, a woman almost two decades his senior. The couple decided to visit France, where Borglum could pursue further studies. Once again, Mrs. Frémont came to his aid, organizing an exhibition of his paintings. The profits from this show helped to fund Borglum's subsequent travels.

Gutzon Borglum in his studio, next to his sculpture "Statue of Aviator." (Photograph courtesy of the Library of Congress.)

The Making of an Artist

Borglum and his wife settled in Paris, and he studied for a time at the Académie Julian as well as at the École des Beaux-Arts. One of those who influenced him to become a sculptor was Auguste Rodin, with whom Borglum became friends during his Paris sojourn. He exhibited a painting in the 1901 Paris Salon, and also had a bronze sculpture accepted for the New Salon. From France, Borglum and his wife traveled to Spain, again relying on the assistance of Mrs. Frémont for introductions. Here he sketched and also researched the early missions that were established back in his home state of California.

Returning to California in 1893, Borglum became part of an effort to preserve the old missions while opposing attempts at restoration. He spent three years in the state, working with his brother Solon, who had also become a sculptor. Relations with his wife were becoming strained however: the age difference was taking its toll, as was Borglum's somewhat lavish lifestyle, which was supported by debt. In 1896, Borglum again left the United States

Borglum's vision of the Newark, New Jersey, War Memorial resulted in a sculpture and reflecting pond.
(Photograph © Bettmann/Corbis.)

and settled for the next five years in England, holding exhibitions at Buckingham Palace and becoming a member of the Royal Society of British Artists. He earned an income of sorts from portraits and busts of children, ultimately gaining critical notice for his murals installed at a hotel in Leeds, England. During this time he and his wife lived increasingly apart.

By the time of his return to the United States in 1901, Borglum had almost completely shifted from painting to sculpture. Once again, luck played a part in his career; big money was available in the country at the turn of the twentieth century, and this big money went in search of big, ostentatious artwork. Borglum's sculpture fit that bill. He set up a studio in New York City, and won acclaim for his 1904 installation for the St. Louis Exposition, "Mares of Diomedes." This was a group of seven racing horses, the foremost of which was ridden by a Native American. Winning a gold medal, the multipiece sculpture was purchased for New York's Metropolitan Museum. This success led to a commission to sculpt the Twelve Apostles for the city's Cathedral of St. John the Divine. Borglum increasingly established himself as an important sculptor for public places, fashioning a large head of Abraham Lincoln for the Capitol in Washington, DC, as well as an equestrian statue of General Philip Sheridan for that same city in 1908.

That same year Borglum finally divorced his first wife, and the following year he married Mary William Montgomery, a woman ten years younger than him whom he had met shortly after returning from England. With his success, he was able to buy a country estate near Stamford, Connecticut, and there the couple raised two children, James Lincoln and Mary Ellis. As an artist of note, Borglum had now "arrived." However, although he made a decent living, his extravagant lifestyle kept him and his family in financial arrears. At the time of his death in 1941, Borglum was $200,000 in debt.

The Stone Mountain Controversy and Mount Rushmore

In 1915 Borglum was approached by a group of Southerners to carve a large head of Confederate General Robert E. Lee to sit at the bottom of a large granite dome near Atlanta, Georgia. The site, called Stone Mountain, appealed to the sculptor, and soon he was proposing a much-more-ambitious project. Borglum conceived of a column of Confederate soldiers a quarter of a mile in length winding across the face of Stone Mountain. At the head of the enormous grouping would be Lee, along with Stonewall Jackson and Jefferson Davis, two other famed Confederates. Work commenced in 1916, but World War I intervened. During his tenure at Stone Mountain, Borglum became connected with members of the Ku Klux Klan who were part of the group helping to finance the sculptures. He not only became a member of the Klan (a fact not revealed until the 1990s in a *New Republic* article), but he also became a cabinet member for the racist organization.

It was not until 1924 that the first part of the stone composition was unveiled: a twenty-foot head of Lee. This sculpture was scarcely displayed before rancor broke out between the parties involved, and Borglum's autocratic, irascible nature was considered largely to blame. The sponsors of the project accused him of misusing funds and of dedicating insufficient time to the work. Indeed, the sculptor was involved in other projects at the time, including the forty-three figures and two horses comprising the Wars of the Americas Memorial in Newark, New Jersey. Never one to shrink from a fight, however, Borglum accused the committee in charge of Stone Mountain of mismanagement and interference. Dismissed from the project, he destroyed all the models so that his successor would not have access to his design. For years the arguments and lawsuits continued. Eventually Borglum's image of Lee was dynamited to make room for newer plans.

Whatever else the result of the Stone Mountain controversy, it did establish Borglum's name as a sculptor on a monumental scale. Thus, when the official historian of South Dakota, Doane Robinson, envisioned a gigantic memorial carved in the side of a mountain, Borglum's name topped the list of potential artists. Robinson had in mind a series of large statues of memorable men and women of the West that might attract tourists; Borglum immediately proposed an alternative: a monument to the nation itself, as exemplified by some of its finest presidents. He first proposed Washington and Lincoln for their name appeal, and the ever-effervescent sculptor eventually managed to persuade U.S. President Calvin Coolidge to come to Mount Rushmore—the site Borglum had personally selected—to win official approval of the plan and also to win federal funding for the project. Coolidge insisted on having four faces: in addition to Washington, there were to be the visages of two Republicans and one Democrat. Thus were added Jefferson and Roosevelt, the latter a personal acquaintance of Borglum's.

Construction began on Mount Rushmore on October 4, 1927, and continued for fourteen more years. Borglum oversaw much of the drilling of holes for

Borglum working on a model of the Mount Rushmore Memorial in his studio, c. 1930. (Photograph courtesy of Underwood & Underwood/Corbis.)

dynamite himself: he would blast out the first bits of granite with dynamite, and then send his crews in with pneumatic drills and chisels to do the finer facial features. Each of the sixty-foot busts was created after models Borglum fashioned in his studio at Mount Rushmore. Originally these figures in rock were meant to extend from head to waist, but as funding dried up during the Great Depression, economies had to be made in the overall plan.

Mount Rushmore was put under the jurisdiction of the National Park Service in 1933, after which Borglum remained continually at odds with Park Service engineers and officials, despising to be under anyone's control. Employing a crew of 400, he supervised the intricate work, a mixture of art and engineering. On July 4, 1934, Washington's face was unveiled and dedicated. Jefferson came next, in 1936, followed by Lincoln in 1937 and Roosevelt in 1939. Each of these unveilings was the occasion for a gala public celebration, as Borglum attempted to keep the project in the public eye and keep funding flowing. Other heads were considered, among them that of President Woodrow Wilson and of the proponent of women's rights and women's suffrage, Susan B. Anthony. However, nothing came of these other possible additions to the site.

Borglum, a vital sixty years of age at the outset of the Mount Rushmore project, did not live to see his memorial completed. In March of 1941 he took time off from his work to travel to Chicago for a minor operation, and during the course of the surgery he died of a coronary embolism. His death came only days before his seventy-fourth birthday. The final touches on the Mount Rushmore Memorial were

Borglum and son work on Jefferson's head from a wooden basket in this 1935 photograph of the construction of the Mount Rushmore memorial. (Photograph © Underwood and Underwood/Corbis.)

added by his son, Lincoln Borglum, and work officially came to an end on October 31, 1941 at a cost of about one million dollars (supplied by federal funds and private donations) and with no loss of life in the fourteen years of work.

Borglum's Legacy

"Rushmore holds a fierce, unbudgeable grip on our national imagination," wrote Jackson. "Rushmore is immovability, overstatement, the symbol of symbols, icon of icons." Yet even during its construction, Mount Rushmore had its critics, from those who descried its spoliation of nature to those who parodied its kitsch quality. Native Americans also raised a legitimate complaint: Mount Rushmore was originally know to the Lakota Sioux as Six Grandfathers, and was given to them, along with the rest of the Black Hills, by treaty in 1868. However, after the Great Sioux War of 1876-77, the United States once again claimed this territory, which was held sacred by the Lakota. In 1971 the monument was occupied by members of the American Indian Movement (AIM) and renamed Mount Crazy Horse. A monument honoring that Native American hero was commemorated in 1998, the work of Korczak Ziolkowski, who had briefly worked for Borglum at Mount Rushmore. Once Borglum's Ku Klux Klan past was made public in the 1990s, there was also a spate of criticism about the hypocrisy of this monument to democracy having been created by an avowed racist and anti-Semite. Yet the monument lives on. In 1991, President George H.W. Bush officially dedicated Mount Rushmore, a half century after its completion.

Regarding Borglum's reputation as an artist, most agree that he was competent as a painter and sculptor, but was not an artist of greatness. However, his unique ability to blend technical engineering know-how with sculpture to create monumental and immense figures in stone guarantees him a place in the annals of art history. Borglum's roughrider spirit in attacking life, participating in non-art matters from the early years of aircraft production to prize fighting, and his signature short stature and pugnacious attitude all combine to make him a fascinating

The completed Mount Rushmore Memorial, as it now appears. (Photograph © J.P. Laffont/Sygma/Corbis.)

Thus quick-tempered Morse is balanced by his assistant, Detective Sergeant Lewis. Cushing Strout, writing in the *Armchair Detective*, compared the relationship between the two to that of Arthur Conan Doyle's Sherlock Holmes and John Watson, calling Dexter's work "the best contemporary English example of adapting and updating Doyle's technique." Strout further noted that, like Holmes, "Morse is a bachelor, [but] in spite of his generally cynical expectations about human nature and the world, unlike Holmes he is always romantically vulnerable (in spite of disappointing experience) to being smitten by love at first sight for some attractive and intelligent, but quite inappropriate woman." Where Morse is contemplative and full of literary and musical allusions, Lewis is down to earth, practical, and solidly working class. And he is usually stuck with the tab at the pubs the duo frequent.

A Series in Full Flower

"Morse's uniqueness as a fictional detective lies in the influence of his particular temperament not only on the tone of the fiction but on each individual case he undertakes, putting the stamp of his personality on each venture," wrote Benstock. This uniqueness continues throughout the series. *The Riddle of the Third Mile* finds Morse investigating a dismemberment death. The body may be that of an elderly Oxford don, and Morse's investigations take him into the labyrinthine world of academia and the sex dens of London's Soho district. With the 1986 addition to the series, *The Secret of Annexe 3*, Morse is awakened much too early on New Year's Day to investigate the death of a reveler in a local hotel. The following year saw the first episode of the television adaptation of the "Morse" books, with the inspector played by British actor John Thaw. Over the next thirteen years, thirty-three of these episode were broadcast, making Morse a household name not only in his native England, but also to viewers of the PBS network in the United States.

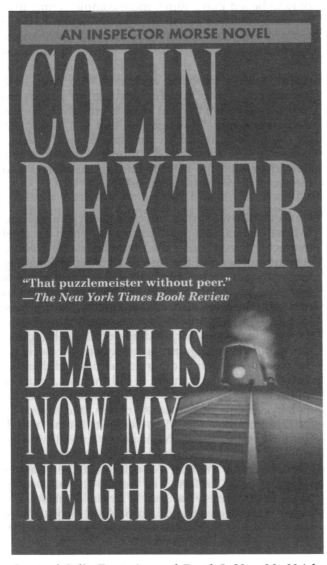

Cover of Colin Dexter's novel *Death Is Now My Neighbor,* **a popular "Inspector Morse" mystery published in 1996.** (Copyright © 1998 by Ivy Books. Used by permission of Ivy Books, a division of Random House, Inc.)

Dexter won a Gold Dagger award for his 1989 work, *The Wench Is Dead*. A complete change of pace from the usual "Morse" novels, this one has Morse hospitalized with a bleeding ulcer. Bored almost to death, he decides to save his sanity by reopening a Victorian murder case that took place in Oxford and employs the hapless Lewis to do the legwork for him. Morse's wits and temper, wrote Marilyn Stasio in the *New York Times Book Review*, "tug the reader into the detective's hospital bed to share his single-minded pursuit of the truth." For *Publishers Weekly* reviewer Sybil Steinberg, *The Wench Is Dead* is a "jolly good read that juxtaposes past and present Oxford with imagination and finesse." In his 1991 series installment, *The Jewel That Was Ours*, Dexter adapted a story idea he had for an episode of the televised *Inspector Morse*. The mystery here surrounds the death of an American tour group member in Oxford and the theft of her rare gem, the Wolvercote Jewel.

More tourists in England figure in *The Way through the Woods*. Here Morse is investigating the disappearance of Karin Eriksson, a Swedish tourist. However, with no body, there is no case; not, that is, until a year later when an anonymous letter reawakens Morse's interest. A *Publishers Weekly* reviewer praised this novel as a "stunning work." Reviewing the same novel for *Entertainment Weekly,*

Dexter contributed to television's *Inspector Morse* series, starring John Thaw and Kevin Whatley. (Photograph courtesy of Carlton UK Productions/Kobal Collection/The Picture Desk, Inc.)

Gene Lyons similarly commented, "Together with his creator, Colin Dexter, [Morse] is rescuing the British mystery from terminal gentility."

Morse's Finale

In a review of the 1994 novel, *The Daughters of Cain,* for the *New York Times Book Review,* Stasio advised readers "to get out their pencils, timetables and aspirin." Indeed, Morse has his hands full in investigating the double deaths of an Oxford don and of the prime suspect in that killing, a former employee of the college, who is later found stabbed to death. *Booklist* contributor Emily Melton termed this "another top-notch read from an outstanding author." For Elizabeth M. Cosin, writing for *Insight on the News, The Daughters of Cain* is "a thick, cerebral story chock-full of literary references and clever red herrings."

If you enjoy the works of Colin Dexter, you may also want to check out the following books:

The mystery novels of Peter Lovesey, including *Diamond Dust,* 2002.
Elizabeth George's *What Came before He Shot Her,* 2006.
Reginald Hill's "Dalziel/Pascoe" series of crime novels, including *The Last National Serviceman,* 2007.

Death Is Now My Neighbor presents more nasty doings at one of Oxford's colleges: the retirement of the head of Lonsdale College sets off a fight for that top position that ultimately leads to murder and mayhem. Morse and Lewis find themselves on the trail of these murders in the least suspected places. In the course of the action, Morse also discovers that he has diabetes. A *Publishers Weekly* contributor noted of this series addition: "A treat for buffs, this is also a good introduction for newcomers to an addictive detective."

Dexter brought the "Inspector Morse" series to a conclusion in 1999 with *The Remorseful Day: The Final Inspector Morse Novel.* As in earlier tales, Morse is called in to re-investigate the two-year-old murder of a local nurse. The plot is complicated by the fact that the victim was a woman with whom he was once romantically involved. During the investigations, Morse's health deteriorates, for though diagnosed with diabetes, he refuses to moderate his love of beer and scotch. "This finale to a grand series," noted a reviewer for *Publishers Weekly,* "presents a moving elegy to one of mystery fiction's most celebrated and popular characters." Similar praise came from *Booklist* contributor Bill Ott, who described it as "an audaciously clever and surprisingly moving finale." Likewise, *New York Times Book Review* writer Stasio dubbed *The Remorseful Day* an "impeccably plotted finale."

Dexter, who himself was diagnosed with diabetes, was frank about the demise of the "Morse" series and, indeed, of Morse himself. As reported in a *Writer* article, he noted of his fictional protagonist, "He is diabetic and drinks too much. So it is no wonder he keels over." However, if Dexter could put on a brave face, his fans could not. *The Remorseful Day* marked the passing of one of the "classics of the mystery genre," as Melton termed the "Inspector Morse" novels.

■ Biographical and Critical Sources

BOOKS

Contemporary Popular Writers, St. James Press (Detroit, MI), 1997.

Dictionary of Literary Biography, Volume 87: *British Mystery and Thriller Writers since 1940, First Series*, Gale (Detroit, MI), 1989.

St. James Guide to Crime and Mystery Writers, 4th edition, St. James Press (Detroit, MI), 1996.

PERIODICALS

Armchair Detective, summer, 1993, review of *The Jewel That Was Ours*, p. 45; summer, 1995, review of *The Daughters of Cain*, p. 342; fall, 1995, Cushing Strout, "In the Footsteps of Peculiar Companions from Doyle to Dexter," pp. 434-437.

Booklist, December 15, 1993, Karen Harris, review of *The Way through the Woods*, p. 772; March 1, 1995, Emily Melton, review of *The Daughters of Cain*, p. 1139; October 1, 1995, Emily Melton, review of *Morse's Greatest Mystery and Other Stories*, p. 212; December 1, 1996, Bill Ott, review of *Death Is Now My Neighbor*, p. 619; April 15, 1999, Bill Ott and Brad Hooper, review of *The Daughters of Cain*, p. 1458; December 1, 1999, Bill Ott, review of *The Remorseful Day: The Final Inspector Morse Novel*, p. 660.

Books, November, 1994, review of *The Daughters of Cain*, p. 16.

Entertainment Weekly, May 1, 1992, Josh Rubins, review of *The Jewel That Was Ours*, p. 48; April 23, 1993, Gene Lyons, review of *The Way through the Woods*, p. 50; April 4, 1997, Nikki Amdur, review of *Death Is Now My Neighbor*, p. 79; December 12, 1997, Tom De Haven, review of *The Way through the Wood*, p. 78.

Insight on the News, May 22, 1995, Elizabeth M. Cosin, review of *Daughters of Cain*, p. 25.

Kirkus Reviews, March 1, 1995, review of *The Daughters of Cain*, p. 270.

Library Journal, February 1, 2000, Fred M. Gervat, review of *The Remorseful Day*, p. 121.

Los Angeles Times Book Review, April 9, 1995, review of *The Daughters of Cain*, p. 12.

New Statesman, September 20, 1996, Boyd Tonkin, review of *Death Is Now My Neighbour*, p. 45; October 25, 1999, Michael Leapman, "Clotted Heart" and review of *The Remorseful Day*, p. 54; November 20, 2000, Andrew Billen, "Requiem for a Cop," p. 47.

New York Times Book Review, May 20, 1990, Marilyn Stasio, review of *The Wench Is Dead*; April 16, 1995, Marilyn Stasio, review of *The Daughters of Cain*, p. 29; March 2, 1997, Marilyn Stasio, review of *Death Is Now My Neighbor*, p. 20; February 20, 2000, Marilyn Stasio, review of *The Remorseful Day*, p. 28.

People, May 8, 1995, Cynthia Sanz, review of *The Daughters of Cain*, p. 46.

Publishers Weekly, March 23, 1990, review of *The Wench Is Dead*, p. 68; April 13, 1990, Rosemary Herbert, "Aiming Higher," p. 30; March 8, 1993, review of *The Way through the Woods*, p. 71; March 13, 1995, review of *The Daughters of Cain*, p. 63; October 9, 1995, review of *Morse's Greatest Mystery and Other Stories*, p. 79; December 30, 1996, review of *Death Is Now My Neighbor*, p. 57; January 24, 2000, review of *The Remorseful Day*, p. 296.

Rapport, August-September, 1992, Steven Rosen, review of *The Jewel That Was Ours*, p. 38.

Time, April 26, 1993, William A. Henry III, review of *The Way through the Woods*, p. 65.

Times Literary Supplement, December 23, 1994, review of *The Daughters of Cain*, p. 21.

Virginia Quarterly Review, autumn, 1992, review of *The Jewel That Was Ours*, p. 131.

Wall Street Journal, April 27, 1995, review of *The Daughters of Cain*, p. A12; March 28, 1997, review of *Death Is Now My Neighbor*, p. A14.

Writer, March, 2001, "@Deadline," p. 12.

ONLINE

BBC Lincolnshire Web site, http://www.bbc.co.uk/ (December 27, 2008), "Famous Yellowbelly—Colin Dexter."

Museum of Broadcast Communications Web site, http://www.museum.tv/ (December 27, 2008), Charlotte Brunsdon, "Inspector Morse."

Public Broadcasting Service Web site, http://www.pbs.org/ (December 27, 2008), Ron Miller, "Finding the Perfect Exit for a Great Detective."

Times Online (London, England), http://entertainment.timesonline.co.uk/ (April 17, 2008), "The 50 Greatest Crime Writers, No 47: Colin Dexter."*

Ted Elliott

(Photograph by Vince Bucci/Getty Images.)

■ Personal

Born 1961.

■ Addresses

Home—Los Angeles, CA. *Agent*—Brian Siberell, Creative Artists Agency, 9830 Wilshire Blvd., Beverly Hills, CA 90212-1825.

■ Career

Screenwriter and producer. Owner (with Terry Rossio) of Scheherazade Productions, Los Angeles, CA. Producer of films, including *Shrek*, DreamWorks, 2001, and *Deja Vu*, Touchstone, 2006. Creative consultant for films, including *Antz*, DreamWorks, 1998, *Sinbad: Legend of the Seven Seas*, DreamWorks, 2003, and *Shrek 2*, DreamWorks, 2004. Appeared as himself in *Epic at Sea: The Making of "Pirates of the Caribbean: The Curse of the Black Pearl,"* 2003. formerly spell-checked movie reviews for News America

Syndicate/Roger Ebert; cofounder (with Craig Mazin) of online screenwriting site *The Artful Writer*; cofounder (with Rossio) of online screenwriting site *Wordplay*.

■ Member

Writers Guild of America (member, board of directors, 2004-06).

■ Awards, Honors

Annie Award for Outstanding Individual Achievement for Writing in an Animated Feature Production, 2001, and Academy Award nomination, and British Academy of Film and Television Arts Award for Best Writing for Screenplay Based on Material Previously Produced or Published, both 2002, all for *Shrek*; People's Choice Award for Favorite Motion Picture, 2003, for *Pirates of the Caribbean: The Curse of the Black Pearl*.

■ Writings

SCREENPLAYS; WITH TERRY ROSSIO

Little Monsters, United Artists, 1989.

(With John Musker and Ron Clements) *Aladdin* (animated), Buena Vista, 1992.

(With David Goyer) *The Puppet Masters* (also known as *Robert Heinlein's The Puppet Masters*), Buena Vista, 1994.

(Uncredited) *Men in Black,* Columbia Pictures, 1997.

(With Gavin Scott and Adam Rifkin) *Small Soldiers,* DreamWorks, 1998.

(Author of story, with Dean Devlin and Roland Emmerich) *Godzilla,* TriStar, 1998.

(With John Eskow; and author of story with Randall Jahnson) *The Mask of Zorro,* TriStar, 1998.

The Road to El Dorado (animated), DreamWorks, 2000.

(With Joe Stillman and Roger Schulman; and coproducer) *Shrek* (based on the children's book by William Steig), DreamWorks, 2001.

(Author of animation story, with Ron Clements and John Musker) *Treasure Planet* (based on the novel *Treasure Island,* by Robert Louis Stevenson), Disney, 2002.

(Author of story, with Stuart Beattie and Jay Wolpert) *Pirates of the Caribbean: The Curse of the Black Pearl,* Disney, 2003.

(Uncredited) *National Treasure,* Disney, 2004.

(Author of story, with Roberto Orci and Alex Kurtzman) *The Legend of Zorro,* Sony Pictures, 2005.

Pirates of the Caribbean: Dead Man's Chest, 2006.

Pirates of the Caribbean: At World's End, Disney, 2007.

(Author of story, with others) *National Treasure: Book of Secrets,* Disney, 2007.

(Uncredited) *The Spiderwick Chronicles* (based on the novel by Holly Black and Tony DiTerlizzi), Paramount, 2008.

(With Marianne Wibberley, Cormac Wibberley, and Tim Firth) *G-Force,* Disney, 2009.

Also screenwriter of short films *Diary of a Producer,* 2003, and *Spirit of the Ride,* 2003.

■ Adaptations

The Mask of Zorro was novelized by Frank Lauria and published by Pocket Books in 1998; *The Legend of Zorro* was novelized by Scott Ciencin and published by HarperEntertainment in 2005. The "Pirates of the Caribbean" series has also been adapted into several story books.

■ Sidelights

Ted Elliott is a hugely successful screenwriter and producer who shares credit with his longtime collaborator, Terry Rossio. The fifteen films they have written together, sometimes with other writers, have earned over two billion dollars in U.S. box-office receipts alone. Three times their films have been ranked number one at the box office worldwide: in 1992, with *Aladdin;* in 2006, with *Pirates of the Caribbean: Dead Man's Chest;* and in 2007, with *Pirates of the Caribbean: At World's End.* Elliott and Rossio have also contributed to screenplays for the hit films *Godzilla, The Mask of Zorro, Shrek, National Treasure: Book of Secrets,* and *Pirates of the Caribbean: The Curse of the Black Pearl,* the last the film that transformed a Disney theme-park ride into a wildly popular film franchise.

The two writers grew up in California and first met in the mid-1970s at Saddleback High School in Santa Ana. Elliott and Rossio were both writers for their high-school paper, the *Saddleback Roadrunner,* and they shared an interest in movies. It was only later that they began collaborating in earnest; as Elliott explained on their Wordplay Web site, "There were a number of reasons. Fear was one. Neither of us really had the slightest idea what we were doing, but we thought—hoped—prayed—that the other guy did. The writing partner as security blanket." At first, they worked other jobs while meeting in coffee shops and passing a writing pad back and forth. They took one of Rossio's unpublished stories, about a boy who discovers that the monsters under his bed are real, and turned it into an original screenplay. It took several years to sell the project, but it was finally made into the film *Little Monsters* in 1989. "Neither of us much like the finished film," Rossio told M.J. Simpson on the *M.J. Simpson Web site.* "A common occurrence for us—people buy the script and throw it out, and what they replace it with is obviously not as good."

Classic Tale Becomes Smashing Success

Despite this disappointment with their first screenplay, Elliott and Rossio considered their career prospects good. They were on contract to Disney Studios, whose animation division was working on a film based on the classic tales of the *Arabian Nights.* "We heard about the project on a Monday, met to pitch our approach on a Wednesday, and were working on Thursday," they recalled to Simpson. "Robin Williams was already cast when we were hired, so we knew the voice and style of acting that needed to be written." Elliott and Rossio collaborated with directors John Musker and Ron Clements throughout the creation of *Aladdin,* which debuted in 1992. The script features Aladdin as a street urchin who can only win the hand of Princess Jasmine by becoming a prince. After he finds a magic lamp with a genie (voiced by comic Williams), he has the ability to make his wishes come

Ted Elliott's film-writing credits include *The Mask of Zorro*, starring Antonio Banderas in the title role. (Photograph courtesy of TriStar/Amblin/Kobal Collection/Torres, Rico/The Picture Desk, Inc.)

true. Later, he thwart the evil plans of the sultan's advisor, Jafar, who is trying to steal Jasmine's kingdom. "*Aladdin* is a ravishing thrill ride pulsing at MTV-video tempo," Richard Corliss noted in *Time*. "You have to go twice—and that's a treat, not a chore—to catch the wit in the decor, the throwaway gags, the edges of the action." *Washington Post* writer Rita Kempley praised the "sophisticated script" and added that "Disney quite simply has outdone itself with this marvelous adaptation of the ancient fairy tale."

Rossio and Elliott's next scripts were science-fiction stories with a darker edge. The 1994 film *The Puppet Masters*, starring Donald Sutherland and Julie Warner, was based on a novel by Robert Heinlein in which reptilian creatures take control of human bodies and minds. The film bombed, a fact Rossio attributes to how films get made in Hollywood: new producers or directors come onto a project and rework the script. When that happened, he noted on the *Wordplay* Web site, "all the work, all the story

meetings, all the studio notes, the original novel, all the drafts done by four or five different writers and writing teams with various executives and producers over the previous two years—all of it was thrown out the window. A draft would be written in two weeks, and that would be the movie that hit the screens." The two had a similar experience with their script for *Godzilla*, a 1998 reworking of the classic Japanese monster movie about a giant, dinosaur-like creature. While the film earned over 100 million dollars at the box office, many die-hard fans maintained that it retained none of the essence of the well-loved original. "The Godzilla film that got made didn't have anything to do with our work," Rossio told Simpson. "Our credit on the film is just another testament to the vagaries of the [Writers Guild of America] credit arbitration process."

Elliott and Rossio returned to more family-oriented action fare with two other 1998 films. *Small Soldiers* focuses on set of plastic toy soldiers who are brought to life through computerization and begin battling each other; two teens are the only thing keeping them from taking over the neighborhood. *The Mask of Zorro* revisits the masked Mexican swordsman who made his first film appearance in 1920 and became the focus of a popular 1950s television series. This film features Anthony Hopkins as the aging hero, Antonio Banderas as his protégé and future replacement, and Catherine Zeta-Jones as the elder Zorro's daughter and young Zorro's love interest. Charles Isherwood reviewed the film in *Variety*, writing that it "stands as a pointed riposte to those who say they don't make 'em like that anymore. The return of the legendary swordsman is well served by a grandly mounted production in the classical style." The film earned almost 100 million dollars at the box office, and Elliott and Rossio also contributed to the story's 2005 sequel, *The Legend of Zorro.*

An Exciting New Venture

In 1996 Rossio and Elliott became the first writers to sign a deal with DreamWorks SKG, a studio set up by director Steven Spielberg, former Disney Anima-tion executive Jeffrey Katzenberg, and film and music producer David Geffen. The first product of that arrangement was the 2000 animated film *The Road to El Dorado*. Katzenberg had suggested the setting—Central America during the Spanish conquest—and the writers "hit on the idea of creating a comedy team," Rossio recalled to Simpson. "There aren't any real comedy teams around any more, and there had never been any animated films with dual comedic leads." The film borrowed its title and theme from the "Road" movies of comic duo Bing Crosby and Bob Hope. Tulio and Miguel are two friends trying to find the legendary treasure of El Dorado, but they get caught up in a series of mishaps and adventures. "This is not a landmark in the history of feature animation," critic Roger Ebert noted on the Chicago *Sun Times* online, "but it's bright and has good energy, and the kinds of witty asides that entertain the adults in between the margins of the stuff for the kids." The film was not a huge success, but the screenwriters were more disappointed that the directors had moved away from their script's original story.

Elliott and Rossio had more success with their next project for DreamWorks. Not only did they write

Elliott's work for Disney includes the animated film *Aladdin*, released in 1992. (Photograph courtesy of Walt Disney Pictures/Kobal Collection/The Picture Desk, Inc.)

the script for *Shrek* with Joe Stillman and Roger Schulman, they served as coproducers on the film. Adapted from the children's story by William Steig, the movie centers on a green ogre named Shrek who rescues a princess and falls in love. As Rossio explained to Simpson, they wanted to write "a story that plays with fairy tale conventions—to do a story set in a world where people are aware of fairy tales, and in fact probably know the people who were in the original stories." The film features the voice of Mike Myers as the title character, who is fleeing from an internment camp being installed for "storybook characters" in his swamp. To get them out of his swamp and back into the kingdom of Lord Farquhar, Shrek must rescue the princess Fiona from a tower guarded by a dragon. During his travels he is aided by a talking Donkey, who tries to get behind the ogre's rough exterior and become his friend. Eventually Shrek falls in love with Fiona, whose hidden secret sets up a clever twist ending.

The film was a smash hit, popular with audiences and critics alike. In *Time* Richard Schickel observed that "it is the hilarious business of *Shrek* . . . to subvert all the well-worn expectations of its genre." *Entertainment Weekly* critic Lisa Schwarzbaum called the film a "charmingly loopy, iconoclastic story," and praised the "nicely barbed script from a team headed by Ted Elliott and Terry Rossio." A *Newsweek* critic called it "the wittiest and most endearing Hollywood animated movie since *Toy Story 2*," and concluded: "The biggest surprise, in the end, is not the hip references . . . or the bathroom humor or the tale's sweet but conventional moral of self-acceptance. It's how good this fractured and funky fairy tale makes you feel." The film made over 260 million dollars at the U.S. box office, won the first Academy award for best animated feature, and earned Rossio and Elliott and their co-writers an Oscar nomination for best adapted screenplay. The two men also served as creative consultants for the sequel, *Shrek 2*, another box-office success.

Their deal with DreamWorks completed, Elliott and Rossio returned to work with Disney. Their story ideas were used for the animated film *Treasure Planet*, a 2002 space-set adaptation of Robert Louis Stevenson's classic adventure novel *Treasure Island*. The two screenwriters had always felt it was possible to make a good pirate movie, and when Disney later approached them about writing a screenplay based on the popular theme-park ride "Pirates of the Caribbean," they jumped at the opportunity. "We grew up in Orange County [California], so Disneyland was always about 15 minutes from the house," Elliott told Scott Holleran of *Box Office Mojo* online. "I spent a lot of time there. Before we started working on the movie, I'd probably been on the ride at least a hundred times." Elliott and Rossio

took certain scenes from the ride and sprinkled them into a story of cursed pirate treasure and star-crossed lovers that included plenty of swashbuckling action. Expectations were low for the movie; critics doubted that a theme-park ride could provide the basis for anything of substance. "The odds were against us," Elliott told Peter Gilstrap in *Variety*. "A friend of mine said taking on a pirate movie based on a ride for Disney isn't so much a job as a dare. But in a way, it was freeing, because there hadn't been a successful pirate movie, and we were able to come in and say, 'We think this is what needs to happen to make this work.'"

An Action-packed Trilogy

With Johnny Depp playing Captain Jack Sparrow, a quirky pirate with a flair for the dramatic, *Pirates of the Caribbean: The Curse of the Black Pearl* surprised Hollywood by earning over 300 million dollars in U.S. box-office receipts. The film follows Sparrow and young blacksmith Will Turner (Orlando Bloom) as they join forces to rescue the governor's daughter, Elizabeth (Keira Knightley), from the nefarious Captain Barbossa (Geoffrey Rush). Barbossa has kidnapped Elizabeth because she has the power to break a curse that has left Barbossa and his crew to walk the earth as the living dead. *Newsweek* reviewer David Ansen wrote that the film is "better than a movie based on a theme-park ride has any right to be," and *Time* critic Richard Corliss called the script by Elliott and Rossio "cunning," adding that "the actors and authors all have fun with the genre without making fun of it. Rather, they revive it." "All in all, *Pirates of the Caribbean* is the best spectacle of the summer: the absence of pomp is a relief, the warmth of the comedy a pleasure," David Denby wrote in the *New Yorker*, praising the "consistently funny" screenplay.

The success of *Pirates of the Caribbean: The Curse of the Black Pearl*, with over 650 million dollars in worldwide box-office receipts, five Oscar nominations, and the 2004 People's Choice Award for Favorite Motion Picture, led to demands for not one but two sequels. Elliott and Rossio were tapped to write both scripts, which were to be filmed back-to-back for release in 2006 and 2007. The first sequel, *Pirates of the Caribbean: Dead Man's Chest*, finds Will and Elizabeth about to be married when they are arrested and sentenced to death for helping Captain Jack Sparrow escape prison. They can earn their freedom if they return with Captain Jack's magic compass, but the wily and eccentric buccaneer has his own problems, mainly a debt he owes to supernatural pirate Davy Jones. Despite the film's two-and-a-half-hour length, it set records for open-

Directed by Gore Verbinski, *Pirates of the Caribbean: Dead Man's Chest* **also features a screenplay coauthored by Elliott and Terry Rossio.** (Photograph courtesy of Walt Disney/Kobal Collection/The Picture Desk, Inc.)

ing day and weekend box office and eventually earned more than one billion dollars worldwide to become the number one movie of the year. "Lively is an odd word for something called *Dead Man's Chest,* but lively it is," remarked *Rolling Stone* critic Peter Travers. "You won't find hotter action, wilder thrills or loopier laughs this summer." Steve Rose noted in the *Guardian Online:* "Despite all the fits, starts, and flaws, there's enough invention and energy here to make you want to see the next installment."

The third franchise installment, *Pirates of the Caribbean: At World's End,* was another popular success. It begins where *Dead Man's Chest* left off, with Will and Elizabeth enlisting the help of an old enemy to rescue Captain Jack from the land of the dead. Then they must call together the pirate lords of the seven seas in order to regain control of Davy Jones' heart—and freedom of the seas—from the sinister Lord Beckett. With a running time of almost 170 minutes and an intricate story line, the film, according to several critics, was overly complicated. "The third and . . . final entry in this screamingly successful Disney franchise is, like its predecessors, big on spectacle: There's so much to look at that you never know where to look," Stephanie Zacharek noted in *Salon.com.* Elliott, however, believed that

audiences would welcome the depth of the story. As he told *UGO.com* interviewer Troy Rogers, "In terms of complexity, I wonder if [critics' complaints of] 'too long' means too much information. On the other hand, I really think that's one of the attractions of the movies themselves is there's a richness to the world." Filmgoers tended to agree with Elliott: the film earned over 960 million dollars worldwide.

For all their experience and success in Hollywood, Rossio and Elliott cannot predict which projects will turn out to be blockbusters. "We don't make hits," Rossio told Gilstrap. "Making them, they don't look like hits. Making them, they look like problems, disasters, things not working. You don't know you're making hits; you just don't." That combination of anticipation and uncertainty is part of the fun of making movies, they believe. "One of the joys of filmmaking—and it is just pure joy—is how different disciplines are brought together," Rossio told Aaron Wallace in an *Ultimate Disney* online interview. When the writing comes together with the design, directing, and acting, Rossio remarked, "you can come up with something that does endure, hopefully, or enters into the popular consciousness. . . . It doesn't always happen but when it does, it's just amazing to be a part of it."

While Rossio has also had success with the 2006 thriller *Deja Vu*, which he co-wrote and co-produced without Elliott, for the most part the pair continues to work as a team. When creating a script, they work out the structure of the story on index cards (a technique called storyboarding), then divide scenes and write them separately. "The reason I became a screenwriter is to make movies," Elliott told Holleran. "If I just wanted to write screenplays, that's all I'd do. If I just wanted to be a writer, I'd never write screenplays. There is much more satisfactory work than writing a screenplay because it's not the final work. You're not actually writing to communicate with your intended audience; you're writing to communicate with the people who are making the movie."

If you enjoy the works of Ted Elliott, you may also want to check out the following films:

Raiders of the Lost Ark, starring Harrison Ford, 1984.
Toy Story, an animated film directed by John Lasseter, 1995.
The Incredibles, an animated adventure film, 2004.

Rossio and Elliott have contributed to another Disney movie, the family film *G-Force*, about a group of guinea-pig secret agents. They also have plans for rebooting the classic character of the Lone Ranger, and perhaps even a fourth "Pirates" movie, if they can find the right story to connect with filmgoers. "Writing stories and making films is great, it's powerful, it's fun," Rossio said on the *Wordplay* Web site. "You get to play God, you get to make whatever fantastic things you want happen up there on screen. Just remember—the audience is listening."

■ Biographical and Critical Sources

PERIODICALS

Entertainment Weekly, June 1, 2001, Lisa Schwarzbaum, review of *Shrek*, p. 50; April 28, 2006, review of *Pirates of the Caribbean: Dead Man's Chest*, p. 82.

Hollywood Reporter, July 7, 2003, Kirk Honeycutt, review of *Pirates of the Caribbean: The Curse of the Black Pearl*, p. 8.

Los Angeles Times, July 8, 1998, Marla Matzer, "Ted and Terry's Excellent Screenwriting Adventures," p. F4.

Newsweek, May 7, 2001, "A Shrek of a Summer," p. 62; July 14, 2003, David Ansen, review of *Pirates of the Caribbean: The Curse of the Black Pearl*, p. 57.

New Yorker, July 28, 2003, David Denby, review of *Pirates of the Caribbean: The Curse of the Black Pearl*, p. 94.

New York Times, November 11, 1992, Janet Maslin, review of *Aladdin*; October 22, 1994, Stephen Holden, review of *The Puppet Masters*; May 19, 1998, Stephen Holden, review of *Godzilla*; July 10, 1998, Janet Maslin, review of *Small Soldiers*; March 31, 2000, Stephen Holden, review of *The Road to El Dorado*; May 16, 2001, Elvis Mitchell, review of *Shrek*; October 28, 2005, Stephen Holden, review of *The Legend of Zorro*; July 9, 2003, Elvis Mitchell, review of *Pirates of the Caribbean: Curse of the Black Pearl*.

Time, November 9, 1992, Richard Corliss, "Aladdin's Magic," p. 74; May 21, 2001, Richard Schickel, "Monstrously Good," review of *Shrek*, p. 86; July 14, 2003, Richard Corliss, review of *Pirates of the Caribbean: The Curse of the Black Pearl*, p. 61; June 4, 2007, Richard Schickel, "Washed Up," p. 69.

Variety, May 25, 1998, Joe Leydon, review of *Godzilla*, p. 55; June 29, 1998, Charles Isherwood, review of *The Mask of Zorro*, p. 37; July 13, 1998, Leonard Klady, review of *Small Soldiers*, p. 54; April 3, 2000, Todd McCarthy, review of *The Road to El Dorado*, p. 35; May 7, 2001, Todd McCarthy, review of *Shrek*, p. 49; November 25, 2002, Andy Klein, review of *Treasure Planet*, p. 14; July 14, 2003, Todd McCarthy, review of *Pirates of the Caribbean: The Curse of the Black Pearl*, p. 22; July 10, 2006, Todd McCarthy, "Sequel Is Waterlogged," p. 21; May 21, 2007, Peter Gilstrap, "Pair of 'Pirates': Scribes Riding Wave of Trilogy's Success," p. 10.

Washington Post, November 25, 1992, Rita Kempley, review of *Aladdin*.

ONLINE

Artful Writer Web log, http://www.artfulwriter.com/ (April 1, 2009).

Box Office Mojo Web site, http://www.boxofficemojo.com/ (May 31, 2007), Scott Holleran, interview with Elliott and Rossio.

Chicago Sun Times Online, http://rogerebert.suntimes.com/ (March 31, 2000), Roger Ebert, review of *The Road to El Dorado*.

Guardian Online (London, England), http://www.guardian.co.uk/ (June 30, 2006), Steve Rose, review of *Pirates of the Caribbean: Dead Man's Chest.*

M.J. Simpson Web site, http://www.mjsimpson.co.uk/ (April, 2000), "Ted Elliott and Terry Rossio."

Rolling Stone Online, http://www.rollingstone.com/ (June 28, 2006), Peter Travers, review of *Pirates of the Caribbean: Dead Man's Chest.*

Salon.com, http://www.salon.com/ (May 25, 2007), Stephanie Zacharek, review of *Pirates of the Caribbean: At World's End.*

Silver Bullet Comic Books Web site, http://www.silverbulletcomicbooks.com/ (June 25, 2006), interview with Elliott.

UGO.com, http://www.ugo.com/ (February 26, 2009), Troy Rogers, "Ted Elliott and Terry Rossio Interview."

Ultimate Disney Web site, http://www.ultimatedisney.com/ (December 19, 2006), Aaron Wallace, interview with Elliott and Rossio.

Wordplay Web site, http://wordplayer.com (February 26, 2009).*

(Photograph courtesy of the Library of Congress.)

Richard Estes

■ Personal

Born May 14, 1932, in Kewanee, IL; son of William (owner of an auto repair shop) and Marie Estes. *Education:* Attended School of the Art Institute of Chicago, 1952-56.

■ Addresses

Home—New York, NY and ME. *Agent*—Marlborough Gallery, 40 W. 57th St., New York, NY 10019; Louis K. Meisel Gallery, 141 Prince St., New York, NY 10012.

■ Career

Artist. Worked as illustrator for publishing and advertising layout work in Chicago, IL, 1956-59; worked in commercial art studios, including Reiss, Cappiello, and Caldwell, and Marstellar Advertising Agency, in New York, NY, 1959-62; lived and painted in Spain, 1962; full-time painter, 1966—. *Exhibitions:* Works included in permanent collec-

tions at Smithsonian American Art Museum, Washington, DC; Solomon R. Guggenheim Museum, New York, NY; Art Institute of Chicago; Museum of Contemporary Art, Chicago; Museum of Fine Arts, Boston, MA; Museum of Modern Art, New York, NY; Metropolitan Museum of Art, New York, NY; National Gallery of Art, Washington, DC; Whitney Museum of American Art, New York, NY; Detroit Institute of Arts; Tate Gallery, London, England; Teheran Museum of Contemporary Art, Teheran, Iran; Museum Ludwig, Cologne, Germany; Yale University Art Gallery, New Haven, CT; Des Moines Art Center, Des Moines, IA; Fonds National d'Art Contemporain, Paris, France; High Museum of Art, Atlanta, GA; Hirshorn Museum and Sculpture Garden, Washington, DC; J.P. Morgan Chase Manhattan Bank, New York, NY; Modern Art Museum of Fort Worth, Fort Worth, TX; Nelson-Atkins Museum of Art, Kansas City, MO; Norton Simon Museum of Art, Pasadena, CA; Portland Art Museum, Portland, OR; San Antonio Museum of Art, San Antonio, TX; Toledo Museum of Art, Toledo, OH; Virginia Museum of Fine Arts, Richmond, VA; and Walker Art Center, Minneapolis, MN. Solo exhibitions include Allan Stone Gallery, New York, NY, 1968; Museum of Contemporary Art, Chicago, IL, 1974; Museum of Fine Arts, Boston, MA, 1978-79; Allan Stone Gallery, New York, NY, 1983; Louis K. Meisel Gallery, New York, NY, 1985; Sert Gallery, Carpenter Center for the Visual Arts, Harvard University, Cambridge, MA, 1990; Hiroshima City Museum of Contemporary Art, Hiroshima, Japan, 1990; Portland Museum of Art, Portland, ME, 1991; touring exhibit across the United States, 1992-95; Grand Palais, Paris, France, 1993; Marlborough Gallery, New York, NY, 1995, 1998, 2006, 2008; Galeria Marlborough, Madrid, Spain, 1998; AMS Marlborough, Santiago, Chile, 2003; and Palazzo Magnani, Reggio Emila, Italy, 2007. Group exhibitions include "Ninety-ninth Exhibition," National Academy Galleries, New York, NY, 1966; "Painting from the Photo," Riverside Museum, New York, NY, 1969; "Twenty-two Realists," Whitney Museum of American Art, New York, NY, 1970; "Radical Realism," Museum of Contemporary Art, Chicago, Il, 1971; "American 1976: A Bicentennial Exhibition," U.S. Department of the Interior touring exhibition, 1976; "Photo-realist Printmaking," Louis K. Meisel Gallery, New York, NY, 1978; "Contemporary American Realism since 1960," Pennsylvania Academy of Fine Arts, Philadelphia, PA, 1981; "Seven Photorealists from New York Collections," Solomon R. Guggenheim Museum, New York, NY, 1981; "American Realism—Twentieth Century Drawings and Watercolors from the Glenn C. Janss Collection," San Francisco Museum of Modern Art, San Francisco, CA, 1986; "The Urban Landscape," Louis K. Meisel Gallery, New York, NY, 1987; "American Realism and Figurative Art: 1952-1990" venues across Japan, 1991; "On the Edge: Forty Years of Maine Painting, 1952-1992," Maine Coast Artists Gallery, Rockport, ME, 1992; "CityScapes," Marlborough Gallery, New York, NY, 1997; "Tools as Art: The Hechinger Collection," venues across the United States, 2002; "Big City: Cityscapes and Urban Life from the Collection," Phoenix Art Museum, Phoenxi, AZ, 2006; "Shock of the Real: Photorealism Revisited," Boca Raton Museum of Art, Boca Raton, FL, 2009; and touring exhibits in the United States and internationally.

■ **Awards, Honors**

National Council of the Arts fellowship, 1971; Achievement in Visual Arts Award, California Arts Council, 1995; MECA Award for Achievement as a Visual Artist, Maine College of Art, 1996.

■ **Sidelights**

American artist Richard Estes is best known for his crisp, precisely rendered paintings of urban scenes, particularly those in New York City, and he is considered one of the founders of the photo-realist movement of the late 1960s. Estes's work, according to Gregory J. Peterson in *ArtInterview*, "exhibits a high finish, fine details and an almost photographic fidelity to reality." Praising the "vividness" of Estes's paintings, *New York Times* critic Roberta Smith cited "the even-handed profusion of detail—backgrounds as clear and present as foregrounds, reflections as solid as anything else—that is the defining characteristic of Mr. Estes's art."

Estes's work—like that of artists such as Malcolm Morley, Chuck Close, and Duane Hanson, who similarly produce work with a high degree of verisimilitude—has been labeled variously as photo-realism, super-realism, neo-realism, or radical realism. All these terms are useful in understanding Estes's style; many of his works look like large photographs. According to Benjamin Genocchio, writing in the *New York Times,* photo-realism "is all about form, technique and surface, a manic, unthinking empiricism—every leaf, every blade of grass is carefully colored and defined." Genocchio added, "Yet to say this is to hit upon what many people admire about the genre, which is the skill of the artists to fashion such an accurate representation of reality. We admire their ability to do something we cannot, while marveling at the work's photographic detail."

Early Experiences Prove Valuable

Estes was born on May 14, 1932, in Kewanee, Illinois, and grew up in nearby Sheffield. As a youngster, Estes spent his time building models and sketching. "I always liked to draw," he remarked to Peterson. "I was not much more than eight or nine years old when I got a Christmas present of an oil painting set." In 1947, his family moved to Evanston, a Chicago suburb, which gave him access to that city's cultural resources. After graduating from high school, Estes worked in the insurance business for a year, earning enough money to travel to Europe, where he visited museums and attended concerts. Returning to the United States, he received art training at the School of the Art Institute of Chicago between 1952 and 1956. Much of his training was in figural and traditional subjects. "I think one of the best things about being a student there was, for example, trying to do a figure painting and then going up into the galleries to see the way El Greco or Degas did it," he told John Arthur in *Richard Estes: The Urban Landscape*. "You can really put your work in the proper perspective that way—and learn from the paintings."

Following his graduation, Estes worked as a graphic designer in Chicago for three years before moving to New York City in 1959. He found employment at

Richard Estes's painting "Soho Scene," which demonstrates his use of reflective surfaces. (From a painting in *Richard Estes* by John Wilmerding, Rizzoli, 2006. Copyright © Richard Estes, courtesy Marlborough Gallery, New York.)

a number of commercial art studios, including Reiss, Cappiello, and Caldwell, and Marstellar Advertising Agency. "When I was in advertising I spent a lot of time doing layouts and quick sketches with magic markers or chalk," he remarked to Athur. "I learned a lot about drawing and developed the ability to do things very quickly." He also performed freelance work, including art for record jackets as well as magazine and book illustrations. Estes told Arthur that the projects didn't require "any emotional energy. That way I wouldn't be drained. I really wanted to paint, and would save all my creative energies for when I got home."

During this time Estes developed his technique of working from photographs that depicted the urban landscape. "Most of Estes' paintings from the early 60's are of New Yorkers engaged in everyday activities," Peterson explained. "It was around 1967 that a shift occurred in his city scenes: he began to paint storefronts and buildings with glass windows partially reflecting images of the street scene in front of the building. These paintings were based on color photographs he would make of his object, which trapped the evanescent nature of the reflections, which would change in part with the lighting and the time of day." The decision to use photographs arose out of necessity, Estes told Peterson: "I went through a phase of going and sitting in cafeterias and drawing and going out and doing drawing, but I knew from all my work in advertising that the illustrators all use photographs, and I said 'Why am I doing all this? It's masochistic.' It just makes it more difficult, not necessarily any better. The photographs are what makes it possible to do all these things with reflections and things that are just there for a moment when the light hits." In 1966 Estes devoted himself full time to his craft, and his first one-man show took place at the Allan Stone Gallery in New York City in 1968.

The Artist at Work

Estes normally uses several photographs in the preparation of a single painted composition. The paintings are not reproductions of photographs, but rather highly organized compositions based on photographs. "In accordance with his stance as an artist," Karl Ruhrberg stated in *Art of the Twentieth Century*, "Estes considers photography a preparatory, auxiliary means. Instead of providing a subject, the photograph, as he says, merely gives the best pointers to the theme he wants to paint. For all their apparent faithfulness, Estes's motifs undergo a degree of imaginative transformation unmatched by most other photo-realists employing related subject matter." As the artist remarked to Arthur, "I can

select what to do or not to do from what's in the photograph. I can add or subtract from it. Every time I do something it's a choice, but it's not a choice involving something creative or reproductive. It's a selection from the various aspects of reality. So what I'm trying to paint is not something different, but something more like the place I've photographed."

Estes's paintings frequently portray anonymous streets or other urban sights, with glass, metal, cars, store fronts, and other reflective surfaces. Often scenes include elaborate signage, curved and reflective architectural shapes, and colored neon, reminiscent of Art Deco. Other details make clear that Estes is not recreating a previous era in his paintings, but rather showing structures that have endured the passage of time. The reflective surfaces concentrate attention not only on what is inside the windows but on what is around the viewer: the context of the image. As a contributor remarked in *Contemporary Artists*, while viewing "one of his front-on store windows we become aware of what is behind us, outside of the painting altogether, through the multiple imagery recorded in the glass. In a painting where the store window is viewed from the side, we are given visual information about what's on the other side of the street. In a way it is all like three-dimensional tic-tac-toe."

Most of the scenes are of Manhattan, but there are also images of Venice, Chicago, and Paris. His scenes show day-light, never night, and suggest vacant and quiet Sunday mornings. He rarely included garbage, people, slush or snow, or other details that might detract from the "structure" of the city. There are numerous details in terms of signs, stickers, and window displays, often viewed backwards because reflected. An Estes painting presents more visual information than can easily be received, and this wealth of familiar detail is essential to the concept of realism in painting. "One has only to look closely at a work by Estes to see how richly painted it is," noted the contributor in *Contemporary Artists*. "The pigment is applied with considerable painterly élan, with virtuoso handling of the brush here and there—as seductive as touches in a Guardi or Vermeer. Just because Estes refers to photographs for pictorial information doesn't preclude his profound interest in composition, drawing, color and form."

Estes mostly works in oils or acrylics, and in constructing a painting he moved from the general to the specific. He uses color slides in the studio but did not project on the canvas as did some other artists. He does, however, plan on the canvas, first sketching out entirely the general composition. His

"42nd Street Crosstown Bus," a painting by Estes that focuses on his native Manhattan. (From a painting in *Richard Estes* by John Wilmerding, Rizzoli, 2006. Copyright © Richard Estes, courtesy Marlborough Gallery, New York.)

Estes's painting "81st Street and Amsterdam," which depicts the city that is home to thousands. (From a painting in *Richard Estes* by John Wilmerding, Rizzoli, 2006. Copyright © Richard Estes, courtesy Marlborough Gallery, New York.)

work in the studio is one of selection and organization. Thus, despite the power of the photographic illusionism, the abstract qualities are strong. The thoughtful viewer is sensitive to forms and shapes, as much as to the tactile quality of the surfaces and objects. As Helen A. Harrison observed in a *New York Times* review of the artist's work, "At first glance Richard Estes's cityscapes appear to be straight translations of photographs. That effect is caused by the preconceptions we bring to such precisely rendered art, but it dissipates as we study the imagery and appreciate the liberties that the artist has taken with his subjects."

Stylistic Choices

Estes admires the early twentieth-century photographer Eugève Atget and eighth-century Venetian *vedute* (view) painters such as Canaletto and Bernardo Bellotto. These artists presented detached views of their surroundings, sensitive to the particularity of places but equally concerned with strong pictorial composition. In an effort to focus on form and color and avoid a narrative quality in his paintings, Estes often eliminates human figures from his works. As he told Arthur, "It changes one's reaction to the painting and destroys the feeling of it to put a figure in because when you add figures then people start relating to the figures and it's an emotional relationship. The painting becomes too literal, whereas without the figure it's more purely a visual experience."

Estes's work emphasizes craftsmanship and traditional conventions of making a two-dimensional canvas look three-dimensional, allowing the viewer to play the impartial observer, so that the sensation of being in that scene determines a more subtle mood. His paintings are far removed from the powerful abstract expressionist tendency in American painting of the post-World War II period. "I think the thing about the Abstract Expressionists was that they were so involved with pure feeling and emotions that they didn't bother with craftsmanship," he stated in his interview with Arthur. "There was no urge to just make something beautiful. The great artists of the past never let their feelings or personalities intrude that much." Estes's relationship to pop art is more complex. He does not share the light-hearted, casual approach of those artists, but does rely on aspects of popular culture in his work. "Photorealism was largely an American movement," a contributor remarked in *Modern Art: Impressionism to Post-modernism*, "and like the Pop art which served as one of its sources it was often interpreted in terms of its subject matter either as a critique or a celebration of lowbrow suburban culture. In its very dependence on readymade imagery, however, it declared its detachment and nonjudgmental scrutiny."

If you enjoy the works of Richard Estes, you may also want to check out the following:

The lifelike sculptures of American artist Duane Hanson (1925-1996).
The art of British-born photorealist painter and sculptor Malcolm Morley (1931—).
The paintings and photographs of Chuck Close (1940—), an American photorealist.

Estes is one of the most accomplished painters in defining and presenting the urban landscape in a super-realist style. "I think the popular concept of the artist is a person who has this great passion and enthusiasm and super emotion," he remarked to Arthur. "He just throws himself into this great masterpiece and collapses from exhaustion when it's finished. It's really not that way at all. Usually it's a pretty calculated, sustained, and slow process by which you develop something." Estes concluded: "I think the real test is to plan something and be able to carry it out to the very end. Not that you're always enthusiastic; its just that you have to get this thing out. It's not done with one's emotions; its done with the head."

■ **Biographical and Critical Sources**

BOOKS

Arthur, John, *Richard Estes: The Urban Landscape,* Museum of Fine Arts/New York Graphic Society (Boston, MA), 1978.

Arthur, John, *Richard Estes: Paintings and Prints,* Chameleon Books (New York, NY), 1993.
Battock, Gregory, *Super Realism, aCritical Anthology,* Dutton (New York, NY), 1975.
Britt, David, editor, *Modern Art: Impressionism to Post-modernism,* Thames & Hudson (New York, NY), 1999.
Contemporary Artists, 5th edition, St. James Press (Detroit, MI), 2001.
Lucie-Smith, Edward, *Art Now: From Abstract Expressionism to Superrealism,* Morrow (New York, NY), 1977.
Lindey, Christine Christine, *Superrealist Painting and Sculpture,* Morrow (New York, NY), 1980.
Marshall, Richard, *Fifty New York Artists: A Critical Selection of Painters and Sculptors Working in New York,* Chronicle Books (San Francisco, CA), 1987.
Meisel, Louis K., *Photo-realism,* Abrams (New York, NY), 1980.
Meisel, Louis K., *Richard Estes: The Complete Paintings 1966-1985,* Abrams (New York, NY), 1985.
Meisel, Louis K., and Linda Chase, *Photorealism and the Millennium,* Abrams (New York, NY), 2002.
Parmeggiani, Sandro, *Richard Estes,* Skira (New York, NY), 2008.
The Prestel Dictionary of Art and Artists in the Twentieth Century, Prestel (New York, NY), 2000.
Ruhrberg, Karl, *Art of the Twentieth Century,* Volume 1, *Painting,* Taschen (New York, NY), 1998.
Wilmerding, John, *The Genius of American Painting,* Morrow (New York, NY), 1973.
Wilmerding, John, *Richard Estes,* Rizzoli (New York, NY), 2006.

PERIODICALS

Art and Artists, August, 1974, Herbert Raymond, interview with Estes.
Art Criticism, volume 8, number 2, Matthew Baigell, "Reflections on/of Richard Estes," pp. 16-25.
Art in America, November-December, 1972, "The Photo-Realists: 12 Interviews."
ArtInterview, August 2, 2002, "A Dialogue between Gregory J. Peterson and Richard Estes."
Christian Science Monitor, April 1, 1974, Mary Lou Kelley, "Pop-Art Inspired Objective Realism."
New York, May 27, 1974, Barbara Rose, "Treacle and Trash."
New York Home, May-June, 2006, Peter Webster, "I Am a Camera: Photorealist Richard Estes Paints a Poetic Vision of Manhattan," pp. 72-74.
New York Times, August 8, 1972, John Canady, "A Critic's Valedictory: The Americanization of Modern Art and Other Upheavals"; May 25, 1974, John Russell, "An Unnatural Silence"; October 11,

1992, Helen A. Harrison, "Richard Estes's Silk-Screen Interpretations of Cityscapes"; May 19, 1995, Roberta Smith, "Art in Review"; January 30, 2005, Benjamin Genocchio, "Photorealism: Is That All There Is?"

OTHER

Richard Estes: A Film Documentary, Southwest Harbor, 1998.*

Terence Fisher

■ Personal

Born February 23, 1904, in London, England; died June 18, 1980, in London, England. *Education:* Educated in Horsham, Sussex, England.

■ Career

Director and editor. Worked as a window-dresser in London, England, 1930; entered film industry as clapper-boy and runner, Lime Grove Studios, Shepherd's Bush, England, 1930; earned first screen credit as clapper-boy on *Falling for You*, 1933; first film as assistant editor, *Brown on Resolution/Born For Glory*, 1935; debut as solo editor, *The Two of Us*, 1936; directorial debut, *Colonel Bogey*, 1947; joined Hammer Film Productions, Bray, England, 1952.

Director of films, including: *Colonel Bogey*, Highbury Productions, 1947; *A Song for Tomorrow*, Highbury Productions, 1948; *Portrait from Life*, Gainsborough Pictures, 1948; *To the Public Danger*, Highbury Productions, 1948; *Marry Me*, Gainsborough Pictures, 1949; *The Astonished Heart*, Gainsborough Pictures, 1950; *So Long at the Fair*, Gainsborough Pictures, 1950; *Home to Danger*, New World Productions, 1951; *The Last Page*, Hammer, 1952; *Wings of Danger*, Hammer, 1952; *Stolen Face*, Hammer, 1952; *Distant Trumpet*, Hammer, 1952; *Mantrap*, Hammer, 1953; *Four Sided Triangle*, Hammer, 1953; *Spaceways*, Hammer, 1953; *Blood Orange*, Hammer, 1953; *Face the Music*, Hammer, 1954; *Murder by Proxy*, Hammer, 1954; *The Stranger Came Home*, Hammer, 1954; *Final Appointment*, Hammer, 1954; *Mask of Dust*, Hammer, 1954; *Children Galore*, Hammer, 1955; *Stolen Assignment*, Hammer, 1955; *The Flaw*, Hammer, 1955; *The Gelignite Gang*, Hammer, 1956; *The Last Man to Hang?*, Hammer, 1956; *Kill Me Tomorrow*, Hammer, 1957; *The Curse of Frankenstein*, Hammer, 1957; *Dracula*, Hammer, 1958; *The Revenge of Frankenstein*, Hammer, 1958; *The Hound of the Baskervilles*, Hammer, 1959; *The Man Who Could Cheat Death*, Hammer, 1959; *The Mummy*, Hammer, 1959; *The Stranglers of Bombay*, Hammer, 1960; *Sword of Sherwood Forest*, Hammer, 1960; *The Brides of Dracula*, Hammer, 1960; *The Two Faces of Dr. Jekyll*, Hammer, 1960; *The Curse of the Werewolf*, Hammer, Hammer, 1961; *The Phantom of the Opera*, Hammer, 1962; *Sherlock Holmes and the Deadly Necklace*, CCC Filmkunst, 1962; *The Horror of It All*, Associated Producers, 1963; *The Gorgon*, Hammer, 1964; *The Earth Dies Screaming*, Lippert Productions, 1965; *Dracula, Prince of Darkness*, Hammer, 1966; *Island of Terror*, Planet Film Productions, 1966; *Frankenstein Created Woman*, Hammer, 1967; *Night of the Big Heat*, Planet Film Productions, 1967; *The Devil Rides Out*, Hammer, 1968; *Frankenstein Must Be Destroyed*, Hammer, 1969; and *Frankenstein and the Monster from Hell*, Hammer, 1974.

Director of television shows, including: *Douglas Fairbanks, Jr., Presents*, 1953-55; *Three's Company*, 1954; *Colonel March of Scotland Yard*, 1956; *The Adventures of Clint and Mac*, 1957; *Sword of Freedom*, 1957; *The Gay Cavalier*, 1957; *The Adventures of Robin Hood*, 1957; and *Dial 999*, 1959.

Editor of films, including: (as T.R. Fisher) *Tudor Rose,* Gainsborough Pictures, 1936; (as T.R. Fisher) *Jack of All Trades,* Gainsborough Pictures, 1936; (as T.R. Fisher) *Where There's a Will,* Gainsborough Pictures, 1936; (as T.R. Fisher) *Everybody Dance,* Gainsborough Pictures, 1936; *Windbag the Sailor,* Gainsborough Pictures, 1936; *Mr. Satan,* Warner Bros./First National Productions, 1938; *That's the Ticket,* Warner Bros./First National Productions, 1940; *George and Margaret,* Warner Bros./First National Productions, 1938; *Atlantic Ferry,* Warner Bros./First National Productions, 1941; *The Peterville Diamond,* Warner Bros./First National Productions, 1942; *Flying Fortress,* Warner Bros./First National Productions, 1942; *Tomorrow We Live,* British Aviation Pictures, 1943; *The Dark Tower,* Warner Bros./First National Productions, 1943; *They Met in the Dark,* Excelsior Film Productions, 1943; *Candlelight in Algeria,* British Aviation Pictures, 1944; *One Exciting Night,* Columbia Productions, 1944; *The Wicked Lady,* Gainsborough Pictures, 1945; and *Master of Bankdam,* Rank Organisation, 1947. *Military service:* British Merchant Marine Service, 1929; attained rank of junior officer.

■ Writings

SCREENPLAYS

(With Paul Tabori; and director) *Four Sided Triangle,* Hammer, 1953.

(With Paul Tabori; and director) *Mantrap,* Hammer, 1953.

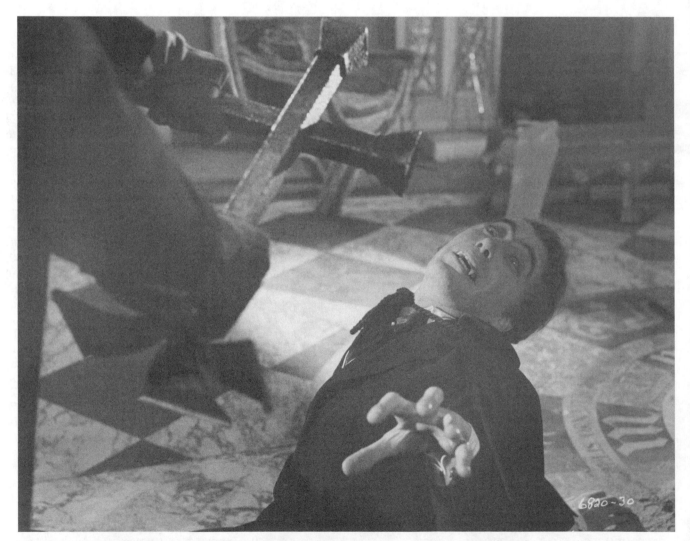

Filmed by Terrence Fisher in 1958 and starring Christopher Lee, *Dracula* was released in the United States as *Horror of Dracula*. (Photograph © Bettmann/Corbis.)

■ Sidelights

A prolific British director of the 1950s and 1960s, Terence Fisher is best known for his association with Hammer Film Productions, for whom he created such horror classics as *The Curse of Frankenstein, Dracula,* and *The Devil Rides Out.* Fisher's "consistently high standards of craftsmanship, and his laidback techniques that accent the robustness of his solid dramatic narratives and their physical and emotional energy, redefined the moribund horror genre and defined the Hammer style," Alan Jones remarked in *The Rough Guide to Horror Movies.* The director's films, according to Paul Leggett, writing in *Terence Fisher: Horror, Myth, and Religion,* "have clearly been a major influence on contemporary cinema." Leggett added, "Fisher has done more to establish the conventions and styles of the modern horror film than any other director."

For his part, Fisher remained humble about his abilities. As he remarked in a *Cinefantastique* interview with Harry Ringel, "All a director is . . . is an interpreter of the written word, or translator of the written word, into visual form. Consequently, if the written word is no bloody good, no director in the world is going to be able to put it into a visual form which is going to be done ably." Fortunately, Fisher often worked with outstanding source material, including Mary Shelley's gothic novel *Frankenstein; or, The Modern Prometheus* and Bram Stoker's horror classic *Dracula.* "My themes remained what I was given. . . . I'm only a working director," Fisher told Ringel, in typically self-effacing fashion. "I'm not a director who can pick what he wants to do."

Arrives Late to Film

Nothing in Fisher's early life suggested that he would eventually enter the film industry. He was born February 23, 1904, in Maida Vale, a district of London, England. Educated in Sussex, at age sixteen he joined the British Merchant Marines, where he spent the next five years, attaining the rank of junior officer. He worked briefly as a window dresser for a London department store before finding employment as a clapper-boy for Lime Grove Studios at the astonishingly late age of twenty-nine. He toiled for three years at various positions before becoming a film editor in 1936; over the next decade, he would edit more than fifteen films for, among others, Gainsborough Pictures and Warner Brothers-First National Productions. Andrew Spicer, writing in *Film Criticism,* noted that Fisher's later directorial efforts were enhanced by the knowledge he gained in the editing room. As Spicer remarked, these "films are often distinguished by their deft cutting. Fisher frequently uses startling juxtapositions, which add a significant dimension to the mise-en-scene and help to create the narrative tempo."

In 1947, as part of a showcase for untested talent, Fisher directed his first film, *Colonel Bogey,* a humorous fantasy about a woman who acts as though her late husband were still alive. In the ensuing years, he would direct such fare as *Mantrap,* a crime film, *The Astonished Heart,* an adaptation of a Noel Coward play, and *So Long at the Fair,* a costume piece. "Fisher's films from this period received virtually no critical attention at the time of their release, and Fisher himself remained an anonymous figure . . . Peter Hutchings noted in his biography of the director. "However, there was something about Fisher's career in what might be termed his 'wilderness years' that, while of no apparent importance at the time, would in retrospect become significant. Of the nineteen low-budget films directed by Fisher up until 1957, eleven were for a small, up-and-coming independent production company called Hammer."

The rise of Hammer Film Productions from a relatively minor studio in Bray, England, to one synonymous with horror films, is one of the great success stories of post-war British cinema. Though the company had begun to cash in during the early 1950s with a few popular science-fiction films, including *Four Sided Triangle,* cowritten and directed by Fisher, it gained prominence after releasing a series of movies that updated the classic monster catalogue popularized by Universal Studios in the 1930s and 1940s. "In 1957, Hammer Films began filming Gothic horror movies in color, bringing life and popularity back to the vintage monsters of the golden age of cinema," Robert Marrero stated in *Vampire Movies: An Illustrated Guide to Seventy-two Years of Vampire Movies.* "What Universal had once concealed in atmospheric shadows or in characters reacting to off-screen supernatural occurrences, Hammer exposed in full light and vivid and colorful close-ups. The effect was stunning."

The Hammer Years

The film that launched the Hammer brand to worldwide fame was *The Curse of Frankenstein,* a remake of the iconic 1931 film starring Boris Karloff. *The Curse of Frankenstein* joined Fisher with screenwriter Jimmy Sangster; the pair would collaborate often over the next several years. Featuring ac-

Fisher directed Christopher Lee in the 1957 motion picture *The Curse of Frankenstein,* **released by Hammer Film.**
(Photograph courtesy of Hammer/Kobal Collection/The Picture Desk, Inc.)

claimed actors Christopher Lee as the Creature and Peter Cushing as Baron Victor Frankenstein, the film, made on a shoestring budget, proved to be box-office gold and shocked audiences with its explicit horror. "It's hard now to imagine what a sea change was represented by this remodeling of Mary Shelley's classic novel as a gory drawing-room melodrama," observed Jones. "Yet it was a sensational novelty to have all the blood in vivid Technicolor—and to cause such disgust." Though Carlos Clarens, writing in *The Illustrated History of Horror and Science-fiction Films,* criticized the garish makeup on Lee, which rendered him "wholly negligible as a dramatic character," he acknowledged that Fisher's version "did restore the action to the original setting of the novel, Switzerland at the beginning of the nineteenth century, and its other assets were Technicolor, excellent sets . . . and the crisp man-

nered performance of . . . Cushing as Doctor Frankenstein." Jones offered further praise for *The Curse of Frankenstein,*, stating that "Fisher's directorial verve gave it the patina of a witty fairy tale and a high scare score."

The next year Fisher completed *Dracula,* "a masterpiece of horror, a classic with an impact that has not diminished even with time," Marrero wrote. Directed by Fisher from a screenplay by Sangster, the film starred Lee as the fiendish Count Dracula, Cushing as his nemesis, the vampire hunter Van Helsing, and John Van Eyssen as Jonathan Harker, a guest at Dracula's castle who falls victim to his bite. According to Jones, "Fisher's shocker might not be the most faithful adaptation of Bram Stoker's novel; but sparsely and crisply scripted by . . . Sangster, . . . it remains one of the finest renderings of the Dracula theme. Of the well-mounted scenes hardly any are without rousing action, erotic frissón or unforgettable suspense, and Fisher's masterly direction set an unmatched standard in romantic gothic horror." Alain Silver and James Ursini, writing in *The Vampire Film*, also complimented the work, particularly noting Fisher's "deceptive introduction of the Count himself. Appearing suddenly at the head of a broad flight of steps, he strides down threateningly towards Jonathan Harker who is aghast at what seems to be the prelude to an attack, only to proffer words of greeting and conduct him upstairs." In 2007 the British Film Institute restored the original print of *Dracula*, and the film received a special Halloween screening at the National Film Theatre. According to *Spectator* contributor Sinclair McKay, "the film still works today because it is an expert piece of taut adaptation—Stoker's 400 pages clock in at 84 minutes. And in giving the film that

sheer pace and urgency—previously horror had been a rather stagey genre—Sangster and Fisher set the Hammer house-style in stone."

With the success of *The Curse of Frankenstein* and *Dracula*, Fisher became Hammer's principal director of horror films. He produced a number of sequels to those two movies, including *The Revenge of Frankenstein* and *The Brides of Dracula*. He also offered his unique take on favorite film monsters in *The Mummy, The Two Faces of Dr. Jekyll, The Curse of the Werewolf*, and *The Phantom of the Opera*. "The importance of Hammer horror to Fisher's career is indisputable," Hutchings observed, adding: "Fisher's importance to Hammer is equally indisputable; he was one of the key contributors in the initial formation of the type of horror upon which Hammer's subsequent success was built."

Christopher Lee (left) and Peter Cushing wrestle in a life-and-death duel in Fisher's spine-tingling early film *The Mummy*, released in 1959. (Photograph courtesy of Hammer/Kobal Collection/The Picture Desk, Inc.)

More horror is served up by Hammer studios via Fisher's 1960 film *The Stranglers of Bombay.* (Photograph courtesy of Hammer/ Kobal Collection/The Picture Desk, Inc.)

Eventually, however, Fisher's brand of horror fell out of favor with audiences, and Hammer chose to work with younger directors. Following his departure from that studio in 1962, Fisher set to work for a number of other production companies, and produced such films as *Island of Terror*, which starred Cushing as a cancer researcher on a remote island whose experiments result in the creation of monstrous beings that feed on bone marrow. "*Island of Terror* was an extremely fine horror thriller, one of the best of the 1960s," Michael R. Pitts wrote in *Horror Film Stars*. Fisher eventually returned to the Hammer fold in the late 1960s, directing such films as *Frankenstein Created Woman* and *Frankenstein Must Be Destroyed*. He was also at the helm of the well-received *The Devil Rides Out*, an adaptation of Dennis Wheatley's novel about black magic. Jeremy Dyson, writing in *Bright Darkness: The Lost Art of the Supernatural Horror Film*, called *The Devil Rides Out* "superb," adding that "the film has the solid structure of a thriller, lending it an adult seriousness many other Hammers lack." *Frankenstein and the Monster from Hell*, Fisher's last film for Hammer, was released in 1974. He died in Twickenham, a district of London, on June 18, 1980.

A Place in Film History

Fisher's career is forever linked to his work at Hammer, which reinvigorated the horror genre with a successful formula incorporating diabolical creatures awash in vivid color and fast-paced action recorded in lurid detail. While popular with audiences, the Hammer films were considered distasteful by a number of critics. In the opinion of Clarens, "the common denominator of their product is not really horror but sadism. The more jaded the public's palate becomes, the ranker the banquet of effects." Clarens added, "Mutilations, beheadings, gougings, burning flesh, and decaying corpses—all of these are arbitrarily spliced into the scenarios at the expense of characterization and plot." Silver and Ursini offered a vastly different take on Fisher's work, however, declaring that his "violence is not gratuitous, not just a titillating bit of *grand guignol.* The authors further noted that in his Dracula films, the director "relies heavily—particularly in relation to other Hammer products—on understatement. By means of finely-drawn characters and a flexible style, Fisher employs shifting moods to elicit tension."

While noting the shortcomings of the Hammer movies, London *Guardian* contributor Derek Malcolm nonetheless viewed Fisher's works favorably. "The conventional view of Hammer films is that they were fun without being particularly good, and it is certainly true that many fall into the poor-to-moderate bracket," Malcolm wrote. "But the best, like *Dracula, The Curse of Frankenstein, The Devil Rides Out* and *Frankenstein Must Be Destroyed*—all directed by Fisher—have a quality unmatched by horror films today." "If any terror theme was Fisher's it was the charisma of evil," Jones remarked in *The Rough Guide to Horror Movies.* The critic concluded, "Fisher translated the classic Universal monster gallery into colour and as one of the originators of the modern vocabulary of horror, such as the use of gore and showing of nastiness, he left an indelible impression on a generation of filmmakers and filmgoers."

If you enjoy the works of Terence Fisher, you may also want to check out the following films:

Rosemary's Baby, directed by Roman Polanski, 1968.
Bram Stoker's Dracula, directed by Francis Ford Coppola, 1992.
Mary Shelley's Frankenstein, directed by Kenneth Branagh, 1994.

Fisher himself remained ambivalent about his legacy. "In his infrequent interviews," observed Hutchings, "he always seemed to prefer discussing matters of technique and the everyday, mundane business of getting films made rather than making any grandiose statements about his films' content or about any ideas he might have wanted to express." Despite such modesty, Fisher's reputation has grown steadily since his death. "The fact that Fisher worked in routine genre films in an unpretentious studio should not blind anyone to the depth and force of his work," Leggett commented. Stephen Jones, writing in *The Essential Monster Movie Guide,* stated that the director "always brought integrity and an uncomplicated style to his best work in the horror genre."

■ Biographical and Critical Sources

BOOKS

Barta, Tony, editor, *Screening the Past: Film and the Representation of History,* Praeger Press (Westport, CT), 1998.
Brosnan, John, *The Horror People,* Macdonald & Jane's (London, England), 1976.

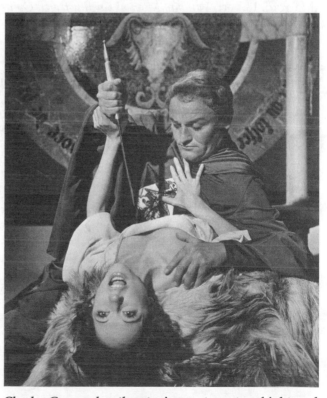

Charles Gray makes threatening gestures to a frightened Nike Arrighi in the Fisher-directed *The Devil Rides Out,* **a film released in 1968.** (Photograph courtesy of Hammer/Kobal Collection/ The Picture Desk, Inc.)

Chibnall, Steve, and Julian Petley, editors, *British Horror Cinema*, Routledge (London, England), 2002.

Clarens, Carlos, *The Illustrated History of Horror and Science-fiction Films*, Da Capo Press (New York, NY), 1997.

Curran, James, and Vincent Porter, editors, *British Cinema History*, Weidenfeld & Nicolson (London, England), 1983.

Dixon, Wheeler W., *The Charm of Evil: The Life and Films of Terence Fisher*, Rowman & Littlefield (Lanham, MD), 1991.

Dyson, Jeremy, *Bright Darkness: The Lost Art of the Supernatural Horror Film*, Cassell (Washington, DC), 1997.

Gifford, Denis, *The British Film Catalogue 1895-1985*, David & Charles (Newton Abbot, England), 1986.

Haining, Peter, *The Dracula Scrapbook*, Longmeadow (Stamford, CT), 1987.

Hutchings, Peter, *Terence Fisher*, Manchester University Press (Manchester, England), 2002.

Jones, Alan, *The Rough Guide to Horror Movies*, Rough Guides (New York, NY), 2005.

Jones, Stephen, *The Essential Monster Movie Guide*, Billboard Books (New York, NY), 2000.

Leggett, Paul, *Terence Fisher: Horror, Myth, and Religion*, McFarland & Company (Jefferson, NC), 2002.

Marrero, Robert, *Vampire Movies: An Illustrated Guide to Seventy-two Years of Vampire Movies*, Fantasia Books (Key West, FL), 1994.

McFarlane, Brian, *An Autobiography of British Cinema*, Methuen (London, England), 1997.

Meikle, Denis, *A History of Horrors: The Rise and Fall of the House of Hammer*, Scarecrow Press (Lanham, MD), 1996.

Petrie, Duncan, *Creativity and Constraint in the British Film Industry*, Macmillan (Basingstoke, England), 1991.

Pirie, David, *A Heritage of Horror: The English Gothic Cinema*, Gordon Fraser (London, England), 1973.

Pitts, Michael R., *Horror Film Stars*, McFarland & Company (Jefferson, NC), 1991.

Silver, Alain, and James Ursini, *The Vampire Film*, Limelight Editions (New York, NY), 1997.

Spicer, Andrew, *Typical Men: The Representation of Masculinity in Popular British Cinema*, I.B. Tauris (London, England), 2001.

Spicer, Andrew, *Film Noir*, Longman (Harlow, England), 2002.

Spicer, Andrew, *Sydney Box*, Manchester University Press (Manchester, England), 2006.

Wolfenstein, Martham and Nathan Leites, *Movies: A Psychological Study*, Free Press (Glencoe, IL), 1950.

PERIODICALS

Cinefantastique, Volume 4, number 3, Harry Ringel, "Terence Fisher: The Human Side," pp. 5-16.

Cinema, July 18, 1951, review of *Home to Danger*, p. 15.

Entertainment Weekly, May 14, 1993, Steve Daly, review of *The Brides of Dracula*, p. 63.

Film Criticism, autumn, 1996, Brian McFarlane, "Pulp Fictions: The British B Film and the Field of Cultural Production," pp. 48-70; winter, 2005, Andrew Spicer, "Creativity and the 'B' Feature: Terence Fisher's Crime Films," p. 24.

Guardian (London, England), August 1, 1996, Derek Malcolm, review of *Dracula*, p. 9; October 26, 2007, Peter Bradshaw, review of *Dracula*, p. 10.

Journal of British Cinema and Television, Volume 1, number 1, Andrew Spicer, "The Production Line: Reflections on the Role of the Film Producer in British Cinema," pp. 33-50.

New York Times, October 21, 2008, Dave Kehr, review of *The Two Faces of Dr. Jekyll*, p. C4.

Observer (London, England), October 16, 2005, Philip French, review of *The Hound of the Baskervilles*; February 8, 2009, Philip French, review of *Dracula, Prince of Darkness*, p. 22.

Spectator, October 20, 2007, Sinclair McKay, review of *Dracula*, p. 28.

Times (London, England), August 29, 2002, Stephen Dalton, review of *The Hound of the Baskervilles*, p. 30.

Today's Cinema, September 27, 1954, review of *Final Appointment*, p. 8.

ONLINE

British Film Institute Web site, http://www.bfi.org (April 15, 2009), "Terence Fisher."

Turner Classic Movies Web site, http://www.tcm.com (April 15, 2009), "Terence Fisher."*

Jeff Foxworthy

(Photograph © Jacques M. Chenet/Corbis.)

■ Personal

Born September 6, 1958, in Atlanta, GA; raised in Hapeville, GA; son of Jim (a computer executive) and Gayle (an advocate for the homeless) Foxworthy; married Pamela Gregg (an actress; name sometimes cited as Pamela Gregg Grethe), September 18, 1985; children: Jordan Lane (daughter), Juliane. *Education:* Graduated from Georgia Institute of Technology, 1979.

■ Addresses

Home—Atlanta, GA. *Agent*—Creative Artists Agency, 2000 Avenue of the Stars, Los Angeles, CA 90067; manager: J.P. Williams, Parallel Entertainment, 9420 Wilshire Blvd., Ste. 250, Beverly Hills, CA 90212.

■ Career

Comedian, performing and recording artist, producer, and author. Worked as computer engineer at IBM, 1979-84, comedian, 1984—. Actor in television series, including *The Jeff Foxworthy Show*, American Broadcasting Company (ABC), 1995-96, National Broadcasting Company (NBC), 1996-97, and *Blue Collar TV*, The WB, 2004-06. Actor in films, including *Blue Collar Comedy Tour: The Movie*, Warner Bros., 2003, (voice of character) *Racing Stripes*, Warner Bros., 2005, and (voice of character) *The Fox and the Hound II*, Buena Vista, 2006.

Host of television specials, including *Annual Academy of Country Music Awards*, NBC, 1995 and 1997, *The Twenty-third Annual American Music Awards*, ABC, 1996, *The CMT Music Awards*, Country Music Television (CMT), 2005, 2006, and 2007, and *Foxworthy's Big Night Out*, CMT, 2006; host of game show *Are You Smarter than a Fifth Grader?*, Fox, 2007—. Has appeared in television specials, including *Jeff Foxworthy: You Might Be a Redneck . . .*, Showtime, 1991, *Jeff Foxworthy: Check Your Neck*, Showtime, 1992, *An Evening with Randy Travis and Special Guests*, The Nashville Network, 1994, *Jeff Foxworthy: Totally Committed*, Home Box Office (HBO), 1998, *Inside TV Land: The Andy Griffith Show*, TV Land, 2000, *An American Celebration at Ford's Theatre*, ABC, 2001, *Comedy Central Roast of Jeff Foxworthy*, Comedy Central, 2005, *Blue Collar Comedy Tour: One for the Road*, Comedy Central, 2006, and *Larry the Cable Guy's Star-studded Christmas Extravaganza*, Comedy Central, 2008. Has appeared in episodes of *Good Morning America*, ABC, *The Tonight Show with Jay Leno*, NBC, *The View*, ABC, *Late Show with David Letterman*, CBS, *Late Night with Conan O'Brien*, NBC, and *Live with Regis and Kathie Lee*, ABC.

Executive producer of *Jeff Foxworthy: Check Your Neck*, Showtime, 1992, executive producer of *Jeff Fox-*

worthy: Totally Committed, HBO, 1998, creator and executive producer of Blue Collar TV, The WB, 2004-06; executive producer of Foxworthy's Big Night Out, CMT, 2006, and producer of Are You Smarter than a Fifth Grader?, Fox, 2007—. Host of The Foxworthy Countdown (syndicated radio show), 1999—.

■ Awards, Honors

Named Funniest Male Comedy Club Stand-up Performer, American Comedy Awards, 1990; People's Choice Award for Favorite Male Newcomer; Comedian of the Year, Nashville Network/Music City News, 1995, 1996, and 1997; Broadcast Personality of the Year nomination, Country Music Association, 2001; CableACE Award; has earned five Grammy Award nominations.

■ Writings

FILM AND TELEVISION

Jeff Foxworthy: Check Your Neck, Showtime, 1992.

(With others)The Jeff Foxworthy Show, American Broadcasting Company (ABC), 1995.

(With Ritch Shydner) Jeff Foxworthy: Totally Committed, Home Box Office (HBO), 1998.

(With Larry the Cable Guy, Bill Engvall, and Ron White) Blue Collar Comedy Tour: The Movie, Warner Bros., 2003.

(With Larry the Cable Guy, Bill Engvall, and Ron White) Blue Collar Comedy Tour Rides Again, Paramount, 2004.

Boyz in the Woodz, The WB, 2004.

(With Larry the Cable Guy, Bill Engvall, and Ron White) Blue Collar Comedy Tour: One for the Road, Comedy Central, 2006.

(With others) Foxworthy's Big Night Out, Country Music Television (CMT), 2006.

BOOKS

You Might Be a Redneck If . . . , illustrated by David Boyd, Longstreet Press (Atlanta, GA), 1989, reprinted, Rutledge Hill Press (Nashville, TN), 2004.

Hick Is Chic: A Guide to Etiquette for the Grossly Unsophisticated, illustrated by David Boyd, Longstreet Press (Atlanta, GA), 1990.

Red Ain't Dead: 150 More Ways to Tell If You're a Redneck, illustrated by David Boyd, Longstreet Press (Atlanta, GA), 1991.

Check Your Neck: More of You Might Be a Redneck If . . . , illustrated by David Boyd, Longstreet Press (Atlanta, GA), 1992.

You're Not a Kid Anymore When . . . , illustrated by David Boyd, Longstreet Press (Atlanta, GA), 1993.

(With Vic Henley) Games Rednecks Play, Longstreet Press (Atlanta, GA), 1994.

Redneck Classic: The Best of Jeff Foxworthy, illustrated by David Boyd, Longstreet Press (Atlanta, GA), 1995.

No Shirt, No Shoes, . . . No Problem!, illustrated by David Boyd, Hyperion (New York, NY), 1996.

Those People: Humorous Drawings, Longstreet Press (Atlanta, GA), 1996.

(With Big Jim Foxworthy) The Foxworthy Down-home Cookbook: No Arugula, No Pate, No Problem!, illustrated by David Boyd, Longstreet Press (Atlanta, GA), 1997.

The Final Helping of You Might Be a Redneck if . . . , illustrated by David Boyd, Longstreet Press (Atlanta, GA), 1999.

There's No Place like a Mobile Home for the Holidays, illustrated by David Boyd, Rutledge Hill Press (Nashville, TN), 2004.

You Might Be a Redneck If . . . This Is the Biggest Book You've Ever Read, illustrated by David Boyd, Rutledge Hill Press (Nashville, TN), 2004.

The Redneck Grill, illustrated by David Boyd, Rutledge Hill Press (Nashville, TN), 2005.

Red Is the Color of My True Love's Neck, illustrated by David Boyd, Rutledge Hill Press (Nashville, TN), 2005.

Redneck Extreme Mobile Home Makeover, illustrated by David Boyd, Rutledge Hill Press (Nashville, TN), 2005.

Jeff Foxworthy's Redneck Dictionary: Words You Thought You Knew the Meaning Of, illustrated by Layron DeJamette, Villard (New York, NY), 2005.

The Redneck Doesn't Fall Far from the Tree, illustrated by David Boyd, Rutledge Hill Press (Nashville, TN), 2006.

How Many Women Does It Take to Change a Redneck?, illustrated by David Boyd, Rutledge Hill Press (Nashville, TN), 2006.

No Redneck Left Behind: Facing the Real World after Gettin' Your Diploma, illustrated by David Boyd, Rutledge Hill Press (Nashville, TN), 2006.

Jeff Foxworthy's Redneck Dictionary II: More Words You Thought You Knew the Meaning Of, illustrated by Layron DeJarnette, Villard (New York, NY), 2006.

Jeff Foxworthy's Redneck Dictionary III: Learning to Talk More Gooder Fastly, illustrated by Layron DeJarnette, Villard (New York, NY), 2007.

Dirt on My Shirt, illustrated by Steve Björkman, HarperCollins Children's Books (New York, NY), 2008.

(With Brian Hartt) *How to Really Stink at Golf*, Villard (New York, NY), 2008.

Jeff Foxworthy's Complete Redneck Dictionary: All the Words You Thought You Knew the Meaning Of, illustrated by Layron DeJarnette, Villard (New York, NY), 2008.

(With Brian Hartt) *How to Really Stink at Work: A Guide to Making Yourself Fire-proof While Having the Most Fun Possible*, illustrated by Layron DeJarnette, Villard (New York, NY), 2009.

RECORDINGS

Too Drunk to Fish, Laughing Hyena, 1989.

Bodacious Tatas, Laughing Hyena, 1989.

You Might Be a Redneck, Laughing Hyena, 1989.

Redneck Stomp, Warner Bros. Records, 1993.

You Might Be a Redneck If . . . , Warner Bros. Records, 1994.

The Redneck Test, Laughing Hyena, 1995.

The Original, Laughing Hyena, 1995.

Sold Out, Laughing Hyena, 1995.

Party All Night, Warner Bros. Records, 1995.

Games Rednecks Play, Warner Bros. Records, 1995.

King of the Rednecks, Laughing Hyena, 1995.

Live, Laughing Hyena, 1996.

Redneck Games, Warner Bros. Records, 1996.

Crank It Up: The Music Album, Warner Bros. Records, 1996.

Totally Committed, Warner Bros. Records, 1998.

Greatest Bits, Warner Bros. Records, 1999.

Big Funny, Dreamworks SKG, 2000.

The Best of Jeff Foxworthy: Double Wide, Single Minded, Rhino Records, 2003.

(With Larry the Cable Guy, Bill Engvall, and Ron White) *Blue Collar Comedy Tour* (original motion picture soundtrack), Warner Bros. Records, 2003.

Have Your Loved Ones Spayed or Neutered, Warner Bros. Records, 2004.

(With Larry the Cable Guy, Bill Engvall, and Ron White) *Blue Collar Comedy Tour Rides Again*, Warner Bros. Records, 2004.

One for the Road, Warner Bros. Records, 2006.

■ **Sidelights**

Comedian Jeff Foxworthy is best known for a litany of gags that begin "You might be a redneck if . . . ." and he has parlayed his southern-flavored but very mainstream routines into a hugely lucrative career that includes platinum-selling albums, bestselling books, and a number of network television series. Though his "redneck" material forms only a portion of Foxworthy's standup routine—which also includes satirical riffs on marriage, child-rearing, and consumer culture—it is clearly responsible for his meteoric rise. Discussing Foxworthy's success in the *New York Times*, A.J. Frutkin noted that the comedian "sends up his Southern roots and pays tribute to them at the same time."

Foxworthy was raised in Hapeville, Georgia, a suburb of Atlanta; he described his hometown to Phil Kloer of the *Detroit Free Press* as "almost like a Mayberry," the mythical burg of television's *The Andy Griffith Show*. His father, an executive at IBM, hardly fits the "redneck" stereotype he has so successfully exploited. Even so, the younger Foxworthy recalled to a *People* reporter, Jim Foxworthy came home from the office, "sat out in the back, drinking a beer and watching the bug zapper."

A class clown who earned good grades, Foxworthy grew up entranced with comedy records by Bob Newhart, Flip Wilson, and especially Bill Cosby, whose bemused observations on domestic life clearly informs his own humor. Indeed, Foxworthy

Jeff Foxworthy, performing on stage at the New York State Fair, 1998. (Photograph courtesy of Michael Okoniewski/Getty Images.)

Comedian and author Foxworthy at work on the road. (Photograph courtesy of the Kobal Collection/The Picture Desk, Inc.)

divulged to Bob Cannon in *Entertainment Weekly*, Cosby was his "No. 1 influence, because he was able to do comedy clean. Part of the art of comedy is finding a way to say things without being dirty. I think it's lazy, otherwise." In the same way that Cosby's gentle, inclusive material helped him escape the tag of "black comedian" in the racially charged 1960s, Foxworthy's avoidance of the politically controversial side of "redneck" culture has guaranteed him mainstream appeal. He also came to admire more daring and less "clean" comics, such as Richard Pryor and George Carlin, particularly for their highly developed sense of character and observation.

Foxworthy played football in high school and was a fierce competitor, though his skinny build cost him dearly. "He doesn't believe in losing," Jim Foxworthy noted to Kloer, calling his son a "kamikaze" and adding: "I don't know how many nights I sat up with him in the hospital." Since a career on the gridiron was unlikely, Jeff attended Georgia Tech and took a page from his father's book by accepting a computer engineer's post at IBM. "I never did

quite fit in to that suit and tie thing," he remarked to Colin Covert in the Minneapolis *Star Tribune*. "Every business had the guy in the break room telling jokes, doing impersonations of the boss and getting caught at it. I was constantly getting caught at it. But I didn't know you could do this for a living."

A Hard-working Comic

Foxworthy's first attempt at stand-up comedy came at The Punch Line, an Atlanta club, in June of 1984. In the audience was former actress Pamela Gregg Grethe; the two would later marry and Gregg, as her husband calls her, became Foxworthy's biggest booster. She supported him with a public relations job and he hit the road, performing as many as 500 gigs a year; they reunited on weekends. "Nobody who's been successful at this has been lazy about it," Foxworthy told Covert. "It's a labor of love, but it's working at your job." Not every performance was magic, however. "I remember playing somebody's office Christmas party," the comic reminisced in his interview with Kloer, "where they're all drunk and you have a Radio Shack microphone."

Though Foxworthy's earliest routine, according to Kloer, was "about his father cutting his toenails with bolt cutters," he didn't come up with his "redneck" gambit until a few years later. While in Michigan, he spied a sign in front of a bowling alley that offered its patrons valet parking. Foxworthy realized that there were no geographical or financial limits to "redneckism," which he defines as "a glorious absence of sophistication." As he told Frutkin, "It's a state of mind—Elvis was a millionaire, and he had carpet on his ceiling." Soon he would bring this epiphany to the nation with his handy pointers for redneck self-diagnosis, such as, "You might be a redneck if your lawn furniture used to be your living room furniture," or, "You go to a family reunion to meet women." As country music and its cultural fallout became a mainstream phenomenon, his material struck a chord. "It was like finding your crowd," he told Cheech Marin in *Newsweek*. Even as his career skyrocketed, Foxworthy learned not to stray far from his roots. "One thing I figured out

from the start," Foxworthy told *Denver Post* contributor Butch Hause, "is that the closer to the truth I kept my stories, the better they worked on stage. Hell, I don't have to exaggerate much of anything I talk about. The fact that I'm a redneck is usually funny enough!"

Foxworthy's success wasn't limited to the stage, however. First came his million-selling books, including *No Shirt. No Shoes . . . No Problem! Red Is the Color of My True Love's Neck*, and *Jeff Foxworthy's Redneck Dictionary: Words You Thought You Knew the Meaning Of.* "Foxworthy honors us with his down-home takes on universal conditions," Benjamin Segedin remarked in a *Booklist* critique of *No Shirt. No Shoes . . . No Problem!* Next came the crossover triumph of his CD *You Might Be a Redneck If . . .*, which came out in 1994 and achieved multi-platinum sales. "The people at Warner Bros. [records] said if it did 100,000, we'd be throwing confetti," Foxworthy informed a *USA Today*

Memorable moments at the 2006 CMT Music Awards included Foxworthy's "Line Dancing with the Stars" skit.
(Photograph courtesy of John Shearer/WireImage/Getty Images.)

interviewer. "Thank God they don't know anything about their business." Alanna Nash praised the album in *Entertainment Weekly*; Foxworthy, she proclaimed, is "almost always amusing" and "hits his stride with the title segment, veering between the zany and the all-too-true."

Transitions to Television and Film

Since a lion's share of successful television sitcoms are built around comics and their best-known routines—Roseanne Barr's cynical homemaker, Tim Allen's hardware fetishist, Jerry Seinfeld's obsessive urbanite—Foxworthy seemed an obvious choice for his own half-hour. Unfortunately, ABC had trouble finding an appropriate pretext for *The Jeff Foxworthy Show*. Initially set in the South with Foxworthy cast as a construction worker, the action moved to Indiana, where his character runs a heating-and-air-conditioning business and gets to sound off about rednecks. Although the show's reviews were uniformly dreadful, Foxworthy was clearly unworried. "I love bein' the underdog," he noted to Kloer.

Although the sitcom lasted just two years, Foxworthy has continued to work in television. He starred in his own Showtime specials, *Jeff Foxworthy: You Might Be a Redneck . . .* and *Jeff Foxworthy: Check Your Neck*, and also served as the host of *The CMT Music Awards*. Additionally, he made numerous appearances on such programs as *The Tonight Show with Jay Leno* and *Late Show with David Letterman*. Foxworthy also branched into film, providing his voice for the animated films *Racing Stripes* and *The Fox and the Hound II*. Some of his biggest screen triumphs, however, evolved from his work on the Blue Collar Comedy Tour, which he began in 2000 with fellow comedians Bill Engvall, Ron White, and Larry the Cable Guy. The tour spawned a best-selling live album, a pair of hit films, and a highly-rated show, *Blue Collar TV*, on The WB network. According to Gillian Flynn, reviewing *Blue Collar TV* in *Entertainment Weekly*, the skits are "aimed at poking fun at the flyover-state lifestyle before those smarty-pants in New York City get a chance to." The critic added, "*Blue* at its best is plain good-natured, the mockery self-inflicted."

In 2007 Foxworthy was picked to host *Are You Smarter than a Fifth Grader?*, a popular game show in which adults match wits with a group of camera-friendly children. Calling Foxworthy "a bang-up host," *New York Times* contributor Virginia Heffernan noted that "his invocations of elementary-school concepts, from wedgies to stolen lunch money, lift *Are You Smarter* out of the current day into some

shared utopia of childhood, spent mostly in the classroom, where popularity and parents' divorces don't trouble anyone." Michael D. Schaffer, writing in the *Philadelphia Inquirer*, also praised the comedian's performance, stating that this "laid-back, folksy personality (just like your favorite teacher's) and his kindly wit make him ideal for a show that relies heavily on children and is meant to be watched by parents and their offspring together." When it first aired, *Are You Smarter than a Fifth Grader?* drew more than twenty million viewers, the biggest series premiere in Fox history.

If you enjoy the works of Jeff Foxworthy, you may also want to check out the following:

Bill Engvall's audio CD *A Decade of Laughs*, 2004.
Ron White's audio CD *You Can't Fix Stupid*, 2006.
Larry the Cable Guy's DVD *Morning Constitutions*, 2007.

Thanks to the success of his books and recordings, Foxworthy no longer needs to tour incessantly, which allows him to spend more time with his wife and daughters at their Atlanta home. "My life is centered around them," he told Kloer in his *Atlanta Journal-Constitution* interview. "I'm a dad and a husband and a brother and a son and a friend. I like what I do, but it's not what I am." Should he ever wish to return to stand-up full time, however, Foxworthy is confident that there will be no shortage of material. As he told Kevin Sack in the *New York Times*, "I do have a theory that when they finally nuke this planet that the only two things that are going to be around are cockroaches and rednecks. I guarantee you that out of the mushroom there's going to be one guy come staggering without a shirt on and a pair of blue jeans going: 'Crank it up! Hoo-eee. Damn, man, that about busted my eardrums.'"

■ Biographical and Critical Sources

PERIODICALS

America, January 13, 1996, George W. Hunt, review of *Redneck Classic: The Best of Jeff Foxworthy*, p. 2.

Foxworthy's efforts at public education include his detailed presentations in the television show *Are You Smarter than a Fifth Grader?* (Photograph courtesy of Frank Micelotta/Getty Images, for FOX.)

Atlanta Journal-Constitution, June 11, 1998, Glenn Hannigan, "Foxworthy Fiction Is More Fun than Fact," p. J15; December 18, 2007, Phil Kloer, "Foxworthy Redefines His Role as Comedian," p. E1; February 28, 2008, Phil Kloer, "The Family Guy," p. E1.

Booklist, Benjamin Segedin, review of *No Shirt, No Shoes . . . No Problem!,* p. 1546.

Country Music, January-February, 1997, Michael Bane, "20 Questions with Jeff Foxworthy," p. 4.

Denver Post, June 17, 1996, Butch Hause, "Cashing in on Redneck Humor Lots of Fun for Jeff Foxworthy," p. F8; March 1, 2001, "You Might Be a Comic If . . . Your Shows Draw Thousands, p. F5.

Detroit Free Press, September 26, 1995, Phil Kloer, interview with Foxworthy, p. 3C.

Entertainment Weekly, October 21, 1994, Alanna Nash, review of *You Might Be a Redneck If . . . ,* p. 67; January 20, 1995, Bob Cannon, "A Stand-up Ovation," p. 51; July 28, 1995, David Browne, review of *Games Rednecks Play,* p. 60; May 31, 1996, Gene Lyons, review of *No Shirt. No Shoes . . . No Problem!,* p. 52; October 6, 1995, review of *The Jeff Foxworthy Show,* p. 51; September 3, 2004, Gillian Flynn, "Trite *Collar,*" p. 65; April 1, 2005, Scott Brown, "Stupid Questions: This Week with . . . Jeff Foxworthy," p. 80.

Houston Chronicle, Tom Zucco, "A Normal Life: Back in Georgia with His Family, Foxworthy Has Come Full Circle," p. 6.

Kansas City Star, July 16, 2004, "*Blue Collar* Comedians Give WB Network a Different Look."

Los Angeles Times, September 20, 1994, Jon Matsumoto, "Laughs on Both Sides of Mason-Dixon Line: Jeff Foxworthy Turns Jokes about Southern Background into His Funny Business," p. F1; March 28, 2003, "Comedy That's Redneck, White, and Blue-Collar," review of *Blue Collar Comedy Tour: The Movie,* p. E8.

Newsweek, August 21, 1995, Cheech Marin, "Bubbapalooza, U.S.A.," p. 68.

New York Times, February 7, 1996, Kevin Sack, "Jeff Foxworthy: 2,000 Ways You Might Be a Redneck"; August 22, 2004, A.J. Frutkin, "Enough with the Fancy Urban Singles," p. L4; June 13, 2005, Ross Johnson, "Red State Humor Turns Blue," p. C1; October 20, 2006, Susan Stewart, "Just a Good Old Boy, Traversing Familiar Old Comic Territory," review of *Foxworthy's Big Night Out,* p. E29; March 8, 2007, Virginia Heffernan, "Too Bad There's No Credit for Lunch and Recess Here," review of *Are You Smarter than a Fifth Grader?,* p. E6.

People, November 7, 1994, "The Bubba Book," p. 124; October 9, 1995, review of *The Jeff Foxworthy Show,* p. 23.

Philadelphia Inquirer, February 3, 2008, Michael D. Schaffer, "*5th Grader* a Smart Play for Foxworthy."

Publishers Weekly, March 17, 2008, review of *Dirt on My Shirt,* p. 70.

School Library Journal, June, 2008, Catherine Threadgill, review of *Dirt on My Shirt,* p. 122.

Star Tribune (Minneapolis, MN), January 21, 2000, Colin Covert, "Crazy like a Fox: True Tales of His Georgia Family Have Kept Blue Collar Comedian Jeff Foxworthy Honest and Funny," p. 14.

TV Guide, March 19, 2007, Jonathan Small, "Jeff Foxworthy," p. 26.

USA Today, July 24, 1995, interview with Foxworthy, p. 4D; March 8, 2007, Gary Strauss, "Fox's *5th Grader* Makes Smart Moves, p. D1; June 25, 2007, Missy Baxter, "Foxworthy takes the *Fifth,*" p. D3; May 7, 2008, "All Seriousness Aside, Whack Away," p. C3.

Variety, December 2, 1991, Kathleen O'Steen, review of *Hot Country Nights,* p. 92; September 11, 1995, Todd Everett, review of *The Jeff Foxworthy Show,* p. 38; October 21, 1996, Jeremy Gerard, review of *The Jeff Foxworthy Show,* p. 212; March 31, 2003, Robert Koehler, review of *Blue Collar Comedy Tour: The Movie,* p. 30.

ONLINE

Comedy Central Web site, http://comedians.comedycentral.com/ (March 15, 2009), "Jeff Foxworthy."

Country Music Television Web site, http://www.cmt.com/ (March 15, 2009), "Jeff Foxworthy."

Jeff Foxworthy Official Web site, http://www.jefffoxworthy.com (March 15, 2009).*

Elizabeth Gaskell

(Illustration courtesy of the Library of Congress.)

■ Personal

Born September 29, 1810, in London, England; died November 12, 1865, in Holybourne, Hampshire, England; daughter of William (keeper of treasury records and writer) and Elizabeth (Holland) Stevenson; married William Gaskell (a minister), August 30, 1832; children: Marianne, Margaret Emily "Meta"), Florence, William, Julia. *Religion:* Unitarian.

■ Career

Writer.

■ Writings

(Published anonymously) *Mary Barton: A Tale of Manchester Life* (novel), two volumes, Chapman & Hall (London, England), 1848, published in one volume, Harper (New York, NY), 1848, new edition, introduction and notes by Shirley Foster, Norton (New York, NY), 2006.

(As Cotton Mather Mills, Esq.) *Libbie Marsh's Three Eras: A Lancashire Tale,* Hamilton, Adams (London, England), 1850.

(Attributed to Charles Dickens) *Lizzie Leigh: A Domestic Tale, from "Household Words,"* Dewitt & Davenport (New York, NY), 1850.

(Published anonymously) *The Moorland Cottage,* Chapman & Hall (London, England), 1850, Harper (New York, NY), 1851.

(Published anonymously) *Ruth: A Novel,* three volumes, Chapman & Hall (London, England), 1853, published in one volume, Ticknor, Reed & Fields (Boston, MA), 1853, new edition published under name Elizabeth C. Gaskell, Oxford University Press (Oxford, England), 1985.

(Published anonymously) *Cranford,* Harper (New York, NY), 1853, new edition published under name Elizabeth C. Gaskell, Oxford University Press (Oxford, England), 1980, with notes by Patricia Ingham, Penguin (New York, NY), 2005.

(Published anonymously) *Lizzie Leigh and Other Tales,* Chapman & Hall (London, England), 1855, Hardy (Philadelphia, PA), 1869.

(Published anonymously) *Hands and Heart and Bessy's Troubles at Home,* Chapman & Hall (London, England), 1855.

(Published anonymously) *North and South,* two volumes, Chapman & Hall (London, England), 1855, published in one volume, Harper (New York, NY), 1855, published under name Elizabeth C. Gaskell, Scholarly Press, 1871, revised edition, Oxford University Press (New York, NY), 1982, new edition, with an introduction by Jenny Uglow, Norton (New York, NY), 2005.

The Life of Charlotte Brontë, Author of "Jane Eyre," "Shirley," "Villette" etc. (biography), two volumes, Appleton (New York, NY), 1857, reprinted, Oxford University Press (Oxford, England), 1975.

My Lady Ludlow: A Novel, Harper (New York, NY), 1858, published as *Round the Sofa,* two volumes, Low (London, England), 1858, published as *My Lady Ludlow and Other Stories,* Oxford University Press (Oxford, England), 1989.

Right at Last, and Other Tales, Harper (New York, NY), 1860.

Lois the Witch and Other Tales, Tauchnitz (Leipzig, Germany), 1861.

Sylvia's Lovers (novel), three volumes, Smith, Elder (London, England), 1863, published in one volume, Dutton (New York, NY), 1863, new edition, edited with an introduction and notes by Andrew Sanders, Oxford University Press (New York, NY), 2008.

A Dark Night's Work, Harper (New York, NY), 1863, published as *A Dark Night's Work and Other Stories,* Oxford University Press (Oxford, England), 1992.

Cousin Phillis: A Tale, Harper (New York, NY), 1864, published as *Cousin Phillis and Other Tales,* Smith, Elder (London, England), 1865, reprinted, Oxford University Press (Oxford, England), 1981.

The Grey Woman and Other Tales, Smith, Elder (London, England), 1865, Harper (New York, NY), 1882.

Wives and Daughters: An Every-Day Story, two volumes, Smith, Elder (London, England), 1866, published in one volume, Harper (New York, NY), 1866, reprinted, Penguin (New York, NY), 2001.

COLLECTIONS

The Works of Mrs. Gaskell, eight volumes, edited by A.W. Ward, Smith, Elder (London, England), 1906–11, published as *The Works: The Knutsford Edition,* Lubrecht & Cramer, 1974.

The Novels and Tales of Mrs. Gaskell, edited by C.K. Shorter, eleven volumes, Oxford University Press (Oxford, England), 1906–19.

The Letters of Mrs. Gaskell, edited by John A. Chapple and Arthur Pollard, Harvard University Press (Cambridge, MA), 1966.

The Letters of Mrs. Gaskell and Charles Eliot Norton, 1855-1865, introduction by Jane Whitehill, Lubrecht & Cramer, 1973.

Elizabeth Gaskell: A Portrait in Letters, edited by J.A.V. Chapple and John Geoffrey Sharps, Manchester University Press (Manchester, England), 1980, reprinted, 2007.

Four Short Stories, Pandora Press (Boston, MA), 1983.

Gothic Tales, Penguin (New York, NY), 2000.

Further Letters of Mrs. Gaskell, edited by John Chapple and Alan Shelston, Manchester University Press (Manchester, England), 2000.

Contributor of stories, essays, and articles to periodicals, including *Cornhill* and Charles Dickens's *Household Words* and *All the Year Round.*

Collections of Gaskell's papers are housed at Harvard University, Leeds University, the Manchester Central Reference Library, Manchester University, Princeton University, and the John Rylands Library.

■ Adaptations

Mary Barton was adapted for a movie, 1964; *Cranford* was adapted for a movie titled *The Followers,* 1939, a British Broadcasting Corporation (BBC) movie, 1951, and a BBC television mini-series, 2007; *North and South* was adapted for a BBC television miniseries, 2004; *Wives and Daughters* was adapted for a 1991 miniseries, and a BBC television miniseries, 1999.

■ Sidelights

Elizabeth Gaskell is most commonly termed a Victorian novelist, yet such a term does little to enlighten or to explicate the work of this writer. Though she was a novelist, perhaps her two best-known works, as T.J. Winnifrith noted in *Reference Guide to English Literature,* are the series of essentially inter-connected short stories that comprise her 1853 work, *Cranford,* as well as the biography *The Life of Charlotte Brontë, Author of "Jane Eyre," "Shirley," "Villette" etc.* According to Winnifrith, these two works "have had an important if adverse effect on Gaskell's standing as a novelist." Another interpretation of Gaskell, as Maureen T. Reddy wrote in the *Dictionary of Literary Biography,* is that of the "conventional, middle-class Victorian wife and mother who accepted the values of her world and who also happened to write books."

Yet such a bland description is dispelled by her novels of social realism and social problems, such as her first novel, *Mary Barton: A Tale of Manchester Life,* which is a searing indictment of the industrial revolution and of labor relations, or *Ruth: A Novel,* about a so-called "fallen woman," or her final work, *Wives and Daughters: An Every-Day Story,* which expounds upon the changing world of society and

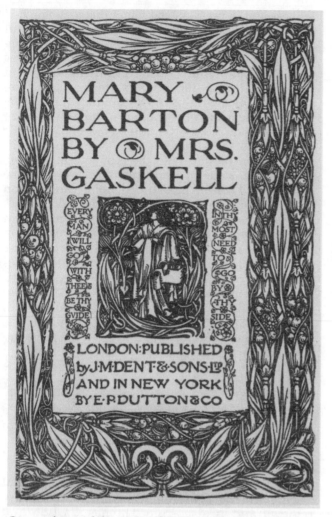

Cover of one of the early editions of Elizabeth Gaskell's popular novel *Mary Barton*, which was first published anonymously in 1848. (Photograph courtesy of the Graduate Library, University of Michigan. Reproduced by permission, PR 4710.M4 1912.)

technology that her characters must adapt to. Those who define Gaskell by these works find incipient Marxist leanings in her writings or see her as a proto-feminist. As Reddy further commented, for these critics, "Gaskell was an unconventional, complicated person, a serious artist who strove to articulate in all of her writings what she understood to be the truth of women's lot—very far indeed from the contented, minor, feminine dove of earlier views." Still others see Gaskell as a provincial artist, a writer on the order of Thomas Hardy or George Eliot who portrays life in rural and regional communities, while some find her an innovator in the short fiction form.

The genius of Gaskell is that she was all these. In addition to the afore-mentioned novels, Gaskell is also remembered for the novels *North and South* and *Sylvia's Lovers*, as well as for a number of short story collections and novellas such as *Cousin Phillis: A Tale*, works which provide the reader with "a renewed appreciation for Gaskell's remarkable gifts as a storyteller and of her sophisticated understanding of psychology," according to Reddy. Gaskell chose as her themes the social changes caused by the industrial revolution, the contrasts between life in industrial cities and in rural communities, and the emotional and social troubles her female characters experienced in a male-dominated world. Although many of her novels were initially published anonymously, by the time of her death in 1865, Gaskell had become part of the British literary canon. Reporting on her death in the *Athenaeum* (as quoted in *Encyclopedia of British Women Writers*), a contributor described the recently deceased author as, "if not the most popular, with small question, the most powerful and finished female novelist of an epoch singularly rich in female novelists." Although Gaskell's reputation flagged for some time in the early twentieth century, by the 1980s her work had made a definite comeback, with new editions of her novels, biography, and short stories, and well-received television adaptations of several of her more popular novels. Renewed critical and academic interest accompanied this literary resurrection.

Unitarian Beginnings

Born Elizabeth Cleghorn Stevenson on September 29, 1810, Gaskell was the second child of Elizabeth Holland Stevenson and William Stevenson, a Unitarian minister. Gaskell's father had, before his daughter's birth, given up a paid ministry, finding it ethically wrong to take money for such work, and instead made his living by writing for various journals on topics such as agriculture and naval history, and also as a civil servant, the keeper of the records of the state treasury. The family made their home in the Chelsea section of London, which at the time was a rural western suburb of the city. Gaskell's mother gave birth to eight children; however, only the first, John, and the last, Elizabeth, survived.

Gaskell grew up without a mother, for hers died just thirteen months after her birth. She knew maternal affection, though, for her mother's sister, Aunt Lumb, adopted her and removed the child to the country village of Knutsford, where she grew up in rural surroundings and was initially educated at home. This education was rigorous, for Unitarians strongly believed in such learning for both boys and girls. At the age of twelve, Gaskell was sent to a boarding school near Stratford-on-Avon, where she learned classics and languages. As Edgar Wright observed in the *Dictionary of Literary Biography,* "[Gaskell] spent five years in surroundings that admirably suited her tastes, intelligence, and love of the country, leaving the school in 1827 an accomplished and—according to the evidence of friends and artists—a vivacious and attractive young woman."

During this time it appears that the young Gaskell did not have much of a relationship with her father, who had since remarried. She was drawn back to London, however, in 1828 with the disappearance of her only sibling, John, who was employed by the East India Company and appears to have been lost on a voyage to India. This tragic event brought Gaskell back into her father's orbit, but there was little love between the stepmother and Gaskell. Despite this, she stayed on in London until the death of her father in 1829. She thereafter returned to Knutsford, but on a visit to the industrial hub of Manchester, she met a young Unitarian minister, William Gaskell, who was the assistant minister at the Cross Street Chapel, an important Unitarian center in the city.

The couple was married in 1832 and settled in Manchester. As Wright noted, "The Gaskells seem to have been two intelligent and sensitive people who respected each other's independence and temperament without denying the basic roles of husband and paterfamilias." According to Unitarian belief, a wife is not the submissive property of her husband; Elizabeth Gaskell was encouraged by her husband to develop her own interests. In the first decade of marriage the couple had four surviving children. Gaskell concentrated on domestic tasks primarily in these years, but also studied poetry and did relief work among the city's poor, for the 1840s were a time of economic depression and dislocation in Manchester, which had become the center for England's industrial revolution, a town of mills and smudgy air. Gaskell witnessed at firsthand the distressing conditions of workers in these mills and factories, and the contrast between the dirty industrial city and the bucolic charm of Knutsford where she had grown up could not have been starker. As Wright observed, Gaskell referred to her adopted city as "dear old dull ugly smoky grim grey Manchester."

Birth of a Writer

In 1845 Gaskell's nine-month-old son, Willie, died of scarlet fever, and Gaskell's husband suggested she write a long story as a way to overcome the sadness and depression she felt at this loss. She had earlier composed a sonnet to a stillborn child, but now she set to work with deeper purpose, finishing her first novel, *Mary Barton,* in 1847. The book was published anonymously the following year and Gaskell collected 100 pounds sterling from the publishers for the rights. As Wright noted, the novel "created a sensation," for it tells a story of romance and murder as a result of industrial action. The title character is the daughter of a Manchester mill worker, John Barton. With the economy in turmoil, labor unrest is rife in Manchester at the time of the story. Finally as a measure of labor and union protest, John is chosen by lot to kill the mill owner's son, who, incidentally, has nearly seduced Mary. Though John Barton does in fact commit the deed, Mary's real love interest, Jem Wilson, becomes the chief suspect in the killing. Finally the truth comes out, via Mary's estranged aunt, Esther, a prostitute, and Mary and Jem leave the grime of Manchester for a new life in Canada. Wright commented, however, that such "a summary of the plot gives little hint of the real force of the novel: the presentation of Manchester life and the pressures that turn John Barton into a murderer." For Winnifrith, the novel "asks many questions, but provides no easy answers." Arthur Pollard, writing in the *Reference Guide to English Literature,* termed this first novel "a powerful, if at times uneven book, justly praised on its appearance and retaining a strong appeal ever since."

Writing in *History Today,* Sue Wilkes observed that "Although *Mary Barton* received good literary reviews and praise from Thomas Carlyle and Charles Dickens, the book attracted savage criticism in the Manchester *Guardian* and the *British Quarterly.*" As Wilkes pointed out, some of the contemporary reviewers complained that Gaskell exaggerated the conflicts between mill owners and workers and only exacerbated the situation with her novel. Writing in the *Edinburgh Review* in 1849, for example, William Rathbone Greg declared that Gaskell "has borne false witness against a whole class,—has most inconsiderately fostered the ill-opinion of them known to exist in certain quarters—and has, unintentionally no doubt, but most unfortunately, flattered both the prejudices of the aristocracy and the passions of the populace." Wilkes, on the other hand, commented: "It is unlikely that *Mary Barton* further inflamed attitudes that were already deeply polarized. Mrs. Gaskell was horrified at suggestions she was stirring up class hatred; her own vision of her novel was a 'tragic poem' rather than a political platform. The novel certainly provoked fierce criticism. Publishing *Mary Barton* in such fractious times took courage. But it was also an act of love, and Gaskell's love of humanity forms the abiding message of this classic tale."

Gaskell established herself as a professional writer with *Mary Barton*, and soon was publishing stories for *Household Words*, a journal founded by the well-known writer Charles Dickens. One of these stories, "Our Society at Cranford," became the first two chapters of the novel *Cranford*, published in 1853. If *Mary Barton* is Gaskell's depiction of urban difficulties and class warfare, her second novel presents something of a rural idyll, reflecting the spirit of old-fashioned Knutsford society where she grew up. Peopled by a group of eccentric characters, the book focuses on the life of kindly Miss Matty and the search for her missing brother. This plot element recalls Gaskell's own despair and action at the disappearance of her brother John a quarter century earlier. However, unlike real life, Gaskell's novel has the long-lost brother finally returning to Miss Matty from India. *Cranford* is a novel of social manners, and has found praise over the years for its intimate style of storytelling. As Wright noted, "The attractiveness of *Cranford* lies in the way in which [Gaskell] recreates with humor and affection a way of life that was already old-fashioned when she was a young girl growing up among the little group of ladies of good birth but small income who constituted Cranford society."

While Gaskell was supplying the eight installments to *Household Words*, that became the novel *Cranford*, she was also working on a darker novel, also published in 1853. *Ruth: A Novel* earned Gaskell 500 pounds sterling, but also embroiled her in a critical and social scandal, for here she looks at a woman who bears a child out of wedlock. Gaskell based the character of the Unitarian minister who helps Ruth raise her child on a family friend. In the end Ruth reclaims her reputation, working as a volunteer nurse during a cholera outbreak and dying of the disease. As Wright noted, the publication of *Ruth* "touched off an immediate reaction from shocked moralists, though many critics and readers praised it for its courage and its quality." Wright further noted, "The strength of the novel lies in its presentation of social conduct within a small Dissenting community when tolerance and rigid morality clash." For Winnifrith, "Ruth's fall from grace is delicately handled, and she appears to modern readers as almost entirely innocent, whereas her seducer . . . seems cruel and callow."

Gaskell returned to the social-problem novel with her 1855 work *North and South*. Here she compares and contrasts directly life in the city versus the country. The involved plot of the novel features John Thornton, a Milton (read Manchester) mill owner, and Margaret Hale, a privileged young woman from Helstone (a stand-in for Knutsford), a small town in the rural south of England. The setting of the novel moves between the south and the industrialized north when Margaret's family moves there. It is not only the city and country that are contrasted in the novel, though, for Gaskell also looks at workers versus employers, wealth versus poverty, and unionists versus nonunionists. Amid all this variety of subplot, John and Margaret fall in love and gain an appreciation of one another's background. Wright thought that with publication of *North and South* "Mrs. Gaskell achieves maturity as a novelist." For Reddy, both *Mary Barton* and *North and South* "depict the problems of the urban poor as infinitely complicated and resistant to simple solutions, and in them Gaskell struggles to reconcile the demands of Christianity with the basic principles of capitalism, refusing to damn capitalism in the facile way some of her contemporaries did."

From Novelist to Biographer

In 1850, while traveling about England and gathering material for *North and South*, Gaskell stopped at the village of Haworth and met for the first time

Gaskell's novel *Cranford*, released in 1853, was published anonymously, as was much of her early work.
(Photograph courtesy of Special Collections Library, University of Michigan. Reproduced by permissionm, PR 4710.C8 1853.)

A rare photograph of Gaskell, taken c. 1860. (Photograph courtesy of Hulton Archive/Getty Images.)

the popular novelist Charlotte Brontë; the two became fast friends. At Brontë's death in 1855, Gaskell consented to the wishes of the other woman's father to write a biography. The result was the 1857 work, *The Life of Charlotte Brontë*, which "remains unparalleled for its intimate, moving, and authentic telling of Brontë's life story," according to *Dictionary of Literary Biography* contributor Barbara Mitchell. The work gained immediate popularity, an *Athenaeum* reviewer calling it "one of the best biographies of a woman by a woman which we can recall to mind." However, the work also drew protests from some of those named in the work. For example, Gaskell took as truth the story of the dismissal of Charlotte's brother, Branwell, as a tutor for refusing to be seduced by the wife of the employer. This later had to be retracted. Also, critics argue that Gaskell tended to sanitize Brontë's emotional and love life. Writing in the London *Guardian* some 150 years after publication of the biography, Tanya Gold stated that "Gaskell took Charlotte Brontë, the author of *Jane Eyre*, the dirtiest, darkest, most depraved fantasy of all time, and, like an angel murdering a succubus, trod on her. . . . Gaskell stripped Charlotte of her genius and transformed her into a sexless, death-stalked saint." Whatever the factual faults of the book, Wright felt that *The Life of Charlotte Brontë* "still

stands as a portrait of a remarkable family and its background, as well as being a detailed study of the development and motivation of its exceptional heroine." Wright also termed the work "one of the great biographies." Likewise, Mitchell felt that "the richness of incident and emotion that makes *The Life of Charlotte Brontë* so enduring is a testament to Gaskell's sympathy with people, power of observation, and love of storytelling."

Short fiction took up much of Gaskell's time for almost the next decade. Gaskell published her work in Dickens' *Household Words*, and also in *Cornhill* magazine. Additionally, collections and novellas including *My Lady Ludlow* and *Lois the Witch*, appeared in these years, as well. Gaskell's next novel, *Sylvia's Lovers*, was published in 1863, and features Sylvia Robson, a young resident of the whaling community of Monkshaven. Wright felt that Sylvia represents "a portrait of passionate intensity without parallel in [Gaskell's] work." Wright went on to observe that "the novel's strength lies in the characters and in the insight into relationships between those characters in their setting."

The novella *Cousin Phillis* was originally serialized in *Cornhill* magazine and appeared in book form in 1864. A contributor in the *Encyclopedia of British Women Writers* deemed this work "Gaskell's crowning achievement in the short novel." The tale is told from the point of view of railroad engineer trainee Paul Manning and is largely concerned with the unrequited love of Phillis for Paul's employer. Also potent in the novella is the setting, a rural district reminiscent of that in the earlier *Cranford*. Industry is the despoiler, as the railroad is beginning to destroy the pastoral beauty of the area. Reddy found this work "Gaskell's most complex, subtle, and finely crafted treatment of her characteristic themes." It also led directly to Gaskell's next, and last, novel.

The Final Work

Wives and Daughters was serialized in a magazine, this time the *Cornhill*, and ran monthly from August 1864 to January 1866. Gaskell died before the final installment could be completed, yet as a novel it is still a finished artistic creation. Once again Gaskell chooses a rural setting reminiscent of Knutsford, calling the fictional locale Hollingford, "a community where society, from the great house to the tradespeople, has to grapple with a changing world, whether in technology or conduct or ideas," as Wright noted. The novel is set in the 1820s and features a large cast of characters, focusing particularly on Roger Hamley, a scientific explorer, and bright and sensitive Molly Gibson. Wright thought that the plot of *Wives and Daughters* is "complex, since it relies far more on a series of relationships between family groups in Hollingford than it does on the dramatic structure, which nevertheless is well controlled and integrated with the themes." Like a Jane Austen novel, *Wives and Daughters* "concerns itself with mobility and change," according to *New Statesman* reviewer Michele Roberts, who also termed the novel "wonderful."

Gaskell died on November 12, 1865, while working on the final installment of her novel. A review by Frederick Greenwood in the *Cornhill* magazine of that last work could also stand as a fitting summation to the author's entire oeuvre: "Mrs. Gaskell was gifted with some of the choicest faculties bestowed upon mankind. . . these grew into

If you enjoy the works of Elizabeth Gaskell, you may also want to check out the following books:

Jane Austen, *Sense and Sensibility*, 1811.
Charlotte Brontë, *Jane Eyre*, 1847.
Emily Brontë, *Wuthering Heights*, 1847.

greater strength and ripened into greater beauty in the decline of her days; and . . . she has gifted us with some of the truest, purest works of fiction in the language." Winnifrith, in evaluating the author's legacy, felt that "Gaskell is hard to place" in the pantheon of British writers. "While obviously not in the first division of novelists she is equally obviously no minor figure. Her novels cover a more varied range than those of Thackeray, are better plotted than those of Dickens, and are more realistic than those of the Brontës." In her half-dozen novels and her short works, as well as her biography of Charlotte Brontë, Gaskell left readers with a picture of mid-nineteenth-century England that is at once charming and incisive. "Critical awareness of Gaskell as a social historian is now more than balanced by awareness of her innovativeness and artistic development as a novelist," concluded the contributor in the *Encyclopedia of British Women Writers*. "While scholars continue to debate the precise nature of her talent, they also reaffirm the singular attractiveness of her best works."

Cover of a new edition of *Cranford*, featuring a cover image taken from the 2007 BBC miniseries. (Cover photo by Nick Briggs Copyright 2007 by British Broadcasting Corporation. Reproduced by permission of Penguin Books, Ltd.)

■ Biographical and Critical Sources

BOOKS

Concise Dictionary of British Literary Biography, Volume 4: *Victorian Writers, 1832-1890,* Gale (Detroit, MI), 1991.

Dictionary of Literary Biography, Gale (Detroit, MI), Volume 21: *Victorian Novelists before 1885,* 1983, Volume 144: *Nineteenth-Century British Literary Biographers,* 1994, Volume 159: *British Short-Fiction Writers, 1800-1880,* 1995.

Encyclopedia of British Women Writers, edited by Paul Schlueter and June Schlueter, Rutgers University Press (Piscataway, NJ), 1999.

Gerin, Winifred, *Elizabeth Gaskell: A Biography,* Clarendon Press (Oxford, England), 1976.

Hopkins, Annette Brown, *Elizabeth Gaskell: Her Life and Work,* Lehmann (London, England), 1952.

Matus, Jill L., editor, *The Cambridge Companion to Elizabeth Gaskell*, Cambridge University Press (New York, NY), 2007.

Pollard, Arthur, *Mrs. Gaskell: Novelist and Biographer*, Manchester University Press (Manchester, England), 1966.

Reference Guide to English Literature, edited by D.L. Kirkpatrick, 2nd edition, St. James Press (Detroit, MI), 1991.

Selig, R.L., *Elizabeth Gaskell: A Reference Guide*, Hall (Boston, MA), 1977.

Spencer, Jane, *Elizabeth Gaskell*, St. Martin's (New York, NY), 1993.

Uglow, Jenny, *Elizabeth Gaskell: A Habit of Stories*, Faber & Faber (London, England), 1993.

Wright, Edgar, *Mrs. Gaskell: The Basis for Reassessment*, Oxford University Press (Oxford, England), 1965.

PERIODICALS

Athenaeum, April 7, 1855, review of *North and South*, p. 403; April 4, 1857, review of *The Life of Charlotte Brontë, Author of "Jane Eyre," "Shirley," "Villette"* etc., pp. 427-429.

Bookman, November, 1908, review of *Cousin Phillis*, pp. 98-99.

Cornhill, January, 1866, Frederick Greenwood, review of *Wives and Daughters: An Every-Day Story*, pp. 11-15.

Edinburgh Review, April, 1849, William Rathbone Greg, review of *Mary Barton: A Tale of Manchester Life*, pp. 402-435.

Fraser's, May, 1857, review of *The Life of Charlotte Brontë*, pp. 569-582.

History Today, November, 2008, Sue Wilkes, review of *Mary Barton*, p. 58.

New Statesman, September 15, 2003, Michele Roberts, review of *Wives and Daughters*, p. 56.

North British Review, May, 1853, J.M. Ludlow, review of *Ruth: A Novel*, pp. 151-174.

Westminster Review, April, 1853, George Henry Lewes, review of *Ruth*, pp. 474-491.

ONLINE

Elizabeth Gaskell House Web site, http://www.elizabethgaskellhouse.org/ (December 28, 2008).

Guardian Online (London, England), http://www.guardian.co.uk/ (March 25, 2005), Tanya Gold, "Reader, I Shagged Him."

Literary Gothic Web site, http://www.litgothic.com/ (December 28, 2008), "Gaskell, Elizabeth."

Spartacus Educational Web site, http://www.spartacus.schoolnet.co.uk/ (December 8, 2008), "Elizabeth Gaskell."

Unitarian Universalist Historical Society Web site, http://www25.uua.org/ (December 28, 2008), "Elizabeth Gaskell Biography."

Victorian Web, http://www.victorianweb.org/ (December 28, 2008), "Elizabeth Cleghorn Gaskell."*

Elizabeth George

(Courtesy of Figge Photography.)

■ Personal

Born February 26, 1949, in Warren, OH; daughter of Robert Edwin (a conveyor salesman) and Anne (a registered nurse) George; married Ira Jay Toibin (a business manager), May 28, 1971 (divorced, November, 1995); married Tom McCabe (a retired firefighter). *Education:* Foothill Community College, A.A., 1969; University of California, Riverside, B.A., 1970; California State University, Fullerton, M.S., 1979; attended University of California at Berkeley. *Politics:* Democratic. *Religion:* "Recovering from Catholicism." *Hobbies and other interests:* Reading, theater, movies, skiing, photography, gardening.

■ Addresses

Home—Whidbey Island, WA. *Agent*—Robert Gottlieb, Trident Media, 41 Madison Ave., Fl. 36, New York, NY, 10010.

■ Career

Writer, novelist, and educator. Mater Dei High School, Santa Ana, CA, teacher of English, 1974-75; El Toro High School, El Toro, CA, teacher of English, 1975-87; Coastline Community College, Costa Mesa, CA, teacher of creative writing, beginning 1988; Irvine Valley College, Irvine, CA, teacher of creative writing, 1989; University of California, Irvine, teacher of creative writing, 1990. Teacher of intensive writing seminars for University of Oklahoma and Book Passage, Corte Madera, CA; visiting professor, University of British Columbia and Exeter College Oxford; Maui Writer's Retreat, creative writing instructor.

■ Awards, Honors

Award for teacher of the year, Orange County Department of Education, 1981; Anthony Award for best first novel, Bouchercon World Mystery Convention, and Agatha Award for best first novel, Malice Domestic, both 1989, Grand Prix de Litterature Policiére, 1990, and Edgar and Macavity award nominations, all for *A Great Deliverance;* MIMI award (Germany), for *Well-schooled in Murder;* honorary degree, California State University, Fullerton.

■ Writings

"INSPECTOR LYNLEY" MYSTERIES

A Great Deliverance, Bantam (New York, NY), 1988.
Payment in Blood, Bantam (New York, NY), 1989.

Well-schooled in Murder, Bantam (New York, NY), 1990.

A Suitable Vengeance, Bantam (New York, NY), 1991.

For the Sake of Elena, Bantam (New York, NY), 1992.

Missing Joseph, Bantam (New York, NY), 1993.

Playing for the Ashes, Bantam (New York, NY), 1994.

In the Presence of the Enemy, Bantam (New York, NY), 1996.

Deception on His Mind, Bantam (New York, NY), 1997.

In Pursuit of the Proper Sinner, Bantam (New York, NY), 1999.

A Traitor to Memory, Bantam Books (New York, NY), 2001.

A Place of Hiding, Bantam (New York, NY), 2003.

With No One as Witness, HarperCollins (New York, NY), 2005.

What Came before He Shot Her, HarperCollins (New York, NY), 2006.

Careless in Red, HarperCollins (New York, NY), 2008.

OTHER

The Evidence Exposed (short stories), Hodder & Stoughton (London, England), 1999.

Remember, I'll Always Love You, ASAP Publishing (Mission Viejo, CA), 2001.

I, Richard: Stories of Suspense, Bantam (New York, NY), 2002.

(Editor) *Crime from the Mind of a Woman*, Coronet (London, England), 2002, published as *A Moment on the Edge: 100 Years of Crime Stories by Women*, HarperCollins (New York, NY), 2004.

Write Away: One Novelist's Approach to Fiction and the Writing Life, HarperCollins (New York, NY), 2004.

Contributor to anthologies, including *Sisters in Crime*, Volume 2, Berkley Books (New York, NY), 1990; *Women on the Case*, Bantam (New York, NY), 1996; and *Murder and Obsession*, Random House (New York, NY), 1999.

A collection of George's manuscripts is housed at the Mugar Memorial Library, Boston University.

■ **Adaptations**

George's "Inspector Lynley" novels were adapted by the British Broadcasting Corporation/WGBH Boston and aired on Public Broadcasting System *Mystery!* television series, including *A Great Deliverance*, 2001; *Well-schooled in Murder*, 2002; *Payment in Blood*, 2002; *For the Sake of Elena*, 2002; *Missing Joseph*,

2002; *Playing for the Ashes*, 2003; *In the Presence of the Enemy*, 2003; *A Suitable Vengeance*, 2003; *Deception on His Mind*, 2003; *In Pursuit of the Proper Sinner*, 2004; *A Traitor to Memory*, 2004; *A Cry for Justice*, 2004; and *If Wishes Were Horses*, 2004. The character of Inspector Lynley has also appeared in other episodes of the PBS *Mystery* series not based on George's novels.

■ **Sidelights**

The first thing to know about the popular British mystery writer Elizabeth George is that she is, in fact, American. The second thing to note is that for George, "the whodunit is less important than the whydunit," as Karl L. Stenger noted in the *Dictionary of Literary Biography*. Both these elements figure in her bestselling "Inspector Lynley" series of books and in their television spinoffs. The series—featuring patrician Detective Superintendent Thomas Lynley of New Scotland Yard; his partner, frank-talking, working-class Detective Sergeant Barbara Havers; pathologist Simon St. James, Lynley's best friend; and Simon's wife Deborah—has garnered fans both in England and in the United States, as well as around the world in translation.

George told *Publishers Weekly* contributor Lisa See that her decision to create a British series was a technical one: "The English tradition offers the great tapestry novel, where you have the emotional aspects of a detective's personal life, the circumstances of the crime and, most important, the atmosphere of the English countryside that functions as another character." Indeed, George does create tapestries with her novels, some of them running over 700 pages, and each full of subplots dealing with the back stories of the ongoing main characters as well as of criminals and victims unique to each title. According to Stenger, George writes "literary mysteries, each of which has outdone the previous one in terms of plotting, character development, and length, have met with considerable commercial and critical success." Stenger further noted, "In George's books, the Golden Age tradition of the English mystery meets contemporary reality." George takes Dorothy Sayers as a model in her use of an aristocratic protagonist. For Sayers it was Lord Peter Wimsey; with George we have Lynley, the eighth earl of Asherton.

George also is reminiscent of the British mystery novelist P.D. James for the depth of her psychological investigation, characterization, and for the sheer length of her novels. And, "like Agatha Christie and Ruth Rendell, George exposes the violence and hatreds beneath the peaceful facade of village life," according to a contributor for *Contemporary Popular Writers*. Reviewing George's 2008 addition to the "Lynley" series, *Careless in Red*, *Booklist* reviewer Connie Fletcher delivered a verdict that could sum up the entirety of the author's work: "George delivers, once again, a mystery imbued with psychological suspense and in-depth characterization."

California Girl

"I have always felt compelled to write," George told Kathy Pohl in an interview for *Writer*. "When I began reading the Little Golden Books as a 7-year-old, I knew that I wanted to write one, too. I wrote tiny stories like that in the beginning." George's beginnings were in Warren, Ohio, where she was born in 1949. However, the family moved west to California when George was eighteen months old, partly to escape the harsh Midwest winters, and, in part, so that her father, Robert Edwin George, could remove the family from his wife Anne's large Italian family. As a result, George grew up in the then-little town of Mountain View away from her extended family, something she wished she had more of. Speaking with *People* contributor Marjorie Rosen, George explained her early interest in books and in writing: "We weren't a family that had a lot of money. We turned to the world of imagination."

George was inspired by her parents' love of books and literature, and soon was writing her own short stories, pounding out tales during her years in elementary school on an old typewriter her mother bought for her. By the age of twelve, she had already written her first mystery novel, inspired by the Nancy Drew books. With the advent of the 1960s and the invasion of British culture spearheaded by the Beatles, George became drawn to things English, including the works of William Shakespeare. She made her first trip to England in 1966 to get ready for a Shakespeare seminar. George felt immediately at home in this new country, and has made regular trips back ever since. By the time of her graduation from Holy Cross High School in Mountain View, she had other unpublished novel-length works to her credit.

Writing as a profession, however, was put on hold for a number of years. George went to college at the University of California at Riverside, where she met her first husband, Ira Toibin. (They would remain married for twenty-four years.) After graduation, she went into teaching; in 1981 she was named Orange County Teacher of the Year, instructing in English at El Toro High School. As part of her

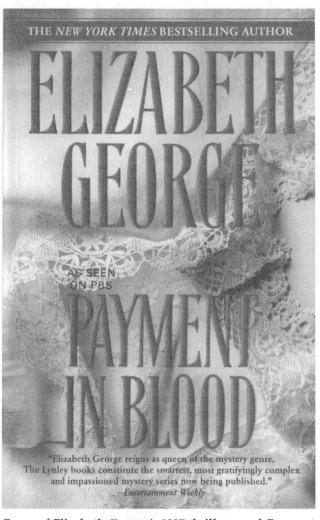

Cover of Elizabeth George's 1997 thriller novel *Payment in Blood*, the second outing of Inspector Lynley. (Bantam Books, 2008. Cover photo copyright © 1997 by Mort Engel Productions. Used by permission of Bantam Books, a division of Random House, Inc.)

instruction, she provided a course in writing mysteries, and by 1983 she was herself writing again. George was able to make fast headway with her writing when her husband bought her one of the first personal computers in the mid-1980s. She finished her first mystery novel in a matter of months. This attempt featured forensic scientist Simon Allcourt-St. James, along with Thomas Lynley, Lord Asherton, a slightly womanizing aristocrat, in a more minor role. The manuscript was rejected by numerous publishers, but George was undaunted. Following a 1984 trip to England, she wrote another novel featuring Allcourt-St. James. This too was rejected (though it was ultimately published in 1991 as *A Suitable Vengeance*), so for her next attempt George shifted focus from the forensic scientist to the New Scotland Yard detective, Lynley. This time, she was successful, and the novel *A Great Deliverance* was purchased by Bantam Books. After this publication, George left a thirteen-year career in teaching in order to devote herself full time to writing.

Thomas Lynley and Company

With *A Great Deliverance*, Lynley teams up with Havers, his polar opposite, whom George created for this work. Lynley could thus be viewed through Havers' eyes, and his aristocratic ticks could be given sharper contrast. Prickly and unable to get along with other police, Havers has been put on street patrol as a punishment; now she is partnered with Lynley, whom she considers a fop. The dynamics between Lynley and Havers, at the heart of most of the "Lynley" books, was thus already in place with George's first published novel. In this debut case they investigate the beheading of a wealthy family's patriarch in Keldale, Yorkshire. The man's daughter wants to confess to the grisly crime, but Lynley and Havers think otherwise, and soon uncover many uncomfortable secrets in the cozy village. *A Great Deliverance* was reviewed well and won the prestigious Anthony and Agatha awards, setting the series off handsomely. However, it also stirred a bit of controversy when Martha Grimes, another American who uses English settings for her works, accused George of lifting parts of her novel from Grimes's own 1985 publication, *Help the Poor Struggler.*

A Scottish manor house converted into a hotel is the setting for George's next novel, *Payment in Blood*, in which Lynley and Havers are sent to a Glasgow estate to investigate the stabbing death of a playwright. Here they discover that the murderer must have passed through a room occupied by an aristocratic woman, Lady Helen Clyde, with whom Lynley is in love. Lynley subsequently becomes distracted by romance, and Havers takes over their inquiry. Lynley's judgment is more than clouded by his love, and he discovers that he is being used in a high-level cover-up. Carolyn Banks, in her review of *Payment in Blood* in the *Washington Post,* noted the novel's "wonderfully drawn tensions and bonds between the characters."

A torture-murder of a thirteen year old attending a prestigious school is at the heart of George's next mystery, *Well-schooled in Murder.* Here Lynley and Havers uncover various criminal and scandalous activities, including blackmail, sadism, and suicide. For *People* contributor Susan Toepfer, this psychological mystery put George "clearly in the running with the genre's master," P.D. James. In *A Suitable Vengeance* the action of which comes chronologically before the preceding novels, Lynley brings his fiancée Deborah Cotton (who later becomes the wife of Simon St. James) home to Cornwall to introduce her to his mother. The visit has unexpectedly violent and tragic results, culminating in the murder of a local newspaper editor. For *Publishers Weekly* contributor Sybil Steinberg, this was a "darkly vibrant modern English mystery." Steinberg also complimented George's "deftly handled plot" and "memorable characters." Further praise came from Charles Champlin, who wrote in the *Los Angeles Times Book Review* that with *A Suitable Vengeance* George gives readers a "sumptuous, all-out reading experience."

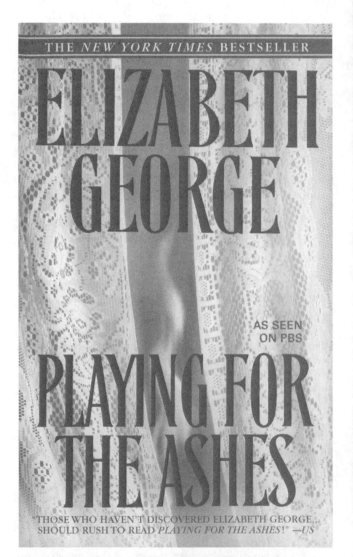

THE *NEW YORK TIMES* BESTSELLER

ELIZABETH GEORGE

AS SEEN ON PBS

PLAYING FOR THE ASHES

"THOSE WHO HAVEN'T DISCOVERED ELIZABETH GEORGE... SHOULD RUSH TO READ *PLAYING FOR THE ASHES*!" —*US*

Another popular novel by George, *Playing for the Ashes*, was first published in 1997. (Bantam Books, 1989. Cover art copyright © 1997 by Jerry Simpson. Used by permission of Bantam Books, a division of Random House, Inc.)

The Series Grows in Stature

George set her fifth "Inspector Lynley" title, *For the Sake of Elena*, at Cambridge University, where her protagonist investigates the bludgeoning death of a coed, deaf long-distance runner Elena Weaver, who is the daughter of a respected professor. Lynley and Havers, the latter who is dealing with personal problems of her own, soon discover that Elena was not such an innocent young woman as people think. Meanwhile, Lynley continues his attempts to court Lady Helen in this "story [that] never fails to engage," as a *Publishers Weekly* reviewer wrote. Further praise came from *Belles Lettres* reviewer Jane Bakerman, who called *For the Sake of Elena* "suspenseful, literate but readily accessible to a wide range of readers, thoughtful and thought provoking . . . an elegant novel." Toepfer, writing in *People*, concluded that "George goes to the head of her genre, with class." Similarly, Mark Harris, reviewing the work in *Entertainment Weekly*, lauded "the skill with which [George] has developed her intriguing sleuths since their debut."

With each new title, George has added additional readers and further critical praise. In the 1993 novel, *Missing Joseph*, St. James and his wife Deborah are featured in a "deftly plotted, highly atmospheric novel" about a fifteen-year-old death of an infant, according to a *Publishers Weekly* contributor. *Playing for the Ashes*, concerning the mysterious death of a star cricket player, was commended by Emily Melton in *Booklist*: "George is a gifted writer who spins rich, colorful, mesmerizing, multifaceted stories." *Playing for the Ashes* is, according to the critic, "another tour de force from one of today's best storytellers."

In the Presence of the Enemy, George's eighth novel, deals with the kidnapping of the illegitimate daughter of a conservative politician. Havers ends up brutally beaten in her attempts to save the child. "George's fully developed characters will live with the readers long after the last page is turned," wrote a *Publishers Weekly* contributor. Similarly, *Entertainment Weekly* reviewer Harris praised this "gripping installment of a series that grows in stature with every new book," while *People* contributor Toepfer termed *In The Presence of the Enemy* "a splendid, unsettling novel."

George features Barbara Havers in *Deception on His Mind*. Recovering from her injuries suffered in the previous novel, Havers finds herself investigating the murder of a Pakistani in a seaside town to which she has gone to recuperate. *Booklist* contributor Stephanie Zvirin called this work an "intelligent, finely nuanced performance," while for a *Publishers Weekly* writer it serves as "an unusually elaborate and intricate mystery." George continued her trend toward more intricate plotting with *In Pursuit of the Proper Sinner*, a story involving murder and sexual perversion among Britain's upper class. Lynley, newly married to Lady Helen, and Havers, facing demotion for insubordination, continue their sometimes bickering, sometimes friendly relationship as criminal investigators in this tale. Zvirin, writing in *Booklist*, stated that "George delivers infinitely more than the requisite deception and murder," and assured fans that the book is "masterfully plotted, thoughtful, and bursting with clever complications." A *Publishers Weekly* reviewer also praised George for combining a taut mystery with fine character development, and doing so "with an engaging mix of subtlety and bravado."

A Traitor to Memory employs multiple viewpoints to tell a "sprawling epic," according to a *Publishers Weekly* reviewer. Here Lynley and Havers are called to London to investigate a hit-and-run case with ties to an older child murder investigation. *Booklist* reviewer Connie Fletcher commented that despite its length of more than seven hundred pages, *A Traitor to Memory* manages to "fairly zip along, keeping the reader on the knife's edge of suspense, thanks to George's skill." Simon St. James and his wife Deborah again take the spotlight in *A Place of Hiding*. Here an unexpected visit from Cherokee River, the brother of Deborah's American friend and roommate China River, reveals that China has been arrested for murder. She is being held on the island of Guernsey, charged with murdering wealthy Guy Brouard, an influential philanthropist with painful connections to the Holocaust. Simon and Deborah accompany Cherokee to Guernsey to try to exonerate China and uncover the identity of the real murderer. Unexpected twists and shocking discoveries await the protagonists as the story darkly unspools. *Entertainment Weekly* reviewer Tina Jordan concluded of this series installment that *A Place of Hiding* "is mystery writing at its most complex and intelligent."

A Surprising Loss

George created a stir among her fans for killing off Lynley's pregnant wife in *With No One as Witness*, which concerns the brutal, ritualistic death of a teenage boy and its link to three other similar deaths. Because all of the victims were black males, and because connections to a serial killer were made very late in the investigation, Scotland Yard Assistant Commissioner Sir David Hillier fears that accusations of racism will be leveled at the department. To combat this image, Hillier promotes black officer Winston Nkata to the rank of sergeant and involves him prominently in public meetings and press briefings. Lynley, Nkata, and Constable Barbara Havers eventually identify the victims and link them to Colossus, a group for troubled youths that is run by a staff with questionable backgrounds. *Booklist* reviewer Zvirin termed *What Came before He Shot Her* a "a riveting installment in a superb series," and similar praise was offered by a *Publishers Weekly* contributor who found *With No One as Witness* "an outstanding and explosive addition to a popular series."

What Came before He Shot Her proceeds from the devastating events of *With No One as Witness,* chronicling the events and characters that led to Lynley's tremendous loss. Twelve-year-old Joel, his teenage sister Ness, and brother Toby Campbell are three mixed-race siblings suffering through a difficult upbringing after their father is murdered and their mother institutionalized. Their Aunt Kendra takes them in, and although she means well, she does not have the means to raise three children. Ness and Joel fight to adjust and survive in their dangerous new surroundings in North Kensington, while Joel helps protect younger, developmentally challenged brother Toby. Despite his good intentions and earnest attempts to help, Joel's decisions are usually followed by tragedy, and Ness's involvement with a vicious, jealous drug dealer endangers the family. A *Publishers Weekly* reviewer called the novel a "stinging indictment of a society unable to respond effectively to the needs of its poorer citizens." For Jordan, writing in *Entertainment Weekly, With No One as Witness* is "absolutely riveting."

Careless in Red finds Lynley recuperating from the loss of his wife in Cornwall, having resigned from Scotland Yard. However, he is drawn back into police work when he discovers the body of a teenager who may have been pushed from the cliffs along the seashore. This one is for readers, as a *Publishers Weekly* contributor noted, "who prefer psychologically sophisticated plots and motivations."

George has also written short fiction as well as the nonfiction work *Write Away: One Novelist's Approach to Fiction and the Writing Life.* However, she continues to be best known for her "Inspector Lynley" books. In the *St. James Guide to Crime and Mystery Writers,* Jane S. Bakerman concluded that George's popularity results from her skillful use of "an intriguing range of continuing characters who are interesting individually as well as in their interactions with one another, gripping plots, well-drawn descriptive passages, and plenty of gore. The crimes

If you enjoy the works of Elizabeth George, you may also want to check out the following books:

The mystery novels of Colin Dexter, including *Death Is Now My Neighbour,* 1996.
Ian Rankin's *A Question of Blood,* 2003.
Peter Robinson's "Alan Banks" series of crime novels, including *Friend of the Devil,* 2007.

depicted in these novels are horrific not only in physical detail but also in their psychological impact upon the cast of characters—and upon the readers." In the same work, the author stated, "My novels tend to hearken back to the Golden Age of the detective story in that they attempt to reflect the glamour of Dorothy L. Sayers's type of writing rather than the grim reality of present day dissections of murder. Nonetheless, the issues they revolve around are very much part of contemporary life."

■ Biographical and Critical Sources

BOOKS

Contemporary Popular Writers, St. James Press (Detroit, MI), 1997.
Dictionary of Literary Biography, Volume 306: *American American Mystery and Detective Writers,* Gale (Detroit, MI), 2005.
St. James Guide to Crime and Mystery Writers, 4th edition, St. James Press (Detroit, MI), 1996.

PERIODICALS

Atlantic Monthly, November, 2006, review of *What Came before He Shot Her,* p. 125.
Belles Lettres, fall, 1992, Jane Bakerman, review of *For the Sake of Elena,* p. 28.
Booklist, May 15, 1994, Emily Melton, review of *Playing for the Ashes,* p. 1645; May 15, 1997, Stephanie Zvirin, review of *Deception on His Mind,* p. 1541; July, 1999, Stephanie Zvirin, review of *In Pursuit of the Proper Sinner,* p. 1893; May 1, 2001, Connie Fletcher, review of *A Traitor to Memory,* p. 1632; May 15, 2004, Stephanie Zvirin, review of *A Moment on the Edge: 100 Years of Crime Stories by Women,* p. 1601; February 1, 2005, Stephanie Zvirin, review of *With No One as Witness,* p. 917;

August 1, 2006, Allison Block, review of *What Came before He Shot Her*, p. 8; February 15, 2008, Connie Fletcher, review of *Careless in Red*, p. 4.

Book, July-August, 2003, Kate Julian, "The Anglo File: A California Girl Writes Spot-on British Mysteries," p. 22.

Books, summer, 1998, review of *Deception on His Mind*, p. R3.

Christian Science Monitor, March 27, 1997, review of *In the Presence of the Enemy*, p. B2; July 31, 1997, Michele Ross, review of *Deception on His Mind*, p. B2, and Robin Whitten, review of *In the Presence of the Enemy*, p. B4.

Clues: A Journal of Detection, fall-winter, 2000, Carl D. Malmgren, "Truth, Justice, the American Way: Martha Grimes and Elizabeth George," p. 47.

Denver Post, July 13, 1997, Carol Kreck, review of *Deception on His Mind*, p. E6.

Entertainment Weekly, September 18, 1992, Mark Harris, review of *For the Sake of Elena*, p. 73; March 15, 1996, Mark Harris, review of *In the Presence of the Enemy*, p. 56; December 12, 1997, Tom De Haven, review of *In the Presence of the Enemy*, p. 77; December 24, 1999, review of *In Pursuit of the Proper Sinner*, p. 144; August 10, 2001, Mark Harris, "Lady Thrillers: Four Popular Women of Mystery Introduce New Chapters in the Lives of Their Hard-boiled Heroines"; August 8, 2003, Tina Jordan, review of *A Place of Hiding*, p. 78; March 18, 2005, Mark Harris, review of *With No One as Witness*, p. 74; October 20, 2006, Tina Jordan, review of *What Came before He Shot Her*, p. 87.

Globe and Mail (Toronto, Ontario, Canada), September 25, 1999, review of *In Pursuit of the Proper Sinner*, p. D15.

Kirkus Reviews, February 1, 2005, review of *With No One as Witness*, p. 151; August 1, 2006, review of *What Came before He Shot Her*, p. 755; March 15, 2008, review of *Careless in Red*.

Knight-Ridder/Tribune News Service, August 6, 1997, Lynn Carey, "Elizabeth George Reveals Why Britain's the Setting for Her Best-selling Mysteries," p. 806.

Library Journal, July, 1999, Francine Fialkoff, review of *In Pursuit of the Proper Sinner*, p. 141; June 1, 2001, Jane la Plante, review of *A Traitor to Memory*, p. 214; August, 2004, Jane la Plante, review of *A Moment on the Edge*, p. 61; March 15, 2005, Jane la Plante, review of *With No One as Witness*, p. 78; April 15, 2006, Douglas C. Lord, review of *With No One as Witness*, p. 123; September 1, 2006, Jane la Plante, review of *What Came before He Shot Her*, p. 136.

Los Angeles Times, June 9, 1996, Dennis McLellen, "Murder She Writes," p. E1.

Los Angeles Times Book Review, August 13, 1989, Charles Champlin, review of *Payment in Blood*, p. 8; July 12, 1992, Charles Champlin, review of *For the Sake of Elena*, p. 8; May 12, 1996, Margo Kaufman, review of *In the Presence of the Enemy*, p. 11; October 31, 1999, review of *In Pursuit of the Proper Sinner*, p. 11.

New York Times, August 26, 1992, Herbert Mitgang, review of *For the Sake of Elena*, p. B2; August 17, 1994, Sarah Lyall, "Making the List," p. C16; December 14, 1999, Mel Gussow, "Golly! A Yank Wrote Those Oh-So-British Mysteries?," p. B1; April 10, 2005, Dwight Garner, review of *With No One as Witness*.

New York Times Book Review, November 12, 1989, Josh Rubins, review of *Payment in Blood*, p. 58; August 12, 1990, Marilyn Stasio, review of *Well-schooled in Murder*, p. 21; June 20, 1993, Marilyn Stasio, review of *Missing Joseph*, p. 21; April 21, 1996, Marilyn Stasio, review of *In the Presence of the Enemy*, p. 39; August 10, 1997, Marilyn Stasio, review of *Deception on His Mind*, p. 18.

People, October 1, 1990, Susan Toepfer, review of *Well-schooled in Murder*, p. 32; August 31, 1992, Susan Toepfer, review of *For the Sake of Elena*, p. 26; August 23, 1993, Marjorie Rosen, "No True Brit," p. 59; March 18, 1996, Susan Toepfer, review of *In the Presence of the Enemy*, p. 34; October 11, 1999, Pam Lambert, review of *In Pursuit of the Proper Sinner*, p. 49; August 6, 2001, review of *A Traitor to Memory*, p. 53.

Philadelphia Inquirer, October 18, 2006, Maxine Clarke, review of *What Came before He Shot Her*.

Publishers Weekly, April 12, 1991, Sybil Steinberg, review of *A Suitable Vengeance*, p. 46; May 11, 1992, review of *For the Sake of Elena*, p. 56; May 3, 1993, review of *Missing Joseph*, p. 296; May 23, 1994, review of *Playing for the Ashes*, p. 80; January 8, 1996, review of *In the Presence of the Enemy*, p. 60; March 11, 1996, Lisa See Kendall, "Elizabeth George: An American in Scotland Yard," p. 38; June 2, 1997, review of *Deception on His Mind*, p. 56; August 2, 1999, review of *In Pursuit of the Proper Sinner*, p. 71; June 4, 2001, review of *A Traitor to Memory*, p. 60; January 1, 2004, review of *Write Away: One Novelist's Approach to Fiction and the Writing Life*, p. 43; February 21, 2005, review of *With No One as Witness*, p. 161; August 7, 2006, review of *What Came before He Shot Her*, p. 31; March 10, 2008, review of *Careless in Red*, p. 56; March 24, 2008, Leonard Picker, "PW Talks with Elizabeth George," p. 56.

School Library Journal, January, 1998, Susan H. Woodcock, review of *Deception on His Mind*, p. 136.

Star-Ledger (Newark, NJ), March 24, 1996, Jessica Cleerdin, review of *In the Presence of the Enemy*, p. 6.

Wall Street Journal, August 9, 1994, Tom Nolan, review of *Playing for the Ashes*, p. A10; July 25, 1997, Tom Nolan, review of *Deception on His Mind*,

p. A12; August 24, 1999, review of *In Pursuit of the Proper Sinner*, p. A16.

Washington Post, August 29, 1989, Carolyn Banks, review of *Payment in Blood*, p. E3; February 29, 1996, James Hynes, review of *In the Presence of the Enemy*, p. C2.

Washington Post Book World, July 15, 1990, Jean M. White, review of *Well-schooled in Murder*, p. 11; October 17, 1999, Katy Munger, review of *In Pursuit of the Proper Sinner*, p. 13.

Writer, September, 2004, Stephanie Dickinson, review of *Write Away*, p. 44; June, 2007, Kathy Pohl, interview with George, p. 20.

ONLINE

BookPage, http://www.bookpage.com/ (January 2, 2007), Jay MacDonald, "The Other Side of the Story," interview with George.

Elizabeth George Home Page, http://www.elizabethgeorgeonline.com (January 5, 2009).

Powells.com, http://www.powells.com/ (December 28, 2008), "Ink Q & A: Elizabeth George."

Washington Post Online, http://www.washingtonpost.com/ (June 27, 2005), "Mystery!: Inspector Lynley," online discussion with George.

Mel Gibson

(Photograph © by Frank Trapper/Corbis.)

■ Personal

Born January 3, 1956, in Peekskill, NY; immigrated to Australia, 1968; son of Hutton (a railroad brakeman) and Anne Gibson; married Robyn Moore (a nurse's aide), 1979 (separated, 2009); children: Hannah, Edward and Christian (twins), Will, Louis, Milo, Thomas. *Education:* National Institute of Dramatic Arts (Australia), graduate, 1977. *Religion:* Roman Catholic.

■ Addresses

Home—CA; CT; Costa Rica. *Agent*—Ed Limato, ICM, 8942 Wilshire Blvd., Beverly Hills, CA 90211.

■ Career

Actor, producer, and film director. Actor in stage performances, including (with South Australian Theatre Company) *Romeo and Juliet, Oedipus, Henry IV,* and *Cedoona.* Actor on Australian television series, including *The Sullivans* and *The Oracle.* Actor in films, including *Summer City,* 1977, *Mad Max,* 1979, *Tim,* 1979, *Attack Force Z,* 1981, *Gallipoli,* 1981, *The Road Warrior,* 1982, *The Year of Living Dangerously,* 1983, *The Bounty,* 1984, *The River,* 1984, *Mrs. Soffel,* 1984, *Mad Max: Beyond Thunderdome,* 1985, *Lethal Weapon,* 1986, *Tequila Sunrise,* 1988, *Lethal Weapon 2,* 1989, *Air America,* 1990, *Hamlet,* 1990, *Lethal Weapon 3,* 1992, *Forever Young,* 1992, *Maverick,* 1994, *Pocahontas,* 1995, *Braveheart,* 1995, *Ransom,* 1996, *Conspiracy Theory,* 1997, *Lethal Weapon 4,* 1998, *Payback,* 1999, *The Billion Dollar Hotel,* 1999, *Chicken Run,* 2000, *The Patriot,* 2000, *What Women Want,* 2000, *We Were Soldiers,* 2002, *Signs,* 2002, *The Singing Detective,* 2003, and *Edge of Darkness,* 2009. Director of films, including *The Man without a Face,* 1993, *Braveheart,* 1995, *The Passion of the Christ,* 2004, and *Apocalypto,* 2006. Producer of films, including *Braveheart,* 1995, *The Singing Detective,* 2003, *The Passion of the Christ,* 2004, *Paparazzi,* 2004, *Leonard Cohen: I'm Your Man,* 2005, and *Apocalypto,* 2006; producer of television films and series, including *The Three Stooges,* 2000, *Invincible,* 2001, *Family Curse,* 2003, *Evel Knievel,* 2004, *Clubhouse,* 2004, *Complete Savages,* 2004-05, *Another Day in Paradise,* 2008, and *Carrier,* 2008. Founding partner, Icon Productions, 1989—.

■ Awards, Honors

Australian Film Institute award for best lead actor, 1979, for *Tim,* and 1981, for *Gallipoli;* People's Choice Awards for favorite motion-picture actor, 1991, 1997, 2001, 2003, and 2004, and for favorite motion picture star in a drama, 2001; ShoWest Awards for male star of the year, 1993, and director of the year, 1996; MTV Awards for Best Action Sequence and Best Duo (with Danny Glover), 1993, for *Lethal Weapon 3;* Academy Awards for best director and best picture, Golden Globe Award for best director of a film, National Board of Review Award for special achievement in filmmaking, and Broadcast Film Critics Association Award for best director, all 1996, all for *Braveheart;* named officer, Order of Australia, 1997; named Hasty Pudding Theatricals Man of the Year, Harvard University, 1997; Blockbuster Entertainment Award for favorite actor in a suspense, 1997, for *Ransom,* and 1998, for *Conspiracy Theory,* and for favorite actor in a drama, 2001, for *The Patriot;* Blockbuster Entertainment Award for favorite actor in a drama, for *The Patriot,* 2000; Global Achievement Award, Australian Film Institute, 2002; Hollywood Film Festival's Hollywood Producer of the Year award, Discovery Award, National Board of Review Freedom of Expression Award, and Golden Knight Film Festival Grand Prix Award, all 2004, and Golden Satellite Award for best director and People's Choice Award for favorite movie drama, both 2005, all for *The Passion of the Christ;* award for outstanding contributor to world cinema, Irish Film and Television Awards, 2008.

■ Writings

SCREENPLAYS

(With Benedict Fitzgerald) *The Passion of the Christ,* Newmarket Films, 2004, edited version released as *The Passion Recut,* 2005.
(With Farhad Safinia) *Apocalypto,* Buena Vista, 2006.

Also author of an episode of the television series *Complete Savages,* 2004.

■ Sidelights

Australian actor and director Mel Gibson first became known to American audiences in the early 1980s with the cult sci-fi hit *Mad Max* and the acclaimed war drama *Gallipoli.* Since then, Gibson has become one of the biggest stars in Hollywood. He has appeared in a number of hit films and proven himself to be more than just another pretty face, playing an ambitious journalist in *The Year of Living Dangerously,* the multidimensional title character in *Hamlet,* and a hero of the American Revolution in *The Patriot.* Gibson has more recently turned to directing, making his mark with his unlikely blockbuster *The Passion of the Christ,* about the last hours of Jesus.

Gibson was born in Peekskill, New York in 1956, the middle child among five girls and six boys. He first heard about Australia through stories from his grandmother, who came to the United States from the country Down Under to become an opera singer. Gibson would soon learn a lot more about Australia; when he was twelve, his father moved his entire family to the continent, using money he received after he was injured at his job. Although it has been rumored that World War II-veteran Hutton Gibson moved the family so his sons could avoid the Vietnam War draft, Gibson told a contributor in the *Sydney Morning Herald:* "The truth was my father had hurt himself and we had friends and family in Australia who could make it easier for us to live while he recovered."

Gibson recalls that growing up in Sydney, New South Wales, Australia, was not that different from growing up in the United States, but it took time before his peers accepted him. "It was an exciting kind of adventure for a kid," he told an interviewer in *Vanity Fair,* "exciting and spooky at the same time. And culturally the two places are not dissimilar, so it was a fairly easy adjustment to make. It got to the point where I began to like it more than America." Still, "there were adjustments to be made," he told a contributor in *Cosmopolitan.* "It's difficult leaving your friends behind and trying to make new ones. The kids made fun of me and called me Yank, and I had a fairly rough time of it."

An Actor's Life

After graduating from a strict Catholic boys' high school, Gibson considered becoming a journalist, or perhaps a chef, but neither profession held much appeal for him. Meanwhile, his sister secretly entered an application in his name to Australia's National Institute of Dramatic Art. When he was asked during the entrance audition why he wanted to become an actor, Gibson recounted to Lynn Hirschberg in *Rolling Stone,* his reply was: "I've been goofing off all my life. I thought I might as well get paid for it." By 1977, before he officially graduated drama school, Gibson had made his film debut in *Summer City,* a low-budget Australian film that, he later told Hirschberg, was "a cheap, nasty flick, an abomination." Still, the film brought him to the attention of director George Miller, who was seeking a lead for *Mad Max,* his film set in a violent future.

Mel Gibson first gained fame among U.S. audiences in the role of Mad Max in 1982's *The Road Warrior.* (Photograph courtesy of Warner Bros/Kobal Collection/The Picture Desk, Inc.)

Gibson was cast as Max Rockatansky, a renegade cop fighting the evil biker gang who murdered his family. While *Mad Max* initially bombed in the United States (where it was screened with another actor's voice dubbed over Gibson's Australian accent), it became a hit around the world, earning more than 100 million dollars.

Gibson followed up with two dramatic performances in the Australian films *Tim* and *Gallipoli,* both of which earned him best actor awards from the Australian Film Institute. A second "Mad Max" film, *The Road Warrior,* earned a respectable twenty-three million in the United States. He gained increasingly larger roles in critically praised films, holding his own on the screen with Oscar-nominated stars like Sigourney Weaver, Sissy Spacek, and Anthony Hopkins. *Mad Max: Beyond Thunderdome* proved he could headline a movie, earning more than thirty-six million dollars in the States. Gibson's popularity really took off with *Lethal Weapon,* the 1987 action film about a detective (Danny Glover) looking forward to his retirement who is teamed on one last case with Gibson, an on-the-edge cop pushed to suicidal tendencies by the violent murder of his family. With the popularity of *Lethal Weapon,* Gibson became of the most sought-after actors in Hollywood, one of the few whose name on the marquee could guarantee box office success. *Lethal Weapon* spawned three sequels; altogether, the series grossed over 890 million dollars worldwide.

In the early 1990s, Gibson moved permanently from Australia to the United States and began to take charge of his career, moving into the areas of producing and directing. With partner Bruce Davey, Gibson had formed Icon Productions in 1989 to secure financing for a production of William Shakespeare's *Hamlet* in which Gibson was to star. The actor told Stephen Galloway of the *Hollywood Reporter* that Icon came about from "a genuine desire to exploit my own creativity; it was not a complete vision. Then Bruce and I both received a baptism of fire when it came to *Hamlet.*" Despite the challenge, Icon co-produced several films in the 1990s, including several of Gibson's star vehicles. Gibson himself began considering the idea of directing his own film.

It felt like a "natural progression," Gibson told Graham Fuller in a 1995 *Interview* article: "In the last twenty years, I've worked with incredible visual directors like Peter Weir and George Miller—I'd also include Richard Donner among them—and as I witnessed them, I just seemed to snap into their talent." Besides, he explained to Galloway, "I find that there's a lot more pleasure in directing than there is in acting. You have a chance to spread your creative wings, and nobody can clip them."

Behind the Camera

Gibson made his directorial debut in 1993 with *The Man without a Face,* a film based on the young-adult novel by Isabelle Holland. Teenager Chuck needs tutoring to achieve his dream of military school, and turns to local recluse Justin McLeon (played by Gibson), a disfigured former teacher, for help. When the locals suspect McLeon of being a criminal and a pedophile, misunderstandings and conflict ensue. The film was a modest success, earning the debut

director good notices. *Chicago Sun Times'* critic Roger Ebert wrote that the film "shows him not only with a good visual sense, but with what is even rarer, the confidence to know what needs to be told and what can be left unsaid." While *Time* writer Richard Schickel found the story maudlin, he noted that "Mel Gibson, directing for the first time, presents this deeply wet material in a reasonably cool and dry manner." "Gibson, as both an actor and a director, has managed to find much humor in the material," Leah Rozen remarked in *People*. "As a director, he gives his actors their moments without overindulging them, and his scenes are well-paced and shaped."

After starring in another hit, 1994's *Maverick,* Gibson settled back in the director's chair, this time for an historical epic set in thirteenth-century Scotland. The 1995 film *Braveheart* is loosely based on the story of William Wallace, the Scottish commoner who led his countrymen in battle against English invaders. Wallace gains control of the English city of York but is later betrayed in battle by his allies. Gibson not only directed the film, he also starred as

Gibson teamed with Danny Glover in the popular film sequel *Lethal Weapon 2*, directed by Richard Donner. (Photograph courtesy of Warner Bros/Kobal Collection/The Picture Desk, Inc.)

Gibson first took on the role of producer in his award-winning 1995 film *Braveheart*. (Photograph courtesy of Icon/Ladd Co./Paramount/ Kohal Collection/The Picture Desk, Inc.)

Wallace, a challenging role that included many battle scenes. As the director remarked to Fuller, "I wanted to make a film that was kinetic, in which the camera is continuously moving on cranes and tracks. There are times when it doesn't move, and it's a blessed relief, let me tell you. It's a very physical action piece, as well as political and romantic. I tried to make a quintessential epic."

Braveheart earned five Academy awards, including two Oscars for Gibson for best director and best film. Owen Glieberman observed in *Entertainment Weekly* that "Gibson, face lit by adrenaline, makes you feel the pulse-quickering rush of war. He makes you feel it as a director, too. *Braveheart* features some of the most enthralling combat sequences in years, and the excessive ferocity of the violence is part of the thrill." At nearly three hours, the film slows in spots, John Simon remarked in *National Review*, "but the fighting—both individual contests and mass battle scenes—is first-rate, barbaric, and sublime." "*Braveheart* is a huge historical epic . . . with a well-

balanced blend of romantic and documentary styles," Jack Kroll noted in *Newsweek*, adding that the film "is an impressive achievement, Gibson's honorable shot at a big, resonant paean to freedom."

Throughout the late 1990s and early 2000s, Gibson continued working as successful actor. He earned a then-record twenty-five-million-dollar salary for the 2000 film *The Patriot,* and had smash hits with the romantic comedy *What Women Want* and the 2002 thriller *Signs.* In the meantime, he was working behind the scenes to secure funding for a pet project about the last hours of Jesus Christ. "It was something that was rambling about in my [head] for quite a few years, and it came to a certain point where I got somebody to sit down, and we wrote it out," he told Galloway. Gibson, a staunch Roman Catholic, felt he had been personally saved from depression by Christ's Passion, and he planned to film it in detail. He co-wrote a script, had the dialogue translated into Latin and Aramaic (languages used at the time), and put nearly twenty five million dollars of his own money into the production, titled *The Passion of the Christ*.

Controversial Epic

Before the film's release, nothing about *The Passion of the Christ* said "blockbuster." As production was winding down, the media began circulating rumors that the film was overly violent and anti-Semitic. The film was graphic, with a nine-minute whipping scene and close-ups of Christ's wounds, but that was his intent, Gibson told Jane Johnson Struck in *Today's Christian Woman*. "I intentionally pushed that edge to show the enormity of Christ's sacrifice. Jesus could have done what he did for us with a finger prick. Instead, he chose to go all the way for us." He had less success countering objections that the film might inflame anti-Jewish sentiments, despite screening the film for Jewish leaders. *The Passion of the Christ* included scenes of Jews calling for Christ's death; as Gibson said in a television interview, as quoted by Michael Lerner in the *International Herald Tribune*, "the Jews' real complaint isn't with my film but with the Gospels." The controversy made some distributors and theaters shy away from the film, but Gibson went on a nationwide promotion tour, talking about the film to religious groups around the country.

Regardless of the controversy, the movie was a smash hit. *The Passion of the Christ* earned 83.8 million dollars its first weekend alone and over 370 million dollars total during its U.S. run, making it the most successful R-rated film ever. Devout Christians, a demograph often ignored by Hollywood, saw the film repeatedly, bringing friends and neighbors to share the experience. The predicted anti-Semitic reaction never happened; the controversy had only served to give the film more publicity. Besides huge box-office receipts, the film earned several awards, including the National Board of Review Freedom of Expression Award, the Golden Knight Film Festival Grand Prix, the Golden Satellite Award for best director, and the People's Choice Award for favorite movie drama.

Released in 2000 and directed by Roland Emmerich, *The Patriot* was one of Gibson's most popular films as an actor.
(Photograph courtesy of Columbia TriStar/Kobal Collection/Cooper, Andrew/The Picture Desk, Inc.)

Not surprisingly, *The Passion of the Christ* generated much discussion among critics, who debated whether the film is too violent and how effective it explores Christ's life. *Nation* contributor Stuart Klawans considered the violence to be overdone, observing that "Gibson directs down to the audience. . . . Everything has to be doubled before Gibson will trust you to get the message." In contrast, John Leo found that some scenes provide "intertwined lessons in forgiveness, in a few seconds, with no words. This is brilliant filmmaking," he wrote in *U.S. News & World Report*, concluding: "It has way too much carnage for my taste, but it's a serious and powerful film." Writing in *Christianity Today*, Peter T. Chattaway faulted the film for emphasizing the violence of Christ's crucifixion over the Resurrection, but added: "By giving us the feeling of experiencing Jesus' thoughts, and by making us privy to the prayers Jesus offers up as he submits to the will of his Father, *The Passion of the Christ* draws us toward Christ's full humanity like no film before." On the other hand, *Variety* contributor Todd McCarthy noted that Gibson's portrayal of the Resurrection is "stunning, for its brevity, poetic simplicity and clarity of intent. . . . It's done in a minute or less and couldn't be bettered as a silent thunderclap of an ending." "In dramatizing the torment of Jesus' last 12 hours, has made a serious, handsome, excruciating film that radiates total commitment," Richard Corliss concluded in *Time*. "Few mainstream directors have poured so much of themselves into so uncompromising a production."

Portrays a Civilization's Demise

The huge success of *The Passion of the Christ*—the profits on its 611-million-dollar, worldwide box-office take went back to Gibson's production company—meant that the actor-director had the clout to do whatever project he might choose. His next film was on another unlikely subject: the Mayan civilization that ruled southern Mexico before the Spanish conquerors arrived in the 1600s. "You're always looking to do something you have a thirst to see in your own heart and mind. And there has always been this shroud of mystery about the Mayan civilization," the director told Allison Hope Weiner and Joshua Rich in *Entertainment Weekly*. In addition, Gibson stated, "I just wanted to fashion a really exciting chase. I wanted something fast and exhilarating. . . . I haven't ever seen a really good foot chase. A foot chase could be really primal, with animals and all sorts of stuff." Gibson cowrote a script, had it translated into Mayan, cast unknowns (many of whom were new to acting), traveled to Mexico to begin shooting the film, titled *Apocalypto*.

Despite its R rating, subtitles, cast of unknowns, and controversy surrounding its director, *Apocalypto*

debuted in December of 2006 at number one, earning an unexpected 15 million dollars in its first weekend. "Gibson is always good for a surprise, and his latest is that *Apocalypto* is a remarkable film," Todd McCarthy wrote in *Variety*. "The long central section . . . is simply great epic cinema, with generous dollops of chilling horror and grisly human sacrifice." "Whatever his shortcomings, Gibson is a director with vision and ambition," Daniel Eagon wrote in *Film Journal International*. "*Apocalypto* takes place on a scale few filmmakers today would attempt, and it is a measure of Gibson's talent and perseverance, as well as his respect for old-fashioned storytelling, that it succeeds as well as it does." *Hollywood Reporter* contributor Kirk Honeycutt deemed the film overly violent, but still described it as "a first-rate epic built around one man's will to survive to rescue his family." The critic added that Gibson "knows how to make a heart-pounding movie; he just happens to be a cinematic sadist." As Ross Douthat concluded in *National Review*, *Apocalypto* "probably isn't to everyone's taste, but it's the work of a filmmaker who understands exactly how to use a moving image to dazzle your eye and pin you to your seat."

Gibson's success as an actor and filmmaker has made him a very wealthy man. The profits generated by the self-financed *The Passion of the Christ* reportedly increased his worth to over 850 million dollar, which would make him the richest actor in the world. He has owned homes in California, Connecticut, and Costa Rica, and purchased the South Pacific island of Mago in late 2004. Although he does not publicize it widely, Gibson donates much of his wealth to charities. After filming *Apocalypto* in Mexico, he donated one million dollars to build homes in the area devastated by Hurricane Stan in 2005. He has contributed large amounts to Healing the Children, a charity that provides medical care to impoverished children around the world; this included a ten-million-dollar donation in 2004 designed to reimburse two Los Angeles hospitals for treating these children. He donated half a million dollars to and served on the board of the Mirador Basin Project, an environmental and archeological project in Guatemala. He has also put several million dollars into the construction of churches in California and Pennsylvania belonging to a Catholic splinter sect.

With a career that has lasted more than thirty years, Gibson has conquered all aspects of the movie business and shows no signs of slowing down. He has taken fewer acting roles; between 2002's *Signs* and 2009's *Edge of Darkness* he took only one or two cameo roles on screen. It is a measure of his enduring popularity that in 2003 and 2004 he won People's Choice awards for favorite motion-picture

Gibson directing his award-winning film *Apocalypto* on location in Mexico. (Photograph courtesy of Icon Ent/Buena Vista/Kobal Collection/ Cooper, Andrew/The Picture Desk, Inc.)

actor, despite not having starred in any films those years. As Gibson told Weiner and Rich, "I think what you have to do is not work too often. You don't want to inflict yourself on the public too much."

If you enjoy the works of Mel Gibson, you may also want to check out the following films:

Rush Hour, starring Jackie Chan and Chris Tucker, 1998.
Gladiator, starring Russell Crowe, 2000.
Black Hawk Down, directed by Ridley Scott, 2001.

While he believes he still has acting challenges ahead of him, directing remains Gibson's passion, as he told *IGN.com* interviewer Todd Gilchrist. "I'm so in love with the storytelling process that I'm passionate to see my vision of it, and that kind of is taking my attention. I didn't plan it that way; it's just kind of gradually evolved into that, and I get

such a kick out of calling the shots and putting what I see in my mind's eye on film. And getting a wonderfully talented group of people together to help me do it and even getting more than what I imagined."

■ Biographical and Critical Sources

BOOKS

International Dictionary of Films and Filmmakers, Volume 3: Actors and Actresses, 4th edition, St. James Press (Detroit, MI), 2000.

McAvoy, Jim, *Mel Gibson*, Lucent Books (San Diego, CA), 2002.

McCarty, John, *The Films of Mel Gibson*, Citadel Press (New York, NY), 2001.

McKay, Keith, *Mel Gibson*, Doubleday (Garden City, NY), 1986.

Pendreigh, Brian, *Mel Gibson and His Movies*, Bloomsbury (London, England), 1997.

Perry, Roland, *Lethal Hero: The Mel Gibson Biography*, Oliver Books, 1993.

Perry, Roland, *Mel Gibson: Actor, Director, Producer*, Pan Macmillan Australia (Sydney, New South Wales, Australia), 1996.

Wheeler, Jill C., *Mel Gibson*, Abdo & Daughters (Edina, MN), 2003.

PERIODICALS

Christianity Today, March, 2004, Peter T. Chattaway, "Lethal Suffering," p. 36.

Cosmopolitan, May, 1983, interview with Gibson.

Entertainment Weekly, May 26, 1995, Owen Gleiberman, review of *Braveheart*, p. 58; December 8, 2000, Rebecca Ascher-Walsh, "Lady and the Chump," p. 26; March 5, 2004, "Faith Healer?," p. 46; December 8, 2006, Allison Hope Weiner and Joshua Rich, "The Year of Living Dangerously," p. 28; December 15, 2006, Lisa Schwarzbaum, "Rogue Warrior," p. 61.

Esquire, February, 2002, Charles P. Pierce, "Gibson: He Has Taken Lives and Academy Awards in Thirteenth-century Scottish Rebellions, the Revolutionary War, and World War I, and Is Now Headed into Vietnam," p. 63.

Film Journal International, January, 2007, Daniel Eagan, review of *Apocalypto*, p. 40.

Hollywood Reporter, November, 2004, Stephen Galloway, "A Lasting Partnership," p. 16; December 4, 2006, Kirk Honeycutt, review of *Apocalypto*, p. 2.

International Herald Tribune (Paris, France), April 1, 2004, Michael Lerner, "Mel Gibson Revives an Old Message of Hate."

Interview, May, 1995, Graham Fuller, "Thistle Do Nicely," p. 66.

Nation, March 29, 2004, Stuart Klawans, "Adaptation," p. 34.

National Review, July 10, 1995, John Simon, review of *Braveheart*, p. 68; December 31, 2006, Ross Douthat, "Old World," p. 51.

Newsweek, May 29, 1995, Jack Kroll, review of *Braveheart*, p. 60; February 16, 2004, Jon Meacham, "Who Killed Jesus," p. 44.

People, August 30, 1993, Leah Rozen, review of *The Man without a Face*, p. 17; July 27, 1998, "Mister Mischief," p. 86; March 8, 2004, Allison Adato, "The Gospel of Mel," p. 82.

Rolling Stone, January 12, 1989, Lynn Hirschberg, interview with Gibson.

Time, August 30, 1993, Richard Schickel, review of *The Man without a Face*, p. 63; March 1, 2004, Richard Corliss, "The Goriest Story Ever Told," p. 64; March 27, 2006, Tim Padgett, "Apocalypto Now," p. 58; December 11, 2006, Richard Schickel, "The Maya Are Us," p. 85.

Today's Christian Woman: March-April, 2004, Jane Johnson Struck, "Mel's Passion," p. 39.

U.S. News & World Report, March 8, 2004, John Leo, "A Film to Excite Passions," p. 18.

Vanity Fair, July, 1989, interview with Gibson.

Variety, February 23, 2004, Todd McCarthy, review of *The Passion of the Christ*, p. 4; December 4, 2006, Todd McCarthy, review of *Apocalypto*, p. 4.

ONLINE

Chicago Sun Times Online, http://rogerebert.suntimes.com (August 25, 1993), Roger Ebert, review of *Man without a Face*.

IGN.com, http://movies.ign.com/ (December 15, 2006), Todd Gilchrist, interview with Gibson.

Sydney Morning Herald Online, http://www.smh.com.au/ (April 6, 2002), "Veteran's Affairs."*

Tyree Guyton

■ Personal

Born August 24, 1955, in Detroit, MI; son of George and Betty Guyton; married Karen Smith, July 19, 1987 (divorced, 1994); married Jenenne Whitfield (an art agent and executive director), October 5, 2001; children: Tyree Jr., Towan, Omar, James, Tylisa. *Education:* Attended Center for Creative Studies, 1980-82; also studied art at Franklin Adult Education program, Wayne County Community College, and Marygrove College; studied with Charles McGee and other artists.

■ Addresses

Office—Heidelberg Project, 3360 Charlevoix, Detroit, MI 48207.

■ Career

Painter, sculptor, and mixed-media artist; president and sculptor, *Heidelberg Project* (an artwork in progress), Detroit, MI, 1987—. Ford Motor Company, Dearborn, MI, inspector, c. 1979-84; Detroit Fire Department, firefighter, c. 1979-84; instructor in master residence art program at Northern High School, Franklin Adult Education program, and Marygrove College. *Exhibitions:* Work shown at Detroit Artists Market, Michigan Gallery, Liberal Arts Gallery, Cade Gallery, and Trobar Gallery, all Detroit, MI; Le Minotaure and Alexa Lee Gallery, both Ann Arbor, MI; Ledis Flam Gallery, New York, NY; and elsewhere around the world, including Ecuador, Hungary, Australia, Brazil, France, Italy, Russia, Japan, and Germany. Work shown and installed at Detroit Institute of Arts, 1990, and at numerous art and academic institutions, including Auburn University, Charles Wright Museum of African-American History, and Harvard University. Work featured on television shows, including *NBC Nightly News, Oprah Winfrey Show,* and *Good Morning America.* Group exhibitions include Urban Institute of Contemporary Art, Grand Rapids, MI, 1994; Center Galleries, Detroit, MI, 1995; and Minnesota Museum of American Art, St. Paul, 1996. *Military service:* U.S. Army, private, 1972.

■ Awards, Honors

David A. Harmond memorial scholarship, City of Detroit, 1989; Spirit of Detroit Award, Detroit City Council, 1989; Commission Resolution Award, Wayne County, 1990; Testimonial Resolution Award, City of Detroit, 1990; Michiganian of Year Award, State of Michigan, 1991; Governor's Arts Award, 1992; Humanity in the Arts Award, Center for Peace & Conflict Studies, Wayne State University, 1992; Volunteer Community Service Award, Youth Volunteer Corps, 1995; Award of Recognition, Detroit Mayor Kwame Kilpatrick, 2002; Wayne County

International Artist Award, 2003; Great Place Award for Place Design, Environmental Design Research Association, 2004; Rudy Bruner Award for Urban Excellence, 2005; Joyce Award, Joyce Foundation (Chicago, IL), 2007; Award for Artistic Excellence, City of Detroit, 2007; Spirit of Giving Award, Franklin Wright Settlements, 2007; Pollack Krasner Award, Pollack Krasner Foundation, 2007; *Heidelberg Project* chosen as one of fifteen projects to represent United States in 2008 Venice Architecture Biennale.

■ Writings

(With Hilda Vest and Jenenne Whitfield) *Connecting the Dots: Tyree Guyton's Heidelberg Project*, Wayne State University Press (Detroit, MI), 2007.

■ Sidelights

Artist Tyree Guyton has proven the old adage that "one man's trash is another man's treasure" by transforming his blighted Detroit neighborhood into a thriving indoor/outdoor art gallery. Guyton began his *Heidelberg Project* over twenty years ago by taking discarded objects he found—everything from old shoes to bicycles to used tires to baby dolls—and using them to embellish abandoned houses, sidewalks, and empty lots. At first, city leaders called his art junk and took a bulldozer to it. Now, however, Guyton is recognized worldwide as an "urban environmental artist" who helps revitalize economically depressed communities through the power of art.

Through his work Guyton has challenged the boundaries between art and life, as did French artist Marcel Duchamp, who took ordinary objects and presented them as art, and American artist Robert Rauschenberg, who combined painting and common objects in collages or "combines." Guyton's work falls outside what is commonly recognized as art. Part of a group of "outsider" artists—Western artists who draw inspiration from sources outside traditional art—Guyton draws from the lives of the

Tyree Guyton seated in front of a part of his *Heidelberg Project*, Detroit, Michigan, 1997. (Photograph courtesy of AP Images.)

urban poor and makes their experiences and human spirit visible to people who have come from all over the world to see his work. He also shows how fragments of city life can be turned into art.

Guyton was born in 1955 in Detroit, Michigan, one of ten children raised by his mother. The east side neighborhood where he grew up was not always rough; at one time it was "really beautiful, with well-kept houses on all the lots and happy kids playing in the street," Guyton told Brad Darrach in *People.* When he was twelve, however, a violent race riot spread through the city. After five days, there were forty-three dead, over 400 injured, and more than 2,000 buildings destroyed by fire. In the aftermath, residents and businesses fled the city for the suburbs, leaving many neighborhoods filled with abandoned homes. Those residents who remained were often too poor to move from the troubled region, and had to deal with dilapidated schools and escalating drug and gang activity.

Artistic Beginnings

Growing up in one such neighborhood, Guyton found his escape in creativity. "When I was a kid, all I had was the art," he told Janet I. Martineau on the *MLive Saginaw News Blog.* "It was my safe haven, my rescuer." His grandfather nurtured young Tyree's artistic inclinations. "Grandpa was a house-painter," Guyton told Darrach. "When I was eight years old, he stuck a paintbrush in my hand. I felt as if I was holding a magic wand." It was his mother, however, who influenced Guyton's graphic style. Because their family was poor, he remarked to Darrach, "Clothes, furniture, everything came from a second-hand store or was given to us. On the floor we had squares of linoleum. On the sofa were stripes. On a chair there were polka dots. Nothing matched, but my mother made it work. Today I paint with stripes and polka dots, and it works too."

As a teenager Guyton attended Northern High School. To further his art education, he took adult art classes at high schools and colleges in Detroit, including the Center for Creative Studies, the Franklin Adult Education Program, and Marygrove College. He also received early encouragement from Detroit artists Charles and Ali McGee. After serving in the U.S. Army for two years in the early 1970s, Guyton supported himself by working as an inspector for the Ford Motor Company in Dearborn, serving as a firefighter with the Detroit fire department, and teaching art at his old high school. However, he continued to think about making art, and with the encouragement of his grandfather, he decided to do just that.

Guyton's *Heidelberg Project* has continued to draw numerous visitors to an unusual inner-city neighborhood. (Photograph courtesy of Jeff Kowalsky/AFP/Getty Images.)

In the mid-1980s Guyton began the *Heidelberg Project,* named after the street where he starting building. In his neighborhood, with its abandoned, drug-infested houses, he gathered discarded objects and used them to decorate the outsides of the houses or make roadside sculptures, transforming his collections into urban art. With the help of his grandfather, Sam Mackey, and first wife Karen Smith, Guyton painted the objects he attached to the exteriors of the houses and surrounded them with everything from tires to toilets to tombstones, depending on his theme for the house. He also filled empty lots with rows of drinking fountains and old appliances. The painted polka dots that became his signature were inspired by his grandfather's love of jelly beans.

Guyton's urban art gallery changed the city blocks on which it was located from deserted combat zones to places where people stopped and stared. In his

The cityscape of dilapidated sections of Motown was graphically altered as a result of Guyton's creative vision.
(Photograph courtesy of Jeff Kowalsky/AFP/Getty Images.)

essay in the book *Art in the Public Interest*, Michael Hall observed: "A stroll down Heidelberg Street (despite the rawness of Detroit's East Side) recalls a stroll down the main street of Disneyland. Guyton, like Disney, delights, entertains and beguiles with his fantasy facades." Part of the fascination surrounding Guyton's works is that they were forever changing due to weather or the environment, or through the artist's whims. The artist saw the attention as something positive. Pointing to one of his works, a former crack house, he remarked to Darrach, "After the fourth [police] raid we couldn't stand it anymore. So we went on over and painted the place. Pink, blue, yellow, white and purple dots and stripes and squares all over it. Up there on the roof we stuck a baby doll and that bright blue inner tube, and on the porch we put a doghouse with a watchdog inside. . . . Now all day long people drive by and stop to stare at the place. Believe me, in front of an audience like that, nobody's going to sell crack out of that house anymore."

Controversy over Heidelburg

Initial public reaction to Guyton's offbeat street works generated considerable controversy in his home city of Detroit. Some neighborhood residents viewed them as eyesores, and the artist was ticketed for littering. In addition, after reported complaints by neighborhood residents reached the ears of Detroit's then-mayor, Coleman Young, four of the abandoned houses Guyton had decorated with objects were suddenly demolished by the city government in 1991. A second demolition occurred in 1999, during the mayoral administration of Dennis Archer. Guyton sued the city for the destruction of his work, but the suit was later dropped when he came to an accommodation with the city government in the early 2000s.

Guyton believed that at least one of these houses, *The Babydoll House*, which, through its use of broken, naked dolls, dealt directly with issues of child abuse, abortion, and prostitution, was demolished because its images were so powerful. The artworks stored in the fallen houses—estimated to be worth as much as 250,000 dollars, based on what Guyton's work was selling for at the time—had been scheduled to be part of an art tour sponsored by the Detroit Council for the Arts. "Each doll represents something," Guyton told a contributor in the Toronto *Globe and Mail*. "They tell the horrors of drugs and the pity of a neglected child."

Guyton has continued to respond to those who have questioned his motives in creating such controversial works. "This is my art," he maintained to Peter

Plagens in *Newsweek*. "Most of the things used are things that I didn't have coming up. We didn't have a phone, we didn't have toys to play with. So a lot of the stuff that I relate to is stuff that has played a part in my life—stuff that I didn't have, stuff that I wanted." Guyton also noted that his art is driven by his need to "talk about life here in this area . . . to talk about the craziness." Many critics agree that his work, while unconventional, is nonetheless art; as *Art News* contributor Sandra Yolles commented, "Guyton's compositions consist of the houses, the vacant lots, the streets, the trees, the telephone poles. The power of his imagery is what touches people—so much so they have composed music about it, held concerts around the works, and given money for new projects." In an essay for the Detroit Institute of Arts Ongoing Michigan Artists Program, Marion E. Jackson compared Guyton's work to the folk-art "bottle trees" made by African-American artists in the South. The critic added: "The fragmentation, isolation, and juxtaposition of the familiar with the unfamiliar may even affect us subliminally," while "difficult themes such as abortion, child abuse, homelessness, and abandonment" become "jarring aspects of a complex and ever-changing mosaic."

The initial controversy surrounding the *Heidelberg Project* also brought Guyton international attention. His work was featured on a segment of the *NBC Nightly News* and Guyton himself has appeared on the *Oprah Winfrey Show* and *Good Morning America*. As news of his work spread beyond Detroit, visitors from New York City, Canada and even Zimbabwe, Kenya, and Japan began coming to view the project. When Jenenne Whitfield (whom Guyton married in 2001) joined the project as executive director in 1993, it began a period of community outreach for Guyton and his work. He began hosting street festivals and participating in exhibitions and projects worldwide. In Detroit, the Heidelberg Project spread to cover two city blocks, as the nonprofit organization purchased abandoned homes to be decorated with Guyton's art.

Reaching Out to the Community

Guyton found himself in demand as an artist and community organizer. In 1996 he was invited to St. Paul, Minnesota, to transform the outside of a house belonging to the widow of the University of Minnesota's former president as part of an exhibition for the Minnesota Museum of American Art. "We live in a time where art can be anything and everything," Guyton told Joe Kimball in the Minneapolis *Star Tribune*. "It's time to shock people back into reality, to make people think. They look at this

Guyton's colorful, folk-art vision continues to inspire others to share his view of the creative possibilities within the urban landscape. (Photograph courtesy of Jeff Kowalsky/AFP/Getty Images.)

and think: Can he really do that? Yes?" In 2001, the artist was invited to create a permanent art installation for the city of Mt. Vernon, New York. In conjunction with a local art center and groups of teenagers and senior citizens, the *Circle of Life* was created to show "that art can be a catalyst [for] social change and leadership" by "making the connection between life and art," Lisa Robb commented in the *Westchester County Business Journal*.

Guyton continued to broaden the reach of his *Heidelberg Project* in the 2000s. Although some critics contended that his work would not be accepted in wealthier, surrounding suburban neighborhoods, in 2002 he was invited to transform a house in a Detroit suburb into a temporary art exhibition. He used polka dots, old shoes and toys, and collaborated with local artists and schoolchildren. The result was "an ephemeral but memorable artwork—jolly, colourful and idiosyncratic," remarked a contributor in the *Architectural Review*. In 2004 Guyton flew halfway across the world to create artwork in Sydney, Australia. He worked with a diverse

group of residents, including aboriginal youth, to transform a school, community center, and skateboard park into a project called *Singing for That Country*. "I am honored to have been invited to play a role in *Singing for That Country*," the artist was quoted as commenting in *PR Newswire*. "If we are capable of landing on the moon, building weapons of mass destruction and fighting wars, I say we are also capable of bringing hope, health and happiness to people all over the world."

Guyton continues to develop his art in his hometown of Detroit as well. In 2003 he began developing *The House That Makes Sense*, a new project to cover a house entirely with pennies, in collaboration with an architectural firm and Youthbuild Detroit, a nonprofit working with young people to help improve their communities. "I want to build a place where kids can come to learn, to be themselves and to see that there are opportunities for them beyond this neighborhood," Guyton told David Lyman in the *Detroit Free Press*. When finished, the house will include a workshop for young artists, a space where their art can be exhibited, and a loft to host visiting artists. "It's still the polka dot," Guyton remarked to Lyman. "It's just got one of our presidents on it now." To help fund the project, Guyton auctioned off art from one of his *Heidelberg Project* buildings.

Guyton has learned to cooperate and collaborate with the government groups that once tried to destroy his work. As the artist told a contributor in the *Detroit Free Press:* "For a long time, I was mad because people didn't understand my work." "I couldn't let that go," he added. "They had to understand it. They had to appreciate it. I kept talking about the future, but I was being held back by the past." His new attitude has brought partnerships with government and civic groups, as well as corporate sponsorships. His success keeps growing. More than twenty years after he started the *Heidelberg Project,* it receives more than 275,000 visitors from around the world each year. The Project sponsors garden projects in the neighborhood and several educational programs for children. This is what his work is about, he told Martineau: "Tapping into new possibilities, transforming perceptions about life and art, building bridges and connecting with people."

If you enjoy the works of Tyree Guyton, you may also want to check out the following:

The large-scale works of Robert Smithson (1938-1973), an American environmental artist.
The works of British environmental artist Andy Goldsworthy (1956—).
The art of Lynne Hull, an American environmental artist.

In a statement on his official Web site, Guyton wrote: "I strive to be a part of the solution. I see and understand how order is needed in the world and in our individual lives. My experiences have granted me knowledge of how to create art and how to see beauty in everything that exists." He added: "For me, art is a way of expressing life. My work is a science that deals with colors, shapes, objects that brings about a rare beauty to the mind and eyes of people, a type of esthete. My art is life, life that lives on with time because the entire creation is an art form."

■ **Biographical and Critical Sources**

BOOKS

Contemporary Black Biography, Volume 9, Gale (Detroit, MI), 1995.
Eckert, Kathryn Bishop, *Buildings of Michigan,* Oxford University Press (New York, NY), 1993.
McLean, Linda K., *The Heidelberg Project: A Street of Dreams,* Nelson Publishing (Northville, MI), 2007.
Raven, Arlene, editor, *Art in the Public Interest,* Da Capo Press (New York, NY), 1993.

PERIODICALS

African American Family, September, 2007, Niran Tunji, "The Evolution of Heidelberg: Tyree Guyton's Vision," pp. 17-19.
American Style, October, 2007, Amy S. Eckert, "Polka Dot Power," pp. 19-21.
Ann Arbor News, February 23, 1996, "A Day with the Polka Dot Man"; July 16, 2005, "Beyond Heidelburg: Guyton Widens His Commentary."
Architectural Review, July, 2002, "Delight: The Redecoration of an Ordinary American House by a Collaboration of Architect and Artist Is a Wild Manifesto for the Rejuvenation of Decayed Property in Imploding Industrial Cities," p. 98.
Art News, October, 1989, Sandra Yolles, "Junk Magic," p. 27; May, 1992, Sandra Yolles, "Shoed Away," pp. 19-20; September, 1995, Roger Green, "Tyree Guyton," p. 148.
Baltimore Sun, May 27, 1999, "Preserving the Works of a Detroit Folk Artist."
Boston Globe, February 5, 1999, "Detroit Trashes Artist's Work It Deemed Junk."
Charlotte Observer, March 12, 2001, "Detroit Artist Guyton Will Speak at Winthrop."
Chicago Sun-Times, June 13, 1999, "Doing Detroit in Polka Dots."
Cincinnati Enquirer, October 1, 1995, "Detroit Street a 'Must See' Neighborhood Artist Shakes up Motown."
Connoisseur, March, 1989, Vicki Goldberg, "Art by the Block," pp. 124-27.
Craft Arts International, 2002-03, "The Heidelberg Project."
Crain's Detroit Business, October 10, 1994, "Benefit Features Artist Who Gets to the Point," p. 7.
Detroit Free Press, July 30, 1994, "Neighbors Are Seeing Spots Before Their Eyes," p. 7B; August 16, 1996, "Urban Cobbler," p. E1; June 6, 2001, "Connect the Dots"; May 24, 2003, Rochelle Riley, "Detroit Spirit Shines Bright in Australia"; September 24, 2003, David Lyman, "Coins Add up to Art."

Detroit News, November 24, 1991, "Art Everybody Took Pride In . . . It's Gone," pp. 1A, 10A; March 18, 1992, "Tyree Guyton: Through Art Made from Cast-offs, He Finds What Detroit Has Lost"; November 30, 1994, "Street Artist Is Facing Littering Charges Again"; March 9, 2001, Joy Hakanson-Colby, "Into His Own" November 27, 2002, Joy Hakanson-Colby, "Tyree Guyton Loves a Parade"; February 18, 2005, "Fundraiser Will Let Artist Pursue a Dream"; August 25, 2006, "The Heidelberg Project Endures: 20-year Party Will Connect Dots."

Essence, May, 1997, "Tyree Guyton: Art for the People."

Globe and Mail (Toronto, Ontario, Canada), September 30, 1989, "One Man's Garbage Is Another Man's Art," p. C4.

Harvard Design, winter/spring, 1999, "Eyesore or Art?"

Independent (London, England), August 9, 1995, "Detroit Days: History Is All Junk in the Pompeii of Motor City."

Johnsonian, March 21, 2001, "The The Art of a Revolution: Controversial Artist Visits Winthrop."

Juxtapoz, fall, 1997, "Welcome to Heidelberg, a Walk through Detroit's Art Ghetto."

Kalamazoo Gazette, September 11, 2005, "Guyton Discusses Heidelberg Project."

Los Angeles Times, May 5, 1995, Duane Noriyuki,"A World Gone Mad," p. E1; June 8, 2003, Stephanie Simon, "An Artist Auctions His Junkscape," p. A22.

Metro Times (Detroit, MI), July 13-19, 1994, "New Hope Grows on Heidelberg Street," pp. 26-27; August 23-29, 2006, "Dot the Eye—The Heidelberg Project Is Still Connecting after 20 Years of Ups and Downs."

Michigan Chronicle, July 27-August 2, 1994, "Controversial Artist Set to Unveil Latest Works"; July 26-August 1, 2005, "The 20th Anniversary Celebration Planned for Heidelberg Project."

Newsweek, August 6, 1990, p. 64, Peter Plagens, Come On-a My House," p. 64.

New York Times, July 2, 1990, "One Man's Treasure, Another's Junkyard"; February 6, 1999, "Art? Maybe. Junk? Perhaps. History? For Sure."

People, August 15, 1988, Brad Darrach, "With Blight Spirit, Tyree Guyton Transforms Trash into Murals and Crack Houses into Ghetto Galleries," pp. 58-60.

PR Newswire, September 9, 2004, "Detroit-based Artist Tyree Guyton Travels Globe for Cultural Exchange."

Public Art Review, fall/winter, 2006, "Guyton Connects Dots in Detroit."

Raw Vision, spring, 1999, "Heidelberg Project Loses Long Battle for Survival"; spring, 2006, "Circles of Hope."

Real Detroit Weekly, February 11-25, 1999, "Goodbye Polka Dot Road, The Heidelberg Project Comes to an End"; August 23-29, 2006, "Connecting the Dots—Heidelberg Turns 20."

Star Tribune (Minneapolis, MN), August 15, 1996, Joe Kimball, "An Artist's Sole Purpose," p. 1B.

TDR, winter, 2001, Wendy S. Walters, "Turning a Neighborhood Inside Out," p. 64.

Time, August 25, 1997, Ron Stodghill II, "Portrait of the Artist as Polka-dotter," p. 4.

Toledo City Paper, March 30-April 5, 2005, "Connecting the Dots: Detroit Artist Tyree Guyton Beautifies Blighted Neighborhood."

Toronto Star, August 24, 1996, "Urban Renewal at Its Funkiest, Artist Tyree Guyton Is Reclaiming Slums with Whimsy and a Vengeance"; April 28, 2001, "Ghetto Art: Tyree Guyton Struggles to Bring a Little Brightness and Whimsy to His Detroit Street."

USA Today, September 21, 1998, Carrie Hedges, "Artist Makes Loud Statement but Detroit's Not Listening."

Wall Street Journal, November 29, 1991, "Are They B.F. Retreads or Part of a Genuine Work?," p. B1.

Washington Post, February 5, 1999, "Out, Out, Darn Dots! Controversial Detroit Art Project Bites the Dust."

Westchester County Business Journal, July 23, 2001, Lisa Robb, "Public Art Project Brings Teens and Seniors Together," p. S10.

ONLINE

Heidelberg Project Official Web site, http://www.heidelberg.org/ (February 1, 2009).

MLive-Saginaw News Web log, http://blog.mlive.com/ (March 25, 2008), Janet I. Martineau, "Tyree Guyton of Detroit's Heidelberg Project Speaks about His Love of Art at Saginaw Valley State University."

Tyree Guyton Home Page, http://www.tyreeguyton.com (February 1, 2009).

OTHER

Come unto Me: The Faces of Tyree Guyton (film), 1998.

Twentieth-Century Art, Tyree Guyton, June 30 through August 19, 1990 (exhibition catalog), Detroit Institute of Arts Ongoing Michigan Artists Program, pp. 3-9.

Additional information for this profile was provided by Jenenne Whitfield, executive director of Heidelberg Project.*

(Courtesy of Ellen Hopkins.)

Ellen Hopkins

■ Personal

Born March 26, 1955, in Long Beach, CA; adopted daughter of Albert and Valeria Wagner; biological daughter of Toni Chandler; married Jerry Vancelette (divorced); married John Hopkins (a television news assignment editor), October 19, 1991; children: Jason, Cristal, Kelly, Orion. *Education:* Attended University of California, Santa Barbara. *Politics:* "Rabid Democrat." *Religion:* Lutheran. *Hobbies and other interests:* Hiking, biking, skiing, gardening, camping, fishing, sports.

■ Addresses

Home—Washoe Valley, NV. *Office*—Juniper Creek Publishing, P.O. Box 2205, Carson City, NV 89702. *E-mail*—ellenhopkins@charter.net.

■ Career

Novelist and nonfiction writer. Valley Video, owner, 1980-85; freelance journalist, 1986-92; *Tahoe Truckee Reader,* reporter and editor, 1992-96; freelance writer, 1996-98; *Northern Nevada Family Magazine,* editor and contributor, 2000-02; founder of Juniper Creek Publishing, Carson City, NV, and *Three Leaping Frogs* (children's newspaper).

■ Member

Society of Children's Book Writers and Illustrators (regional advisor), Ash Canyon Poets.

■ Awards, Honors

Charlotte's Web pin for outstanding contributions to children's literature by a new author, Society of Children's Book Writers and Illustrators, 2001; Sierra Arts Foundation professional artist award, 2001 and 2004; Quick Picks for Reluctant Young Adult Readers selection, American Library Association (ALA), Books for the Teen Age selection, New York Public Library, and National Book Award nominee, 2006, all for *Crank;* Silver Pen Award, Nevada Writers Hall of Fame, 2006; Best Book for Young Adults selection, ALA, 2007, for *Burned;* Best Book for Young Adults selection and Quick Picks for Reluctant Young Adult Readers selection, both ALA, both 2008, both for *Impulse.*

■ Writings

Air Devils: Sky Racers, Sky Divers, and Stunt Pilots, Perfection Learning (Logan, IA), 2000.

Orcas: High Seas Supermen, Perfection Learning (Logan, IA), 2000.

Tarnished Legacy: The Story of the Comstock Lode, Perfection Learning (Logan, IA), 2001.

Into the Abyss: A Tour of Inner Space, Perfection Learning (Logan, IA), 2001.

The Thunderbirds: The U.S. Air Force Aerial Demonstration Squadron, Capstone Press (Mankato, MN), 2001.

The Golden Knights: The U.S. Army Parachute Team, Capstone Press (Mankato, MN), 2001.

Fly Fishing, Capstone Press (Mankato, MN), 2002, revised edition, 2008.

Freshwater Fishing, Capstone Press (Mankato, MN), 2002, revised edition, 2008.

Canopies in the Clouds, Perfection Learning (Logan, IA), 2002.

Countdown to Yesterday, Perfection Learning (Logan, IA), 2002.

United States Air Force, Heinemann Library (Crystal Lake, IL), 2003.

United States Air Force Fighting Vehicles, Heinemann Library (Crystal Lake, IL), 2003.

United States Special Operations Forces, Heinemann Library (Crystal Lake, IL), 2003.

All for Our Country: Check out Nevada!, Juniper Creek Publishing (Carson City, NV), 2003.

Light Shows: Comets, Meteors, and Asteroids, Perfection Learning (Logan, IA), 2003.

Mysteries of Space, Perfection Learning (Logan, IA), 2003.

Are We Alone? The Case for Extraterrestrial Life, Perfection Learning (Logan, IA), 2003.

Inside a Star, Perfection Learning (Logan, IA), 2003.

Telescopes: Exploring the Beyond, Perfection Learning (Logan, IA), 2003.

Storming the Skies: The Story of Katherine and Marjorie Stinson, Pioneer Women Aviators, Avisson Press (Greensboro, NC), 2004.

(Editor, with Leah Wilson) *A New Dawn: Your Favorite Authors on Stephenie Meyer's Twilight Series*, Borders (Ann Arbor, MI), 2008.

Contributor of articles to local, regional, and national periodicals.

YOUNG-ADULT FICTION

Crank, Simon & Schuster (New York, NY), 2004.

Burned, Margaret K. McElderry Books (New York, NY), 2006.

Impulse, Margaret K. McElderry Books (New York, NY), 2007.

Glass (sequel to *Crank*), Margaret K. McElderry Books (New York, NY), 2007.

Identical, Margaret K. McElderry Books (New York, NY), 2008.

Tricks, Margaret K. McElderry Books (New York, NY), 2008.

Contributor of short stories to anthologies, including *Does This Book Make Me Look Fat?*, 2008.

■ **Sidelights**

Although Ellen Hopkins writes free-verse novels, according to a *Publishers Weekly* reviewer, hers is "not your typical verse." There are no fanciful flights of imaginative reconstruction of nature, no flowery descriptions of emotions. Instead, Hopkins offers hard-hitting verse narration of teen problems. In her best-selling novels, she has tackled edgy subjects, including crystal meth addiction in *Crank* and its sequel, *Glass*; physical and spiritual abuse in *Burned*; attempted suicide in *Impulse*; eating disorders and drug and alcohol abuse in *Identical*; and teenage prostitution in *Tricks*.

Hopkins uses social networking sites as *MySpace* and *FaceBook* to stay in touch with her teen readers and keep current with the problems young adults face. Hopkins wrote her first young-adult novel, *Crank*, which was loosely based on her own daughter's struggle with crystal meth, and she now views dealing with difficult topics as her writer's mission. Speaking with *Publishers Weekly* contributor Kate Pavao, the author noted, "I really believe I was put on sort of a path to write about subjects a lot of authors don't want to look at." "I feel it's important to shed light on these issues," Hopkins further explained in her interview, "because that's the only way we're going to develop empathy for people who are going through them."

A California Childhood

Hopkins was born in 1955, in Long Beach, California. She was adopted by Albert and Valeria Wagner and grew up in Palm Springs. (Hopkins discovered her birth mother in 2000 and was amazed to find that she, too, was a writer and poet.) Her father was seventy-two years old at the time of the adoption and her adopted mother forty-two. As Hopkins noted on her home page, "Having older parents definitely presented some challenges, as well as many, many great things." From her adopted father Hopkins developed a work ethic and sense of honesty, while from Valeria, who read to her every night, she gained a love of language. She lived a privileged childhood in Palm Springs, a neighbor to celebrities such as Kirk Douglas and Elvis Presley. She rode horses and participated in gymkanas. Bal-

Ellen Hopkins describes the dedication of a group of brave U.S. military pilots in *The Thunderbirds*, a nonfiction book released in 2001. (Capstone Press, 2001. Photograph courtesy of U.S. Air Force Thunderbirds/SSgt. Kevin J. Gruenwald. Reproduced by permission.)

let and jazz dance lessons were part of her weekly routine. In addition, Hopkins also began to write poetry, publishing her first poem in the local newspaper when she was nine. Summers were spent in somewhat cooler Napa, California, amid the vineyards, and also at Lake Tahoe.

When Hopkins was a freshman in high school, the family moved to the Santa Ynez Valley, just inland from Santa Barbara. "High school was neither awful nor wonderful for me," she related on her home page. She continued to write and dance, and became involved in theater, as well as some sports, such as middle-distance track events. She later attended the nearby University of California, Santa Barbara, where she majored in journalism. However, she did not finish her degree, leaving school in 1977 to marry her first husband. Hopkins had three children and started her own business before that marriage ended in divorce. She met her current husband, John Hopkins, in 1984. Together, they moved to Tahoe, where Hopkins went back into journalism, taking a job with a local newspaper and freelancing

for other periodicals. Then, in 1998, a visit to the Smithsonian Air and Space Museum changed her career trajectory.

At the Smithsonian Hopkins saw an exhibit on women in aviation that piqued her interest in the subject. She decided to focus on book-length freelance work targeted at young readers. Her debut title, *Air Devils: Sky Racers, Sky Divers, and Stunt Pilots*, recounts the history of flight and covers such topics as dirigibles, early airplanes, military planes, and even airplane pylon races. According to *Booklist* contributor Catherine Andronik, the work is "easy to read, contemporary, and not condescending." In her next publication, *Orcas: High Seas Supermen*, Hopkins brings to readers the world of the Orca, or killer whale. Information about whale habitats, survival mechanisms, and communication is interspersed with color and black-and-white photographs, diagrams, and sidebars. Noting that whale habitats are "expertly explained," *Booklist* critic Roger Leslie concluded: "Always captivating, this book is sure to please" young naturalists.

Personal Life Informs Fictional Works

Hopkins wrote a score of nonfiction works before she published her first young-adult novel, taking inspiration from her own daughter's addiction to methamphetamine for the 2004 title, *Crank.* Written in free verse, the book details the devastation wrought by the drug, also called crank, on the life of sixteen-year-old Kristina, who is introduced to meth on a visit to her estranged father. When Kristina feels smothered by her boring home, she turns to crank, calling herself Bree when under the influence of the drug. This alter ego takes over and the teen begins hanging out with some unsavory characters, resulting in an unwanted pregnancy. Although her family helps Kristina through the pregnancy and subsequent adoption, Hopkins allows for no easy happy endings, for, as with many addicts, Kristina returns to her crank habit after the birth.

Crank garnered strong reviews, a *Kirkus Reviews* critic calling it a "powerful and unsettling" novel in which "hypnotic and jagged free verse wrenchingly chronicles" Kristina's plight. Similar praise came from *School Library Journal* contributor Sharon Korbeck, who found the novel "a stunning portrayal of a teen's loss of direction and realistically uncertain future." For *Kliatt* contributor Claire Rosser, *Crank* tells a "devastating story." Rosser went on to note: "We aren't used to YA novels that end in such despair, but we have to face the truth that many addicts do not recover." Likewise, *Booklist* reviewer Gillian Engberg predicted that "readers won't soon forget smart, sardonic Kristina . . . [or] her chilling descent into addiction." A *Publishers Weekly* contributor further commended Hopkins for "creat[ing] a world nearly as consuming and disturbing as the titular drug."

Hopkins continues the journey of Kristina in *Glass,* which "walks readers forward from where *Crank* leaves off," as Hopkins explained to a *Powells.com* contributor. Hopkins further remarked that *Glass* "follows Kristina as she returns to the lair of the 'monster' drug, crystal meth. The book is a brutally honest portrait of addiction, and just how low even a 'good girl' will go when caught in the snare of this terrible substance." Hopkins' own daughter spent two years in prison as a result of her addiction, but has been mostly clean since 2002.

Glass begins on a positive note, with Kristina clean from her addiction and living with her family in Reno, having given birth to a baby which was the result of a rape. However her post-birth figure and a dead-end job at a convenience store depress her. Soon she weakens and, under the influence of an abusive man, goes back to her meth habit in this "heartrending and intimately honest" novel, as Engberg called it. Kristina's mother thereafter kicks her out of the house and takes custody of the baby. Although *School Library Journal* reviewer Johanna Lewis was unimpressed with this sequel, finding that "minor characters are flat, and Kristina's overblown self-pity elicits little empathy," the critic also believed that "reluctant readers, may appreciate the spare style and realism." A more positive assessment was offered by a *Publishers Weekly* reviewer who termed *Glass* a "hard-hitting free-verse novel" in which Hopkins "expertly relays both plot points and drug facts through verse." For a *Kirkus Reviews* contributor, the same novel is "hypnotically sad, with a realistic lack of closure."

Other Tales of Teenage Struggle

Another sixteen-year-old girl is at the center of Hopkins's young-adult novel *Burned.* With this work, Hopkins turns her attention from drugs to the influence of religion and domestic violence on a teen's life. Once again using free verse, Hopkins presents

Cover of Hopkins' young-adult verse novel *Burned*, which finds a teen confronting domestic violence. (Jacket Illustration © by Sammy Yuen, Jr. Reprinted with the permission of Margaret K. McElderry Books, an imprint of Simon & Schuster Children's Publishing Division.)

young Pattyn, whose first-person narrative details the repression and violence she experiences as a female member of the Mormon Church and the daughter of an alcoholic, abusive father. Sent to her aunt's desert ranch as punishment for questioning her father and her religion, Pattyn matures with her newfound freedom and engages in a love affair with a young boy that ends in pregnancy. A critic for *Kirkus Reviews* called *Burned* "sharp and heartbreaking." Writing in *Booklist*, Frances Bradburn deemed the work a "troubling but beautifully written novel," while *School Library Journal* contributor Kathy Lehman observed that Hopkins "has masterfully used verse to re-create the yearnings and emotions of a teenage girl trapped in tragic circumstances."

Impulse takes on the difficult topic of teenage attempted suicide. Here Hopkins has three such young patients of a psychiatric relate their stories in free verse. "Their lives unfold in alternating chapters, revealing emotionally scarred family relationships," noted Vicki Reutter in a *School Library Journal* review. Bipolar or uncaring parents, drug addiction, questions of sexual identity, and failed love affairs have all contributed to these failed attempts at suicide. "Mature fans of the verse format will devour this hefty problem novel," Reutter thought. A *Publishers Weekly* contributor also praised the "artful free verse" Hopkins employs in these interweaving tales, further noting, "By book's end, readers may well feel the effects of each protagonist's final choice." Writing for *Kirkus Reviews* a contributor similarly described *Impulse* as "a fast, jagged, hypnotic read."

In *Identical* "Hopkins's gift with free verse reaches new heights in this portrait of splintered identical twins," as a *Kirkus Review* contributor noted. The twins, Kaeleigh and Raeanne, come from a home torn asunder. Their father is an alcoholic who sexually abuses one twin while his wife escapes the home for a career in politics. The girls resort to sex, drugs, and bulimia as a refuge from their problems. The *Kirkus Reviews* writer added further praise, calling the work "sharp and stunning, with a brilliant final page." Likewise, a *Publishers Weekly* critic felt that Hopkins "takes readers on a harrowing ride into the psyches of 16-year-old identical twins," and Joyce Adams Burner, reviewing the novel in *School Library Journal*, concluded: "Gritty and compelling, this is not a comfortable read, but its keen insights make it hard to put down."

"I write books for young adults because I truly connect with them on some very deep level," Hopkins remarked in her *Powells.com* interview. "They are our hope, our future, and inspiring them to be the best they can be is very important to me." Asked by Pavao if she had intentions of taking her writing in a different direction or writing for a different audience, Hopkins replied: "For now, I don't see a reason to go in a different direction. I've got so many topics I'd like to write about, and my readership is drawn to the format. I like what I'm doing and my readers are waiting for the next book." On her home page, Hopkins also offered this advice for those who want to become writers: "Try to write every day, even if it's just a sentence or two in a journal, a short poem or a character sketch. If you miss a day, don't beat yourself up. Writing should be something you love to do, not something you have to do."

If you enjoy the works of Ellen Hopkins, you may also want to check out the following books:

Melvin Burgess, *Smack*, 1998.
Alex Flinn, *Breaking Point*, 2002.
Gail Giles, *What Happened to Cass McBride?*, 2006.

■ **Biographical and Critical Sources**

PERIODICALS

Booklist, July, 2000, Catherine Andronik, review of *Air Devils: Sky Racers, Sky Divers, and Stunt Pilots*, p. 2016; November 1, 2000, Roger Leslie, review of *Orcas: High Seas Supermen*, p. 528; November 15, 2004, Gillian Engberg, review of *Crank*, p. 595; June 1, 2006, Frances Bradburn, review of *Burned*, p. 62; October 1, 2007, Gillian Engberg, review of *Glass*, p. 45.

Bulletin of the Center for Children's Books, June, 2006, Deborah Stevenson, review of *Burned*, p. 455.

Kirkus Reviews, October 1, 2004, review of *Crank*, p. 96; April 1, 2006, review of *Burned*, p. 348; December 1, 2006, review of *Impulse*, p. 1221; July 15, 2007, review of *Glass*; July 1, 2008, review of *Identical*.

Kliatt, May, 2000, review of *Air Devils*, p. 38; September, 2004, Claire Rosser, review of *Crank*, p. 21; January, 2007, Myrna Marler, review of *Impulse*, p. 14; November, 2008, Janis Flint-Ferguson, review of *A New Dawn: Your Favorite Authors on Stephenie Meyer's Twilight Series*, p. 35.

Publishers Weekly, November 1, 2004, review of *Crank*, p. 63; January 22, 2007, review of *Impulse*, p. 186; August 13, 2007, review of *Glass*, p. 69; July 7, 2008, review of *Identical*, p. 59.

School Library Journal, November, 2004, Sharon Korbeck, review of *Crank*, p. 145; May, 2005, Elizabeth Stumpf, review of *Storming the Skies: The Story of Katherine and Marjorie Stinson, Pioneer Women Aviators*, p. 152; July, 2006, Kathy Lehman, review of *Burned*, p. 105; February, 2007, Vicki Reutter, review of *Impulse*, p. 118; September, 2007, Johanna Lewis, review of *Glass*, p. 198; August, 2008, Joyce Adams Burner, review of *Identical*, p. 122.

Voice of Youth Advocates, April, 2005, Valerie Ott, review of *Crank*, p. 14.

ONLINE

Ellen Hopkins Home Page, http://www.ellenhopkins.com (December 15, 2008).

Powells.com, http://www.powells.com/ (January 5, 2008), interview with Hopkins.

Publishers Weekly Online, http://www.publishersweekly.com/ (August 9, 2007), Kate Pavao, interview with Hopkins.*

Robert E. Howard

■ Personal

Born January 22, 1906, in Peaster, TX; died June 12, 1936, in Cross Plains, TX, from a self-inflicted gunshot wound; son of Isaac Mordecai (a doctor) and Hester Jane Howard. *Education:* Attended Howard Payne Commercial School, c. 1927. *Hobbies and other interests:* Boxing, history.

■ Career

Writer. Previously worked odd jobs, including as a private secretary in a law office, geologist assistant, public stenographer, and drugstore clerk.

■ Writings

SHORT STORY COLLECTIONS

Skull-Face and Others, Arkham House (Sauk City, WI), 1946, published as *Skull-Face Omnibus,* Spearman (Sutton, NE), 1976, published as *The Valley of Worms and Others* (England), 1976, published as *The Shadow Kingdom,* 1976.

The Dark Man and Others, Arkham House (Sauk City, WI), 1963.

(With Lin Carter) *King Kull,* Lancer (New York, NY), 1967, material by Howard published separately as *Kull, the Fabulous Warrior King,* 1978, new edition published as *Kull: Exile of Atlantis,* illustrated by Justin Sweet, Del Rey (New York, NY), 2006.

Wolfshead, Lancer (New York, NY), 1968.

Red Shadows, Donald M. Grant (West Kingston, RI), 1968.

(With Tevis Clyde Smith) *Red Blades of Black Cathay,* illustrations by David Karbonik, Donald M. Grant (West Kingston, RI), 1971.

Marchers of Valhalla, illustrations by Robert Bruce Acheson, Donald M. Grant (West Kingston, RI), 1972.

The Sowers of the Thunder, illustrations by Roy G. Krenkel, Donald M. Grant (West Kingston, RI), 1973.

The Incredible Adventures of Dennis Dorgan, introduction by Darrell C. Richardson, Fax (West Linn, OR), 1974.

The Lost Valley of Iskander, illustrations by Michael William Kaluta, Fax (West Linn, OR), 1974.

The People of the Black Circle, Donald M. Grant (West Kingston, RI), 1974.

Tigers of the Sea, Donald M. Grant (West Kingston, RI), 1974.

Worms of the Earth (includes *Bran Mak Morn*), Donald M. Grant (West Kingston, RI), 1974.

Red Nails, illustrations by George Barr, Donald M. Grant (West Kingston, RI), 1975.

Swords of Shahrazar, illustrations by Michael William Kaluta, Fax (West Linn, OR), 1976.

Black Vulmea's Vengeance, and Other Tales of Pirates, illustrations by Robert James Pailthorpe, Donald M. Grant (West Kingston, RI), 1976.

The Devil in Iron, illustrations by Dan Green, Grosset & Dunlop (New York, NY), 1976.

Rogues in the House, Donald M. Grant (West Kingston, RI), 1976.

The Iron Man and Other Tales of the Ring, illustrated by David Ireland, Donald M. Grant (West Kingston, RI), 1976.

Son of the White Wolf, illustrations by Marcus Boas, Fax (West Linn, OR), 1977.

The People of the Black Circle, Berkley (New York, NY), 1977.

Queen of the Black Coast, Donald M. Grant (West Kingston, RI), 1978.

The Gods of Bal-Sagoth (collected stories), Ace (New York, NY), 1979.

Hawks of Outremer, edited by Richard L. Tierney, illustrations by Rob MacIntyre and Chris Pappas, Donald M. Grant (West Kingston, RI), 1979.

The Road to Azrael, illustrations by Roy G. Krenkel, Donald M. Grant (West Kingston, RI), 1979.

Lord of the Dead, illustrations by G. Duncan Eagleson, Donald M. Grant (West Kingston, RI), 1981.

The Last Cat Book, illustrations by Peter Kuper, Dodd, Mead (New York, NY), 1984.

The Dark Barbarian: The Writings of Robert E. Howard, edited by Don Herron, Greenwood Press (Westport, CT), 1984.

Pool of the Black One, Donald M. Grant (West Kingston, RI), 1986.

Cthulhu: The Mythos and Kindred Horrors, Baen Books (New York, NY), 1989.

The Complete Action Stories, edited by and with an introduction by Paul Herman, Wildside Press (Holicong, PA), 2001.

Bran Mak Morn: The Last King, illustrated by Gary Gianni, Wandering Star (London, England), 2001, Del Rey/Ballantine Books (New York, NY), 2005.

Waterfront Fists and Others, introduction by Mark Finn, edited by Paul Herman, Wildside Press (Holicong, PA), 2003.

Graveyard Rats and Others, introduction by Don Herron, edited by Paul Herman, Wildside Press (Holicong, PA), 2003.

The Savage Tales of Solomon Kane, illustrated by Gary Gianni, Del Rey/Ballantine Books (New York, NY), 2004.

Gates of the Empire and Other Tales of the Crusades, Wildside Press (Holicong, PA), 2004.

Lord of Samarcand and Other Adventure Tales of the Old Orient, edited by Rusty Burke, introduction by Patrice Louinet, University of Nebraska Press (Lincoln, NE), 2005.

The Black Stranger and Other American Tales, edited and with an introduction by Steven Tompkins, University of Nebraska Press (Lincoln, NE), 2005.

Boxing Stories, edited and with an introduction by Chris Gruber, University of Nebraska Press (Lincoln, NE), 2005.

The Best of Robert E. Howard, illustrated by Jim and Ruth Keegan, Ballantine Books, (New York, NY), 2007.

The Horror Stories of Robert E. Howard, illustrated by Greg Staples, Del Rey (New York, NY), 2008.

Other omnibus volumes include *The Book of Robert E. Howard*, 1976; *The Second Book of Robert E. Howard*, 1976; *The Robert E. Howard Omnibus*, 1977; *Sword Woman*, 1977; and *Black Canaan*, 1978. Contributor of short stories and novellas to pulp magazines, including *Spicy Adventure, Action Stories, Thrilling Adventures, Weird Tales, Top Notch, Strange Detective, Oriental Stories, Fight Stories*, and *Argosy*.

NOVELS

Almuric, Ace (New York, NY), 1964.

A Witch Shall Be Born, illustrations by Alicia Austin, Donald M. Grant (West Kingston, RI), 1975.

"CONAN" FANTASY NOVELS

Conan the Conqueror, Gnome Press (New York, NY), 1950, published as *The Hour of the Dragon*, Putnam (New York, NY), 1977.

(With L. Sprague de Camp) *The Treasure of Tranicos*, with introduction and essays by de Camp, Ace (New York), 1980.

"CONAN" SHORT-STORY COLLECTIONS

The Sword of Conan, Gnome Press (New York, NY), 1952.

The Coming of Conan, Gnome Press (New York, NY), 1953, new edition illustrated by Mark Schultz, Del Rey (New York, NY), 2005.

King Conan, Gnome Press (New York, NY), 1953.

Conan the Barbarian, Gnome Press (New York, NY), 1954.

(With L. Sprague de Camp) *Tales of Conan*, Gnome Press (New York, NY), 1955.

(With L. Sprague de Camp) *Conan the Adventurer*, Lancer (New York, NY), 1966.

(With L. Sprague de Camp and Lin Carter) *Conan*, Lancer (New York, NY), 1967.

(With L. Sprague de Camp) *Conan the Warrior*, Lancer (New York, NY), 1967.

(With L. Sprague de Camp) *Conan the Usurper*, Lancer (New York, NY), 1967.

(With L. Sprague de Camp) *Conan the Freebooter*, Lancer (New York, NY), 1968.

(With L. Sprague de Camp and Lin Carter) *Conan the Wanderer*, Lancer (New York, NY), 1968.

(With others) *Conan the Avenger,* Lancer (New York, NY), 1968.

(With L. Sprague de Camp and Lin Carter) *Conan of Cimmeria,* Lancer (New York, NY), 1969.

Conan: The Tower of the Elephant, Grosset & Dunlap (New York, NY), 1975.

Conan: The People of the Black Circle, edited by Karl Edward Wagner, Berkley (New York, NY), 1977.

Jewels of Gwahlur, illustrated by Dean Morrissey, Donald M. Grant (West Kingston, RI), 1979.

Black Colossus, illustrated by Ned Dameron, Donald M. Grant (West Kingston, RI), 1979.

The Conan Chronicles, 1989.

The Bloody Crown of Conan (includes *The People of the Black Circle, The Hour of the Dragon,* and *A Witch Shall Be Born*), illustrated by Gary Gianni, Del Rey (New York, NY), 2004.

The Complete Chronicles of Conan, Gollancz (London, England), 2004.

The Conquering Sword of Conan, Del Rey/Ballantine Books (New York, NY), 2005.

Contributor of Conan stories to periodicals, including *Weird Tales.*

WESTERN SHORT STORIES

A Gent from Bear Creek, Jenkins (Grove City, PA), 1937, selections published as *The Pride of Bear Creek,* Donald M. Grant (West Kingston, RI), 1966.

The Vultures; Showdown at Hell's Canyon, Fictioneer, 1973.

Vultures of Whapeton, Zebra (New York, NY), 1975.

The Last Ride, Berkley (New York, NY), 1978.

Mayhem on Bear Creek, illustrated by Tim Kirk, Donald M. Grant (West Kingston, RI), 1979.

The Riot at Bucksnort and Other Western Tales, edited and with an introduction by David Gentzel, University of Nebraska Press (Lincoln, NE), 2005.

The End of the Trail: Western Stories, edited and with an introduction by Rusty Burke, University of Nebraska Press (Lincoln, NE), 2005.

Contributor of western stories to periodicals, including *Argosy, Cowboy Stories,* and *Zane Grey Western.*

POETRY

Always Comes Evening: The Collected Poems of Robert E. Howard, Arkham House (Sauk City, WI), 1958.

Etchings in Ivory, Glenn Lord, 1968.

Singers in the Shadows, illustrations by Marcus Boas, Donald M. Grant (West Kingston, RI), 1970.

Echoes from an Iron Harp, illustrations by Alicia Austin, Donald M. Grant (West Kingston, RI), 1972.

A Song of the Naked Lands, Squires, 1973.

The Gold and the Grey, Squires, 1974.

Shadows of Dreams, Donald M. Grant (West Kingston, RI), 1989.

LETTERS

Selected Letters, 1923-1930, Necronomicon Press (West Warwick, RI), 1989.

Selected Letters, 1931-1936, Necronomicon Press (West Warwick, RI), 1991.

Dear August: Letters, Robert E. Howard to August Derleth, 1932-1936, Robert E. Howard Properties, 2002.

Dear HPL: Letters, Robert E. Howard to H.P. Lovecraft, 1930-1936, Robert E. Howard Properties, 2002.

■ Adaptations

Howard's fictional character Conan was the basis for novels by writers such as Bjorn Nyberg, L. Sprague de Camp, Lin Carter, Andrew J. Offutt, Robert Jordan, and Steve Perry; in addition, the character was featured in the Marvel comics *Conan the Barbarian* and *The Savage Sword of Conan.* Conan has appeared in videogames, role-playing games, television series (animated and live action), and in films such as 1982's *Conan the Barbarian* and 1984's *Conan the Destroyer,* which starred Arnold Schwarzenegger. The "Conan" stories have also been adapted for the sound recording *Robert E. Howard's Conan,* Moondance Productions (Wilmington, VT), 1976. Other films based on Howard's characters include *Red Sonja,* 1985, and *Kull the Conqueror,* 1997. Film rights to Howard's collected works were purchased in 2006 by Paradox Entertainment. Marvel Comics adapted Kull of Atlantis, Solomon Kane, and other characters for a comic-book format. Howard's stories have been adapted for television, including "Pigeons from Hell" for *Boris Karloff's Thriller.*

■ Sidelights

Robert E. Howard ranks among the most prominent, and prolific, writers in the genre of fantastic, sword-and-sorcery fiction, and he is widely known as the creator of the heroic barbarian character Conan. "Howard is very nearly a major cultural figure," a critic wrote in the *St. James Guide to Fantasy Writers.* "His influence on 20th-century fantasy is simply inescapable. While he may have had his antecedents, he effectively created and defined the sword-and-sorcery story. His barbarian hero is a pop archetype, as instantly recognizable as Tarzan or Sherlock Holmes."

Howard was born in 1906 in Peaster, Texas. Without siblings or many playmates, he spent much of his childhood reading. His family settled in Cross Plains, a small rural town in West Texas, when Howard was thirteen years old. Unable to afford a college education, he pursued financial independence by writing. In 1924, when he was still in his teens, he sold his first story, "Spear and Fang," to *Weird Tales.* This magazine would prove to be the

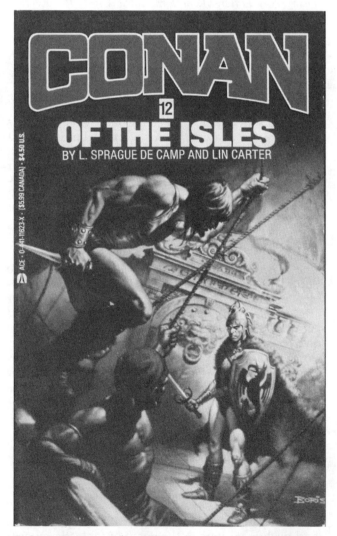

Robert E. Howard's "Conan" series inspired many novels, such as *Conan of the Isles,* coauthored by Lin Carter and L. Sprague de Camp. (Ace Books, 1968. All rights reserved. Reproduced by permission of the illustrator, Boris Vallejo.)

principal publisher of Howard's writings throughout the brief remainder of his life.

Howard was considered strange by many of his neighbors, sitting in isolation at his typewriter and producing as many as 12,000 words a day. After being victimized by gangs as a youth, he devoted himself to physical fitness. As one local told Carlton Stowers in the *Houston Chronicle,* Howard was "a big, strong guy who looked like a boxer." Nonetheless, his contemporary said, "I never heard of him getting into any fights. He didn't play ball, didn't go to dances. He didn't like many people." When he was not writing, Howard would wander the local countryside with his dog, Patches. On the occasions he went out, it was usually by himself: to the local library, the movie theater, or sometimes to a boxing exhibition or football match. He did befriend a local teacher and aspiring writer, Novalyne Price Ellis, but his close relationship with his mother discouraged any romance. (In 1986 Ellis wrote a memoir of their relationship, *One Who Walked Alone: Robert E. Howard, The Final Years;* it was made into a film, 1997's *The Whole Wide World.*) As Ellis told the Los Angeles *Daily News,* "Maybe he was a little different from other men, but a lot of writers are. Bob was a nice person; very peculiar, but I think we all are. He was very kind. He wanted to be kind."

Sword-and-Sorcery Tales

Howard worked a few odd jobs while starting out as a writer; by his own account, he had little inclination to be a post-office secretary, store clerk, stenographer, or geologist's assistant. Luckily, he showed himself to be a speedy and imaginative writer whose best stories were inevitably propelled by action, and he was soon making a good living writing for pulp magazines. Many of his fast-paced tales featured recurring heroes. In the late 1920s, for instance, he produced stories centering on Solomon Kane, a morose figure dedicated to the eradication of evil. During that same period, Howard also wrote about Steve Costigan, a vigorous sailor with considerable prowess as a boxer. In the sword-and-sorcery genre, he had already written several atmospheric tales featuring King Kull, an adventurer hailing from the underwater kingdom of Atlantis.

In 1932 Howard introduced Conan the Barbarian to *Weird Tales* readers in "By This Ax I Rule!" and "The Phoenix and the Sword." In these tales, and the many that followed, Conan roams the primitive lands of Cimmeria, where all manner of helpless maidens, evil sorcerers, and gruesome serpents might be found. Conan himself is a crude figure

Former bodybuilder Arnold Schwarzenegger rose to fame with the help of his starring role in the film adaptation of Howard's *Conan the Barbarian.* (Photograph courtesy by De Laurentiis/Kobal Collection/The Picture Desk, Inc.)

whose powers in combat far outweigh his prowess as a reasoning individual, and in dangerous situations he inevitably favors brutal retaliation over deliberation. Howard, as quoted in *The Last Celt: A Bio-Bibliography of Robert Ervin Howard*, described Conan as "a combination of a number of men I have known, and I think that's why he seemed to step full-grown into my consciousness when I wrote the first yarn of the series." He added that he "took the dominant characteristics of various prize-fighters, gunmen, bootleggers, oil field bullies, gamblers, and honest workmen . . . and combining them all produced the amalgamation I call Conan the Cimmerian."

It was in the "Conan" tales that Howard produced what he described in *The Last Celt* as "the bloodiest and most sexy weird story I ever wrote." That tale, "Red Nails," featuring the strong-willed female warrior Red Sonja, is among the most prominent of the "Conan" series, which also includes such titles as "The Hour of the Dragon," "The Tower of the Elephant," "The Slithering Shadow," "The People of

the Black Circle," and "Beyond the Black River." As fantasy writer L. Sprague de Camp noted in his book *Literary Swordsmen and Sorcerers: The Makers of Heroic Fantasy*, "Howard envisaged the entire life of Conan, from birth to old man, and made him grow and develop as a real man does. At the start, Conan is merely a lawless, reckless, irresponsible, predatory youth with few virtues save courage, loyalty to his few friends, and a rough-and-ready chivalry toward women. In time he learns caution, prudence, duty, and responsibility, until by middle age he has matured enough to make a reasonably good king."

Howard's stories were praised for their simple, energetic prose and action-packed plots. Writing in *Amra*, Fritz Leiber declared himself "impressed with Howard's simple, youthful, melodramatic power." Howard, Leiber continued, "painted in about the broadest strokes imaginable. A mass of glimmering black for the menace, an ice-blue cascade for the hero, between them a swathe of crimson for battle, passion, blood—and that was the picture, or story, rather, except where a vivid detail might chance to

Vincent D'Onofrio performed the role of Howard in the 1997 biographical film *The Whole Wide World*. (Photograph © Corbis SYGMA.)

obtained Howard's incomplete manuscripts and notes and completed many of the stories. The de Camp continuations appeared in such 1960s volumes as *Conan the Adventurer, Conan the Warrior,* and *Conan the Usurper.* In 1965 editor and publisher Glenn Lord approached Howard's estate and offered his services as an agent. "I had begun reading the Conan stories in the early '50s," he told Stowers, "and really liked his writing. At the time there was really very little known about Howard, so I set out to learn as much as I could about him and see if I might find other things he'd written—simply because I wanted to read more of what he'd done."

Posthumous Success

In the following years Howard's reputation grew, not only in the United States but across the globe. New editions gathered many of Howard's 400 stories into themed collections, and they were translated into at least thirty languages. Standout characters included not only Conan but Kull of Atlantis, a barbarian warrior who becomes king; Solomon Kane, a seventeenth-century Puritan who wanders the Earth battling evil; and Bran Mak Morn, the last king of the Picts, an ancient tribe that lived in Scotland until the tenth century. Marvel Comics also produced series based on Kull, Solomon Kane, and Conan, and Conan was featured in dozens of sword-and-sorcery novels by other writers, including de Camp, Lin Carter, Andrew J. Offutt, Robert Jordan, and Steve Perry. In addition, the Barbarian of Cimmeria was played by Arnold Schwarzenegger in two feature films, *Conan the Barbarian* and *Conan the Destroyer.* Other characters from the "Conan" series have also received their own movie or comic treatments, including Red Sonja and Thulsa Doom.

More than seventy years after Howard's death, his stories continue to be recollected and reprinted, often in expensive collector's editions with lavish illustrations. *The Bloody Crown of Conan,* published in 2004, includes not only stories of the warrior but also the author's notes and early drafts. Conan remains popular outside the United States as well. The British collection titled *The Complete Chronicles of Conan* was published in 2005 and was deemed "an absolute must buy" in a review in the *Bookseller.* Conan's resurgence continued with new books, comics, films, and games based on Howard's timeless character. "He is the original American fantasy hero," one game developer told Mike Snider of *USA Today,* while another noted that Conan "is the sort of character that everyone, in some deep corner of their mind, wants to be, even for just a little while."

spring to life, or a swift thought-arabesque be added." Because Howard churned out tales so quickly, however, his works do have their flaws, including "inconsistencies, anachronisms, and other examples of careless craftsmanship," de Camp remarked.

Howard had long suffered from depression and written of suicide; his close relationship with his mother prevented him from taking any such action. In 1936, told by doctors that his mother was hours from death, Howard killed himself. In the ensuing decade, his stories seemed to fall into literary obscurity. However, in 1950 "The Hour of the Dragon" was published as *Conan the Conqueror,* and two years later a collection of "Conan" tales were published as *The Sword of Conan.* By the middle of the 1950s, Howard's "Conan" tales were back in print. The Conan revival continued when de Camp

While his adventure tales remain most prominent among Howard's writings, he also worked in other genres, including westerns, detective tales, horror stories, and even poetry. His verse, for example, is featured in several publications, including *Always Comes Evening: The Collected Poems of Robert E. Howard, Etchings in Ivory, Singers in the Shadows, Echoes from an Iron Harp,* and *The Gold and the Grey.* "Like his prose, his verse is vigorous, colorful, strongly rhythmic, and technically adroit," de Camp noted.

A 2008 collection, *The Horror Stories of Robert E. Howard,* brings together sixty stories, sketches, and poems covering various styles of horror. Roland Green, writing in *Booklist,* praised the author's "vivid depiction of lurking nightmare" as well as his "equally fine use of regional settings." "These tales are often beautifully literate," Jonathan Pearce

Cover of Roy Thomas's *The Chronicles of Conan, Volume One: Tower of the Elephant and Other Stories,* **a graphic novel based on Howard's characters and featuring cover art by Barry Windsor-Smith.** (Dark Horse Books, 2003. Concrete is a registered trademark, and all other prominently featured characters. Reproduced by permission. Conan is a registered trademark of Conan Properties International, LLC.)

similarly noted in *Library Journal,* adding that Howard's "vocabulary and language structure transport the reader in time and place."

If you enjoy the works of Robert E. Howard, you may also want to check out the following books:

John Maddox Roberts, *Conan and the Manhunters,* 1994.
Leonard Carpenter, *Conan the Gladiator,* 1995.
Robert Jordan, *The Conan Chronicles,* 1995.

Howard's fantastic legends of sorcery and swordplay have inspired legions of imitators, but the author himself remains a major figure in the field. "Howard was, in my opinion, a writer of superior ability," commented Darrell Schweitzer in *Conan's World and Robert E. Howard.* In an *American Fantasy* essay, Jessica Amanda Salmonson stated that "Howard was a great storyteller. Perhaps not a skilled writer in technical terms, but nonetheless, his fiction is powerful in an awkward, honest, direct manner—not unlike many of his heroes." Salmonson added that Howard "could do what few adventure writers can do even today; that is, depict a strong woman. Further, he did it in an atmosphere of rank misogyny: the male-defined pulp era of writing." As de Camp concluded in his book, "Howard's stories . . . bid fair to be enjoyed for their action, color, and furious narrative drive for many years to come."

■ Biographical and Critical Sources

BOOKS

De Camp, L. Sprague, *Literary Swordsmen and Sorcerers: The Makers of Heroic Fantasy,* Arkham House (Sauk City, WI), 1976.

Ellis, Novalyne Price, *One Who Walked Alone: Robert E. Howard, The Final Years,* Donald M. Grant (West Kingston, RI), 1986.

Lord, Glenn, editor, *The Last Celt: A Bio-bibliography of Robert E. Howard,* Berkley (New York, NY), 1976.

St. James Guide to Fantasy Writers, St. James Press (Detroit, MI), 1996.

Schweitzer, Darrell, *Conan's World and Robert E. Howard*, Borgo Press (San Bernardino, CA), 1978.

Thomas, Roy, *Conan: The Ultimate Guide to the World's Most Savage Barbarian*, DK Publishing (New York, NY), 2006.

Twentieth-Century Literary Criticism, Volume 8, Gale (Detroit, MI), 1982.

Weinberg, Robert, *The Annotated Guide to Robert E. Howard's Sword and Sorcery*, Starmont House (West Linn, OR), 1976.

PERIODICALS

American Fantasy, February, 1982, Jessica Amanda Salmonson, "Dark Agnes: A Critical Look at Robert E. Howard's 'Swordsmen'" pp. 4-6.

Amra, Volume II, number 17, Fritz Leiber, "Howard's Style."

Booklist, October 15, 2008, Roland Green, review of *The Horror Stories of Robert E. Howard*, p. 30.

Bookseller, December 9, 2005, review of *The Complete Chronicles of Conan*, p. 30.

Daily News (Los Angeles, CA), January 24, 1997, "The Gentle Side of Conan Creator," p. L3.

Hollywood Reporter, February 7, 2006, "Writings of 'Conan' Author at Paradox," p. 6.

Houston Chronicle, March 7, 1999, Carlton Stowers, "Conan's Creator," p. 6.

Library Journal, April 15, 2004, Michael Rogers, review of *Gates of the Empire and Other Tales of the Crusades*, p. 132; August 1, 2004, Michael Rogers, review of *The Bloody Crown of Conan*, p. 131; August 1, 2008, Jonathan Pearce, review of *The Horror Stories of Robert E. Howard*, p. 76.

Publishers Weekly, October 18, 2004, review of *The Bloody Crown of Conan*, p. 52.

USA Today, October 16, 2007, Mike Snider, "'The Original American Fantasy Hero' Rides Again," p. 1D, and "Conan: The Games Begin," p. 6D.

ONLINE

Cross Plains Web site, http://www.crossplains.com/ (April 1, 2009), biography of Robert E. Howard.

Official Robert E. Howard Web site, http://www.rehoward.com (April 1, 2009).

Robert E. Howard United Press Association Web site, http://www.rehupa.com/ (April 1, 2009).*

(Photograph courtesy of AP Images.)

Philip Johnson

■ Personal

Born July 8, 1906, in Cleveland, OH; died January 25, 2005 in New Canaan, CT; son of Homer M. (a lawyer) and Louise Pope (a homemaker and arts patron) Johnson. *Education:* Harvard University, B.A., 1930, B.Arch., 1943.

■ Career

Architect and writer. Museum of Modern Art, New York, NY, founding director of department of architecture, 1930-36, 1946-54; in private practice, Cambridge, MA, 1942-46; architect with Landis Gores, 1946-53; in private practice, New York, NY, 1954-64; architect with Richard Forster, New York, NY, 1964-67; architect with John Burgee, New York, NY, 1967-87; consultant to John Burgee Architects, beginning 1987; architect with Alan Ritchie, New York, NY, c. 1994-2004. *Military service:* U.S. Army Engineering Corps, 1943-44.

■ Member

American Institute of Architects (fellow), Academy of Arts and Letters.

■ Awards, Honors

Medals of Honor, Architectural League of New York, 1960 and 1965; American Institute of Architects (AIA) Honor Awards, 1961, 1975 and 1977; Bronze Medallion, City of New York/AIA New York, 1978; AIA Gold Medal, 1978; Pritzker Prize, 1979; Fellows Award, Rhode Island School of Design, 1983; Herbert Adams Medal, National Sculpture Society, 1984; Lifetime Achievement Award, New York Society of Architects, 1993.

■ Writings

(With Henry-Russell Hitchcock) *The International Style: Architecture since 1922*, Norton (New York, NY), 1932, second edition, with new foreword by Johnson, 1996.

(With Henry-Russell Hitchcock, Jr., Alfred H. Barr, Jr., and Lewis Mumford) *Modern Architects*, Norton (New York, NY), 1932.

(With Henry-Russell Hitchcock, and others) *Mies van der Rohe*, [New York, NY], 1947, 3rd edition, Museum of Modern Art (New York, NY), 1978.

Writings, foreword by Vincent Scully, introduction by Peter Eisenman, Oxford University Press (New York, NY), 1978.

(Editor) John Bracken and Linda Stone, *Restoring the Victorian House and Other Turn-of-the-Century Structures*, Chronicle Books (San Francisco, CA), 1981.

(With Mark Wigley) *Deconstructive Architecture*, Little, Brown (New York, NY), 1988.

The Glass House, edited by David Whitney and Jeffrey Kipnis, Pantheon (New York, NY), 1993.

■ Sidelights

When asked what people would most likely remember from a career that spanned over sixty years and led to the design of more than 100 buildings, architect Philip Johnson remarked to Tom Buckley in *Esquire*, "I think the Glass House will endure, but it may be that I will be best remembered as a gadfly, an encourager of younger architects, and as an *arbiter elegantiarum*—the man who introduced the glass box and then, fifty years later, broke it." Johnson was one of the most unpredictable and influential architects of the twentieth century. He is considered one of the principal forces behind the modernist movement, which dominated American architecture for decades.

Johnson's "Glass House"—a house made entirely of glass, which he built for himself on an estate in Connecticut—and New York City's Seagram Building, which he designed with Mies van der Rohe, are classic examples of modernist style. But in the 1970s, when unadorned glass skyscrapers dotted the country, Johnson decided it was time for a change. The architect threw his considerable influence behind what was becoming known as the postmodernist movement—an effort to reach back into the past for an eclectic assortment of architectural details. Johnson's AT&T Building, built in the early eighties and nicknamed the "Chippendale skyscraper" because of the ornamentation on its top that recalls the works of well-known furniture designer Thomas Chippendale, is considered a prime example of the postmodern style. Never one to stay on course for long, in his later years Johnson moved toward deconstructivism, a movement influenced by Russian modernist architecture of the 1920s.

Johnson was born in Cleveland, Ohio, in 1906, one of four children of Homer Johnson, a successful attorney, and Louise Pope Johnson. Although Johnson had every advantage his parents could give him—private schools, world travel—he had a lonely childhood, as he recalled in an interview on the Academy of Achievement Web site: "I was a spoiled brat. I was insufferable, very unpopular at school, very unpopular with the girls. Couldn't dance, couldn't mix. I was a loner and family practically gave up on me, wanted to give up on myself. You know the usual, 'Oh goodness, what good am I?' bit, that every young person goes through, but I thought it

naturally was unique and that I alone suffered." Architecture became an interest of Johnson's during these years. He was aware of the works of Frank Lloyd Wright, for his mother had long expressed a desire to live in a house designed by the famed architect (a request denied by Johnson's father). Later, she exposed her son to the great buildings of Europe during trips to the continent. Many of them inspired an emotional reaction, he told the Academy of Achievement online interviewer: "I don't see how anybody can go into the nave of Chartres Cathedral and not burst into tears, because I thought that's what everybody would do. That's the natural reaction I had."

Develops Interest in Architecture

Johnson traces the beginnings of his architectural career to a college trip to Europe, when he visited the ancient monuments at Greece's Parthenon.

Philip Johnson, holding a model of his 580 California building. (Photograph © Bernd Settnik/dpa/Corbis.)

"Ephiphanies that move you to tears or leave you feeling exalted for weeks don't translate into words very well, but I had it twice, at Chartres and the Parthenon," Johnson told Buckley. "Before that I had been rather straightforward, interested in philosophy and rationalism and intellectual things, but without a single devoted passion. After I saw the Parthenon, I had a call, as religious people might put it, and I've never changed." Johnson majored in philosophy at Harvard University and took seven years to complete his degree. At first he attributed his frequent breaks from Harvard to bouts of depression; later in life he acknowledged it was due to his struggle to come to terms with his homosexuality.

When Johnson first entered Harvard, his father had given him some stock in an obscure aluminum company called ALCOA; by the time he graduated in 1930, the stock had made Johnson wealthier than his father. He then pursued his interest in architecture through two visits to the Bauhaus, the center of the emerging modernist school in Germany. When he returned to New York City, his friend Alfred Barr, director of the newly formed Museum of Modern Art, named Johnson head of its architecture department. Fortunately for the fledgling museum, which was struggling in the midst of the Great Depression, Johnson did not require a salary. He then proceeded to bring the avant-garde architecture he had found in Germany to the United States via what is widely regarded as the most influential architecture exhibition of the twentieth century. With Henry-Russell Hitchcock, a young art instructor at Wesleyan University who had accompanied Johnson to Germany, he wrote a guide to the show titled *The International Style: Architecture since 1922.* It covered the work of such major modern figures as Swiss-French architect and designer Le Corbusier and architects Walter Gropius and Ludwig Mies van der Rohe.

Having turned the architectural world on its ear, Johnson then made one of the abrupt jumps that were to characterize his life: he resigned from the museum and began dabbling in fascist politics. When he visited Germany in 1934, he had been impressed by the economic improvements Chancellor Adolf Hitler was making there. He supported Huey Long's presidential ambitions in the United States and eventually served as a correspondent for Father Charles Coughlin, an anti-semitic and anti-capitalist radio commentator. When correspondent William Shirer called him "an American fascist" in his book, *Berlin Diary,* Johnson was snubbed by many who knew him. He later explained to television interviewer Charlayne Hunter-Gault on the *PBS Newshour* that his political involvement was due to a desire to change things: "I didn't like the

fact that this was a rich, rich country, and there were people actually going hungry." He called his failure to grasp the extent of Nazi persecution of the Jews "one of those regrets so strong you can't put it into words. It's just unbearable. You don't sleep."

Ultimately, Johnson left politics and returned to Harvard to study architecture; he waited until his thirties to begin studying the art because "I couldn't draw, so I knew I couldn't be an architect," as he told the *Academy of Achievement* interviewer. Fortunately, "Harvard didn't care whether I could draw or not. It seemed like a good idea. By that time, I'd worked for some years at the Museum of Modern Art on architecture, so I decided what the hell, I might as well be one." After graduating in 1943, he was drafted into the U.S. Army and spent two years serving his country. Although he was older than his fellow soldiers and not very physically fit, he saw the experience as valuable. "That got me out of my namby-pamby spoiled kid position in the world. . . . That I lived through it at all was a triumph. It was the most wonderful thing that ever happened. That was a moment of the purest pleasure that I could get along with these kids."

Fantastic, Enduring Buildings

When World War II was over, Johnson began his career as an architect in earnest, establishing himself as a modernist in the tradition of Gropius and van der Rohe. In 1946 he began another term at the Museum of Modern Art and also formed a partnership with Landis Gores. Among Johnson's notable buildings from this period is the home he built in New Canaan, Connecticut, in 1949. The Glass House, as it is known, was inspired by the designs of van der Rohe: a simple box shape made entirely of glass and supported with black steel pillars. The only walls enclosed a small central room that hid a bathroom and utilities; otherwise, there was no impediment to seeing the landscape outside. The Glass House was acknowledged as a pure example of modernism, as well as being Johnson's masterpiece. As Joseph Giovannini commented in the *New York Times,* "Because he was his own client and willing to live in an architectural ideal uncompromised by conventional notions of privacy and convenience, he was able to create a pure Miesian vision: a classically proportioned frame with meticulously detailed, finely proportioned steel limbs." Johnson would live in the Glass House all his life, and he donated it to the National Trust for Historic Preservation for use as a museum after his death.

Although his first architectural commissions were mostly residential, Johnson soon began designing more public buildings. He created the Rockefeller

Johnson's Glass House, located in New Caanan, Connecticut and constructed in 1949 as the architect's home. (Photograph courtesy of AP Images.)

sculpture garden for the Museum of Modern Art 1953, and collaborated with van der Rohe on New York City's Seagram Building, which was completed in 1958. The Seagram Building is a union of bronze, glass, and steel that is generally regarded as one of the finest examples of modernist design. With "a design approach characterized by the straightforward use of modern materials such as glass and steel, and emphasizing function and structure over ornamental decoration," a critic wrote in Johnson's *Real Estate Weekly* obituary, "International Style" as epitomized by buildings like the Seagram "became the guiding spirit of our city skylines for fifty years, and continue . . . to heavily influence contemporary designs." Johnson recognized that skyscrapers had to combine art and commerce; as he told the *Academy of Achievement* interviewer, "The only goal is building a beautiful building, but if you don't know your functions, if the Seagram building didn't work

and make piles of money for everybody, it wouldn't be a success because all skyscrapers are money-making machines."

Most of Johnson's projects during the 1950s and 1960s were institutional, including Ivy League school buildings and museums, a nuclear reactor, a roofless church, and several hospital buildings. In 1964 Johnson entered into a brief partnership with Richard Foster, with whom he collaborated on such buildings as the New York State Pavilion in Flushing and the New York State Theater at Lincoln Center in New York City. After breaking with Foster in 1967, Johnson began a twenty-year partnership with John Burgee, an architect twenty-eight years his junior. Johnson's partnership with Burgee enabled the elder architect to make a "quantum leap," as called it in *Insight*. In addition, Burgee's organizational abilities enabled the firm to begin operating on a much grander scale. "Philip and I had the same objective—to build the best buildings in the world," Burgee later explained to Buckley. "When he proposed the partnership, he said that I was young enough that he didn't have to be jealous of me. I had heard that he could be pretty stormy, and I told myself I'd give it a year and see how it worked out. The first time I made a suggestion, he said, 'That's the stupidest thing I ever heard,' and I said to myself, 'Uh, oh.' But the next time, he said, 'That's brilliant. Why didn't I think of that?'"

The first major project the new partners tackled was the Investors Diversified Services Center in Minneapolis. Built in 1973, it featured a smoke-blue facade and one of the first glass-covered galleries of shops and restaurants in the country. Next was Pennzoil Place in Houston, which they built with developer Gerald D. Hines. Its twin thirty-six-storey glass towers have sloped tops set at right angles to each other so that the closest corners are only ten feet apart. Another Johnson-Burgee design from the 1970s was the Crystal Cathedral, which they built for the Reverend Robert H. Schuller near Anaheim, California. It is built entirely of glass—10,000 panes set in a network of steel.

Postmodernist Leanings

Although these projects made no abrupt break with modernist principles, subtle changes were apparent. Johnson was beginning to be influenced by a new generation of architects who found the prevailing styles to be cold and unappealing. "Johnson had long before broken with the modernist tenet that form should follow function," wrote Craig Unger in *New York* magazine. Several of his buildings from the 1960s drew on historical influences, and he also found inspiration in the works of younger architects, such as Robert Venturi and Robert A.M. Stern. Johnson's merging of his modernist inclinations with his appreciation for classical designs created the combination of old and new that would become known as "postmodernist." The architect was famous for telling students "You cannot not know history." As he explained in his *Academy of Achievement* interview, after World War II people believed that "science will take care of everything and no input of cultural history was of any importance. I never believed it and I still don't. So I claim that you've got to have a feel for the history of architecture."

The KIO towers, a design by Johnson that is located in Puerta de Europa. (Photograph © by Carl and Ann Purcell/Corbis.)

After working together successfully on Pennzoil Place, the team of Johnson and Burgee went on to complete several grand projects in the postmodernist vein. For Pittsburgh Plate Glass, they built a cut-glass complex evoking Britain's Houses of Parliament in downtown Pittsburgh. And in Houston, they put up the Republic Bank Center, a pink granite tower reminiscent of Flemish Gothic architecture, which New York Times critic Paul Goldberger called "a highly electric and altogether splendid romantic composition, its profile truly lyrical against the Texas sky." Goldberger also found many of Johnson's postmodernist designs glib and superficial, however: "So much of this recent work is facile, easy, quick. It seems to come from a single, fast idea, as if someone leaped up at a meeting and shouted, 'I have it! Let's make the PPG building a glass version of the Houses of Parliament!' When it works, it is because Mr. Johnson and Mr. Burgee have not stopped there, but have gone back to the basics and been able to make their buildings succeed on more fundamental levels as well."

Johnson and Burgee continued to build in the postmodernist style across the country, from Crescent Court and Momentum Place in Dallas, Texas, to 580 California Street in San Francisco. Then, in the late 1980s, Johnson became fascinated by a new tendency in the architectural world, called deconstructivism, which he brought to the public eye through an exhibition at the Museum of Modern Art in 1988. That show presented the work of designers throughout the world—among them, Frank Gehry and Bernard Tschumi—who are linked by their similarities to constructivism, the Russian modernism of the twenties. The influence of this unorthodox approach can be seen in Johnson's design for the Canadian Broadcasting Centre in Toronto. Johnson himself recognized that his changing styles were sure to breed controversy. As he told a contributor in People: "I guess I can't be a great architect. Great architects have a recognizable style. But if every building I did were the same," he added, "it would be pretty boring."

Johnson not only helped younger architects by promoting their careers, he continued his work as a critic, proving himself to be an incisive observer and analyst of trends and developments in his field. He collected his stylistic pronouncements in the 1978 book Writings. According to Mark Wigley in Artforum International, Johnson "was famously supportive of the generations before and after him, which is almost unheard of in the field. He helped connect architects to clients; underwrote organizations, research, and publications; and even gave direct financial aid to some designers."

While Johnson admired the work of young postmodernist architects, and supported it by recommending them for commissions, it was he who had the credibility to make a case for it in the corporate world. In 1979, he convinced AT&T's board of directors to back his postmodernist plans for their lavish New York headquarters. Johnson decided that he wanted the headquarters to evoke the great granite buildings that characterized New York in the 1890s and 1920s. In order to give it a massive, solid feeling, he set the windows into granite as much as ten inches thick, using 13,000 tons in all. Some charge that this and other extravagant features made the AT&T building (now known as Sony Tower), on a per-square-foot basis, one of the most expensive buildings ever built. But the feature that caused the most fuss and landed Johnson on the cover of Time was a graceful pediment with a hole in its center. "That broken pediment, as it is called, has caused more argument than any other empty space twenty feet or so in diameter in the history of architecture," Buckley wrote. "Some critics have hailed it as spirited and imaginative, the crowning touch of another Johnson masterpiece. . . . Equally reputable critics damned the building, from its broken pediment on down, as a display of extravagance, arrogance and perversity."

Even into his nineties, Johnson remained a force in his field. He stopped working with John Burgee in 1991, but found a new partner in Alan Ritchie, with whom he formed Philip Johnson-Alan Ritchie Architects. He consulted on many projects and even after his official retirement in 2004 remained active in writing and talking about architecture. One of his last projects was to design an interfaith peace chapel for the Cathedral of Hope, a congregation catering to gay and lesbian Christians in Dallas. At first, Johnson thought he was too old for the project, but he soon became excited by the social statement the building would make. "What is fascinating about Mr. Johnson today . . . ," wrote Goldberger, "is not his potential as a poster boy for architects' longevity but the qualities that have fascinated us all along: his extraordinary ability to be at the center of everything, to produce architecture that engages the public while commanding the attention, if not always the respect, of critics; his way of taking from what is around him and synthesizing it into something that is entirely his own."

A Legendary Figure

Johnson was ninety-eight years old when he died at his home in New Canaan, Connecticut. With his partner of forty-five years, art connoisseur David Whitney, Johnson had expanded his art collection and built seven more buildings on his property to serve as galleries. As he remarked to the Academy of

Johnson's work includes the Crystal Cathedral, located in Garden Grove, California. (Photograph © by J.P. Laffont/Sygma/Corbis.)

Achievement interviewer, "I'm only proud of the buildings I built in my own place, really, because there was nobody to stop me, no financing, no troubles, and if they're bad, at least I don't know it." The New Canaan complex reflected the progression of his career, and opened to sold-out tours, run by the National Trust Historical Preservation Society, in 2007.

Upon his death, Johnson was recognized as a singular figure in the history of architecture. "Was he the greatest architect of the 20th century?" Robert A.M. Stern, dean of the Yale School of Architecture, asked in *Architectural Record*. "I'll leave that assessment to others. What I will say is that not one building by Johnson has failed to give me pride in being an architect, in knowing what an architect can accomplish. I have learned something from every one of his buildings—and they have given me a great deal of pleasure." According to *New York Times* contributor Herbert Muschamp, "Johnson's entire oeuvre can also be seen as a procession, or at least a magical mystery tour, a series of surprises, many of them pleasant. The stops along the way include not only his own buildings but also the spaces between them: the anticipation of where he'll go next." Critic Charles Jencks believed that Johnson's influence was not always to the good, telling Robert Booth in *Building Design*, "He pre-empted and then distorted the three powerful movements of the 20th century and led them astray." Nonetheless, the critic praised Johnson for insisting "that architecture is an art, as a cultural form that can't be subsumed in functionalism. . . . He saved architecture from this reductivist lie that architecture is a form of social amelioration and engineering."

If you enjoy the works of Philip Johnson, you may also want to check out the following:

The landmark buildings of Walter Gropius (1883-1969), the founder of the Bauhaus School.
The works of German architect Ludwig Mies van der Rohe (1886-1969), including the Seagram Building.
The designs of innovative Swiss artist and architect Le Corbusier (1887-1965).

Johnson himself acknowledged a desire for his buildings to be remembered. "To me," the architect once said, as reported by Fred A. Bernstein in the *Advocate*, "the drive for monumentality is as inbred as the desire for food and sex." More important to Johnson was the creation of beauty: "The practice of architecture is the most delightful of all pursuits," he noted in his Pritzker Prize acceptance speech. "Also, next to agriculture, it is the most necessary to man. One must eat, one must have shelter. Next to religious worship itself, it is the spiritual handmaiden of our deepest convictions." The world may change, even decline, Johnson told the *Academy of Achievement* interviewer, but great architecture "will always last and always inspire. . . . [Decadence] maybe is coming, but maybe not. If it's coming, architecture will go on anyhow. If it's not coming, architecture will go on anyhow and create its own richnesses. You can't stop people from doing architecture. You can't stop people from writing poetry."

Johnson (left) was awarded the prestigious Pritzker Architecture Prize by Cesar Pelli in 1979. (Photograph © by Bettmann/Corbis.)

■ **Biographical and Critical Sources**

BOOKS

Blake, Peter, *Philip Johnson*, Birkhauser Verlag (Boston, MA), 1996.

Hitchcock, Henry-Russell, *Philip Johnson: Architecture, 1949-1965,* Holt, Rinehart & Winston (New York, NY), 1966.

International Dictionary of Architects and Architecture, St. James Press (Detroit, MI), 1993.

Lewis, Hillary, and John O'Connor, *Philip Johnson: The Architect in His Own Words,* Rizzoli (New York, NY), 1994.

Schulze, Franz, *Philip Johnson: Life and Work,* Knopf (New York, NY), 1994.

PERIODICALS

Architectural Record, July, 2001, Clifford A. Pearson, "Still the Bad Boy, Philip Johnson Looks ahead at Age 95," p. 59.

Commonweal, September 13, 1996, Christopher Thomas, review of *The International Style: Architecture since 1922,* p. 40.

Esquire, December, 1983, Tom Buckley, "Philip Johnson: The Man in the Glass House," p. 270.

Harper's Bazaar, November, 1992, Cathleen McGuigan, "The Irrepressible Mr. Johnson," p. 161.

Insight, February 23, 1987, interview with Johnson.

New York, November 15, 1982, Craig Unger, profile of Johnson; June 3, 1996, Peter Blake, "Magic Johnson," p. 30.

New Yorker, June 3, 1996, Dodie Kazanjian, "Built to Last," p. 30.

New York Times, June 29, 1986, Paul Goldberger, "Philip Johnson, at 80, Is Dean and Gadfly of the Profession"; July 16, 1987, Joseph Giovannini, "Johnson and His Glass House"; June 7, 1996, Roberta Smith, "Philip Johnson and the Modern"; July 7, 1996, Herbert Muschamp, "A Building That Echoes a Protean Journey," and Paul Goldberger, "Philip Johnson Work in Progress"; April 5, 1998, Eleanor Charles, "At 91, Philip Johnson Ruminates in His Glass House"; November 29, 1998, Herbert Muschamp, "Regent and King in a Procession of New Forms."

New York Times Book Review, December 5, 1993, Martin Filler, review of *The Glass House,* p. 80.

People, December 26, 1983, "The Grand Bold Man of Architecture Comes Full Circle," p. 62.

Vanity Fair, November, 1998, George Wayne, "The Godfather," p. 164.

ONLINE

Academy of Achievement Web site, http://www.achievement.org/ (February 28, 1992), "Interview: Philip Johnson, Dean of American Architects."

Public Broadcasting Service Web site, http://www.pbs.org/ (February 20, 2009), "Philip Johnson"; Charlayne Hunter-Gault, "Portrait of an Artist."

Pritzker Prize Web site, http://www.pritzkerprize.com/ (February 20, 2009), "Philip Johnson, 1979 Laureate: Acceptance Speech."

■ Obituaries

PERIODICALS

American Scholar, spring, 2005, Stanley Abercrombie, "A Few Good Buildings," p. 117.

Architectural Review, March, 2005, p. 30.

Artforum, May, 2005, p. 35.

Art in America, March, 2005, p. 35.

Building Design, February 4, 2005, Robert Booth, "Jencks on Johnson," p. 9.

Chicago Tribune, January 27, 2005, section 1, pp. 1, 5.

Houston Chronicle, January 27, 2005, p. 1.

New York Times, January 27, 2005, pp. A1, C19.

Real Estate Weekly, February 2, 2005, p. 1.

Times (London, England), January 28, 2005, p. 69.

USA Today, January 27, 2005, p. 3D.

Washington Post, January 27, 2005, pp. A1, A6.

ONLINE

Architectural Record Online, http://archrecord.construction.com/ (May, 2005), Robert A.M. Stern, "Philip Johnson: An Essay."*

Gwyneth A. Jones

(Reproduced by permission.)

■ Personal

Born February 14, 1952, in Manchester, England; daughter of Desmond (a garment cutter) and Rita (a headmistress) Jones; married Peter Wilson Gwilliam (a teacher), April 19, 1976; children: Gabriel. *Education:* University of Sussex, B.A. (with honors), 1973. *Politics:* "Green." *Religion:* Roman Catholic. *Hobbies and other interests:* Mountain climbing, gardening, Web site upkeep.

■ Addresses

Home—Brighton, England. *Agent*—Anthony Goff, David Higham Associates Ltd., 5-8 Lower John St., Golden Square, London W1R 4HA, England. *E-mail*—gwyneth.jones@ntlworld.com.

■ Career

Writer. Manpower Services Commission, Whitehall, England, executive officer in Hove, England, 1975-77; author of books for young people and adults, 1977—.

■ Awards, Honors

First prize, *Manchester Evening News* children's story competition, 1967, for "The Christmas Church Mice"; London *Guardian* Children's Fiction Award runner-up, 1981, for *Dear Hill;* James Tiptree, Jr., Award, 1991, for *White Queen;* Dracula Society Children of the Night Award, 1996, for *The Fear Man;* World Fantasy Award, 1996, for both *Seven Tales and a Fable* and *The Grass Princess;* Richard Evans Award, 2001; Arthur C. Clarke Award, 2002, for *Bold as Love;* Philip K. Dick Award, 2005, for *Life.*

■ Writings

FICTION; UNLESS OTHERWISE NOTED

Water in the Air, Macmillan (London, England), 1977.

The Influence of Ironwood, Macmillan (London, England), 1978.

The Exchange, Macmillan (London, England), 1979.

Dear Hill, Macmillan (London, England), 1980.

Escape Plans, Allen & Unwin (London, England), 1986.

Kairos, Unwin Hyman (London, England), 1988.

Identifying the Object (short stories), Swan Press (Austin, TX), 1993.

Seven Tales and a Fable (short stories), Edgewood Press (Cambridge, MA), 1995.

Deconstructing the Starships: Science, Fiction, and Reality (essays), Liverpool University Press (Liverpool, England), 1999.
Life, Aqueduct Press (Seattle, WA), 2004.
Grazing the Long Acre (short stories), PS Publishing (Hornsea, England), 2008.
Spirit: The Princess of Bois Dormant, Gollancz (London, England), 2008.

"*DIVINE ENDURANCE*" SERIES

Divine Endurance, Allen & Unwin (London, England), 1984, Tor (New York, NY), 1989.
Flowerdust, Headline (London, England), 1993, Tor (New York, NY), 1996.

"*ALEUTIAN NOVEL TRILOGY*"

White Queen, Gollancz (London, England), 1991, Tor (New York, NY), 1993.
North Wind, Gollancz (London, England), 1994, Tor (New York, NY), 1995.
Phoenix Café, Tor (New York, NY), 1998.

"*BOLD AS LOVE*" SERIES

Bold as Love, Gollancz (London, England), 2001, NightShade Books (San Francisco, CA), 2005.
Castles Made of Sand, Orion/Gollancz (London, England), 2002.
Midnight Lamp, Gollancz (London, England), 2003.
Band of Gypsys, Gollancz (London, England), 2005.
Rainbow Bridge, Gollancz (London, England), 2006.

Contributor of numerous short stories to periodicals and anthologies. Author of blog, *Bold as Love.*

CHILDREN'S BOOKS; UNDER PSEUDONYM ANN HALAM

Ally, Ally Aster, Allen & Unwin (London, England), 1981.
The Alder Tree, Allen & Unwin (London, England), 1982.
King Death's Garden, Orchard (London, England), 1986.
The Hidden Ones, Women's Press (London, England), 1988.
Dinosaur Junction, Orchard (London, England), 1992.
The Haunting of Jessica Raven, Orion (London, England), 1994.
The Fear Man, Orion (London, England), 1995.
The Powerhouse, Orion (London, England), 1997.
Crying in the Dark, Orion (London, England), 1998.

The Nimrod Conspiracy, Orion (London, England), 1999.
Don't Open Your Eyes, Orion (London, England), 2000.
The Shadow on the Stars, Barrington Stoke (Edinburgh, Scotland), 2000.
Dr. Franklin's Island, Orion (London, England), 2001, Wendy Lamb Books (New York, NY), 2002.
Taylor Five, Orion (London, England), 2002, Wendy Lamb Books (New York, NY), 2004.
Finders Keepers, Barrington Stoke (Edinburgh, Scotland), 2004.
Siberia, Wendy Lamb Books (New York, NY), 2005.
Snakehead, Wendy Lamb Books (New York, NY), 2007.

"*INLAND TRILOGY*"; FOR CHILDREN; UNDER PSEUDONYM ANN HALAM

The Daymaker, Orchard (London, England), 1987.
Transformations, Orchard (London, England), 1988.
The Skybreaker, Orchard (London, England), 1990.

■ Sidelights

British writer Gwyneth A. Jones is, as Barry Forshaw noted in the London *Independent,* one of England's "finest science fiction practitioners, a writer of visionary skills with a striking and poetic narrative style, . . . the most acclaimed British female science-fiction writer since Ursula le Guin." The winner of the James Tiptree, Jr., Award, the Arthur C. Clarke Award, and the Philip K. Dick Award, among others, Jones has published critically acclaimed science fiction under her own name and an equal number of fantasy fiction and science-fiction novels for children and young adults under the pseudonym Ann Halam. Among Jones' best-known works for adults are the "Aleutian Trilogy" and the "Bold as Love" series, while writing as Halam, her "Inland Trilogy" and stand-alone titles such as *Siberia* and *Snakehead* have impressed reviewers and readers alike.

In her works Jones tackles political themes as well as class issues, not the usual fare for science fiction. As a contributor in *Contemporary Novelists* stated, "Her fiction is famous for its feminist approach and its recurring themes of the importance of community and of respect for the Earth. Her fantasy novels are unconventional, primarily for showing that happy endings are difficult to achieve." Gender issues also play a role, as does music, which informs the entirety of Jones' "Bold as Love" sequence. "I'm in a fairly lonely position as a British woman writing science fiction," she told Chris Mitchell in a *Spike* online interview.

Jones was born in 1952 in Manchester, England, the daughter of Desmond and Rita Jones. As the author noted on her home page, "I spent my childhood in an atmosphere of privilege," because her family was considered "minor aristocracy in the parish of Mount Carmel, Blackley, Manchester." Her childhood memories include the fully stacked bookshelves in her father's study, the family piano, and playing imaginative games. "I loved being outdoors, but I was often ill when I was a child," she noted in an essay for the *St. James Guide to Young-Adult Writers.* I had bronchitis every winter, which meant I would spend long days in bed, alone, reading. It was good preparation for a writer's life because you do spend a lot of time on your own."

Although the family did not have much money, they were far from poor. "Shabbiness, in the ideal world of my books, was the ultimate sign of being the people who don't have to prove anything to anyone," Jones wrote. Books were an integral part of her young life, as well. "My childhood was informed—given its psychic structure—by the golden age of children's literature. . . . I absorbed, without question, the ethos of the ideal English middle class family which pervades that fiction. A family that inhabits a misty historical period in the last decades of Empire: modestly well bred, devoid of material aspirations, delighting in hardship, gentle but wary in their dealings with lesser mortals; full of casual erudition about famous explorers, sailing, falconry, mountain climbing."

Makes Literary Debut

Jones had a convent education and then studied European history at the University of Sussex. She began her career as a writer with 1977's *Water in the Air,* a book for younger readers. She wrote several more novels for that audience before turning her hand to science fiction for adults with the 1984 work *Divine Endurance. Divine Endurance* follows the adventures and misadventures of a female android, Derveet, in Southeast Asia. Since then, Jones has relegated her juvenile writing to the pseudonymous Halam. In the first Halam novel, *Ally, Ally Aster,* a group of children struggle with an ancient family secret and an ice being; in the second, *The Alder Tree,* a young girl confronts a dragon that has taken on human form.

King Death's Garden, another book for children, focuses on a sickly, unpleasant boy named Maurice and Maurice's friend Moth, who may be a spirit or merely an imaginary friend. Of *King Death's Garden,* Maureen Speller commented in the *St. James Guide to Fantasy Writers* that "this ambiguity and uncertainty is what gives the novel much of its power, as we observe Maurice retreating increasingly into the world he has created for himself." *The Haunting of Jessica Raven* utilizes a similar theme, as a young girl with a seriously ill brother finds herself involved with a group of people who may or may not be ghosts. A *Books for Keeps* contributor remarked on Jones' fine, sensitive writing, calling the book "superb." A *Junior Bookshelf* reviewer was also impressed, declaring *The Haunting of Jessica Raven* to be "a moving story, told with a simplicity which in no way weakens its emotional appeal. . . . Above all it is a story about people, vulnerable, sad, volatile, at the mercy of events but still capable of influencing them."

One of Jones' most ambitious projects was her "Inland Trilogy," a trio of books described by Jessica Yates in *Books for Keeps* as "a feminist and environmentalist saga of science fantasy." The plot involves the collapse of civilization due to the depletion of known energy sources, and the renaissance of magic. The heroine, a girl named Zanne, is fascinated by the relics of ancient, dead technology. Her affinity for machinery puts her at odds with her culture. Eventually, she disables a power station, discovers a mine filled with radioactive material, and travels to another land, where she discovers a rocket ship. Speller declared that Jones' "socialist vision of a magic which affects the balance of the world and which should be operated only by common consent is very much at odds with the more traditional view of magic as a power which resides in the few and is used at their discretion, without consultation. The series is all the more refreshing for that. She captures very well Zanne's dilemma in that she loves the bygone technology and recognizes how it might help her people but simultaneously understands that this moment is not right for its use, when the cost is too terrible."

More recent books from Jones, writing as Halam, have also stretched the bounds of juvenile fiction. In *Dr. Franklin's Island,* the author presents a "nightmarish thriller of white-knuckle intensity," according to a *Publishers Weekly* reviewer. Here a group of teens are stranded on an island controlled by a mad doctor, creating a "fantastical tale of survival and genetic mutation," according to *Booklist* contributor Debbie Carton. Also praised by reviewers for its mix of fantasy and science fiction, *Taylor Five* finds a fourteen-year-old girl learning that she was one of the first human clones. Before the girl can deal with her anger against her parents, rebel forces attack the Borneo nature reserve where Taylor and her family live, forcing her to flee with her younger brother,

Donny, and a half-tame orangutan named Uncle into the jungle in hopes of surviving. The novel's "taut suspense and Taylor's gritty intensity will compel many YAs," noted Jennifer Mattson in *Booklist*, and *School Library Journal* critic Ellen Fader dubbed *Taylor Five* an "action-packed survival story."

In *Siberia* Jones offers readers a "a future world of ecological and cultural disaster," as *Kliatt* reviewer Claire Rosser noted. A *Kirkus Reviews* contributor found this novel to be "gripping and thoughtful." With *Snakehead*, the author moves from dystopian themes to a retelling of the Greek myth of Perseus and Andromeda, creating a "stylish makeover," according to a *Kirkus Reviews* writer. Writing in *Kliatt*, Rosser had further praise, noting that, "in Halam's careful hands, this ancient myth is told to modern YA readers with all the guts of adolescent struggle intact."

Ambitious Novels Explore Difficult Issues

Although she did not write them as a trilogy, Jones refers to three of her novels about an alien Aleutian invasion of Earth. *White Queen*, winner of the James Tiptree, Jr., Award, tells the story of the first contact the Aleutians make with Earth. Published three years later, *North Wind* explores the consequences of the Aleutian empire on Earth, while *Phoenix Café* relates the process of the Aleutians leaving the planet. Mitchell quoted Jones as explaining: "These three books are a sort of parallel version of the European invasion of Africa in the last century. . . . What happens when a people gets invaded and dominated by a bigger culture and a snazzier technology." Character development is one of the strong points of Jones' writing, and this element, as presented in this trio was again praised by a *Publishers Weekly* critic writing about *Phoenix Café*. The same reviewer remarked that Jones also displays a uniquely "sophisticated understanding of politics, both sexual and general." *Booklist* reviewer John Mort, also writing about *Phoenix Café*, described Jones' trilogy as "a dark blend of Aldous Huxley and Joanna Russ."

Bold as Love, the first work in Jones' series of the same name, appeared in 2001. The book's title is borrowed from one of famed guitarist Jimi Hendrix's albums, *Axis: Bold as Love*. The title also reflects the nature of its protagonist, Ax Preston, a mixed-race guitarist, whom Jon Courtenay Grimwood described in the London *Guardian* as a "flamboyant guitar hero." *Bold as Love*, which won the Arthur C. Clarke Award, tells a futuristic story

of a group of musicians led by Preston, who suddenly find themselves in a position of political power as Great Britain falls into extreme disarray due to the devastating effects of pollution, global warming, massive outbreaks of disease, and terrorism. Other major characters in the novel and ongoing series are Sage Pender and Fiorinda, a teen rock star with a mysterious past. "Since Jones is a good and subtle writer," *Guardian* reviewer Francis Spufford stated, "the texture of this unlikely story is wonderfully maintained."

The heroine of *Bold as Love*, Fiorinda, becomes the "driving force" of Jones' second work in the series, *Castles Made of Sand*, according to Grimwood. *Castles Made of Sand* also takes its name from a Hendrix song; it is important to be aware of this, Grimwood stated, because Jones "weaves lines" from Hendrix's music throughout the novel. Grimwood also pointed out the relationship between Jones's story and the tale of King Arthur, specifically the love triangle between the king, Sir Lancelot, and Lady Guinevere as reenacted by Ax, Sage, and Fiorinda. Grimwood concluded that this second book of the saga is perhaps even better than the first.

The "Bold as Love" series continued with its third installment, *The Midnight Lamp*, in which Ax and Sage attempt reconciliation, dropping out of the political and rock scene to venture into Mexico. Soon events in the United States send the pair into the thick of things once again, and they join Fiorinda in her attempt to stop development of the deadly Neurobomb. "The lively prose can be beautiful, but mostly serves to tell a rollicking yarn very skillfully," noted Justina Robson in the London *Guardian*. "It switches viewpoint and mode freely, dashing from one idea to the next—sex to politics to ecology to drugs to mysticism to rock 'n' roll, all in the space of two pages, or even two sentences."

Band of Gypsys, the fourth novel in the series, takes its name from Hendrix's own band (with the same misspelling). Here the three protagonists find themselves in and out of power in England, and like unwanted royals, imprisoned. The series concluded with *Rainbow Bridge*, another nod to Hendrix's music. Writing for *Strange Horizons*, Sherryl Vint deemed the entire series "a thoughtful and thorough meditation on the political options facing us in the 21st century." Vint went on to note: "Jones is at her intellectual and enigmatic best in these works, offering both a compelling and absorbing personal saga and an astute and engaging political analysis. The series is never short on intrigue and difficult personal choices, but at the same time never collapses into sentimentality, insisting instead on an often painful pragmatism."

Jones has also written numerous critically acclaimed stand-alone titles. The award-winning *Life* is a novel set in the near future in which gender discrimination is about to be fought in a strange, new manner by the science of genetics. *Library Journal* reviewer Jackie Cassada found this book to be "beautifully written and elegantly paced," while *SF Site Reviews* online contributor David Soyka termed the same novel "one of the best things Jones has written." In her 2008 novel *Spirit: The Princess of Bois Dormant,* Jones presents an updated retelling of Alexandré Dumas's *The Count of Monte Cristo,* while also returning to the setting of her "Aleutian Trilogy." Writing in the London *Times,* Lisa Tuttle called *Spirit* "a memorable combination of cutting-edge science with old-fashioned, swash-buckling romance from one of the most intelligent and unsettling of modern science-fiction writers."

If you enjoy the works of Gwyneth A. Jones, you may also want to check out the following books:

Emma Bull, *War for the Oaks,* 1987.
Lisa Goldstein, *Travellers in Magic,* 1994.
Nancy Kress, *Crossfire,* 2003.

The ideas for Jones' fiction come from a variety of sources, as she noted on her home page: "I get a lot of inspiration from other books and stories, films and tv, and from science news: but often it's an incident in my real life that starts me off: a strange place or situation. In real life, no weird adventure follows, but I write the story of what might have happened, to somebody different." According to a contributor in the *St. James Guide to Science-Fiction Writers* " Jones writes some of the most intelligent and intriguing science fiction around, a science fiction that exploits the possibilities of the genre to make informed and pertinent points in a way that illustrates the strength of the genre as a medium for commenting upon our world." Jones was quoted in the *St. James Guide to Fantasy Writers* as saying: "Fiction without any non-real element seems to me tainted with a deeply buried absurdity. Fiction happens in the mind of the reader and the writer, not in the material world—and in the mind, as in fantastic fiction, the apparently immutable rules of the physical world are constantly broken."

■ Biographical and Critical Sources

BOOKS

Contemporary Novelists, 7th edition, St. James Press (Detroit, MI), 2001.

St. James Guide to Fantasy Writers, St. James Press (Detroit, MI), 1996.

St. James Guide to Science-Fiction Writers, 4th edition, St. James Press (Detroit, MI), 1996.

St. James Guide to Young-Adult Writers, 2nd edition, St. James Press (Detroit, MI), 1999.

PERIODICALS

Booklist, June 1, 1995, Carl Hays, review of *Flowerdust,* p. 1736; January 1, 1996, Carl Hays, review of *North Wind,* p. 799; December 1, 1997, John Mort, review of *Phoenix Café,* p. 612; July, 2002, Debbie Carton, review of *Dr. Franklin's Island,* p. 1838; February 15, 2004, Jennifer Mattson, review of *Taylor Five,* p. 1051; June 1, 2005, Jennifer Mattson, review of *Siberia,* p. 1809; October 1, 2005, Regina Schroeder, review of *Bold as Love,* p. 43; April 14, 2008, Holly Koelling, review of *Snakehead,* p. 41.

Bookseller, December 9, 2005, review of *Rainbow Bridge,* p. 35.

Books for Keeps, November, 1993, Jessica Yates, "Journeys into Space," p. 28; September, 1995, review of *The Haunting of Jessica Raven,* p. 12.

Guardian (London, England), August 25, 2001, Francis Spufford, "Visions of Albion," p. 8; August 10, 2002, Jon Courtenay Grimwood, "The Crazy World of Gwyneth Jones," p. 21; December 20, 2003, Justina Robson, "Are You Ready to Rock?: The Counter Culture Lives On," review of *Midnight Lamp,* p. 28; January 17, 2009, Karen Joy Fowler, "Swashbucklers in Space," review of *Spirit: The Princess of Bois Dormant,* p. 10.

Independent (London, England), December 12, 2003, Barry Forshaw, "Gwyneth Jones: The Music of the Future," p. 20.

Junior Bookshelf, December, 1994, review of *The Haunting of Jessica Raven,* p. 237.

Kirkus Reviews, January 15, 2004, review of *Taylor Five,* p. 83; June 1, 2005, review of *Siberia,* p. 637; May 15, 2008, review of *Snakehead.*

Kliatt, July, 2002, Paula Rohrlick, review of *Dr. Franklin's Island,* p. 10; May, 2005, Claire Rosser, review of *Siberia,* p. 12; July, 2008, Claire Rosser, review of *Snakehead,* p. 12.

Library Journal, September 15, 2004, Jackie Cassada, review of *Life,* p. 52.

Magazine of Fantasy and Science Fiction, February, 1994, John Kessel, review of *White Queen,* p. 39; December, 2005, James Sallis, review of *Life,* p. 38.

New York Times Book Review, March 15, 1998, Gerald Jonas, review of *Phoenix Café,* p. 36.

Publishers Weekly, May 17, 1993, review of *White Queen,* p. 70; December 18, 1995, review of *North Wind,* p. 44; December 22, 1997, review of *Phoenix Café,* p. 43; May 6, 2002, review of *Dr. Franklin's Island,* p. 59; March 15, 2004, review of *Taylor Five,* p. 76; September 12, 2005, review of *Bold as Love,* p. 48; June 23, 2009, review of *Snakehead,* p. 55.

School Library Journal, May, 2002, Sharon Rawlings, review of *Dr. Franklin's Island,* p. 152; April, 2004, Ellen Fader, review of *Taylor Five,* p. 154.

Times (London, England), December 31, 2008, Lisa Tuttle, review of *Spirit.*

Utopian Studies, spring, 2000, Marleen S. Bar, "Deconstructing the Starships: Science, Fiction, and Reality," p. 271.

Yearbook of English Studies, July, 2007, Wendy Gay Pearson, "Postcolonialism/s, Gender/s, Sexuality/ies, and the Legacy of 'The Left Hand of Darkness'; Gwyneth Jones's Aleutians Talk Back," p. 182.

ONLINE

Bold as Love Web site, http://www.boldaslove.co.uk/ (January 4, 2009).

Gwyneth Jones Home Page, http://homepage.ntlworld.com (January 5, 2009).

Infinity Plus, http://www.infinityplus.co.uk/ (October 27, 2001), Chris Butler, review of *Bold as Love.*

SF Site Reviews Online, http://www.sfsite.com/ (January 5, 2009), Lisa DuMond, review of *North Wind* and *Phoenix Café;* David Soyka, reviews of *Bold as Love* and *Life;* Stuart Carter, review of *Rainbow Bridge.*

Spike Online, http://www.spikemagazine.com/ (February 1, 1997), Chris Mitchell, interview with Jones.

Strange Horizons Web site, http://www.strangehorizons.com/ (January 10, 2007), Sherryl Vint, review of *Rainbow Bridge.**

(Courtesy of Victoria Birkinshaw.)

Elizabeth Knox

Personal

Born February 15, 1959, in Wellington, New Zealand; daughter of Ray (a journalist) and Heather (a librarian) Knox; married Fergus Barrowman (a publisher), 1989; children: Jack. *Education:* Victoria University, B.A., 1986.

Addresses

Home—Wellington, New Zealand. *Agent*—Natasha Fairweather, A.P. Watt, Ltd., 20 John St., London WC1N 2DR, England.

Career

Writer. *Sport* (magazine), assistant editor, 1988-93; Victoria University, Wellington, New Zealand, tutor in film studies, 1989-95; worked variously as a clerk, printer, insurance underwriter, computer operator, editor, Web page editor, publicity officer, and shop assistant. Writer-in-residence at Victoria University of Wellington, 1997.

Awards, Honors

PEN award, 1988, for *After Z-Hour;* PEN fellowship, 1991; New Zealand Book Award nomination, 1992, for *Treasure;* Queen Elizabeth II scholarship in letters, 1993; writing fellowship, Victoria University, 1997; Montana New Zealand Book Awards' Deutz Medal for Fiction, Readers' Choice award, Booksellers' Choice Award, and Orange Prize shortlist, all 1999, and Tasmania Pacific Region Prize, 2001, and Prix Ville de Saumur shortlist, all for *The Vintner's Luck;* Katherine Mansfield writing fellowship, 1999; Arts Foundation of New Zealand Laureate Award, 2000, 2002; named officer, New Zealand Order of Merit, 2002; ICI young writers bursary; Deutz Medal for Fiction shortlist, 2002, for *Billie's Kiss;* Commonwealth Writers Prize for Best Book in the South Pacific and South East Asian Region shortlist, 2004, for *Daylight;* Esther Glen Award, Library and Information Association of New Zealand Aotearoa, 2005, and Best Books for Young Adults selection, American Library Association (ALA), 2006, both for *Dreamhunter;* Michael L. Printz Honor Book Award and Best Books for Young Adults selection, both ALA, both 2008, both for *Dreamquake.*

Writings

After Z-Hour, Victoria University Press (Wellington, New Zealand), 1987.
Paremata (first novel in "High Jump" trilogy; also see below), Victoria University Press (Wellington, New Zealand), 1989.

Treasure, Victoria University Press (Wellington, New Zealand), 1992.

Pomare (second novel in "High Jump" trilogy; also see below), Victoria University Press (Wellington, New Zealand), 1994.

Glamour and the Sea, Victoria University Press (Wellington, New Zealand), 1996.

Tawa (third novel in "High Jump" trilogy; also see below), Victoria University Press (Wellington, New Zealand), 1998.

The Vintner's Luck, Farrar, Straus (New York, NY), 1998.

The High Jump: A New Zealand Childhood (contains *Paremata, Pomare,* and *Tawa*), Victoria University Press (Wellington, New Zealand), 2000.

Black Oxen, Farrar, Straus (New York, NY), 2001.

Billie's Kiss, Ballantine (New York, NY), 2002.

Daylight, Ballantine (New York, NY), 2003.

Dreamhunter (first volume in "Dreamhunter Duet"), HarperCollins (Wellington, NZ), 2005, Farrar, Straus (New York, NY), 2006.

Dreamquake (second volume in "Dreamhunter Duet"), Farrar, Straus (New York, NY), 2007.

The Invisible Road: Dare to Sleep, Dare to Dream (contains *Dreamhunter* and *Dreamquake*), Harper-Collins (Pymble, New South Wales, Australia), 2008.

Contributor to *Privacy: The Art of Julia Morrison* (Jonathan Jensen Gallery), 1994; and *Cherries on a Plate: New Zealand Writers Talk about Their Sisters,* edited by Marilyn Duckworth, Random House, 1996. Short stories represented in anthologies, including *Now See Hear!,* edited by Ian Wedde and Gregory Burke, Victoria University Press, 1990; *Soho Square 4,* edited by Bill Manhire, Bloomsbury, 1991; *Pleasures and Dangers,* edited by Wystan Curnow and Trish Clark, Moet & Chandon/Longman Paul, 1992; *Into the Field of Play,* edited by Lloyd Jones, Tandem, 1992; and *The Picador Anthology of Contemporary New Zealand Fiction,* edited by Fergus Barrowman, Picador, 1996. Author of screenplay *The Dig,* 1994. Contributor to periodicals, including *Landfall, Metro, New Zealand Listener, Sport,* and *Stout Centre Review.*

■ Adaptations

The Vintner's Luck was adapted for film by Nicky Caro; *Dreamhunter* was optioned for a film by Forward Films.

■ Sidelights

Elizabeth Knox is, according to a contributor to the Arts Foundation of New Zealand Web site, "one of New Zealand's most well-known writers." The award-winning author of a dozen novels, Knox is difficult to label, for she writes in a number of genres and formats. As she told an online contributor for *LeafSalon:* "Each book has a way in which, it seems to me, while thinking it over, it wants to be written. I don't think about genre, but about whatever the story can use—what it can use from life and art." However, as James Urquhart noted in London's *Independent on Sunday,* one constant in Knox's titles is a sense of fantasy. As the novelist told Urquhart: "I think of my fantasy as fantastic naturalism, a fantastic element in a world that is very real, and so the fantastic things have to be very real too. . . . I like fantasy for some deep aesthetic reason, but I also like it because it provides a way of dealing with the awe and the terror without actually tying down these experiences to things that everybody recognizes."

Knox is known for creating novels and stories that feature intricate plots, detailed settings, and elements of mystery and the supernatural. While she first became known for adult novels such as *After Z-Hour, Black Oxen,* and *The Vintner's Luck,* other novels, such as *Billie's Kiss* and her "Dreamhunter Duet" fantasy sequence, have proved popular with sophisticated teen readers. Critics have referred to Knox's prose as intense and poetic, while her themes, according to a *Contemporary Novelists* essayist, reflect "the human groping for understanding in a world that often defies comprehension . . . and the eventual connections between people that ultimately give meaning to life despite the distances between them."

Success in Her Homeland

Knox was born in 1959 in Wellington, New Zealand, where she still makes her home. The daughter of a journalist father and a mother who was a librarian, she was exposed to books and reading at an early age. She graduated from college in 1986, and became an editor at a New Zealand magazine for several years. Meanwhile, she was also beginning her career as an author, publishing her first novel *After Z-Hour* in 1987.

In *After Z-Hour* an abandoned house becomes the central location from which six characters experience hauntings of both a supernatural and psychological nature. In examining the house guests' memories, as well as the memories of a dead soldier who haunts the house, Knox illustrates "how the horrors of the past, whether personal or national, both inform and allow passage into the future," as the *Contemporary Novelists* contributor noted.

Knox followed up her debut novel with several other books that received local rather than international attention. *Treasure* looks at charismatic

Christians through the lens of a campus love story, and it is set in her native Wellington as well as in the United States. This novel was shortlisted for the New Zealand Book Award for Fiction. With *Glamour and the Sea*, Knox returns to a Wellington setting during World War II to tell a mystery which, like her other novels, is characterized by lack of a linear plot line and a multiplicity of voices, times, and settings. Knox has also written a trilogy of semi-autobiographical novels featuring two sisters growing up near Wellington in the 1960s. These were compiled in the year 2000 work, *The High Jump: A New Zealand Childhood*.

Achieves International Recognition

The first of Knox's novels to be published in the United States, *The Vintner's Luck* takes place in nineteenth-century France, as winemaker Sobran Jodeau is visited by the angel Xas and the two develop an intense friendship. Arranging for their annual reunion, Sobran hopes that Xas will become his guardian angel. For his part, however, the powerful yet sensual Xas is no guide; instead the angel takes over the roles of friend, lover, and storyteller, causing Sobran's earthly relationships to diminish in value. In the *New York Times*, Richard Bernstein deemed *The Vintner's Luck* a "sophisticated, supernaturally tinged mystery," and Megan Harlan wrote in *Entertainment Weekly* that Knox's "imagistic" novel explores "the spiritual worth of sensual pleasure."

Daylight, a rather noirish piece of magical realism, draws readers to southern France, where the vacation of an Australian cop is disrupted by an unusual discovery. The body of a drowned woman discovered nearby reminds Brian Phelan of a woman he met years earlier and sets him on a search that involved a soon-to-be sainted member of the Italian Resistance, a literary scholar, and a 200-year-old vampire. Praised as an "illuminating tour-de-force" by a *Publishers Weekly* contributor, *Daylight* also drew comparisons to *The Vintner's Luck* due to Knox's quirky mix. As a *Kirkus Reviews* writer noted, the author's "bizarre narrative impasto" is "at times as entertaining as it is certifiably insane."

Black Oxen is set in the near future, as Carme Risk seeks therapy to overcome a strained relationship with her absent father. Carme's treatment includes keeping a journal about her errant parent, and much of the novel concerns these journal entries and her therapist's responses to them. Knox's story also veers into the supernatural, particularly in scenes set in the fictional Latin-American country of

Cover of Elizabeth Knox's haunting historical novel *Billie's Kiss*, featuring artwork by Royce M. Becker. (Cover design and photo manipulation: Royce M. Becker. Cover photo of woman Copyright © Liz Hampton/Graphistock. Used by permission of Ballantine Books, a division of Random House, Inc.)

Lequama, a land of black magic and revolution. Carme's father, whom she dubs Abra Cadaver, is a healer whose body contains excess phosphorus which he uses for fuel. Ann B. Stephenson wrote in *Book* that *Black Oxen* is "brimming with intense, poetic language" and "leaves readers with the feeling that they've lived through a dense and, at times, magical history." A *Publishers Weekly* critic stated that "Knox's lush, hyperinventive story telling is anything but traditional, and this time-traveling tale is as exuberantly unorthodox as its predecessor," while *Library Journal* contributor David W. Henderson described the novel's plot as a "fascinating, albeit tangled, web . . . for those who enjoy both the unusual and the intelligent."

Recalling the work of British novelists Emily Brontë and Jane Austen, Knox's historical novel *Billie's Kiss* is a tale of romance and mystery set in a Scottish castle in the year 1903. The central character, Billie Paxton, is one of only a few survivors after an explosion at a Scottish port sinks the Swedish steamer *Gustav Edda*. The accident killed Billie's pregnant sister, Edith, and seriously injures her brother-in-law, Henry, a tutor whose new job at Kiss Castle was the reason for the voyage. Murdo Hesketh, the cousin of the lord of the castle, suspects that Billie might have been behind the explosion, but as he investigates the accident he finds himself falling in love with her. In addition to this central story, Knox examines the lives of the island's residents from Billie's perspective and explores the many meanings of the word "kiss." In a review of the novel, a *Publishers Weekly* critic commented that, while it falls short of Brontë's classics, *Billie's Kiss* will leave "many romance fiction fans . . . well satisfied." Praising Knox's "vibrant comic imagination," a *Kirkus Reviews* writer noted that, despite its melodramatic plot, *Billie's Kiss* "reward[s] . . . the bedazzled reader with a stunning climactic confrontation."

Cover of Knox's young-adult novel *Dreamhunter*, an award-winning fantasy set on a remote island during the early twentieth century. (Farrar, Straus & Giroux, 2005. Photograph of forest scene © by Jason Frank Rothenberg/ Photonica; photograph of girl © by Gerlach/Corbis. Reproduced by permission of Farrar, Straus & Giroux, LLC.)

Turns to Young Adult Fiction

Written for a teen audience and compared to the books of well-known Australian writer Margaret Mahy, *Dreamhunter* is the first novel in Knox's "Dreamhunter Duet." Taking place in the early twentieth century, the novel introduces Rose Tiebold and Laura Hame, two fifteen year olds who live in Southland, a remote island nation wherein dreaming is considered dangerous. Both girls have inherited the lucrative skill that enables them to train to become a Dreamhunter: one who ventures into The Place, a dry, arid, invisible otherworld that is "eerily suffused with atmosphere and powerfully portrayed," according to *School Library Journal* reviewer Sue Giffard. Searching The Place, where dreams are born, Dreamhunters acquire visions and then bring them back to share with wealthy audiences at the island's Rainbow Opera. Like films, some dreams are inspiring and others are illuminating. Still others exist only to terrify. Charged with retrieving their first dreams, Laura succeeds, while her cousin Rose fails. When Tziga Hame, Laura's Dreamhunter father, disappears shortly thereafter, the teen receives a letter that sets her on an perilous journey. The second novel of the series, *Dreamquake*, finds Laura joined by others in her efforts to uncover the mystery underlying The Other, a mystery that involves a secret government plot, a regulator army known as the Rangers, and a series of mysterious disappearances.

Explaining her shift to young-adult fantasy fiction, Knox told the *LeafSalon* interviewer: "I came back to reading YA fiction at 25 when I picked up *Charmed Life* by Diana Wynne Jones (my favourite YA writer). I began to read a great deal of YA when I realised that that is where the best fantasy is. I've even given talks to classes studying YA at university, without having written it and without having ever done a paper on it. (I tutored film too, when my only real credentials were being a serious film buff). I always thought I'd write a YA book if I got the right idea." Her move to young-adult fantasy novels was also broached by Kimberly Rothwell in an interview for *Stuff* online. "One of the really attractive things about really good young adult fiction is that sense of something about to happen, or how you can be responsible for something," Knox explained. "They are often saving the world, these young people. It also reflects when you're a teenager, you're teetering between being a hero and being lost in the crowd. It moves all the time."

Reviewers responded well to Knox's duet of novels. In *Publishers Weekly*, a critic wrote of *Dreamhunter* that the author's "fully imagined world will surely lure readers back for multiple readings," while *Horn*

Book contributor Deirdre F. Baker praised the novel as an "engrossing blend of Edwardian civility, family love, and powerfully imagined dreamscape." Noting Knox's sophisticated use of metaphor and vocabulary, Baker added that her "writing is rich and interesting," while in *Kliatt* Michele Winship called Knox's storyline "intriguing and thought provoking, a perfect blend of fantasy and suspense." Citing the novel's "nightmare climax," a *Kirkus Reviews* contributor described *Dreamhunter* as "a lyrical, intricate and ferociously intelligent fantasy."

Reviews for *Dreamquake* were equally positive. *Resource Links* reviewer K.V. Johansen termed the second part of the duet "an excellent alternate-world fantasy," while *School Library Journal* contributor Emily Rodriguez found it to be "richly layered and thoroughly enthralling." Further praise came from Baker, who deemed *Dreamquake* "outstanding in its ability to make us think both poetically and analytically about human nature." For *Booklist* contributor Jennifer Mattson, the two books of the "Dreamhunter Duet" constitute "an organic whole that will be considered among youth fantasy's most significant recent works." Knox received a Michael L. Printz Honor Book Award for *Dreamquake*, while her earlier *Dreamhunter* took New Zealand's equally prestigious Esther Glen Award.

If you enjoy the works of Elizabeth Knox, you may also want to check out the following books:

Jody Lynn Nye, *Waking in Dreamland*, 1998.
Ian McEwan, *Atonement*, 2001.
Charles de Lint, *The Blue Girl*, 2004.

Queried by *Shaken & Stirred* online interviewer Gwenda Bond about her creative process, Knox offered the following: "My books usually start this way. I'll notice that I've begun to think about some character's possible predicament, a dramatic event, or a setting—place, period, atmosphere. Once I've noticed I'm musing I find myself coming up with various proposals, like a kid proposing a bit of action in a game. 'Let's say that,' 'I think,' or, 'What if . . . .'" Knox further explained to Bond: "I usually have a number of ideas for novels circling in a holding pattern. I'm never sure which idea is the first in the queue. And I don't begin writing till I get what I call 'a book-starting idea', the idea that makes it possible for a cluster of notions for a novel to consolidate and start generating their own heat. The book-starting idea is like a starter motor in a car, it makes the big engine of a novel turn over."

■ Biographical and Critical Sources

BOOKS

Contemporary Novelists, 7th edition, St. James Press (Detroit, MI), 2001.

PERIODICALS

Book, July, 2001, Ann B. Stephenson, review of *Black Oxen*, p. 78.
Booklist, December 1, 1998, Mary Ellen Quinn, review of *The Vintner's Luck*, p. 651; January 1, 2002, Kristine Huntley, review of *Billie's Kiss*, p. 810; April 1, 2006, Jennifer Mattson, review of *Dreamhunter*, p. 43; January 1, 2007, Jennifer Mattson, review of *Dreamquake*, p. 92.
Bulletin of the Center for Children's Books, April, 2006, April Spisak, review of *Dreamhunter*, p. 361.
Contemporary Fiction, spring, 2002, Joseph Dewey, review of *Black Oxen*, p. 127.
Economist, May 15, 1999, review of *The Vintner's Luck*, p. 14.
Entertainment Weekly, January 8, 1999, Megan Harlan, review of *The Vintner's Luck*, p. 63.
Horn Book, May-June, 2006, Deirdre F. Baker, review of *Dreamhunter*, p. 321; March-April, 2007, Deirdre F. Baker, review of *Dreamquake*, p. 195.
Independent on Sunday (London, England), August 7, 2005, James Urquhart, "Fantasy: The Way to Deal with Terror."
Kirkus Reviews, January 1, 2002, review of *Billie's Kiss*, p. 11; January 15, 2003, review of *Daylight*, p. 106; March 1, 2006, review of *Dreamhunter*, p. 232; March 1, 2007, review of *Dreamquake*, p. 225.
Kliatt, March, 2006, Michele Winship, review of *Dreamhunter*, p. 13; March, 2007, Michele Winship, review of *Dreamquake*, p. 15.
Library Journal, November 15, 1998, Francisca Goldsmith, review of *The Vintner's Luck*, p. 91; June 15, 2001, David W. Henderson, review of *Black Oxen*, p. 104.
Los Angeles Times Book Review, December 27, 1998, Richard Eder, review of *The Vintner's Luck*, p. 2; August 28, 2001, Michael Harris, review of *Black Oxen*, p. E10; May 2, 2002, Paula Friedman, review of *Billie's Kiss*, p. 3.

New York Times, December 23, 1998, Richard Bernstein, "A Randy Angel Meddles, Literally, in Earthly Affairs," p. E10.

New York Times Book Review, February 21, 1999, Nina Auerbach, "He's No Clarence," p. 15.

Publishers Weekly, October 26, 1998, review of *The Vintner's Luck*, p. 43; June 25, 2001, review of *Black Oxen*, p. 46; February 11, 2002, review of *Billie's Kiss*, p. 165; March 17, 2003, review of *Daylight*, p. 59; April 3, 2006, review of *Dreamhunter*, p. 75.

Resource Links, October, 2006, Angela Thompson, review of *Dreamhunter*, p. 35; June 2007, K.V. Johansen, review of *Dreamquake*, p. 34.

School Library Journal, March, 2006, Sue Giffard, review of *Dreamhunter*, p. 225; June, 2007, Emily Rodriguez, review of *Dreamquake*, p. 53.

Voice of Youth Advocates, February, 2006, Laura Woodruff, review of *Dreamhunter*, p. 499.

Washington Post Book World, March 24, 2002, Liza Featherstone, review of *Billie's Kiss*, p. 6; August 10, 2003, Douglas E. Winter, review of *Daylight*, p. 8.

ONLINE

Arts Foundation of New Zealand Web site, http://www.artsfoundation.org.nz/ (January 9, 2009), "Elizabeth Knox: 2000 Laureate."

Kids Friendly New Zealand Web site, http://www.kidsfriendlynz.com/ (January 9, 2009), interview with Knox.

LeafSalon Web site, http://www.leafsalon.co.nz/(October 22, 2005), interview with Knox.

New Zealand Book Club Web site, http://www.bookclub.co/nz/ (September, 2003), interview with Knox.

New Zealand Writers Web site, http://www.bookcouncil.org.nz/ (January 8, 2009), "Elizabeth Knox."

Shaken & Stirred Web log, http://gwendabond.typepad.com/ (November 8, 2007), Gwenda Bond, "WBBT Stop: Elizabeth Knox."*

Jaclyn Moriarty

■ Personal

Born in Australia; married Colin McAdam (a writer); children: Charlie. *Education:* University of Sydney, B.A.; Yale University, M.A.; Cambridge University, Ph.D.

■ Addresses

Home—Sydney, New South Wales, Australia; and Montreal, Quebec, Canada.

■ Career

Writer and lawyer. Media and entertainment lawyer practicing in Sydney, New South Wales, Australia.

■ Writings

Cicada Summer ("Paradise Point" series), Pan Australia (Sydney, New South Wales, Australia), 1994.

Feeling Sorry for Celia, Pan Macmillan (Sydney, New South Wales, Australia), 2000, St. Martin's Press (New York, NY), 2001.

Finding Cassie Crazy, Pan Macmillan (Sydney, New South Wales, Australia), 2003, published as *The Year of Secret Assignments,* Arthur A. Levine (New York, NY), 2004.

I Have a Bed Made of Buttermilk Pancakes (adult novel), Picador (Sydney, New South Wales, Australia), 2004.

(With Paul Mallam and Sophie Dawson) *Media and Internet Law and Practice,* Thomson Lawbook (Pyrmont, New South Wales, Australia), 2005.

The Betrayal of Bindy Mackenzie, Pan Macmillan (Sydney, New South Wales, Australia), 2006, published as *The Murder of Bindy Mackenzie,* Arthur A. Levine (New York, NY), 2006.

The Spell Book of Listen Taylor, Arthur A. Levine (New York, NY), 2007.

Moriarty's works have been translated into German and Dutch.

■ Adaptations

The Year of Secret Assignments was adapted for an audiobook, Recorded Books, 2005.

■ Sidelights

Australian author Jaclyn Moriarty writes humorous and often poignant books for young adults, pushing the boundaries of that genre with sophisticated themes, situations, and language. Moriarty is, as Roger Sutton noted in the *New York Times Book*

Review, "a complex humorist with a taste for experimentation" who employs a "found-letters format (e-mail, instant messages, faxes, etc.) with wit and authority" in several of her books about young teens at high school. *Feeling Sorry for Celia, The Year of Secret Assignments,* and *The Murder of Bindy Mackenzie* all feature an overlapping cast of characters. In *I Have a Bed Made of Buttermilk Pancakes,* Moriarty turns her hand to adult fiction, but she also has adapted that work for young adults in *The Spell Book of Listen Taylor.* "The first thing I wanted to be was an author," Moriarty told Medeia Senka in a *Maelstrom* online interview. The route to that goal, however, was not a direct one.

Moriarty began writing and reading at an early age. As she reported to Senka, her youthful ambitions changed with age: "I wanted to be a school teacher, a flight attendant, an astronomer. For a while I wanted to be a concert pianist, but I have absolutely no ear for music, no sense of rhythm, and I almost failed all of my piano exams. So I became a lawyer." She was inspired to study law by one of her favorite books, Harper Lee's *To Kill a Mockingbird* and attended the University of Sydney in her native Australia for her bachelor's degree before earning a master's from Harvard University and her doctorate from Cambridge University. When she received her law degree, she also received a congratulations card from an old English teacher that read: "P.S. But remember you are really a writer." "I sat down and wrote a short story the same day," Moriarty recalled to *Teenreads.com* interviewer Lucy Burns. "And that's why I started writing again."

From Law to Literature

For several years, Moriarty continued her career as an entertainment lawyer while writing on the side. After completing a work for the "Paradise Point" teen fiction series, she wrote *Feeling Sorry for Celia,* which is told entirely through letters, Post-it notes, and other messages in written form. As the story opens, Elizabeth Clarry, whose mother is an advertising executive and whose best friend has run away to join the circus, is having a rough year. Her father has reappeared in Elizabeth's life, and she is also receiving anonymous letters from a secret admirer. It seems as though an assignment from her English teacher to write to a girl at a nearby high school will only make things worse, but Elizabeth's pen-pal Christina ends up being someone who can recognize her true talents. "Moriarty poignantly captures the trials of adolescent friendships," wrote Elsa Gaztambide in her *Booklist* review. Miranda Doyle, writing for *School Library Journal,* called *Feeling Sorry for Celia* "a light, enjoyable novel about a memorable young woman," while *Kliatt* reviewer Paula Rohrlick noted: "Here's hoping this first-time author will continue writing for YAs."

Moriarty began writing *Feeling Sorry for Celia* as a traditional narrative that included the occasional letter. She explained to Burns, "The straight narrative got smaller and smaller until one night—it was the middle of the night and I was working on the book—I had this revelation. Why does there need to be a third person narrative at all? Why can't I write all of it in letters?" Moriarty further told Burns that she wanted to write this book "for teenagers like Elizabeth who are worried that they are not doing a good job of being a teenager." Moriarty further explained, "I wanted to remind them that some girls haven't even kissed a boy when they're 16 and some girls have had sex—there is nothing wrong with either approach as long as you are doing exactly what you think is right for yourself."

Novels of Teen Angst and Humor

This modern epistolary style of narrative worked so well that the book took off on its own, and Moriarty again used the storytelling style for her second novel, *Finding Cassie Crazy.* In this novel, which was published in the United States as *The Year of Secret Assignments,* Em, Lyd, and Cassie are part of the same pen-pal exchange program that Elizabeth participated in *Feeling Sorry for Celia.* Instead of finding a listening ear and a female friend, however, all three girls are paired up with boys. Cassie and her mother are still recovering from the death of Cassie's father, and sadly, Cassie is paired with a boy who threatens her, causing her to become increasingly vulnerable. It is up to Em, Lydia, and their pen-pals Charlie and Seb to help Cassie overcome her grief. "Who can resist Moriarty's biting humor?" asked a *Kirkus Reviews* contributor, while Gillian Engberg, writing for *Booklist,* commented on the book's "exhilarating pace, irrepressible characters, and a screwball humor that will easily attract teens." A *Publishers Weekly* reviewer noted that *Finding Cassie Crazy* contains "elements of mystery, espionage, romance, and revenge," while in *School Library Journal* Janet Hilbun commented that the friends' adventures are "funny, exciting, and, at times, poignant." Claire Rosser, writing for *Kliatt,* called the book "intelligent fun," while a reviewer for *Horn Book* noted that Moriarty's novel contains "enormous depth, wit, and poignancy.""

Moriarty features a minor character from her earlier books, Bindy Mackenzie, in *The Murder of Bindy Mackenzie* (published in Australia as *The Betrayal of*

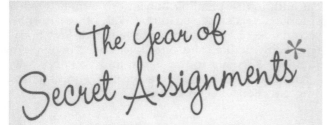

Bindy Mackenzie). Writing in *Blurb* online, Karin van Heerwaarden described Bindy as "a straight A student who believes she's modest and popular but discovers on her first day of year 11 [junior year in high school] that she's in fact the most unpopular girl in school." Thereafter, Bindy decides, as van Heerwaarden commented, "to recreate herself as somebody ruthless and takes it upon herself to tell her classmates what they're really like." This has rather surprising results, one of which is that Bindy begins to feel like a teenager for the first time in her life. Moriarty again tells her story with e-mails and journal entries that give the longish book a fast pace. Eccentric and nerdy, Bindy is also a very lonely girl; her family has lodged her with relatives and only communicates with her through secretaries. Although she excels in academics and has a part-time job at a local store, she is without social skills and manages to annoy fellow classmates and adults alike. However, when she is enrolled in a friendship

and development course at high school, Bindy learns some home truths about relationships that are put to the test when she believes she is being mysteriously poisoned.

Writing in *Resource Links,* Leslie L. Kennedy observed that while *The Murder of Bindy Mackenzie* "might be called humorous and certainly contains a fantastically imaginative mystery, . . . it is also a satire of a society that often thinks teenagers are just slightly shorter versions of adults." Further praise for the novel came from *School Library Journal* contributor Rhona Campbell, who termed it "an enjoyable, well-paced read with an emotional delicacy weaving through the light humor." Similarly, *Booklist* reviewer Gillian Engberg felt that "Bindy's unforgettable, earnest, hilariously high-strung voice . . . will capture and hold eager readers," while a *Kirkus Reviews* contributor found the book "as memorably unique as Bindy herself." According to Rosser, "it is the intelligent YA reader who loves mysteries and puzzles who will thoroughly enjoy this story."

The Zany Zings

After the success of her teen novels, Moriarty focused solely on her writing, taking inspiration and also emotional support from her Canadian-born writer husband Colin McAdam. Moriarty chose a more traditional narrative form for *I Have a Bed Made of Buttermilk Pancakes,* which is something of a fairy tale for adults. The Zing family is surrounded by magic as well as state-of-the-art technology. Each Zing has a special ability: exceptional speed, grace, or slipperiness. As well as these talents, the adult Zings have a family secret, and the mystery of what they hide forms the core of the novel as the youngest family members, Listen and Cassie, go about solving the riddle. Michele Perry, writing for *Blurb* online, called *I Have a Bed Made of Buttermilk Pancakes* "a delightful read for adults wishing to let their imaginations be stretched," and described the story itself as "a very ingenious and witty idea brought to the page by Moriarty."

Moriarty kept tinkering with *I Have a Bed Made of Buttermilk Pancakes* even after it was finished. With a fourth draft of the book, she reworked it as *The Spell Book of Listen Taylor* by focusing more on the story's preteen character. Moriarty maintains the same cast as with the adult novel, including twelve-year-old Listen; sisters Marbie and Fancy Zing; Fancy's daughter Cassie and Cassie's second-grade teacher, Cath Murphy; and Marbie's boyfriend, Nathaniel. However, whereas Nathaniel was the older brother of Listen in *I Have a Bed Made of Buttermilk Pancakes*, in *The Spell Book of Listen Taylor* he is her father and the family has recently moved in with Marbie. The Zing family secret figures heavily in the young-adult adaptation, as does an affair between Cath and another teacher. As for the title character, Listen is shunned by the other children at her new school, and she begins to find solace in an old book of spells she discovers. As Connie Terrell Burns pointed out in *School Library Journal*, "this is not really [Listen's] story." Instead, as Burns stated, "It is more the story of the Zing family." Burns went on to term *The Spell Book of Listen Taylor* "a clever, fun romp, better suited for older teens."

Most reviewers concurred with Burns' assessment of *The Spell Book of Listen Taylor*. *Booklist* reviewer Kathleen Isaacs praised Moriarty's "clever plotting" and "complexity of the adult relationships," while a *Publishers Weekly* contributor observed that this "whimsical though rigorously plotted novel offers an intellectual puzzle that may engage YA readers." However, the same reviewer thought that the complications of the adult-centered plot "may test the patience of its target audience," and Ann Ketcheson in the *Canadian Review of Materials* concluded: "Although the details aren't too lurid for teen readers, almost 500 pages of non sequiturs and quite unbelievable and complicated plots make [*The Spell Book of Listen Taylor*] challenging for all but the most determined of young adult readers." Other reviewers showed less concern for the novel's complexity and difficulties. *Teenreads.com* reviewer Norah Piehl, for example, termed *The Spell Book of Listen Taylor* "a magical, sprawling, complicated saga that will have you flipping pages back and forth, and back again, as you discover new angles, new delights and new connections that shed light on old mysteries." In *Horn Book* Jennifer M. Brabander called Moriarty's novel a "madly convoluted, over-the-top comedy-drama-mystery . . . [whose] end result is magically uplifting."

If you enjoy the works of Jaclyn Moriarty, you may also want to check out the following books:

Ann Brashares, *The Sisterhood of the Traveling Pants*, 2001.
Blake Nelson, *The New Rules of High School*, 2003.
Barry Lyga, *The Astonishing Adventures of Fanboy and Goth Girl*, 2006.

In addition to penning books for younger readers, Moriarty is also the coauthor, with other attorneys, of a book on media and entertainment law. Speaking with Senka, she offered advice for aspiring authors: "Try not to fret if you find you are always changing directions in your writing. I think changing directions is a good thing."

■ Biographical and Critical Sources

PERIODICALS

Booklist, November 15, 2000, Elsa Gaztambide, review of *Feeling Sorry for Celia*, p. 621; January 1, 2004, Gillian Engberg, review of *The Year of Secret Assignments*, p. 858; October 15, 2006, Gillian Engberg, review of *The Murder of Bindy Mackenzie*, p. 41; October 1, 2007, Kathleen Isaacs, review of *The Spell Book of Listen Taylor*, p. 47.
Canadian Review of Materials, May 30, 2008, Ann Ketcheson, review of *The Spell Book of Listen Taylor*.
Horn Book, March-April, 2004, Jennifer M. Brabander, review of *The Year of Secret Assignments*, p. 185; September-October, 2007, Jennifer M. Brabander, review of *The Spell Book of Listen Taylor*, p. 582.
Kirkus Reviews, January 15, 2004, review of *The Year of Secret Assignments*, p. 86; September 15, 2006, review of *The Murder of Bindy Mackenzie*, p. 962; August 15, 2007, review of *The Spell Book of Listen Taylor*.
Kliatt, March, 2002, Paula Rohrlick, review of *Feeling Sorry for Celia*, p. 17; January, 2004, Claire Rosser, review of *The Year of Secret Assignments*, p. 10; September, 2006, Claire Rosser, review of *The Murder of Bindy Mackenzie*, p. 15.
Library Journal, March 15, 2001, Rebecca Sturm Kelm, review of *Feeling Sorry for Celia*, p. 106.
New York Times Book Review, November 11, 2007, Roger Sutton, review of *The Spell Book of Listen Taylor*, p. 34.
Publishers Weekly, February 2, 2004, review of *The Year of Secret Assignments*, p. 78; December 18, 2006, "And Then What Happened?," p. 65; September 17, 2007, review of *The Spell Book of Listen Taylor*, p. 56.
Resource Links, February, 2007, Leslie L. Kennedy, review of *The Murder of Bindy Mackenzie*, p. 40.
School Library Journal, May, 2001, Miranda Doyle, review of *Feeling Sorry for Celia*, p. 156; March, 2004, Janet Hilbun, review of *The Year of Secret Assignments*, p. 220; January, 2007, Rhona Campbell, review of *The Murder of Bindy Mackenzie*, p. 134; November, 2007, Connie Terrell Burns, review of *The Spell Book of Listen Taylor*, p. 132.

ONLINE

Blurb Online, http://www.theblurb.com.au/ (July 12, 2005), Michele Perry, review of *I Have a Bed Made of Buttermilk Pancakes;* (January 6, 2009) Karin van Heerwaarden, review of *The Betrayal of Bindy Mackenzie* and interview with Moriarty.

Chapters.indigo.ca, http://www.chapters.indigo.ca/ (January 6, 2009), Alice Hou, interview with Moriarty.

Jaclyn Moriarty Home Page, http://www.jaclyn moriarty.com (January 6, 2009).

Jaclyn Moriarty Web log, jaclynmoriarty.blogspot.com (January 6, 2009).

Maelstrom, http://maelstrombooks.blogspot.com/ (February 28, 2008), Medeia Senka, interview with Moriarty.

Scholastic Web site, http://www2.scholastic.com/ (January 6, 2009), "Jaclyn Moriarty."

Teenreads.com, http://www.teenreads.com/ (January 6, 2009), Lucy Burns, interview with Moriarty; Sarah A. Wood, review of *The Murder of Bindy Mackenzie;* Norah Piehl, review of *The Spell Book of Listen Taylor.*

Writers Read, http://whatarewritersreading. blogspot.com/ (November 30, 2008), Marshal Zeringue, interview with Moriarty.*

Naomi Novik

■ Personal

Born 1973, in New York, NY; married Charles Ardai. *Education:* Brown University, B.A., Columbia University, M.S.

■ Addresses

Home—New York, NY. *E-mail*—webmaster@ temeraire.org.

■ Career

Writer, novelist, computer programmer, and game designer. Worked on design and development of computer games, including *Neverwinter Nights: Shadows of Undrentide.*

■ Awards, Honors

Locus Award, and Compton Crook Award for best first novel, both 2007, both for *Temeraire: His Majesty's Dragon;* John W. Campbell Award for best new writer, 2007.

■ Writings

"TEMERAIRE" SERIES; FANTASY NOVELS

Temeraire: His Majesty's Dragon, Del Rey Books (New York, NY), 2006.

Throne of Jade, Del Rey Books (New York, NY), 2006.
Black Powder War, Del Rey Books (New York, NY), 2007.
Empire of Ivory, Del Rey Books (New York, NY), 2007.
Victory of Eagles, Del Rey Books (New York, NY), 2008.

Novik's works have been translated into German, Dutch, Spanish, and Russian

■ Adaptations

The books in the "Temeraire" series have been adapted for audiobook by Books on Tape. Film rights to the first three books of the "Temeraire" series were sold to Peter Jackson, 2006.

■ Sidelights

"Is there anything more to say about dragons?" queried *Washington Post Book World* contributor Rachel Hartigan Shea. Answering her own question, Shea further noted: "No one needs any more fantastical medieval theme parks, full of dragons and swords and sorcerers." However, in her "Temeraire" series of fantasy and alternative history novels, former computer game programmer Naomi

Novik has revealed a new and innovative interpretation of one of fantasy's most venerable creatures: the dragon. She puts these mythical creatures to use in a novel series similar to the "Horatio Hornblower" books or Patrick O'Brian's "Master and Commander" series. *New York Times* contributor Julie Bosman described Novik's "Temeraire" books as the "Napoleon-era adventures of a swashbuckling ship captain and a heroic dragon named Temeraire who fight to rescue Britain from a French invasion." Of this sage, Shea was prompted to comment: "All hail Naomi Novik for seizing on an entirely different set of literary conventions for her fantasy."

Speaking with Michael McCarty and Terrie Leigh Relf for *Sci Fi Weekly* online, Novik explained her inspiration for the award-winning series: "I've loved the Napoleonic era in general for a long time: The Jane Austen books are set in that time period, and the Patrick O'Brian books are a big favorite of mine. I really love the flavor of the language. The comedy of manners and the social aspects combined with the swashbuckling adventure of the age itself." Novik's "method of weaving this overworked fantasy lizard into a real world context is meticulously thought out and entirely believable," maintained T.M. Wagner for *SF Reviews* online. Frieda Murray, writing in *Booklist*, lauded the "Temeraire" series for its "excellent plotting, engrossing characters, and sheer page-turning excitement."

From Computer Nerd to Fantasy Guru

Born in 1973, Novik was raised on Long Island. The daughter of Polish immigrants, she grew up listening to her parents reading Polish fairy tales to her. Novik began reading independently at an early age; as a six year old she had already completed J.R.R. Tolkien's "Lord of the Rings" trilogy. From fantasy, the young Novik moved on to an obsession with the novels of Jane Austen. Speaking with Bosman, she described herself as a "stereotypical nerd" in high school, earning straight A's and keeping her nose buried in books. She earned her undergraduate degree in literature at Brown University, thinking that she might pursue a career in journalism. She began writing what is known as fan fiction during these years—that is, taking the characters from her favorite authors and developing her own scenarios for them. However, Novik finally opted for computer programming, earning a graduate degree at Columbia University. Thereafter she worked programming computer games. However, when she reached the age of thirty, she gained a realization, as she told Bosman: "This isn't the life I want at this stage in my career."

In late 2003, a friend suggested that Novik try writing novels. After seeing the film adaptation of O'Brian's seafaring novels, she tried reading the actual books. Within two weeks she had read all twenty, and two months later she had written her own first novel, blending an historical plot with fantasy to produce *Temeraire: His Majesty's Dragon.* The first book in a series set in the Napoleonic era of the early nineteenth century, *Temeraire* introduces a world in which dragons are a well known and accepted part of military life. The formidable flying creatures are controlled by the mysterious Aerial Corps, whose members tame, harness, and ride the dragons as powerful air combat forces. As the story opens, British naval captain Will Laurence has boarded a French ship and discovered an unhatched dragon's egg, which he discovers was intended as a gift for Napoleon himself. When the egg hatches, the dragonling refuses the ritual harnessing by anyone but Captain Laurence, thus forging the beginnings of a deep and permanent bond between human and dragon.

Laurence names the sentient, talking dragon Temeraire, and the story focuses on their growing adventures and deepening friendship as Laurence leaves his beloved naval command to join the Aerial Corps. As the elegant dragon matures and learns about the world, Laurence teaches it responsibility and duty. Laurence laments what his departure from the navy has cost him: his father's respect, his career, and the chance to marry the woman he loved. Yet there is nothing to compare to being friend and equal to a magnificent dragon. The two share combat experiences, political maneuvering, and more serene moments of simple camaraderie such as reading together. The manuscript for this novel was quickly sold to Del Ray, and upon the success of the first title, they immediately contracted for two more works in the trilogy.

Critical response to Novik's debut was very positive. "Novik knows that for the story to work, we have to believe the relationship between Laurence and Temeraire wholeheartedly. And we do," Wagner remarked. *Library Journal* critic Jenne Bergstrom called *Temeraire* a "perfect blend of the familiar and the fantastical." Murray offered "bravos for a most promising new author" and her "superbly written, character-driven series." Reviewer Michelle West, writing in the *Magazine of Fantasy and Science Fiction,* dubbed the book "a joy of a first novel, a wonderful take on dragons, on those who fly them, and on the relationship that unfolds." For Shea, it is "Novik's characterization of the dragon, who speaks in perfect 19th-century English, that makes the book hum." "Novik gets Temeraire's tone just right," Shea further noted: "slightly petulant when [the dragon] doesn't get his way but innocently curious and eager to please." Further praise for this novel came from *Time* magazine reviewer Lev Grossman, who found it "enthralling reading," while a *Publishers Weekly* reviewer noted that "Novik seamlessly blends fantasy into the history of the Napoleonic wars." Likewise, *Kliatt* reviewer Ginger Armstrong termed *Temeraire* "a delight, and readers who enjoy dragon tales will especially enjoy the details of various dragon breeds, the eccentricities of dragon behavior, the humanity of the dragons, and the excitement of dragon battles." As a result of this work, Novik was awarded the Locus Award and Compton Crook Award for best first novel, as well as the John W. Campbell Award for best first novelist.

The World of Temeraire

In *Throne of Jade,* the second book in the series, Laurence discovers that Temeraire is among the rarest and finest of dragons, a Chinese Celestial, and that the Chinese want the dragon back. Temeraire agrees to go only if accompanied by Laurence, and after an eventful sea voyage, they arrive in China, where they face political pressures and other dangers from the Chinese imperial court. Further surprises regarding Temeraire's lineage await them, as they observe firsthand how luxuriously and referentially dragons are treated in China, as opposed to the near-servitude they endure in Europe. As Laurence worries that Temeraire will prefer to take up a pampered life in the Orient, the dragon himself struggles to reconcile his birthright with the military life he has forged with Captain Laurence.

Black Powder War concerns the further adventures of Temeraire and Captain Laurence. The duo faces conflict with both the Turks, who have failed to produce three dragon eggs purchased by the English, and with Temeraire's new blood enemy, Lien, the albino celestial dragon he encountered in the previous novel. In a review of these two works, Murray again had praise for Novik and her creation, remarking that the author's "magical eighteenth century, peopled with sympathetic characters, induces avid reading." In *Maclean's,* Brian Bethune noted another aspect of Novik and her world of dragons and war: "Novik is not just an American fantasy writer mining British history, she's also a girl geek, one who was obsessed with Jane Austen novels as a young teen." Thus, as Bethune pointed out, in addition to Novik's facility with history and battle scenes, "she's also brilliant at the social details." Wagner concluded: "With a multilayered plot that balances adventure, intrigue, war, and rich moments of character-driven drama, *Black Powder War* brings a great trilogy to an explosive finale . . . with the promise of more to come." Further kudos followed the wrap up of the first three books in the series; Peter Jackson, who directed the film adaptation of *The Lord of the Rings,* purchased the rights to Novik's "Temeraire" series. "It's great inspiration for me," the author stated in an online interview for *Ain't It Cool News.* "That kind of affirmation, knowing that somebody really believes in the property that much is just so encouraging as a writer. It really gets me wildly excited to keep going!"

With *Empire of Ivory,* Novik continues her series of novels focusing on the exploits of Laurence and Temeraire. Here they head off to Africa in search of a cure for a mysterious ailment that is affecting the dragons of Europe. In Africa, Laurence soon learns to his own discomfort that the dragons protect the villagers against incursions by British slave traders. A *Publishers Weekly* contributor commended the "richness of Novik's developing world—and characters" in this fourth work in the series. Murray, writing in *Booklist,* also had high praise for the novel, commenting that "Novik's alternate early nineteenth century is so realistic that it drowns disbelief." Murray deemed *Empire of Ivory* "first-class in every respect, including . . . whetting appetites" for the next adventure.

That next series installment, *Victory of Eagles,* returns to the Napoleonic war of earlier titles. Here the French are attacking England. Temeraire believes that Laurence is dead and resolves to lead other dragons into battle. When Laurence returns, Temeraire uses his newly earned command position to sue for not only dragon freedom but also pay for his tireless followers. "Followers of Temeraire's travels will be richly rewarded by the satisfying conclusion of his return to home ground," wrote a *Publishers Weekly* reviewer. Bergstrom, writing in *Library Journal,* observed that "fans of military historicals . . . will likely enjoy the detailed points of military strategy . . . but fantasy readers will still find their sense of wonder." Similarly, a reviewer for the London *Independent* lauded *Victory of Eagles* as a "swashbuckling adventure with added firepower."

One of Novik's literary heroes, O'Brian, stretched his adventure series out to a score of novels, and some have wondered if that is Novik's plan as well. Asked by an online interviewer for *Ain't It Cool News* if she intended to continue with fantasy novels, Novik replied: "Fantasy and science fiction are where I grew up in, in a way. That's really my first love. I'd like to play around with some different kinds of fantasy, not just historical fantasy. I'm thinking about an urban fantasy set in New York and some more science fictional stuff."

If you enjoy the works of Naomi Novik, you may also want to check out the following books:

The "Darkness" series by Harry Turtle-dove, including *Into the Darkness*, 1999.
J. Gregory Keyes, *Empire of Unreason*, 2000.
Paul Park, *The Tourmaline*, 2006.

Speaking with McCarty and Relf about her self-described "geek" qualities and whether they were still in place after her literary successes, Novik replied, "Being a geek in certain ways is about having deep passions in weird areas and being able to follow them. That is very much what I am." In an online interview for *SFFWorld*, she shared her recipe for success as a writer: "I have a deep affection for my own characters, which I try to share with the reader; I think a writer can't hope to engage her audience if she isn't herself deeply engaged with the work."

■ Biographical and Critical Sources

PERIODICALS

Booklist, February 1, 2006, Frieda Murray, review of *Temeraire: His Majesty's Dragon*, p. 38; April 1, 2006, Frieda Murray, review of *Throne of Jade*, p. 29; April 1, 2006, Frieda Murray, review of *Black Powder War*, p. 29; September 15, 2007, Frieda Murray, review of *Empire of Ivory*, p. 54; July 1, 2008, Frieda Murray, review of *Victory of Eagles*, p. 50.
Bookmarks, November-December, 2006, review of *Throne of Jade*, p. 58.
Bookseller, December 9, 2005, review of *Temeraire*, p. 31; December 15, 2005, Alison Bone, "There Be Dragons," review of *Temeraire*, p. 38; October 27, 2006, "Success for Novik Trilogies," p. 39.
Entertainment Weekly, review of *Victory of Eagles*, p. 64.

Independent (London, England), August 10, 2008, review of *Victory of Eagles*.
Kliatt, July, 2006, Ginger Armstrong, review of *Temeraire*, p. 24.
Library Journal, April 15, 2006, Jenne Bergstrom, review of *Temeraire*, p. 71; June 15, 2008, Jenne Bergstrom, review of *Victory of Eagles*, p. 61.
Maclean's, June 30, 2008, Brian Bethune, "Here Be Dragons, Doing Naval Battle," p. 54.
Magazine of Fantasy and Science Fiction, September, 2006, Michelle West, review of *Temeraire*, p. 38.
New York Times, October 11, 2006, Julie Bosman, "A New Writer Is Soaring on the Wings of a Dragon," p. E1.
Publishers Weekly, January 23, 2006, review of *Temeraire*, p. 192; August 20, 2007, review of *Empire of Ivory*, p. 54; May 19, 2008, review of *Victory of Eagles*, p. 40.
Time, March 13, 2006, Lev Grossman, review of *Temeraire*, p. 63.
Washington Post Book World, June 25, 2006, Rachel Hartigan Shea, "The Beasts of War," p. 6.

ONLINE

Ain't It Cool News Online, http://www.aintitcool.com/ (January 8, 2007), interview with Novik.
Naomi Novik Web site, http://www.temeraire.org (January 7, 2009).
Random House Web site, http://www.randomhouse.com/ (January 7, 2008), "Author Spotlight: Naomi Novik."
SciFi Dimensions Web site, http://www.scifidimensions.com/ (June 1, 2006), Carlos Aranaga, interview with Novik.
Sci Fi Weekly Online, http://www.scifi.com/ (September 17, 2007), Michael McCarty and Terrie Leigh Relf, interview with Novik.
SFFWorld Web site, http://www.sffworld.com/ (February 15, 2006), interview with Novik.
SF Reviews Online, http://www.sfreviews.net/ (January 2, 2007), T.M. Wagner, review of *Temeraire*; T.M. Wagner, review of *Throne of Jade*; T.M. Wagner, review of *Black Powder War*.
Strange Horizons Web site, http://www.strangehorizons.com/ (August 14, 2006), Rose Fox, interview with Novik.*

David Poyer

■ Personal

Born November 26, 1949, in DuBois, PA; son of Charles and Margaret Poyer; married Lenore Elizabeth Hart (a novelist); children: Naia Elizabeth. *Education:* U.S. Naval Academy, B.S. (with merit), 1971; George Washington University, M.A.

■ Addresses

Home—Nassawadox, VA.

■ Career

Writer, educator, and Navy officer. U.S. Navy, 1971-2001, line officer on frigates and amphibious ships, 1971-77; transferred to U.S. Naval Reserve, 1977-2001, became commander. Instructor or lecturer at various educational institutions, including U.S. Naval Academy, Flagler College, University of Pittsburgh, Old Dominion University, Armed Forces Staff College, University of North Florida, and Christopher Newport University; Wilkes University, Wilkes-Barre, PA, instructor in MA/MFA in creative writing program. Guest on PBS's *Writer to Writer* series and on Voice of America.

■ Member

Authors Guild, U.S. Naval Institute, American Society of Naval Engineers, U.S. Naval Academy Alumni Association, SERVAS, Tidewater Writers Workshop (founding member).

■ Writings

NOVELS

White Continent, Jove (New York, NY), 1980.
The Shiloh Project, Avon (New York, NY) 1981.
(As David Andreissen) *Star Seed*, Donning (Norfolk, VA), 1982.
The Return of Philo T. McGiffin, St. Martin's Press (New York, NY), 1983.
Stepfather Bank, St. Martin's Press (New York, NY), 1987.
The Only Thing to Fear, Forge (New York, NY), 1995.

"TALES OF THE MODERN NAVY/DAN LENSON" SERIES

The Med, St. Martin's Press (New York, NY), 1988.
The Gulf, St. Martin's Press (New York, NY), 1990.
The Circle, St. Martin's Press (New York, NY), 1993.
The Passage, St. Martin's Press (New York, NY), 1994.
Tomahawk, St. Martin's Press (New York, NY), 1998.
China Sea, St. Martin's Press (New York, NY), 2000.
Black Storm, St. Martin's Press (New York, NY), 2002.
The Command, St. Martin's Press (New York, NY), 2004.
The Threat, St. Martin's Press (New York, NY), 2006.
Korea Strait, St. Martin's Press (New York, NY), 2007.
The Weapon, St. Martin's Press (New York, NY), 2008.

"HEMLOCK COUNTY" SERIES

The Dead of Winter, Tor (New York, NY), 1988.
Winter in the Heart, Tor (New York, NY), 1993.

As the Wolf Loves Winter, Forge (New York, NY), 1996.

Thunder on the Mountain, Forge (New York, NY), 1999.

Winter Light (contains *Winter in the Heart* and *As the Wolf Loves Winter*), Forge (New York, NY), 2001.

"TILLER GALLOWAY" SERIES

Hatteras Blue, St. Martin's Press (New York, NY), 1989.

Bahamas Blue, St. Martin's Press (New York, NY), 1992.

Louisiana Blue, St. Martin's Press (New York, NY), 1994.

Down to a Sunless Sea, St. Martin's Press (New York, NY), 1996.

"CIVIL WAR AT SEA" SERIES

Fire on the Waters: A Novel of the Civil War at Sea, Simon & Schuster (New York, NY), 2001.

A Country of Our Own, Simon & Schuster (New York, NY), 2003.

That Anvil of Our Souls: A Novel of the Monitor and the Merrimack, Simon & Schuster (New York, NY), 2005.

OTHER

(Editor) *Command at Sea*, 4th edition, U.S. Naval Institute Press (Annapolis, MD), 1983.

Contributor of stories to periodicals, including *Analog*, *Galileo*, *Isaac Asimov's Science Fiction Magazine*, *Mike Shayne's Mystery Magazine*, and *Unearth*.

■ Adaptations

Film rights to *The Return of Philo T. McGiffin* were bought in 1991 by Universal.

■ Sidelights

The author of several successful sea-based action fiction series as well as novels that stick closely to the land, David Poyer writes of what he knows best. A member of the U.S. Navy and of the Naval Reserve for many years, Poyer uses his hard-won firsthand knowledge in his novels of the sea and the world of sailors and divers, earning him special praise because of his books' realism. Speaking of Poyer's "Tales of the Modern Navy" series in *Booklist*, Roland Green called the saga "one of the outstanding bodies of nautical fiction in English during the last half-century" and praised Poyer for balancing "hardware description and an extremely well-drawn cast of characters with enormous skill."

"I am no creature of the shore," Poyer wrote in an article for *Water's Edge*. The author went on to enumerate what the sea means to him: "Certainly, to me the sea at first meant freedom. . . . To me the sea means solitude. . . . To me the sea means discipline; for without discipline, resolution, self-mastery, one can face neither fire, nor combat, nor the sea itself. And it also means technique. . . . But after all of these, the sea remains unexplained, unplumbed, unmeasured. For so far, my groping divinations derive not from the essence of the thing, but from our responses to it. And so I cast away the last drifting handhold and strike out, into the blue."

Join the Navy and See the World

Born in 1949, Poyer grew up in Pennsylvania, where he developed an early love for literature. The author once commented: "My sister, my brother, and I grew up in vicious poverty but always with books around, thanks to our mother." Poyer further noted in an interview on his home page: "I can't recall if I was three or four, but I remember the moment clearly. My mother was reading to me, and suddenly I understood what books were, what stories were, and realized that I was put here to write them." First, he needed an education and also wanted to see something of the world. Thus, he applied to the Naval Academy and was accepted. Graduating in 1971, Poyer served on destroyers and amphibious ships in the Atlantic, the Mediterranean, the Caribbean, and the Arctic. He would later use these settings for his novels.

Poyer recalled: "I spent the next six years at sea, married, divorced, and finally asked for transfer to the Reserves. It was time to try for the dream." He lived for a time in the South Seas, attempting to become a novelist, and then returned to the United States. To support his writing, he found work developing a nuclear submarine design for a shipbuilding firm located in Newport News, Virginia, and then rejoined the U.S. Navy as a reserve officer. Eventually, however, he found steady publication in regional magazines and became a partner in a guidebook publishing company. Poyer also earned a master's degree in writing, giving him a firm foundation in his chosen career. Thereafter, he began writing novels again, publishing *White Continent* and *the Shiloh Project* and initiating a career that has seen the publication of almost a novel a year since 1980. It was not until 1988, however, with the publication of *The Med*, that Poyer achieved real success.

Tales of the Modern Navy

The Med, which looks at the Cypriot crisis of 1974, was highly praised by critics for its non-stop action and three-dimensional characterization. The best seller also became the first title in Poyer's "Tales of the Modern Navy" series, which features U.S. Navy officer Dan Lenson, an Annapolis graduate whose career leads him through many assignments and adventures. Lenson is not without his faults: he drinks too much and has difficulty maintaining relationships, but he always manages to get the job done. Though the novels provide plenty of excitement, they also address real issues. For instance, the second novel in the series, *The Gulf*, deals with a conflict in the Persian Gulf. The timely work appeared in 1990, the same year the Gulf War began. The Arctic Ocean above Greenland figures in *The Circle*, while the fourth title in the series, *The Passage*, looks at a possible conflict with Cuba and also deals with the role of gays in the military. Reviewing *Tomahawk*, Green commented: "Poyer's Lenson novels are so character driven that calling them thrillers is misleading, and here Poyer includes a solid cast of secondary characters who are thoroughly individualized yet serve to raise the ethical questions Poyer always brings to the fore. This demanding, excellent novel is probably the best so far in a major contemporary seafaring saga." The success of this series allowed Poyer to become a full-time writer.

China Sea finds Lenson ordered to deliver an outmoded frigate to the Pakistani government as part of a trade. On the voyage, he faces conflicts between the American and Pakistani crews, a serial killer stalking the ship, and an unexpected detour to battle a Chinese pirate organization. "Poyer displays a fine sense of pace and plot when the focus is on seagoing affairs, and the battle scenes are scintillating and satisfying," according to a critic for *Publishers Weekly*. Patrick J. Wall, reviewing *China Sea* in *Library Journal* found that "Poyer's characters are as good as ever, and the action scenes are lively."

Lenson returns in *Black Storm*, a novel set during the Gulf War of 1991. American intelligence has learned that Saddam Hussein has a secret weapon

he plans to use against Israel; Lenson and a crew of special operations experts is sent to Baghdad to locate and destroy the weapon before it can be unleashed. Robert Conroy, writing in *Library Journal*, noted that "Poyer captures the technical and emotional feel of such a dangerous mission, which ranges across the bleak desert and through the claustrophobic sewers of Baghdad." Green labeled *Black Storm* "one of the strongest books in an outstanding series."

Lenson earns a promotion to commander in *The Command*, after which he takes charge of the U.S.S. *Thomas Horn*, a helicopter-capable destroyer. On top of his new duties as the top officer of the Spruance-class *Horn*, Lenson is also charged with being the host ship for the U.S. Navy's initial experiments with integrating women into service aboard a warship. Resentment and opposition simmer throughout the ranks of officers and enlisted, but Lenson sees the integration as a welcome and logical step in the evolution of the military. He even welcomes the presence of his new female executive officer. Unfortunately, new female crewmembers clash with the old crew and the group of Navy SEALS recently assigned to the *Horn*. As the ship's mission is underway, considerable turmoil erupts, including a suspicious fire in the female barracks, an unexpected pregnancy, and a severed goat's head meant to intimidate. As the ship travels from the United States into foreign waters and the Persian Gulf, Navy criminal investigator Aisha Ar-Rahim follows an investigation of her own to the *Horn*, where the enormous destroyer makes a tempting target for local foes with destructive aspirations and nuclear capabilities. "Poyer packs story with both dense technical info and welcome local color," observed a *Kirkus Reviews* critic in reviewing *The Command*.

The Threat takes Lenson to unfamiliar territory in Washington, DC, where he joins the National Security Council and becomes the carrier of the "football," a case containing the vital codes to be used by the president in a nuclear conflict. Working with a president known for his womanizing, and who is detested by the military establishment, Lenson struggles to get used to the Washington bureaucracy while doing his best in a menial assignment with an anti-drug task force. Though he demonstrates great competence, even excellence, in dealing with the machinations of a Colombian drug lord, Lenson's superiors still look on him with suspicion and disdain. Abruptly, Lenson finds himself reassigned and in possession of the nuclear codes and closely aligned with a president whose handling of military matters is dubious at best. Making matters worse, his domestic life is in disarray as he experiences conflict with his higher-

Cover of David Poyer's novel *Korea Strait*, featuring artwork by Alan Ayers. (St. Martin's Press, 2007. Illustration © by Alan Ayers. Reproduced by permission.)

ranking wife, Blair, and realizes that she may be a target of the philandering president's affections. In the background, an assassination plot unfolds through the machinations of unknown parties. A *Kirkus Reviews* critic called *The Threat* "a gloomy story, but Poyer remains the most thoughtful of the military-thriller set and a master of authentic detail." In assessing the novel, *Booklist* reviewer David Pitt named Poyer "a superior writer."

After foiling the assassination plot on his commander in chief in *The Threat*, the thirty-nine-year-old Lenson finds himself, in *Korea Strait*, in the unenviable position of being pushed toward retirement by his commanding officer. Lenson has no intention of leaving his post, however, and thus is reassigned to an uninspiring mission: he is to command a tactical analysis group and gather information from war games held in the Korea Strait and carried out jointly by South Korea, Australia, and

Japan. Acting as an observer and stationed aboard the South Korean flagship *Chung Nam*, Lenson is also tasked with escorting retired military and U.S. civilians. During the war games, Lenson's mission becomes critical when the *Chung Nam* is attacked by unidentified submarines. Lenson quickly disobeys an order from the South Korean commander to leave the ship, and instead tries to help the commander, despite the fact that he has no authority to do so. Soon a typhoon adds to the troubles of the *Chung Nam*, and Lenson helps below decks to repair damage from the subs. Finally, however, he must propose a startling maneuver in order to save the day.

The tenth installment in the "Tales of the Modern Navy" series won kudos from reviewers. *Mostly Fiction* online contributor Kirstin Merrihew, noting that in *Korea Strait* "Poyer has a reputation as one of America's best military fiction authors," went on to observe that the "thriller is highly engrossing in many respects besides the tautly told main plot of battle against uncertain foe and turbulent sea." For Merrihew, *Korea Strait* is "an expert tale of the modern Navy, authored by a real pro." Similar praise came from a *Publishers Weekly* reviewer who termed the novel "taut" and added that "Poyer's tech talk throughout is nicely turned, and Dan Lenson remains a winningly weary hero." A *Kirkus Reviews* critic also commended *Korea Strait*, concluding that it is "well up to Poyer's excellent standards. No bluster, no dazzle, just real naval engagements that we may well see before long." In *Library Journal* Robert Conroy pointed out that "fans of modern naval warfare will relish the details and sea action, as well as the insights into the Korean situation and the Korean people."

The Weapon finds Lenson and his crew attempting to purchase a new rocket torpedo developed by the Russians. When the deal goes sour, Lenson decides to hijack a container ship sailing to China and carrying one of the weapons. When that operation in turn fails, he resorts to taking an Iranian submarine that is carrying one of these new weapons. Thereafter, Lenson and his crew must dodge an Iranian ship steaming after them in this "fine military thriller," as a *Publishers Weekly* contributor termed this addition to the series. The same reviewer also commended the author for providing a "tight structure, plenty of authentic technological detail and a hero who acts like a man rather than a cartoon superhero."

From Civil War Yarns to Tales of the Deep

With *Fire on the Waters: A Novel of the Civil War at Sea* Poyer began a new series of nautical adventures, this time set during the U.S. Civil War. Elisha Eaker is a wealthy young man who has joined the navy to escape his domineering father and an unwanted marriage to his headstrong cousin. Assigned to protect Union forces at Fort Sumter in South Carolina, Eaker finds that as the South secedes from the Union, his position becomes more perilous. Along with a crew of varying loyalty to the besieged Union, he eventually battles not only Confederate forces but storms at sea before venturing to the Chesapeake Bay on a secret mission. A *Publishers Weekly* reviewer commented that *Fire on the Waters* has "plenty of meat on the bones for Civil War and naval buffs," and Margaret Flanagan, writing in *Booklist*, called the novel "a solid introduction to a promising new series." Poyer's second novel in the series, *A Country of Our Own*, moves the spotlight to Confederate navy lieutenant Ken Custis Claiborne, a Virginian who goes south after Sumter, first defending his state on the banks of the Potomac, then commanding a sea-raider that attacks Yankee trade from Brazil to Boston.

That Anvil of Our Souls: A Novel of the Monitor and the Merrimack, the third of the "Civil War at Sea" books, provides a fictionalized account of the origins of ironclad warfare with the storied U.S. Civil War ships *Monitor* and *Merrimack*. Poyer follows the basic true story of the two ships, covering the origins of the *Merrimack* and its capture and refitting as a southern ship named the *Virginia,* and the initial reactions to the smaller and seemingly ineffectual *Monitor*. On board the *Virginia* is Lieutenant Lomax Minter, brash perhaps to the point of being foolhardy, arrogant and handsome. Other crew members distrust Minter and fear that his attitude toward warfare will bring them and the ship to harm. Minter's counterpart on the *Monitor*, Chief Engineer Theo Hubbard, is stalwart and duty-bound, determined and reliable in combat. Real civil war figures and fictional characters interact as the story unfolds from the perspective of these two contrasting military men. A *Kirkus Reviews* contributor praised the novel as the "series best, and for those who see the U.S. Civil War as this country's defining drama, simply not to be missed." With his work, "Poyer makes readers see and feel the blockade and the men who tried to maintain it," observed a *Publishers Weekly* reviewer.

Several of Poyer's nautical novels feature deepwater diver Tiller Galloway, a maverick drifter who, although he is frequently depicted as self-centered and unlikable, is nonetheless "the perfect denizen of the undersea world: tough, stubborn, solitary, out of place on land," in the opinion of a *Publishers Weekly* writer. As Poyer remarked on his home-page interview, "After I go into the angst and the soul-searching of one of the Lenson novels, it's nice to do a Tiller Galloway book, which is pure action/

adventure, male camaraderie, diving; it's faster paced, and I let myself have a little fun with it." Reviewing *Louisiana Blue,* a *Publishers Weekly* critic noted that "the biggest thrills in this well-written and subtly plotted novel come from the way Poyer brings alive the dangerous, claustrophobia-inducing world of deep-sea diving."

Tiller reappears in *Down to a Sunless Sea,* rated "one of [Poyer's] best novels yet" by a *Publishers Weekly* critic. Once again, the realistic descriptions of undersea escapades were singled out by the reviewer as "particularly memorable," especially the "extensive, harrowing" passages about "cave dives, which are riveting enough to terrify experienced divers and hydrophobes alike." Thomas Gaughan echoed this sentiment in *Booklist*: "The cave-diving scenes are riveting, claustrophobic, terrifying, and beautiful. And Tiller has grown into one of the most spectacularly flawed and failed characters ever to seek redemption in popular fiction."

Speaking of his nautical adventure novels in an interview posted on his home page, Poyer explained that his greatest problem in writing was how to use naval terminology so that the general reader would not be overwhelmed: "I start out defining my military terms in context; then, as the book goes on, I introduce more and more of them, especially in dialogue, because that's the really critical area. So by the end, the characters are speaking pretty unadulterated naval jargon, but you can understand it because you've been gradually introduced to it."

Landlubber Novels

While Poyer's nautical books have proven to be popular, his land-based novels have also been praised as engrossing and thought-provoking works, particularly the "Hemlock Country" series. These ecological thrillers feature an unlikely collection of heroes, including W.T. Halvorsen, an elderly, retired oil-driller, and his sidekick, high school student Phil Romanelli. In *Winter in the Heart,* Halvorsen becomes seriously ill after being splashed by contaminated snow. When he discovers that several other residents in his area have been similarly affected, he begins to investigate who is behind the illegal dumping of toxic waste. It turns out to be a bigger project than he expected, as everyone from the Mafia to the federal government struggles to cover up the crimes. A *Publishers Weekly* reviewer called *Winter in the Heart* an "absorbing tale" enlivened by "vividly imagined and deftly rendered characters, each one possessing real depth and a credible place in the story's richly evoked milieu."

A sequel, *As the Wolf Loves Winter*, was praised by a *Publishers Weekly* critic for its "superb storytelling and characterization." *Thunder on the Mountain* is set in 1935, when young Bill Halvorsen finds himself entangled in unionizing efforts in the Pennsylvania oil fields. Violence erupts when ruthless communist organizers clash with corrupt businessmen, leading to sabotage, bribery, and death. *Thunder on the Mountain* is "violent, touching, and incredibly sad as the story careens to its explosive conclusion," Karen Anderson wrote in *Library Journal*. "Poyer's chilling look into the heart of the early union movement is dramatic and suspenseful, full of despair and hope," according to Melanie Duncan in *Booklist*. Similar praise was offered by a critic for *Publishers Weekly*, who found the novel to be "a stunning period tale."

Poyer has also written a half dozen stand-alone novels, among which is *The Only Thing to Fear*. Here he speculates on the wartimes activities of the future U.S. president John F. Kennedy as he embarks on a secret mission to protect President Franklin D. Roosevelt from assassination. The book follows this storyline while constructing a comprehensive fictional portrait of Kennedy, including issues surrounding his health, his military service, and his role as the scion of a famous and prominent family. Green remarked that Poyer's depiction of Kennedy is "one of the most fully realized presentations of JFK to appear in fiction."

The Rewards of a Literary Life

In an essay in *Shipmate*, Poyer addressed his motivation for writing: "I sometimes tell those who ask that the only worthwhile reason to write is to get even. . . . Getting even—which is my shorthand phrase for transforming despair into art, and attempting to at least speak out for justice in an unjust world—is a powerful motivator. But to drive us through the long apprenticeship, and the long labor of creation after that, it must be combined with something else. It has to become a duty." Poyer added that in order to become a successful author, one must possess "a burning sense of outrage, a monomaniacal perfectionism, a compulsion to escape into fantasy on an hourly basis, a long steeping in some form of fiction and drama, a lifetime feeling of being an outsider and an impostor, and a Moses-like ability to keep the faith through forty years in the desert."

Discussing his novels, Poyer once commented: "I admire strong stories with characters who must decide between good and evil—and situations where the choice is not as easy as it may sound. I

don't like fantasy, and my work leans toward realism. I value accurate backgrounds, believable characters, and realistic dialogue and dislike wordiness, schlock, and digression. My goal is very simple—to write a novel, someday, that will satisfy me."

If you enjoy the works of David Poyer, you may also want to check out the following books:

The "Jake Grafton" novels by Stephen Coonts, including *Under Siege,* 1990.
Robert N. Macomber, *At the Edge of Honor,* 2002.
James L. Nelson, *Glory in the Name,* 2003.

Nearly three decades after the publication of his first book, Poyer feels satisfied with the direction of his career. "I've finally found the person I was meant to find," he noted in his home-page interview. The author further explained: "My early novels, frankly, weren't very good; I was writing in several genres and looking for my voice. Now I've identified the worlds I feel comfortable in—the Navy, present and historical; diving, and northwestern Pennsylvania—and can write about believably."

■ Biographical and Critical Sources

PERIODICALS

Analog Science Fiction-Science Fact, February, 1983, Tom Easton, review of *Star Seed,* p. 164.
Booklist, March 15, 1992, Ray Olson, review of *The Circle,* p. 1316; December 15, 1994, Roland Green, review of *The Passage,* p. 736; April 15, 1995, Roland Green, review of *The Only Thing to Fear,* p. 1481; October 15, 1996, Thomas Gaughan, review of *Down to a Sunless Sea,* p. 407; April, 1998, Roland Green, review of *Tomahawk,* p. 1305; March 1, 1999, Melanie Duncan, review of *Thunder on the Mountain,* p. 1151; January 1, 2000, Roland Green, review of *China Sea,* p. 878; July, 2001, Margaret Flanagan, review of *Fire on the Waters: A Novel of the Civil War at Sea,* p. 1983; May 1, 2002, Roland Green, review of *Black Storm,* p. 1509; May 15,

2005, Jay Freeman, review of *That Anvil of Our Souls: A Novel of the Monitor and the Merrimack*, p. 1649; September 15, 2006, David Pitt, review of *The Threat*, p. 32; April 1, 2007, David Pitt, review of *The Threat*, p. 85.

Kirkus Reviews, May 1, 2004, review of *The Command*, p. 419; April 15, 2005, review of *That Anvil of Our Souls*, p. 445; August 15, 2006, review of *The Threat*, p. 806; September 15, 2007, review of *Korea Strait*.

Library Journal, November 15, 1982, review of *Star Seed*, p. 2192; May 1, 1983, A.J. Anderson, review of *The Return of Philo T. McGiffin*, p. 921; April 15, 1988, Edwin B. Burgess, review of *The Med*, p. 96; August 1, 1990, Elsa Pendleton, review of *The Gulf*, p. 145; May 1, 1992, Elsa Pendleton, review of *The Circle*, p. 119; April 1, 1995, Stacie Browne Chandler, review of *The Only Thing to Fear*, p. 125; March 15, 1999, Karen Anderson, review of *Thunder on the Mountain*, p. 110; February 1, 2000, Patrick J. Wall, review of *China Sea*, p. 118; May 15, 2001, Loretta Davis, review of *Fire on the Waters*, p. 165; April 15, 2002, Robert Conroy, review of *Black Storm*, p. 126; September 15, 2007, Robert Conroy, review of *Korea Strait*, p. 53; November 1, 2008, Robert Conroy, review of *The Weapon*, p. 59.

New York Times Book Review, September 23, 1990, Newgate Callendar, review of *The Gulf*, p. 16; July 26, 1992, Newgate Callendar, review of *The Circle*, p. 13.

Officer, June, 2005, David R. Bockel, review of *The Command*, p. 47.

Publishers Weekly, April 15, 1983, review of *The Return of Philo T. McGiffin*, p. 42; March 4, 1988, review of *The Med*, p. 95; August 3, 1990, review of *The Gulf*, p. 64; March 16, 1992, review of *The Circle*, p. 66; February 7, 1994, review of *Louisiana Blue*, p. 70; November 14, 1994, review of *The Passage*, p. 54; February 27, 1995, review of *The Only Thing to Fear*, p. 87; March 4, 1996, review of *As the Wolf Loves Winter*, p. 54; October 7, 1996, p. 63; February 16, 1998, review of *Tomahawk*, p. 202; February 1, 1999, review of *Thunder on the Mountain*, p. 77; January 31, 2000, review of *China Sea*, p. 83; June 18, 2001, review of *Fire on the Waters*, p. 56; May 6, 2002, review of *Black Storm*, p. 34; June 13, 2005, review of *That Anvil of Our Souls*, p. 32; September 18, 2006, review of *The Threat*, p. 34; September 24, 2007, review of *Korea Strait*, p. 43; September 22, 2008, review of *The Weapon*, p. 38.

School Library Journal, September, 1983, review of *The Return of Philo T. McGiffin*, p. 143.

Shipmate, July-August, 1999, David Poyer, "Why They Write."

Tribune Books (Chicago, IL), April 3, 1988, review of *The Med*, p. 5.

Virginia Quarterly Review, autumn, 1995, review of *The Only Thing to Fear*, p. 131.

Voice of Youth Advocates, December, 1987, review of *Stepfather Bank*, p. 245; August 1, 1988, review of *The Dead of Winter*, p. 135.

Water's Edge, July, 1999, David Poyer, "The Abyss."

ONLINE

Armchair Critic Web site, http://thearmchaircritic.blogspot.com/ (December 13, 2006), review of *The Threat*.

David Poyer Home Page, http://www.poyer.com (January 14, 2009).

Mostly Fiction Web site, http://www.mostlyfiction.com/ (January 10, 2008), Kirstin Merrihew, review of *Korea Strait*.

Mystery Gazette Online, http://themysterygazette.blogspot.com/ (November 30, 2007), Harriet Klausner, review of *Korea Strait*.*

Rick Riordan

■ Personal

Born June 5, 1964, in San Antonio, TX; married; children: two sons.

■ Addresses

Home—San Antonio, TX. *E-mail*—rick@rickriordan. com.

■ Career

Writer. Middle school English teacher in San Francisco, CA, 1990-98; former teacher in San Antonio, TX, beginning 1998; currently full-time freelance writer. Presenter at workshops for educational organizations, including Texas Library Association, National Council for Teachers of English, International Reading Association, California Association of Independent Schools, and Colonial Williamsburg Teacher Institute.

■ Awards, Honors

Anthony Award for Best Original Paperback, and Shamus Award for Best First Private Eye Novel, both 1997, both for *Big Red Tequila*; Anthony Award for Best Original Paperback, Edgar Allan Poe Award for Best Original Paperback, and Shamus Award nomination, all 1998, all for *The Widower's Two-step*; Shamus Award nomination for Best Hardcover P.I. Novel, 2002, for *The Devil Went down to Austin*; Master Teacher Award, Saint Mary's Hall, 2002; inducted into Texas Institute of Letters, 2003; Cooperative Children's Book Council Choice Award, and Notable Children's Book citation, National Council for Teachers of English, both 2006, both for *The Lightning Thief*.

■ Writings

"PERCY JACKSON AND THE OLYMPIANS" SERIES; FOR YOUNG ADULTS

The Lightning Thief, Hyperion Books for Children (New York, NY), 2005.
The Sea of Monsters, Hyperion Books for Children (New York, NY), 2006.
The Titan's Curse, Hyperion Books for Children (New York, NY), 2007.
The Battle of the Labyrinth, Hyperion Books for Children (New York, NY), 2008.
(Editor, with Leah Wilson) *Demigods and Monsters: Your Favorite Authors on Rick Riordan's "Percy Jackson and the Olympians" Series*, Benbella Books (Dallas, TX), 2008.
The Last Olympian, Hyperion Books for Children (New York, NY), 2009.

Percy Jackson: The Demigod Files, Hyperion Books for Children (New York, NY), 2009.

"TRES NAVARRE" MYSTERY SERIES

Big Red Tequila, Bantam (New York, NY), 1997.
The Widower's Two-Step, Bantam (New York, NY), 1998.
The Last King of Texas, Bantam (New York, NY), 2000.
The Devil Went down to Austin, Bantam (New York, NY), 2001.
Southtown, Bantam (New York, NY), 2004.
Mission Road, Bantam (New York, NY), 2005.
Rebel Island, Bantam Books (New York, NY), 2007.

OTHER

Cold Springs (novel), Bantam (New York, NY), 2003.
Thirty-nine Clues: The Maze of Bones (children's novel), Scholastic Press (New York, NY), 2008.

Contributor of short stories to magazines, including *Ellery Queen's Mystery Magazine* and *Mary Higgins Clark Mystery Magazine.*

■ **Adaptations**

The Lightning Thief was adapted as a sound recording available on cassette and CD by Listening Library/Books on Tape, 2005, and was optioned for film by Twentieth Century-Fox. Other titles in the "Percy Jackson and the Olympians" series have also been adapted for audiobook. Film rights to *Thirty-nine Clues: The Maze of Bones* were sold to Steven Spielberg and DreamWorks.

■ **Sidelights**

Rick Riordan, a teacher turned award-winning author, has scored successes in two very divergent genres: adult detective fiction and young-adult fantasy. His novels featuring the private investigator Tres Navarre have won prestigious Shamus, Anthony, and Edgar awards and have been hailed by a *Kirkus Reviews* contributor for their "brisk pacing, smart plotting, and an immensely likable protagonist." Similarly, Riordan's "Percy Jackson and the Olympians" series for younger adult readers have been praised for their inventiveness and action. *Booklist* contributor Diana Tixier Herald

dubbed Riordan's books for teens a "clever mix of classical mythology, contemporary teen characters, and an action-packed adventure."

Discussing the popularity of Riordan's two series, Edward Nawotka noted in the Milwaukee *Journal Sentinel* that, "while Tres Navarre brought Riordan critical acclaim and modest success, Percy Jackson offered a far larger audience." Indeed, after the first two titles in the "Percy Jackson and the Olympians" series sold over 400,000 copies in hardcover and softcover, the third work, *The Titan's Curse,* had a whopping print run of 150,000 copies and became a *New York Times* bestseller. The fourth title, *The Battle of the Labyrinth,* had a first printing of one million copies. Meanwhile the first novel in the series, *The Lightning Thief,* went into production as a Twentieth Century-Fox feature film.

Writing in the *San Antonio Express-News,* Bryce Milligan wondered about the immense popularity of Riordan's young-adult works, stating: "Exactly how it is that Rick Riordan can consistently write novels that, although they begin with dire prophecies and end with narrow escapes from cosmic oblivion, are such delightful romps to read—well, 'tis a mystery not unlike his unlikely hero Percy 'Perseus' Jackson, a 21st-century ADHD middle-schooler who happens to be the bona fide son of the Greek god Poseidon." According to Nawotka, "The appeal of the Percy Jackson books can be attributed to Riordan's savvy adaptation of Greek myths to a contemporary setting." Nawotka further noted, "Percy has dyslexia and attention-deficit hyperactivity disorder, which have helped him attract 'reluctant readers,' especially boys, who identify with the hero." As a result, Riordan has increasingly focused on young-adult books, scoring a further success with *Thirty-nine Clues: The Maze of Bones,* an interactive title that was optioned by Steven Spielberg and DreamWorks.

A Lone Star State Investigator

Growing up in San Antonio, Texas, Riordan used to dream about becoming a teacher and a writer. He began writing as a teenager, submitting short stories for publication. In high school he edited the school paper and after graduating from college, he began teaching middle school in San Francisco, California. It was there he also began writing on the side. Homesick for Texas, he decided to set a detective series in his native state, and thus was born Tres Navarre.

Riordan's first mystery, *Big Red Tequila,* introduces Navarre, who has a doctoral degree in medieval studies from the University of California at Berkeley.

He also has earned a few degrees from the streets and has an interest in the martial art of Tai Chi Chuan. Failing at academia, Navarre becomes a private investigator in the San Francisco Bay area. An alarming phone call from an old girlfriend sends Navarre back to his hometown of San Antonio, Texas, to investigate the unsolved murder of his father, who was the former sheriff of Bexar County. As the investigation proceeds, Tres stirs up a hornet's nest of politicians, mobsters, and crooked businessmen. "Riordan writes so well about the people and topography of his Texas hometown that he quickly marks the territory as his own," commented critic Dick Adler in the *Chicago Tribune*.

Riordan spent eight years teaching English in San Francisco before following in his hero's footsteps and returning to his hometown of San Antonio in the summer of 1998. The author uses his own Tex-Mex style to describe the scenery, people, and popular places of southern Texas. In *The Widower's Two-step*, an old friend hires Tres—who is still an apprentice waiting for his P.I. license—to follow a musician suspected of stealing a demo tape of a budding young singer named Miranda Daniels. While Navarre is on stakeout, the musician is gunned down, drawing the sleuth into the arena of dirty dealings, double-crossings, greed, and murder in the country music business. Navarre must extricate Miranda from a tangle of music-industry power games and professional grudges. At times Navarre finds himself on the wrong side of the law; local enforcers and the FBI are hot on his trail as he uncovers illegal dealings between local rednecks and European businessmen who have enough of a stake in country music to warrant murder. As a *Publishers Weekly* reviewer commented of *The Widower's Two-step*, "Riordan showed real talent in *Big Red Tequila*, but here, he's relaxed enough to make it look easy."

The Last King of Texas involves an investigation by Navarre into a web of murderous family rivalries, missing persons, and heroin trafficking, while *The Devil Went down to Austin* begins with the P.I. renovating his great-grandfather's ranch. He learns, however, that older brother Garrett has mortgaged the property in the hopes of funding his failing software company. Tres goes to Austin to confront his brother, only to find Garrett arrested for the murder of his friend and business partner. As *Booklist* contributor Jenny McLarin wrote, "Navarre just may have become the most appealing mystery hero in Texas. His latest is pure heaven for mystery fans." A *Publishers Weekly* reviewer called *The Devil Went down to Austin* "a book sure to enhance the author's solid reputation."

Navarre also appears in the novels *Southtown* and *Mission Road*. In the former title, the P.I. is pitted against a murderer who is also a rapist, kidnapper, immigrant trafficker, and escaped prisoner. Although a *Publishers Weekly* critic admitted that Will Stirman makes for "a fairly standard villain," the reviewer declared *Southtown* to be a "superb" addition to the series "that should delight old Riordan fans and win new ones." A *Kirkus Reviews* contributor credited Riordan with helping to revive "the shamus subgenre" through "brisk pacing, smart plotting, and an immensely likable protagonist." *Booklist* contributor Connie Fletcher was slightly less enthusiastic about *Southtown*, reporting that the author "slips badly in handling his characters." Some critics also had reservations about the next Navarre novel, *Mission Road*, which a *Publishers*

Cover of Rick Riordan's novel *The Lightning Thief*, featuring artwork by John Rocco.

Weekly reviewer described as a "relatively weak" installment. In this tale, Navarre tries to prove the innocence of former criminal Ralph Arguello, whose wife has been murdered and who police believe to be guilty both of that crime and of another killing eighteen years before. The *Publishers Weekly* critic felt that Riordan falls back too much on "sitcom-like" characterizations, while a *Kirkus Reviews* writer declared the novel to be merely "competent." In stark contrast to these opinions, Mike Shea asserted in *Texas Monthly* that *Mission Road* is "the most fully realized of [Riordan's] six Tres Navarre novels."

In *Rebel Island,* Tres has just retired as a private investigator and has married Maia, his longtime girlfriend. Although he is talked into a honeymoon on Rebel Island, located in the Texas Gulf, by his brother Garret, it is hardly the romantic time Tres was looking forward to. In the midst of a hurricane, a U.S. marshal at the hotel is killed and soon the body count mounts in this "entertaining" crime novel, as a *Publishers Weekly* contributor termed it. Similarly, Steve Glassman, writing for *Booklist,* thought that the author's "strong narrative voice . . . is alive in well in this thriller." Further praise came from *Fresh Fiction* reviewer Brenda Wilch, who termed *Rebel Island* "a fast-paced mystery."

Riordan started branching out as an author in his first nonseries adult title, *Cold Springs.* Still drawing on his experience as an educator in California and Texas, the author writes about a former teacher named Chadwick who has left San Francisco to work at Laurel Heights boarding school in rural Texas. The school is really a boot camp for disturbed students, many of whom have problems with drugs and violence. Chadwick himself is a troubled figure, having lost his own daughter, Katherine, to a drug overdose. To make things even more complicated, Chadwick is in love with the head of the school, Ann Zedman, for whom he was about to leave his wife when his daughter died. Matters become worse when Ann's own daughter comes to the school and Chadwick learns that a series of killings might lead all the way back to Katherine's death. A *Publishers Weekly* contributor commended *Cold Springs,* especially for its "believable and absorbing" characters.

Updating the Greek Myths

With *The Lightning Thief,* Riordan ventures farther afield with a fantasy novel for young readers. Despite the abrupt change in genre, critics had considerable praise for this novel about a dyslexic boy who discovers that he is the son of the god Poseidon. In the author's hands, the Greek gods of classical literature are all alive and well and very active in the modern world. Young Percy (short for Perseus) Jackson is thrust into their complex machinations and rivalries when he is charged with locating Zeus's lightning bolt, which the king of the gods believes was stolen by Percy's father. *Booklist* contributor Chris Sherman called the story "fresh, dangerous, and funny," and Patricia D. Lothrop wrote in the *School Library Journal* that it is "an adventure-quest with a hip edge."

Riordan developed the concept for his Greek mythology fantasy as the result of a creative-writing project he developed when he was a sixth-grade teacher. He had his students "create their own demigod hero, the son or daughter of any god they wanted, and have them describe a Greek-style quest for that hero," as he explained in an interview on the *Miss Erin* Web log. When Riordan's son Haley was in the second grade and was studying some of the Greek myths, he asked his father one night to tell him bedtime stories about the Greek gods. Riordan had taught the myths for many years and began relating those tales. When he finished, Haley wanted more, and then Riordan remembered the creative writing project he had developed. At this time, Haley had just been diagnosed with ADHD and dyslexia, and Riordan was happy to see his son fix his attention on these stories of the Greek gods. He began to fabricate a modern retelling of the myths, focusing on a young boy named Percy, who also suffers from ADHD. Percy's quest was to retrieve the lightning bolt of Zeus from twenty-first-century America. Over several nights, Riordan spun out this tale, and then his son begged him to write it down. Thus was the genesis of *The Lightning Thief.*

Riordan continues his "Percy Jackson and the Olympians" series with *The Sea of Monsters.* This book finds Percy finishing up the seventh grade and preparing to attend a summer camp that is specially designed for children such as himself who are the product of one of the Greek gods and a mortal. However, before school even ends, strange things start to happen. First Percy has a horrible dream in which his friend Grover, a satyr, is in some kind of danger. Then the gym is attacked by monsters at his school. Teaming up with Tyson, a homeless boy who is also a Cyclops, and Annabeth, the daughter of Athena and a half-blood like himself, Percy heads to camp hoping to discover what is going on, only to find the camp itself under attack. The tree that serves as a guardian of the camp is dying and in order to heal it, Percy and his friends must find the legendary Golden Fleece. They take off in search of the Fleece with a little help from Hermes, and end up at the Sea of Monsters, a perilous place where they face danger after danger, many of which resemble the trials Odysseus tackled

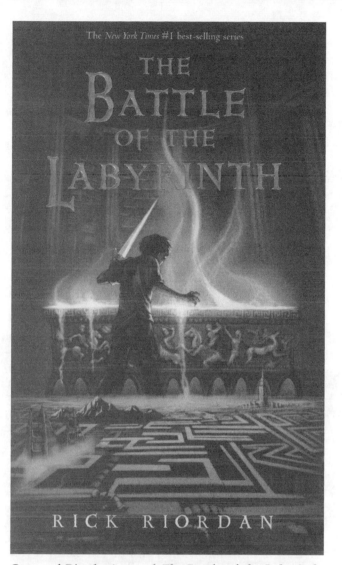

Cover of Riordan's novel *The Battle of the Labyrinth*, featuring artwork by John Rocco. (Illustration © 2006 by John Rocco. Reprinted by permission of Disney Book Group. All rights reserved.)

on his journey home after the Trojan War, though Riordan's characters are transported by way of the Bermuda Triangle.

The Sea of Monsters garnered generally strong reviews. Paula Rohrlick, writing in *Kliatt,* noted that the book is most enjoyable when read after its predecessor, but concluded that it is "an entertaining retelling of Greek myths, and a good bet for adventure and fantasy fans as well as reluctant readers." A contributor for *Kirkus Reviews* opined that in some instances the humor is a bit overly sophisticated for the book's intended readers, but concluded that "Percy's sardonic narration and derring-do will keep the pages turning." A reviewer in *Publishers*

Weekly declared that, "with humor, intelligence and expert pacing, the author uses this tale of believable teens and their high-stakes struggle to bring the mythical lore up to date."

In *The Titan's Curse*, the third work in the series, Percy, now fourteen, is dismayed to learn that his good friend Annabeth has vanished. She is not the only one, either. Artemis, goddess of the hunt, has also apparently gone missing. Along with his friend Grover, Percy sets out to join the search party, despite the promise of danger ahead and a disturbing prophecy that has been revealed by the Oracle. To make the situation worse, giant monsters of legend have begun to grow restless, rising from their sleep after thousands of years and threatening all of Olympus with certain destruction if Percy and his friends cannot stop them. *The Titan's Curse* introduces two new half-bloods as well, Nico and Bianca, who serve to further flesh out Percy's fighting force. Herald, again reviewing for *Booklist,* commented that "Riordan takes it from strength to strength with this exciting installment, adding even more depth to the characters." A contributor for *Kirkus Reviews* felt that "the contests between the gods will have readers wondering how literature can be this fun," and Alison Follos concluded in *School Library Journal* that, "all in all, *The Titan's Curse* is] a winner of Olympic proportions and a surefire read-aloud."

In *The Battle of the Labyrinth*, Riordan's fourth book in his "Percy Jackson and the Olympians" series, Percy learns that Kronos has plans to reassemble his body and, once at his full strength, take over the underworld to gain the support of all of the evil forces that dwell there. Along with Annabeth, and Rachel Elizabeth Dare—a mortal girl—Percy sets out into the mysterious labyrinth to put an end to Kronos's plot. Within the labyrinth's walls, the trio encounters all manner of adventures, including giants, the Sphinx, Daedalus, Hephaestus, Calypso, and Kronos himself. A contributor for *Kirkus Reviews* praised *The Battle of the Labyrinth*, noting that "the often-philosophical tale zips along with snappy dialogue, humor and thrilling action." Similar praise came from a *Publishers Weekly* reviewer who found this title, along with its three predecessors, to contain "high-octane clashes with dark forces, laced with hip humor and drama." Milligan, in a review of *The Battle of the Labyrinth*, also commended the entire series: "Aside from the hilarious puns, inane situations, the treasure trove of mythological allusions, and the breathtaking pace of the narrative, there is throughout all of these novels a strong undercurrent of relevance."

Riordan also created another winning young-adult title with his *Thirty-nine Clues: The Maze of Bones*, "a sensational mix of reading, online gaming, card-collecting, and even a grand-prize sweepstakes," according to *Booklist* contributor Ian Chipman. Ten books, each by a different author, are scheduled for this series, with Riordan providing the debut work. The story arc involves the legacy of Grace Cahill, a member of the world's richest family. She will give each descendant a million dollars or the opportunity to participate in the search for a world-shattering secret, receiving one of thirty-nine clues in this quest. "This ought to have as much appeal to parents as it does to kids," noted a *Publishers Weekly* contributor who described the work as "a rollicking good read."

If you enjoy the works of Rick Riordan, you may also want to check out the following books:

The Monkey's Raincoat, 1987, and other detective novels by Robert Crais.
One False Move, 1998, from the "Myron Bolitar" series by Harlen Coben.
The "Spencer" mysteries by Robert B. Parker, including *Bad Business*, 2004.

In an online interview for *Teen Libris*, Riordan expounded on the differences between writing for adult and young adults: "Writing for kids has taught me a lot about writing well. Kids insist on clear narrative, gripping plot, great characters, humor and action. Adults will put up with a lot of extraneous information. They will bear with you even if your storytelling gets sloppy. But not kids. They will let you know right away if you lose their interest. That's why I like writing for them. They keep me on my toes!" Riordan also encourages youngsters to write for themselves, and on the *Puffin Books Web site,* he offered a number of tips for aspiring authors: "Read a lot! This is where you'll get your inspiration, your 'fuel' for your writer's engine. Write a little bit every day. Writing is like a sport. The more you practice, the better you get. Don't get discouraged! Rejection is part of writing, but if you stick with it, you will succeed."

■ Biographical and Critical Sources

PERIODICALS

Booklist, May 1, 2001, Jenny McLarin, review of *The Devil Went down to Austin,* p. 1640; April 15, 2004, Connie Fletcher, review of *Southtown,* p. 1428; September 15, 2005, Chris Sherman, review of *The Lightning Thief,* p. 59; July 1, 2006, Diana Tixier Herald, review of *The Sea of Monsters,* p. 52; May 15, 2007, Diana Tixier Herald, review of *The Titan's Curse,* p. 62; August, 2007, Steve Glassman, review of *Rebel Island,* p. 48; October 15, 2008, Ian Chipman, review of *Thirty-nine Clues: The Maze of Bones,* p. 39.

Chicago Tribune, July 6, 1997, Dick Adler, review of *Big Red Tequila,* p. 7.

Guardian (London, England), June 9, 2007, Philip Ardagh, review of *The Titan's Curse.*

Horn Book, May-June, 2006, Anita L. Burkam, review of *The Sea of Monsters,* p. 326; May-June, 2006, Anita L. Burkam, review of *The Titan's Curse,* p. 290; July-August, 2008, Anita L. Burkam, review of *The Battle of the Labyrinth,* p. 456.

Houston Chronicle, September 13, 2007, Tom Pilkington, review of *Rebel Island.*

Journal Sentinel (Milwaukee, WI), June 1, 2007, Edward Nawotka, "Talking with Rick Riordan of Childhood Heroes Not Named Harry."

Kirkus Reviews, March 1, 2004, review of *Southtown,* p. 203; May 15, 2005, review of *Mission Road,* p. 566; April 1, 2006, review of *The Sea of Monsters,* p. 355; April 1, 2007, review of *The Titan's Curse;* April 1, 2008, review of *The Battle of the Labyrinth;* September 1, 2008, review of *Thirty-nine Clues.*

Kliatt, March 1, 2006, Paula Rohrlick, review of *The Sea of Monsters,* p. 16.

Publishers Weekly, March 23, 1998, review of *The Widower's Two-step,* p. 96; April 30, 2001, review of *The Devil Went down to Austin,* p. 59; April 7, 2003, review of *Cold Springs,* p. 45; April 5, 2004, review of *Southtown,* p. 44; May 16, 2005, review of *Mission Road,* p. 40; April 24, 2006, review of *The Sea of Monsters,* p. 61; June 18, 2007, review of *Rebel Island,* p. 34; April 14, 2008, review of *The Battle of the Labyrinth,* p. 55.

School Library Journal, August, 2005, Patricia D. Lothrop, review of *The Lightning Thief,* p. 134; May, 2006, Kathleen Isaacs, review of *The Sea of Monsters,* p. 135; May 1, 2007, Alison Follos, review of *The Titan's Curse,* p. 142; September 22, 2008, review of *Thirty-nine Clues,* p. 58.

Texas Monthly, July, 2005, Mike Shea, review of *Mission Road,* p. 64; June, 2007, "Rick Riordan," p. 60.

ONLINE

Bookreporter.com, http://www.bookreporter.com/ (May 7, 2004), "Rick Riordan."

Bri Meets Books Web log, http://bribookblog. blogspot.com/ (July 22, 2007), "Interview: Rick Riordan."

Cynsations Web log, http://cynthialeitichsmith. blogspot.com/ (December 27, 2005), "Author Interview: Rick Riordan on *The Lightning Thief*."

Fresh Fiction Web site, http://freshfiction.com/ (August 15, 2007), Brenda Wilch, review of *Rebel Island*.

Kidsreads.com, http://www.kidsreads.com/ (January 7, 2009), Norah Piehl, review of "The Titan's Curse."

Miss Erin Web log, http://misserinmarie.blogspot. com/ (March 24, 2007), interview with Riordan.

Mystery One Bookstore Web site, http://www. mysteryone.com/ (January 7, 2009), interview with Riordan.

Myth and Mystery: The Official Blog of Rick Riordan, http://rickriordan.blogspot.com (January 13, 2009).

New Mystery Reader Web site, http://www. newmysteryreader.com/ (January 7, 2009), Kathryn Lawson, review of "Rebel Island."

Percy Jackson Web site, http://www.percyjackson.co. uk/ (January 13, 2009).

Puffin Books Web site, http://www.puffin.co.uk/ (January 9, 2009), "Rick Riordan."

Rick Riordan Home Page, http://www.rickriordan. com (January 13, 2009).

San Antonio Express-News Online, May 4, 2008, Bryce Milligan, review of *The Battle of the Labyrinth*.

Scholastic Web site, http://www2.scholastic.com/ (January 13, 2009), "Rick Riordan."

Teen Libris Web site, http://www.teenlibris.com/ (January 7, 2009), "Rick Riordan."

Write Away Web site, http://www.writeaway.org. uk/ (January 7, 2009), Nikki Gamble, "Rick Riordan" (interview).*

Jennifer Roberson

■ Personal

Born October 26, 1953, in Kansas City, MO; daughter of Donald and Shera (a literary agent's reader) Roberson; married Mark O'Green (a designer-manager in the computer games systems), February 16, 1985 (divorced). *Education:* Northern Arizona University, B.S., 1982. *Religion:* Christian. *Hobbies and other interests:* Breeding and exhibiting Cardigan Welsh Corgis, mosaic artwork.

■ Addresses

Office—c/o Children of the Firstborn, 610 N. Alma School Rd., Ste. 18, Box 104, Chandler, AZ 85224. *Agent*—Russell Galen, Scovil Chichak Galen Literary Agency, 276 5th Ave., Ste. 708, New York, NY 10001. *E-mail*—jennifer@cheysuli.com.

■ Career

Writer and journalist. *Wyoming Eagle,* Cheyenne, investigative reporter, 1976; Farnam Companies, Phoenix, AZ, advertising copywriter, 1977; writer, 1982—. Speaker at schools, colleges, professional writers' organizations, and science-fiction conferences.

■ Member

Cardigan Welsh Corgi Club of America, Flagstaff Kennel Club.

■ Awards, Honors

Named best new fantasy author, *Romantic Times,* 1984, for *Shapechangers;* Junior Alumni Achievement Award, Northern Arizona University, 1985; named best new historical author, *Romantic Times,* 1987; named outstanding young woman of America, 1988; reviewer's choice annual top fantasy novel designation, *Science Fiction Chronicle,* 1989, for *Sword-Dancer* and *Sword-Singer,* and 1990, for *Sword-Maker;* certificate of appreciation, City of Tempe, AZ, 1990, for outstanding volunteer service to the community; Jubilee Year Distinguished Alumnus Award, Northern Arizona University, 1990.

■ Writings

"CHRONICLES OF THE CHEYSULI" FANTASY SERIES

Shapechangers, DAW (New York, NY), 1984.
The Song of Homana, DAW (New York, NY), 1985.
Legacy of the Sword, DAW (New York, NY), 1986.
Track of the White Wolf, DAW (New York, NY), 1987.
A Pride of Princes, DAW (New York, NY), 1988.
Daughter of the Lion, DAW (New York, NY), 1989.
Flight of the Raven, DAW (New York, NY), 1990.
A Tapestry of Lions, DAW (New York, NY), 1992.
Shapechanger's Song (contains *Shapechangers* and *The Song of Homana*), DAW (New York, NY), 2001.

Legacy of the Wolf (contains *Legacy of the Sword* and *Track of the White Wolf*), DAW (New York, NY), 2001.

The Lion Throne (contains *A Pride of Princes* and *Daughter of the Lion*), DAW (New York, NY), 2001.

Children of Lion (contains *Flight of the Raven* and *A Tapestry of Lions*), DAW (New York, NY), 2001.

"SWORD-DANCER SAGA" FANTASY SERIES

Sword-Dancer, DAW (New York, NY), 1986.
Sword-Singer, DAW (New York, NY), 1988.
Sword-Maker, DAW (New York, NY), 1989.
Sword-Breaker, DAW (New York, NY), 1991.
Sword-Born, DAW (New York, NY), 1998.
Sword-Sworn, DAW (New York, NY), 2002.

The Novels of Tiger and Del: Volume 1 (includes *Sword-Dancer* and *Sword-Singer*), DAW (New York, NY), 2006.

The Novels of Tiger and Del: Volume 2 (includes *Sword-Maker* and *Sword-Breaker*), DAW (New York, NY), 2006.

The Novels of Tiger and Del: Volume 3 (includes *Sword-Born* and *Sword-Sworn*), DAW (New York, NY), 2006.

"KARAVANS" FANTASY SERIES

Karavans, DAW (New York, NY), 2006.
Deepwood, DAW (New York, NY), 2007.

OTHER

Smoketree (romantic suspense), Walker & Co. (New York, NY), 1985.

(Under pseudonym Jay Mitchell) *Kansas Blood*, Zebra Books (New York, NY), 1986.

(As Jennifer O'Green) *Royal Captive*, Dell (New York, NY), 1987.

Lady of the Forest, Zebra Books (New York, NY), 1992.

(With Melanie Rawn and Kate Elliot) *The Golden Key*, DAW (New York, NY), 1996.

(Editor) *Return to Avalon: A Celebration of Marion Zimmer Bradley*, DAW (New York, NY), 1996.

Lady of the Glen: A Novel of Seventeenth-Century Scotland and the Massacre of Glencoe, Kensington (New York, NY), 1996.

Highlander: Scotland the Brave, Warner Books (New York, NY), 1996.

(Editor) *Highwaymen: Robbers and Rogues*, DAW (New York, NY), 1997.

Lady of Sherwood, Kensington (New York, NY), 1999.

(Editor) *Out of Avalon: Tales of Old Magic and New Myths*, New American Library (New York, NY), 2001.

Guinevere's Truth and Other Tales, Five Star (Waterville, ME), 2008.

Work represented in anthologies, including *Sword and Sorceress*, Volumes 1-8, edited by Marion Zimmer Bradley, DAW (New York, NY), 1984-91; *Spell Singers*, edited by A.B. Newcomer, DAW, 1988; *Herds of Thunder, Manes of Gold*, edited by Bruce Coville, Doubleday (New York, NY), 1989; *Horse Fantastic*, edited by Martin Greenberg and Rosalind Greenberg, DAW, 1991; *Christmas Bestiary*, edited by M. Greenberg and R. Greenberg, DAW, 1992; *The Merlin Chronicles*, 1995; *Tales from Jabba's Palace*, 1995; *Tales from the Mos Eisley Cantina*, 1995; *Return to Avalon*, 1996; and *DAW's 30th Anniversary Fantasy Anthology*, edited by Elizabeth W. Wollheim and Sheila E. Gilbert, DAW, 2002.

Columnist, under name Jennifer Roberson O'Green, for *Corgi Quarterly* and *AKC Gazette*; contributor to periodicals, including *Fantasy, Writer*, and *Aboriginal Science Fiction*.

Roberson's works have been published in France, Japan, China, Poland, England, Israel, Russia, Italy, Sweden, and Germany.

■ Adaptations

Several of Roberson's novels have been optioned for film rights.

■ Sidelights

Jennifer Roberson is the author of over two dozen fantasy novels, the bulk of which are published in three main series: "Chronicles of the Cheysuli," the "Sword-Dancer Saga," and "Karavans." These fantasy worlds are distinct from one another, but all share the author's unique and at times, feminist vision. She has, in addition to her series work, written several well-received historical novels, including the companion pieces about Maid Marian and Robin Hood, *Lady of the Forest* and *Lady of Sherwood*, as well as the Scottish tale of a bloody battle between clans, *Lady of the Glen: A Novel of Seventeenth-Century Scotland and the Massacre of Glencoe*. Roberson has also written numerous short stories for anthologies and her own collections, such as *Guinevere's Truth and Other Tales*. Writing for *Suite*

101.com, Debbie Ledesma termed Roberson "a talented story teller, filling her novels with memorable characters, adventure, romance and many other qualities that bring readers to explore her wonderful Fantasy worlds." In her novels and short stories, as a *Publishers Weekly* reviewer noted, "Roberson quietly illuminates the fascinating, terrifying and perhaps inevitable gulf between women's destinies and men's desires."

Born in 1953, in Kansas City, Missouri, Roberson and her family moved to Phoenix, Arizona, when she was four, and she grew up in that emerging Southwest city. Roberson had the perfect environment for the development of a writer: a family of readers and a mother who was a professional reader for a literary agent. As Roberson once commented, "I was fortunate to grow up in a family of readers; our genealogical chart is filled with bookaholics, including the renowned English author Thomas Hardy. An only child of divorced parents, I discovered very young that siblings and best friends were available at all times between the pages of favorite novels. It was not at all unusual for three generations—grandfather, mother, and daughter—to gather in the living room and wile away the hours engrossed in our books of the moment."

An Early Interest in Writing

Her family's supportive environment also helped foster Roberson's enjoyment of writing. By age fourteen, she had already completed her first novel and received her first rejection slip. This desire to write was also fueled by one particular incident, as she related to a contributor for *Literaturschock:* "When I was 14, I read a book about a girl and her horse written by a local author. I felt it could have been much better, and told my mother I could write a better one. She challenged me to do it. So I wrote my first novel. It was never published, though." Even though Roberson was hurt by the rejection, she did not allow it to quell her desire to become an author. During the next years, she wrote three more unpublished novels before settling into the fantasy genre. Her first fantasy series, "Chronicles of Cheysuli," was begun while in college; it was during her final semester, while studying in England, that she received notice of the sale of her first book, *Shapechangers.*

Shapechangers was followed by seven other novels in the series, including *Legacy of the Sword* and *Flight of the Raven.* The Cheysuli are a race of people in which each member has the power to communicate with a given animal through telepathy as well as the power to assume that animal's form. The series chronicles the struggles between the oppressed Cheysuli—banished by a jealous ruler after his wife left him for his bodyguard—and a race called the Ihlini. The story continues over several generations, with many love affairs and rivalries as well as much use of sorcery and supernatural power. The story progression is in part propelled by a prophecy that one day a child will be born that will unite the many warring groups. Each successive tale in the series thus brings that generation closer to the realization of the prophecy. "The action is swift, constant and exciting," commented Debora Hill in the *St. James Guide to Fantasy Writers.* Roberson's original series featuring the Cheysuli concluded with *A Tapestry of Lions.* However, when editing an omnibus edition for the series about a decade after the publication of that title, she was inspired to revisit her fantasy world again and saw how the series could be expanded to investigate the further adventures of some of the major characters. More volumes in the series are expected.

Of Swords and Sorcery

Roberson is noted for creating strong female characters, both in her "Chronicles of Cheysuli," series and the "Sword-Dancer Saga" books, her next series. Roberson has said she wanted to feature characters who would help break the traditional, sexist female role that had often been assigned by other fantasy authors. The novelist once explained: "I wanted to write about a man who, in meeting up with a strong, competent woman in the same line of work, has his consciousness raised during a dangerous journey that taxes them physically as well as emotionally. My personal description was 'Conan the Barbarian meets Gloria Steinem'; the true title was *Sword-Dancer*, and it was published in 1986."

Roberson has since written five other novels featuring what she calls "my Tracy/Hepburn-like duo"— Tiger, a male sword-dancer, or soldier of fortune, and Delilah (Del for short), a female sword-dancer. When they meet, Del is wanted for killing the man who trained her in the art of sword-fighting. She also is searching for her brother, who was taken prisoner by a band of criminals who murdered their parents and raped Del. Over the course of the series, Tiger joins Del in the quest for her brother and on her journey to face her accusers. Along the way, they meet demonic dogs, powerful wizards, false messiahs, and various other strange beings that inhabit their desolate world. "It adds up to a thoroughly enjoyable and well-written series, with pleasing characters and situations," Hill observed.

Sword-Sworn, the final title in the series, finds Tiger and Del taking refuge on the island of Skandi, where the ultimate battle between Tiger and Abbu

Bensir, who has pursued him for years, takes place, and where Del finally recognizes her true feelings for Tiger. Roberson explains in an endnote why she chose to tell the stories in the first person, and writes that she has been pleased by the male readers who have contacted her to tell her that the series has changed their view of women. As a *Publishers Weekly* contributor wrote, "Sensitive readers of both sexes should appreciate how Roberson rises above the usual genre cliches."

From Sherwood Forest to the Scottish Highlands

Roberson expanded her work into other genres by writing a Western novel from a woman's viewpoint and then a contemporary romantic suspense novel.

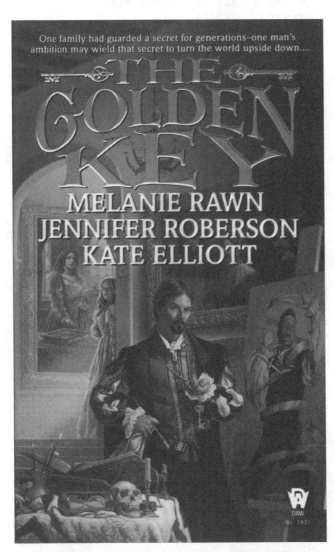

Cover of *The Golden Key*, a novel coauthored by Jennifer Roberson and featuring cover art by Michael Whelan. (Daw Books, 1997. Copyright © 1996 by Melanie Rawn, Jennifer Roberson, and Kate Elliott. All rights reserved. Reproduced by permission.)

"But one thing I'd always wanted to try—another 'someday' dream—was a big, sprawling, mainstream historical epic," she once remarked. . . . I proposed to write a reinterpretation of the Robin Hood legend, but with a twist—I wanted to emphasize Marian's point of view and contribution to the legend." The result was *Lady of the Forest*, which took Roberson a year to research and write. She described it as "in actuality, a 'prequel' to the familiar legend. I wanted very much to write the story of how the legend came to be; the tale of how seven very different people from a rigidly stratified social structure came to join together to fight the inequities of medieval England. To me, the key was *logic*—I interwove historical fact with the fantasy of the classic legend, and developed my own interpretation of how things came to be. I wanted to come to know all of these people; to climb inside their heads and learn what motivated them to do what they did." Reviewing the novel in *Library Journal*, Betsy Larson remarked that "Roberson's extensive research is apparent throughout, yet she does not overwhelm the reader with facts." Larson further praised the "colorful and active" writing that made *Lady of the Forest* "difficult to put . . . down."

In *Lady of Sherwood*, Roberson returns to the characters Marian and Robin Hood to tell the story of what happened after the death of King Richard the Lionhearted, the monarch who had pardoned the Robin Hood gang for their robberies. Suddenly, the sheriff of Nottingham is once again on their trail. Writing in *Library Journal*, Jackie Cassada noted that Marian and Robin Hood "strive to hold onto their love without sacrificing their honor" in this "rousing story." A reviewer for *Publishers Weekly* praised Roberson's portrayal of Marian in particular, finding the character to be "thoroughly independent but not burdened with anachronistic feminist ways." Also impressive, the reviewer continued, is Roberson's "incorporation of historical detail" and her presentation of Marian and Robin's relationship. "Exciting and satisfying," the same contributor concluded, "Roberson's genre-blending novel may be her best yet."

Roberson also sets historical romances and fantasies in the rugged countryside of Scotland. With *Lady of the Glen*, she offers the story of Cat Campbell and Dair MacDonald. King William has issued an order to destroy the MacDonald clan, and this provides the background for their romance. A *Publishers Weekly* reviewer described this book as "a pleasure." *Highlander: Scotland the Brave*, features protagonist Highlander Duncan MacLeod (from the 1990s film series), who shares a past with giant, red-headed Shakespearean actor James Douglas. *Magazine of*

Fantasy and Science Fiction contributor Michelle West wrote that "the prose is taut and clean, staccato when it needs to be, and lyrical when it can."

Roberson collected a quarter-century's worth of short stories in *Guinevere's Truth and Other Tales.* Here are tales from the fantasy worlds of Roberson's series and from other inspirations, including Arthurian legend. Writing for *Genre Go Round Reviews,* Harriet Klausner noted that the volume contains "twenty well-written feminist fantasy tales from an author renowned as one of best authors of the sub-genre." Likewise, *Library Journal* reviewer Cassada commented that *Guinevere's Truth and Other Tales* "offers a sampling of high fantasy, sword and sorcery, and modern myth by the multitalented author."

Return to Series Fiction

In 2006 Roberson began a new fantasy-adventure series, "Karavans." In an online interview for *Fantasy Book Critic,* Roberson expounded on her techniques for setting up a new series or novel: "I definitely work up a rough outline for major plot and subplot issues, and I know what the ending will be, but then I turn my imagination loose. I'm a very organic writer, and I'm well aware that my subconscious often has more intriguing ideas than my outline does! I absolutely give myself the freedom to jettison outline elements on the fly, and to let the story go off in a new direction if the momentum carries me that way."

Karavans is the first book in Roberson's series. The land of Sancorra has been conquered by the Hecari, and a pregnant Audrun, her husband, Davyd, and their four children, journey aboard a "karavan" to a new land that proves to be even more dangerous. The karavan guide, Rhuan, has promised to protect them, and Ilona, who is a palm reader, fears that much danger lies ahead, including the threat of a living forest that is home to magical and threatening creatures. *Booklist* contributor Frieda Murray wrote that "high-quality characterization and world building abet Roberson's novel conception," and a *Publishers Weekly* reviewer added further praise by noting that "the pieces are in place for what promises to be a story of epic proportions."

Roberson carried her "Karavans" series forward with *Deepwood,* in which the magical living forest from the first installment is featured. Alisanos, a sentient, mysterious forest that captures humans and transforms them into nightmarish beasts, surrounds Audrun and her family. Audrun and her children (increased in number to five after Audrun has given premature birth to a daughter) are separated now from Davyd and team with Rhuan, their guide, to fight off the deepwood that attacks them. Murray, writing in *Booklist,* had praise for this series addition, citing "lots of action, competently drawn characters, and a world in which anything can happen." Similarly, a *Publishers Weekly* reviewer concluded that "readers will be impatient to see what happens in the next volume."

If you enjoy the works of Jennifer Roberson, you may also want to check out the following books:

Marion Zimmer Bradley, *The Mists of Avalon,* 1982.
Will Shetterly, *Elsewhere,* 1991.
Michael Stackpole, *A Secret Atlas,* 2005.

Roberson once remarked: "One thing I have learned along the way is that a writer, to be successful, must *write;* she cannot be satisfied with what she has already done, but must look ahead to what she will do. A writer completely satisfied with her work ceases to grow, and stunts her talent. It is far more important to *write* than it is *to have written.*" Roberson further told the *Fantasy Book Critic* online interviewer that she believes her work has demonstrated her development as an author, stating, "I feel I have grown and matured tremendously as a writer, in the technical sense. . . . I work hard to improve at least one element of my writing with every book. I constantly push myself to be better than last time. . . . I was a reader long before I became a writer, and I know what it means to find an author whose work you love. I am grateful when my work can transport readers to another world in the same fashion certain books transported me away from the mundane."

■ Biographical and Critical Sources

BOOKS

St. James Guide to Fantasy Writers, St. James Press (Detroit, MI), 1996.

PERIODICALS

Booklist, April 15, 2006, Frieda Murray, review of *Karavans*, p. 34; July 1, 2007, Frieda Murray, review of *Deepwood*, p. 41; December 1, 2008, Frieda Murray, review of *Guinevere's Truth and Other Tales*, p. 38.

Library Journal, February 15, 1984, Susan L. Nickerson, review of *Shapechangers*, p. 390; August 1, 1992, Betsy Larson, review of *Lady of the Forest*, p. 152; November 15, 1999, Jackie Cassada, review of *Lady of Sherwood*, p. 101; February 15, 2002, Jackie Cassada, review of *Sword-Sworn*, p. 181; November 15, 2008, Jackie Cassada, review of *Guinevere's Truth and Other Tales*, p. 64.

Magazine of Fantasy and Science Fiction, April, 1997, Michelle West, review of *Highlander: Scotland the Brave*, p. 132.

Publishers Weekly, February 26, 1996, review of *Lady of the Glen: A Novel of Seventeenth-Century Scotland and the Massacre of Glencoe*, p. 87; August 19, 1996, review of *The Golden Key*, p. 57; November 1, 1999, review of *Lady of Sherwood*, p. 78; January 7, 2002, review of *Sword-Sworn*, p. 51; February 27, 2006, review of *Karavans*, p. 38; May 15, 2006, Kaite Mediatore Stover, "Happily Ever After," June 11, 2007, review of *Deepwood*, p. 43; September 22, 2008, review of *Guinevere's Truth and Other Tales*, p. 42.

Science Fiction Chronicle, December, 1986, review of *Legacy of the Sword*, p. 50; January, 1987, review of *Sword Dancer*, p. 40; October, 1987, review of *The Song of Homana*, p. 27; December, 1989, review of *Sword-Singer*, p. 39.

ONLINE

Fantasy Book Critic Web log, http://fantasybookcritic.blogspot.com/ (March 23, 2007) interview with Roberson.

Genre Go Round Reviews online, http://genregoroundreviews.blogspot.com/ (October 6, 2008), Harriet Klausner, review of *Guinevere's Truth and Other Tales*.

Jennifer Roberson Home Page, http://www.cheysuli.com (January 10, 2009).

Literaturschock Web site, http://www.literaturschock.de/ (February 2, 2002), interview with Roberson.

SFReviews.net, http://www.sfreviews.net/ (March 3, 2007), review of *Karavans*.

Suite101.com, http://www.suite101.com/ (March 17, 2000), Debbie Ledesma, "Jennifer Roberson."*

Sax Rohmer

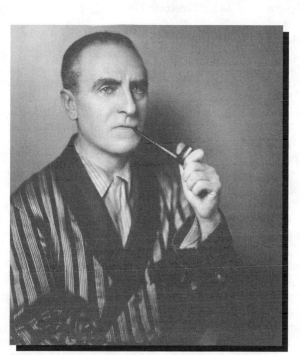

(Photograph © by Bettmann/Corbis.)

■ Personal

Born Arthur Henry Ward, February 15, 1883, in Birmingham, Warwickshire, England; died in London, England, June 1, 1959, from complications following a bout of Asiatic flu; son of William (an engineer) and Margaret Mary Ward; married Rose Elizabeth Knox, January 14, 1909.

■ Career

British novelist, playwright, journalist, and songwriter. Also worked briefly as a bank clerk and held other administrative positions. *Commercial Intelligencer,* London, England, cub reporter. *Military service:* British military intelligence, attained rank of officer.

■ Member

Hermetic Order of the Golden Dawn.

■ Awards, Honors

The Sax Rohmer Society was founded in 1968.

■ Writings

(Published anonymously) *Pause!*, Greening (London, England), 1910.

The Mystery of Dr. Fu-Manchu, Methuen (London, England), 1913, published as *The Insidious Dr. Fu-Manchu,* McBride, Nast (New York, NY), 1913.

The Sins of Severac Bablon, Cassell (London, England), 1914.

The Romance of Sorcery, Methuen (London, England), 1914.

The Yellow Claw, McBride, Nast (New York, NY), 1915.

The Devil Doctor, Methuen (London, England), 1916, published as *The Return of Dr. Fu-Manchu,* McBride (New York, NY), 1916.

The Exploits of Captain O'Hagan, Jarrolds (London, England), 1916.

The Si-Fan Mysteries, Methuen (London, England), 1917, published as *The Hand of Fu-Manchu,* McBride (New York, NY), 1917.

Brood of the Witch-Queen, Pearson (London, England), 1918.

Tales of Secret Egypt, Methuen (London, England), 1918.

The Orchard of Tears, Methuen (London, England), 1918.

The Quest of the Sacred Slipper, Pearson (London, England), 1919.

Dope: A Story of Chinatown and the Drug Traffic, Cassell (London, England), 1919.

The Golden Scorpion, Methuen (London, England), 1919.

The Dream Defective, Being Some Account of the Methods of Moris Klaw, Jarrolds (London, England), 1920, Doubleday, Page (New York, NY), 1925.

The Green Eyes of Bast, Cassell (London, England), 1920.

The Haunting of Low Fennel, Pearson (London, England), 1920.

Bat-Wing, Cassell (London, England), 1921, Doubleday, Page (New York, NY), 1921.

Fire-Tongue, Cassell (London, England), 1921, Doubleday, Page (New York, NY), 1922.

Tales of Chinatown, Cassell (London, England), 1922, Doubleday, Page (New York, NY), 1922.

Grey Face, Cassell (London, England), 1924, Doubleday, Page (New York, NY), 1924.

Yellow Shadows, Cassell (London, England), 1925, Doubleday, Page (New York, NY), 1926.

Moon of Madness, Doubleday, Page (New York, NY), 1927.

She Who Sleeps, Doubleday, Doran (New York, NY), 1928.

The Emperor of America, Doubleday, Doran (New York, NY), 1929.

The Day the World Ended, Doubleday, Doran (New York, NY), 1930.

Daughter of Fu Manchu, Doubleday, Doran (New York, NY), 1931.

Yu'an Hee See Laughs, Doubleday, Doran (New York, NY), 1932.

Tales of East and West, Cassell (London, England), 1932, published with different contents, Doubleday, Doran (New York, NY), 1933.

The Mask of Fu Manchu, Doubleday, Doran (New York, NY), 1932.

Fu Manchu's Bride, Doubleday, Doran (New York, NY), 1933, published as *The Bride of Fu Manchu,* Cassell (London, England), 1933.

The Trail of Fu Manchu, Doubleday, Doran (New York, NY), 1934.

The Bat Flies Low, Doubleday, Doran (New York, NY), 1935.

President Fu Manchu, Doubleday, Doran (New York, NY), 1936.

White Velvet, Doubleday, Doran (New York, NY), 1936.

Salute to Bazarada and Other Stories, Cassell (London, England), 1939.

The Drums of Fu Manchu, Doubleday, Doran (New York, NY), 1939.

The Island of Fu Manchu, Doubleday, Doran (New York, NY), 1941.

Seven Sins, McBride (New York, NY), 1943.

Egyptian Nights, Hale (London, England), 1944, published as *Bimbashi Barak of Egypt,* McBride (New York, NY), 1944.

Shadow of Fu Manchu, Doubleday, Doran (New York, NY), 1948.

Hangover House, Random House (New York, NY), 1949.

Nude in Mink, Fawcett (New York, NY), 1950, published as *Sins of Sumuru,* Jenkins (London, England), 1950.

(As Michael Furey) *Wulfheim,* Jarrolds (London, England), 1950.

Sumuru, Fawcett (New York, NY), 1951, published as *Slaves of Sumuru,* Jenkins (London, England), 1952.

The Fire Goddess, Fawcett (New York, NY), 1952, published as *Virgin in Flames,* Jenkins (London, England), 1953.

The Moon Is Red, Jenkins (London, England), 1954.

Return of Sumuru, Fawcett (New York, NY), 1954, published as *Sand and Satin,* Jenkins (London, England), 1955.

Sinister Madonna, Jenkins (London, England), 1956.

Re-Enter Fu Manchu, Fawcett (New York, NY), 1957, published as *Re-Enter Dr. Fu Manchu,* Jenkins (London, England), 1957.

Emperor Fu Manchu, Jenkins (London, England), 1959.

The Secret of Holm Peel and Other Strange Stories, Ace (New York, NY), 1970.

The Wrath of Fu Manchu and Other Stories, Stacey (London, England), 1973.

The Fu-Manchu Omnibus: Volume One, Allison & Busby (London, England), 1997.

The Fu-Manchu Omnibus: Volume Two, Allison & Busby (London, England), 1997.

The Hand of Fu Manchu, edited by John Michael, toExcel (San Jose, CA), 1999.

The Return of Dr. Fu Manchu, edited by John Michael, toExcel (San Jose, CA), 1999.

The Fu-Manchu Omnibus: Volume Three, Allison & Busby (London, England), 2000.

The Fu-Manchu Omnibus: Volume Four, Allison & Busby (London, England), 2000.

PLAYS

(With Julian and Lauri Wylie) *Round in Fifty,* produced in London, England, 1922.

The Eye of Siva, produced in London, England, 1923.

Secret Egypt, produced in London, England, 1928.

(With Michael Martin-Harvey) *The Nightingale,* produced in London, England, 1947.

OTHER

(Uncredited) Harry Relph, *Little Tich: A Book of Travels and Wanderings,* Greening (London, England), 1911.

Contributor of numerous stories to a wide variety of pulp magazines and periodicals.

■ Adaptations

Many films have been made featuring the character of Dr. Fu Manchu. *The Mystery of Dr. Fu-Manchu* (15 two-reel episodes) was filmed by A.E. Coleby and Frank Wilson and released by Stoll in 1923; *The Further Mysteries of Fu Manchu* was filmed by Fred Paul and released by Stoll in 1924; *The Mysterious Dr. Fu Manchu* was filmed by Rowland V. Lee, starred Warner Oland, and was released by Paramount Pictures in 1929; *The Return of Fu Manchu* starred Oland and was released by Paramount Pictures in 1930; *Daughter of the Dragon* starred Oland and was released by Paramount in 1931; *The Mask of Fu Manchu* starred Boris Karloff, was filmed by Charles Brabin, and was released by Metro-Goldwyn-Mayer in 1932; *The Drums of Fu Manchu* was filmed by John English and William Witney and released by Republic Pictures in 1940 and 1943; *The Face of Fu Manchu* starred Christopher Lee, was filmed by Don Sharp, and was released by Seven Arts in 1965; *The Brides of Fu Manchu* starred Lee, was filmed by Don Sharp, and was released by Seven Arts in 1966; *The Vengeance of Fu Manchu* starred Lee, was filmed by Harry Alan Towers, and was released in 1968; *The Blood of Fu Manchu* starred Lee, was filmed by Harry Alan Towers, and was released in 1969; *The Castle of Fu Manchu* starred Lee, was filmed by Harry Alan Towers, and was released in 1969; *The Fiendish Plot of Fu Manchu*, a comedy, starred Peter Sellers and was released by Warner Bros. in 1980; the film *The Children of Fu Manchu* was scheduled for release in 2009. *The Adventures of Fu Manchu*, a television series, was filmed by Hollywood Television Productions and broadcast 1955-56.

The Yellow Claw was filmed by Rene Plaisetty in 1921. The "Sumuru" series inspired the films *The Million Eyes of Sumuru*, 1967, *The Seven Secrets of Sumuru*, 1969, and *Sumuru*, 2003.

Some of Rohmer's stories were adapted for radio, including *The Day the World Ended*, 1929, *Daughter of Fu Manchu*, 1930, and *Yu'an Hee See Laughs*, 1931; the *Fu Manchu* radio show was broadcast on CBS, 1932-33; the *Dr. Fu Manchu* radio show was broadcast in England, 1936-38; *The Shadow of Fu Manchu*, a syndicated radio show, was broadcast 1939-40; *The Insidious Dr. Fu-Manchu* was adapted for an episode of the *NBC Molle Mystery Theatre*, 1944. The "Fu Manchu" daily comic strip, distributed by the Bell Syndicate, appeared 1931-33.

■ Sidelights

Contemporary thriller writers owe a debt of gratitude to the English author who wrote under the pen name of Sax Rohmer. His creation of the clever and evil Dr. Fu Manchu initiated the trope of the maniacal and sinister character intent on world domination. No small prizes for Fu Manchu; instead, he wants the entire world. His character gave rise to the larger-than-life villains cast in Ian Fleming's "James Bond" novels and to countless other adversaries in the pages of thriller fiction. The baker's dozen of "Fu Manchu" novels found their way into popular culture through books, comics, radio, movies, and later television, making Rohmer one of the most popular and successful novelists of the early twentieth century. In Fu Manchu and his adversaries, Denis Nayland Smith and sidekick, Dr. Petrie (named after noted Egyptologist Flinders Petrie), and in the beautiful and enigmatic Karamaneh, Rohmer created archetypes of evil vs. good that captivated the reading public on both sides of the Atlantic.

Twenty-nine years of age when he created Fu Manchu, Rohmer went back to the creative well with this character off and on for almost half a century. Despite his successes, however, Rohmer, like one of the minor bumbling characters of his fiction, lived in near poverty at times because of his business ineptitude. In addition to the novels featuring Fu Manchu, Rohmer also wrote over a score of other mysteries featuring detectives such as Gaston Max, Morris Klaw (who used occult powers to solve his crimes), the female sleuth Sumuru, Paul Harley, and Chief Inspector Red Kerry, among others. Yet it is for Fu Manchu, the Chinese mastermind criminal, that Rohmer is remembered. The tales and novels featuring him proved so popular with audiences that the name of Rohmer came to be synonymous with that of his sinister protagonist. Thus, according to *Dictionary of Literary Biography* contributor Will Murray, Rohmer "owes his continued renown principally to the international popularity of the character of Dr. Fu Manchu, whom he created in 1911."

Early Interests Lead to Writing

Rohmer was born Arthur Henry Ward to Irish parents living in Birmingham, England, in 1883. William and Margaret Mary Ward and their family moved to London when Rohmer was a young child, and he left school in 1901, the year that his mother, an alcoholic, died. About this time, also, Rohmer adopted the middle name of Sarsfield and stopped

Warner Oland starred as Sax Rohmer's scheming mastermind in the 1929 film version of *The Mysterious Dr. Fu Manchu.* (Photograph © by John Springer Collection/Corbis.)

using the name Henry. His mother had told the young Rohmer that she was descended from a famous Irish general named Patrick Sarsfield, precipitating this first name change. Rohmer went to work first as a bank clerk, having failed the civil service examination. After leaving his bank job, he tried his hand at writing, but his short stories were rejected by all the London magazines. Thereafter he worked in lowly jobs for several businesses before serving, for a time, as a reporter for the *Commercial Intelligence,* a weekly newspaper. Meanwhile, Rohmer was also educating himself in his chosen fields: Egyptology, Islamic culture, and also the Orient. He began to collect a personal library of Egyptology as well as books on occult subjects. A life-long seeker of occult knowledge, he eventually became a member of the Hermetic Order of the Golden Dawn, among whose members were Aleister Crowley and William Butler Yeats. He is also reputed to have been a member of the Rosicrucians.

Despite early failures with his short stories, Rohmer continued to write and at age twenty, his first story, "The Mysterious Mummy," was accepted by *Pearson's Magazine.* Although the story was never actu-

ally published, it broke Rohmer's streak of rejection, and he was soon publishing stories in many British magazines. His second story appeared in *Chambers's Journal* in 1904. "Both stories were steeped in mysticism and showed evidence of Rohmer's interest in Egyptology," Murray noted. These early tales were published under the pen name Sarsfield Ward. He had enough success with these tales to prompt an editor from *Pearson's Magazine* to commission three stories, a sale that promptly gave Rohmer a case of writer's block. In an attempt to break this block with new material, he set out for Holland and when he returned he began using a new pseudonym: Sax Rohmer. He continued to write under both Ward and Rohmer until about 1912, after which he published exclusively as Rohmer. Most of these early stories focused on his personal interest in psychic phenomenon and the occult, of which he had strong beliefs. These themes would show up later in his work, culminating in a nonfiction book titled *The Romance of Sorcery,* a historical treatise of the occult.

The Birth, Death, and Resurrection of Fu Manchu

In 1909 Rohmer married Rose Elizabeth Knox, but because of his small earnings at the time, they kept the marriage secret for two years and also lived apart. Finally, however, the couple was able to take up residence in London. Rohmer's big break occurred in 1913 when a collection of his short stories was published as a novel *The Mystery of Dr. Fu-Manchu* (published in the United States as *The Insidious Dr. Fu-Manchu*). The work was an instant hit with readers, and Rohmer achieved the financial success he needed to support himself and his wife. From that time forward Rohmer continued writing "Fu Manchu" novels. The character became so famous that readers demanded its consistent return, and publishers pressured Ward to produce novels featuring Fu Manchu.

Fu Manchu was inspired by an individual known as Mr. King, supposedly a notorious gambler and drug dealer in Limehouse, London's Chinatown district. Rohmer reported that he saw the man in the flesh one night while researching an article in Chinatown. The sight of King gave the writer a real-life picture of Fu Manchu's characteristics. Rohmer's next two novels, *The Devil Doctor,* published in 1916, and *The Si-Fan Mysteries,* published in 1917, both feature Fu Manchu pitted against his nemesis, British agent Denis Nayland Smith. As Murray noted: "The books are, in essence, an extended narrative of two adversaries. . . . When introduced, Fu Manchu is the agent of a Chinese secret society with sinister political aims, and Nayland Smith . . .

Boris Karloff takes a turn as Rohmer's famous character in the film *The Mask of Fu Manchu.* (Photograph courtesy of MGM/Kobal Collection/The Picture Desk, Inc.)

is an agent of the British government." Murray further explained: "Over the years, as Fu Manchu becomes head of the Si-Fan and Nayland Smith is knighted, their relationship remains bitter but always mutually respectful."

This dynamic between Rohmer's characters prompted some critics to compare the "Fu Manchu" stories to those of Arthur Conan Doyle, with his famous characters Sherlock Holmes and Dr. Moriarty. As Conan Doyle had done to Sherlock Holmes, Rohmer kills off Fu Manchu in *The Si-Fan Mysteries*, but the character made a literary comeback due to popular demand.

Despite the presence of Smith and other adversaries, it is Fu Manchu who is the featured protagonist. This was not a new device in thriller or mystery fic-tion in its day, nor was Rohmer the only one using the "Yellow Peril" fears of the day to posit a devil-ishly clever Chinese plot for world domination. However, Rohmer's genius, a contributor noted in the *St. James Guide to Crime & Mystery Writers*, "was to find just the right variations on the theme, the proper ingredients for widespread popular success. First of all, Rohmer provided an assortment of vividly described and exotically appointed settings for his stories: perfumed apartments, strewn with cushions, furnished with carved teakwood tables and lacquer cabinets, and lit by brass lamps of strange design. Against such backgrounds the vil-lains' whispered threats and the confidences of imperiled heroines seemed not at all out of place." As Murray further noted, "Rohmer produced unforgettable results, as witnessed by the fact that his Fu Manchu stories have remained in print."

Rohmer's famous character has a new face—Christopher Lee—in the 1966 film *The Brides of Fu Manchu*. (Photograph courtesy of the Kobal Collection/The Picture Desk, Inc.)

In the following years Rohmer explored different literary forms, including plays and screenplays. While he achieved a certain amount of success in other genres, he eventually returned to the novel. Although critics would offer praise for certain works, but these departures from Fu Manchu were not well received by Rohmer's audience. The author achieved some literary success with his novel *Brood of the Witch-Queen*, published in 1918, which drew upon his personal interest in the occult. Here the main character discovers sorcery secrets of ancient Egypt and uses them destructively. Rohmer's other pursuits included a musical parody of Jules Verne's *Around the World in Eighty Days*, titled *Round in Fifty*; the play *Secret Egypt*; and two collections of short stories, *The Haunting of Low Fennel* and *Tales of Chinatown*. However, his editor soon urged him to produce another "Fu Manchu" book, which resulted in *Daughter of Fu Manchu*, published in 1931, almost twenty years after the first "Fu Manchu" novel appeared. *Tales of Chinatown* involves the re-activation of the criminal organization, Si-Fan, by Fu Manchu's daughter, Fah Lo Suee. Fu Manchu himself does not appear in the novel until near the end.

During the decade that Rohmer retired Fu Manchu, his books were adapted as several films, increasing the demand for the sinister character. He followed *Daughter of Fu Manchu* with *The Mask of Fu Manchu*, about the title character's attempts to stir up trouble in the Middle East by posing as a long-dead Islamic prophet. The next in the series was *Fu Manchu's Bride*, which many consider to be the best of the "Fu Manchu" novels. It details Fu Manchu's desire to father a child with a white French woman, Fleurette, who is also wooed by the narrator, Alan Sterling. When *Trail of Fu Manchu* was published, *New York Times* critic Isaac Anderson spoke of the popularity of the series, yet also implied that it was growing stale: "The battle between Fu Manchu and Nayland will, presumably, go on as long as Sax Rohmer is able to punch the keys of a typewriter. It is all very exciting, but it is beginning to remind one a little too much of those screen and radio serial dramas that go on and on, world without end." This review reveals the paradox Rohmer faced during his entire literary career. While his editors and fans pushed for the continuation of Fu Manchu, Rohmer suffered some criticism for it. Following the publication of *President Fu Manchu* in 1936, another *New York Times* critic bemoaned that "the story is no more than stereotyped Sax Rohmer despite its flutter in politics of the near future." The novel focuses on Fu Manchu's thwarted attempt to take over the United States.

Peter Sellers turns the Fu Manchu character toward comedy in his film parody *The Fiendish Plot of Dr. Fu Manchu.* (Photograph courtesy of Orion/Playboy/Kobal Collection/The Picture Desk, Inc.)

Interestingly, there were also critics who would criticize Rohmer when Fu Manchu was missing from his work. With the publication of *White Velvet*, *New York Times* critic E.O. Beckwith stated that "the author's favorite bogyman, Fu Manchu, seems to be enjoying a leave of absence, and in most of his work starring that yellow arch-fiend Sax Rohmer has presented more interesting entertainment than his latest book contains." When Rohmer returned again to "Fu Manchu" novels, he produced *The Drums of Fu Manchu*, which plots Fu Manchu's international battles with world leaders. A writer for the *Boston Transcript* echoed the sentiment of many Rohmer fans by writing: "It isn't very often that the same sort of thing we enjoyed back in the pig-tail days is still as enjoyable and thrilling. . . . The old excitement and horror are still present in Mr. Rohmer's writing." Rohmer would write one more Fu Manchu novel before he abandoned writing to work for British military intelligence during World War II. Published in 1941, *The Island of Fu Manchu* is set during the war and revolves around espionage along with elements of the occult. It drew kudos from a *Saturday Review of Books* critic who dubbed the novel a "thriller de luxe" and contended that "Dr. Fu's inventiveness knows no end."

Fu Manchu's Legacy

Rohmer continued to write in different genres during his later life. He dabbled in plays, short stories, and novelizations of radio series. However, he always reluctantly returned to Fu Manchu for financial reasons. Before his death in 1959, four more novels and two short stories that featured Fu Manchu were published. "Rohmer created in Fu Manchu a compelling *living* being, one who has not been tarnished or cheapened by the imitations of lesser authors, by his transformation from an archetype into a stereotype by the popular mind, or by the forward march of history, which has dated the attitudes and situations in even the later books," wrote Murray.

Rohmer's Fu Manchu also inspired a 1984 sequel, *Ten Years beyond Baker Street*, written by Cay Van Ash, Rohmer's biographer, in which the Evil Doctor fights Sherlock Holmes. In addition there are radio and comic-book adaptations, a television series from the 1950s, and several movies starring, among others, actors such as Boris Karloff, Christopher Lee, and Peter Sellers in the central role. Sinister Fu Manchu stereotypes appear in wide numbers in popular fiction, the best known the title character from Ian Fleming's 1958 "James Bond" novel *Doctor No*.

Social critics often point to the non-literary impact of Rohmer's oriental invention. As Urmila Seshagiri noted in *Cultural Critique*, "The central, recurring conflict of these thrillers—Dr. Fu-Manchu's schemes for global domination—rewrote the master narrative of modern England, inverting the British Empire's racial and political hierarchies to imagine a dystopic civilization dominated by evil Orientals." Similarly, Clive Bloom commented in *Cult Fiction: Popular Reading and Pulp Theory*: "Here, perhaps, lies one of the secrets of Fu Manchu's power to fascinate. The Sinophobic message of Rohmer's books is underpinned by three theories: the notion of conspiracy which is based upon a corporate, international secret society acting out of Limehouse, the notion of a parallel supernatural plane of existence and the notion of eternal recurrence." Indeed, from the very outset, Fu Manchu played neatly into the

"Yellow Peril" anxieties of both British and Americans who were fearful of world domination by the huge population of China and Japan. As many have pointed out, such fears were baseless at the time: The population of Chinese in Western countries in the early twentieth century was at low levels, and their infamous opium dens were, in fact, in part the unexpected result of Western incursion in China during the Boxer Rebellion. Nonetheless, such racial fears persisted, and for almost half a century Fu Manchu fed into such fears and also fed them.

If you enjoy the works of Sax Rohmer, you may also want to check out the following books:

Maurice Leblanc, *Arsène Lupin, Gentleman Burglar*, 1910.
The "Shadow" novels by Maxwell Grant, including *The Romanoff Jewels*, 1975.
The League of Extraordinary Gentlemen, a graphic novel by Alan Moore, 2001.

In spite of their politically incorrect assumptions, Rohmer's books continue to attract new readers, and most now take such opinions as an historical curiosity. Four omnibus editions have been published of the "Fu Manchu" novels, introducing the eternal rivalry between Nayland Smith and Fu Manchu to a new generation of readers. In the end, it is the character and not his political and social connotation that attracts new fans. As Murray concluded, "Dr. Fu Manchu is an original creation in every sense, and, like Sherlock Holmes, Dracula, Tarzan, and a very few other popular characters, he has achieved a universal acceptance and popularity which will not be forgotten."

■ Biographical and Critical Sources

BOOKS

Anolik, Ruth Bienstock, and Douglas L. Howard, editors, *The Gothic Other: Racial and Social Constructions in the Literary Imagination*, McFarland (Jefferson, NC), 2004.

Bloom, Clive, *Cult Fiction: Popular Reading and Pulp Theory*, Palgrave Macmillan (New York, NY), 1998.

Day, Bradford M., *Sax Rohmer: A Bibliography*, Science-Fiction & Fantasy Publications (Denver, CO), 1963.

Dictionary of Literary Biography, Volume 70: *British Mystery Writers, 1860-1919*, Gale (Detroit, MI), 1988.

Encyclopedia of Mystery and Detection, McGraw (New York, NY), 1976.

Nevins, Francis M., Jr., editor, *The Mystery Writer's Art*, Bowling Green University Popular Press (Bowling Green, OH), 1970.

Penguin Companion to English Literature, McGraw (New York, NY), 1971.

St. James Guide to Crime and Mystery Writers, 4th edition, St. James Press (Detroit, MI), 1996.

St. James Guide to Horror, Ghost, and Gothic Writers, St. James Press (Detroit, MI), 1998.

Soister, John T., *Up from the Vault: Rare Thrillers of the 1920s and 1930s*, McFarland (Jefferson, NC), 2004.

Squire, J.C., *Life and Letters*, Doran & Company (New York, NY), 1921.

Supernatural Fiction Writers, Scribner (New York, NY), 1985.

Twentieth-Century Crime and Mystery Writers, St. Martin's Press (New York, NY), 1980.

Twentieth-Century Literary Criticism, Volume 28, Gale (Detroit, MI), 1988.

Van Ash, Cay, and Elizabeth Sax Rohmer, *Master of Villainy: A Biography of Sax Rohmer*, Popular Press (Bowling Green, OH), 1971.

PERIODICALS

Bookman, November, 1913, Ralph Hobart Phillips, review of *The Insidious Dr. Fu Manchu*, pp. 305-306.

Boston Sunday Herald, March 8, 1931, Carl Warton, "Houdini Saved the Day for Sax Rohmer."

Boston Transcript, July 8, 1939, review of *The Drums of Fu Manchu*, p. 2.

Cultural Critique, winter, 2006, Urmila Seshagiri, "Modernity's (Yellow) Perils: Dr. Fu-Manchu and English Race Paranoia," p. 162.

New York Times, September 30, 1934, Isaac Anderson, review of *The Trail of Fu Manchu*, p. 20; June 7, 1936, review of *President Fu Manchu*, p. 15; November 29, 1936, E.O. Beckwith, review of *White Velvet*, p. 26.

New York Times Book Review, May 9, 1915, review of *The Yellow Claw*; July 6, 1919, review of *Tales of Secret Egypt*.

Rohmer Review, 1968-81.

Saturday Review of Literature, March 15, 1941, review of *The Island of Fu Manchu*, p. 20.

ONLINE

Page of Fu Manchu Web site, http://www.njedge.net/~knapp/FuFrames.htm/ (January 9, 2009).*

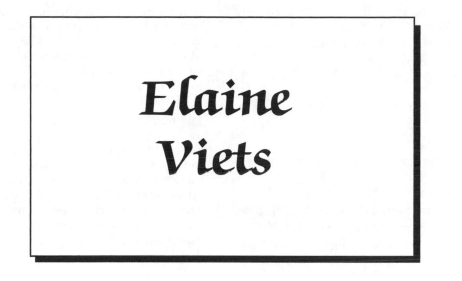

Elaine Viets

■ Personal

Born February 5, 1950, in St. Louis, MO; daughter of Henry Frederick (an electrician) and Elaine (a homemaker) Viets; married Don Crinklaw (a writer, journalist, and actor), August 6, 1971. *Ethnicity:* "German-American." *Education:* Attended University of Missouri—St. Louis, 1968-70; University of Missouri—Columbia, B.J., 1972. *Hobbies and other interests:* Reading, walking.

■ Addresses

Home—Fort Lauderdale, FL. *Agent*—David Hendin, 411 E. 57th St., New York, NY. *E-mail*—eviets@aol.com.

■ Career

Novelist and freelance journalist. *St. Louis Post-Dispatch*, St. Louis, MO, fashion writer, beginning 1972, became youth page editor, and then columnist, beginning 1979. Host, *Viets' Beat*, (television show), and *Travel Holiday Magazine* (syndicated radio show).

■ Member

Mystery Writers of America (president of Florida chapter, 2000; former member of national board), Sisters in Crime (former member of national board).

■ Awards, Honors

Local Emmy Award, St. Louis, MO, 1989 and 1990; named Florida Author of the Year, Pompano Beach Friends of the Library; Agatha Award, and Anthony Award for best short story, both 2005, both for "Wedding Knife"; Elaine Viets Day named in Maplewood, MO, 2005; Lefty Award for Most Humorous Mystery, Left Coast Crime Conference, 2008, for *Murder with Reservations*.

■ Writings

"FRANCESCA VIERLING" MYSTERY SERIES

Backstab, Dell (New York, NY), 1997.
Rubout, Dell (New York, NY), 1998.
The Pink Flamingo Murders, Dell (New York, NY), 1999.
Doc in the Box, Dell (New York, NY), 2000.

"DEAD-END JOB" MYSTERY SERIES

Shop till You Drop, Signet (New York, NY), 2003.
Murder between the Covers, Signet (New York, NY), 2003.
Dying to Call You, Signet (New York, NY), 2004.
Just Murdered, Signet (New York, NY), 2005.

Murder Unleashed, New American Library (New York, NY), 2006.

Murder with Reservations, New American Library (New York, NY), 2007.

Clubbed to Death, New American Library (New York, NY), 2008.

Killer Cuts, New American Library (New York, NY), 2009.

"JOSIE MARCUS, MYSTERY SHOPPER" MYSTERY SERIES

Dying in Style, Signet (New York, NY), 2005.

High Heels Are Murder, Signet (New York, NY), 2006.

Accessory to Murder, Signet (New York, NY), 2007.

Murder with All the Trimmings, Signet (New York, NY), 2008.

OTHER

How to Commit Monogamy: A Lighthearted Look at Long-term Love (essays), Andrews McMeel (Riverside, NJ), 1997.

Contributor to anthologies, including *Blood on Their Hands,* edited by Lawrence Block, Berkley (New York, NY), 2003; *Show Business Is Murder,* edited by Stuart Kaminsky, Berkley (New York, NY), 2005; and *Drop-Dead Blonde,* Signet (New York, NY), 2005. Contributor to periodicals, including *Alfred Hitchcock's Mystery Magazine.* Syndicated columnist, 1997-2000.

■ Adaptations

Backstab, Rubout, The Pink Flamingo Murders, and *Doc in the Box* were adapted as audiobooks read by Viets, Americana Publishing; the essay "An Unimportant Town" was included in *Spirit of the American Voice* (audiobook), Americana Publishing.

■ Sidelights

Novelist, journalist, and columnist Elaine Viets is best known as the author of the "Dead-End Job" mystery series. "I am an addict," admitted Viets on her home page. "I have to have a mystery to read at all times. I get twitchy if I can't find a good one. It's not easy feeding my habit. I read between four and five books a week. . . . I like mysteries with strong, smart women. I hate bimbos who wander half-clad into the house where the serial killer is hiding." Viets additionally noted, "I also like a little humor. Murder is a serious business, but a laugh can get you through the grim times." All of which add up to the kinds of mysteries Viets herself writes.

The author's "Dead-End Job" novels are anchored in the world of low-paying jobs with little hope of advancement, often in the service industry that form the background for series regular Helen Hawthorne's sleuthing. Viets is also the author of the "Josie Marcus, Mystery Shopper" series about a secret shopper who ensures that stores make shopping a pleasurable experience for customers. In her initial series, the "Francesca Vierling" mysteries,

Cover of Elaine Viets' entertaining mystery *High Heels Are Murder.*

Viets stays closer to her own professional interests in a quartet of books featuring a St. Louis columnist and amateur sleuth.

From Columnist to Author

Born in St. Louis, Missouri, in 1950, Viets began her love of mysteries at an early age. As she explained in an interview for the *Aunt Agatha's Web site:* "I read the classics as a kid: Agatha Christie, Conan Doyle, and my mother's old set of Nancy Drew mysteries. I was fascinated that Nancy always powdered her nose before she went detecting, and drove a red roadster. We didn't have roadsters in Florissant, Missouri, but I figured they must be something cool, like a Corvette." Writing mysteries as a profession came much later. After graduating from the University of Missouri, Viets became a journalist for twenty-five years in St. Louis, writing for the *Post-Dispatch* on local issues and human interest features. She eventually became a local celebrity, hosting a television show, *Viets Beat,* which won two Emmy awards. Viets ultimately left St. Louis, moving with her actor-husband to Washington, DC, where she wrote a syndicated column for United Media.

In 1997, Viets began her career as an author with a work of nonfiction, *How to Commit Monogamy: A Lighthearted Look at Long-term Love,* in which she addresses a serious topic in an amusing way. Married to the same man since 1971, she draws from her personal experience as well as research to explain the many joyful merits of a healthy, stable, monogamous relationship. A *Publishers Weekly* reviewer commented that "the author goes a long way toward clearing monogamy's bad name."

Chick-Lit Mysteries

Viets quickly moved from nonfiction to writing about female sleuths. Her first mysteries feature Francesca Vierling, a St. Louis columnist who becomes a reluctant detective. She investigates everything from the death of readers of her newspaper in the series debut, *Backstab,* to an investigation of the disappearance of a male stripper and the mysterious series of killings of medical personnel in the series finale, *Doc in the Box.*

In the course of writing those works, Viets moved to South Florida, which became the setting of her next series, the "Dead-End Job" mysteries. "My first mystery series was set in St. Louis," the author noted on her home page. "But readers expect the Midwest to have standards, morals, and taste. South

Florida has none of these handicaps." In the debut work, *Shop till You Drop,* high-powered business-woman Helen Hawthorne finds an unpleasant surprise when she comes home one day: her stay-at-home husband and the next-door neighbor in a romantic clinch. Overwhelmed with anger, she takes a crowbar to her husband's car, then later finds herself ordered to pay alimony to the cad because of his position as househusband. Bitterly refusing to do so, Helen quits her job and goes into hiding, fleeing to Ft. Lauderdale and working low-pay, cash-only jobs in seedy shops and dubious businesses just to make ends meet. Notably, Viets researched such jobs first hand, taking positions and performing tasks in order to add depth and verisimilitude to her storytelling. Reviewing *Shop till You Drop,* Piper Jones Castillo commented in the *St. Petersburg Times* that Viets's use of a "humorous tone intermingled with local color and believable characters" in this "hilarious look at life in Fort Lauderdale."

The second book in the "Dead-end Job" series, *Murder between the Covers,* finds Helen at work in a book store and ultimately investigating the murder of her little-loved employer. Writing in the *Orlando Sentinel,* Nancy Pate termed this "a witty, deftly plotted story that also provides an inside look at the publishing and book-selling world." Next in the series is *Dying to Call You,* involving telemarketing and for which Viets worked herself as a telemarketer. In *Just Murdered,* the fourth book in the series, Helen has found a job in an upscale bridal salon, but working at Millicent's is no more fun than the other jobs she has had. Weddings, it seems, transform otherwise normal and pleasant people into monstrous jerks. Kiki, for example, is a wealthy mother determined to attract more attention to herself than her daughter on her daughter's wedding day. Obnoxious and almost universally disliked, Kiki makes enemies with abandon, oblivious to the distress she inflicts and shielded behind her money. When the wedding day rolls around, Kiki is found murdered and stuffed into a closet. Few people mourn this turn of events, but Helen feels the pressure to dive in and solve the case, especially since the police consider her the prime suspect in the killing. A reviewer for *MBR Bookwatch* called *Just Murdered* a "hilarious chick-lit mystery."

Murder Unleashed finds Helen working at an exclusive pet boutique. With a clientele that includes some of the area's richest, and craziest, dog owners, she is challenged just keeping up with the demands of people who see their pets as members of the family. The star dog-groomer at the Pampered Pet Boutique, Jonathan, is a local celebrity and object of desire for the city's women, but he is also petty and

NATIONAL BESTSELLING SERIES

Murder with Reservations

A DEAD-END JOB MYSTERY

"Humorous and socially conscious...rollicking fun."
—Publishers Weekly

Elaine Viets
Author of Clubbed to Death

OBSIDIAN

Cover of Viets' novel *Murder with Reservations,* **part of her popular "Dead-End Job" series.** (An Obsidian Mystery, 2007. All rights reserved. Used by permission of Penguin Group (USA), Inc.)

prone to outbursts of anger. When Helen drives out to the gated community where Tammie Grimsbie lives to deliver the woman's newly buffed and shined Yorkie, she discovers Grimsbie dead, stabbed with a pair of dog-grooming shears. Terrified and panicked, Helen flees the scene without reporting the crime. Later, a confrontation with Willoughby Barclay ends with Helen and boutique owner Jeff being threatened with a lawsuit over letting Barclay's prize "labradoodle" get dognapped. After Barclay also ends up a victim of murder, Helen takes up the case in order to find out who is slaying the dogs' best friends. "Viets has a wry way with humor," commented a *Kirkus Reviews* contributor, who concluded that "the snapshots of lunatic dog owners are priceless."

In *Murder with Reservations* Helen is a maid at Sybil's Full Moon Hotel. When one of her coworkers turns up dead in a dumpster and the police do not seemed overly anxious to investigate, Helen takes it upon herself to find the perpetrator. Complications arise, however, when her ex-husband, Rob, comes to Florida and takes a room in the Full Moon Hotel. Donna Gehrke-White, writing for the *Miami Herald* found *Murder with Reservations* to be "one of Viets's most satisfying novels." Further praise came from a *Kirkus Reviews* contributor who called the "Dead-End Job" books an "offbeat series . . . [with] a healthy balance between the banal and the bizarre." Reviewing the same work in *Romantic Times* online Stephanie Schneider praised Viets's "uncanny ability to mix humor, quirky characters and murder into an entertaining page-turner."

Viets suffered a massive, life-threatening stroke in 2007, but she did not let it hold her back from continuing her writing. The seventh installment in the Helen Hawthorn saga, *Clubbed to Death,* appeared in 2008. Here Helen is working as a complaint clerk at a fancy country club, one of whose members turns out to be her ex-husband. He is newly married to Marcella, a.k.a. the "Black Widow," a woman whose numerous spouses seemed to have a knack of dying on her. When the bodies of two club members are discovered in Helen's office and Rob disappears, Helen becomes a prime suspect, and she joins forces with Marcella in order to clear her name. A *Publishers Weekly* reviewer concluded of *Clubbed to Death* that "the romantic ending will leave fans eager for the next installment in this superior cozy series."

Murder at the Market

In 2005 Viets launched a third series, "Josie Marcus, Mystery Shopper," moving the action back to St. Louis and featuring a single mother who enjoys the flexibility of her undercover job, vetting shopping conditions for management. In the series opener, *Dying in Style,* Josie is taking a look at the three branches of a high-profile designer handbag business that is in the process of being purchased by a larger conglomerate. When the owner of the stores, Danessa Celedine, is found murdered, Josie also finds herself in the middle of the investigation, for the murder weapon, a snakeskin belt used to strangle Danessa, is covered with Josie's fingerprints. As in her other series, Viets uses her usual blend of humor and mystery. Writing in *Reviewing the Evidence,* P.J. Coldren dubbed *Dying in Style* "amusing," and Jo Peters, reviewing the same work for *Romantic Times,* commented that "witty and winsome Josie is irresistible, and her family and friends are equally entertaining." Likewise, Harriet Klausner, in an online review, termed *Dying in Style* "a fun cozy starring a delightful protagonist who enjoys debunking crummy sales people and managers."

Josie returns in the second novel in the series, *High Heels Are Murder,* in which she gets an employee at a high-class shoe boutique fired for inappropriate behavior. When he later turns up dead, Josie becomes involved, as this employee also had a relationship with a former classmate of Josie's. Carroll Johnson, writing for *Reviewing the Evidence,* found *High Heels Are Murder* to be "a light and sometimes humorous read." Similar praise came from *Romantic Times* critic Pat Cooper, who predicted that the novel would "keep readers flipping pages until the wee hours." Klausner called *High Heels Are Murder* "one of the funniest amateur sleuth mysteries to come along in ages."

Josie lusts after a designer scarf but instead finds herself embroiled in mystery in *Accessory to Murder.* When the designer of the scarf is killed in a carjacking, and then the husband of her best friend is subsequently arrested for the murder, Josie once again turns to sleuthing in this "pleasant third outing," according to *Reviewing the Evidence* online contributor Linnea Dodson. Klausner had similar praise, noting that "Viets has written a well thought out who done it starring a sleuth who is totally believable and a bit quirky." In *Murder with All the Trimmings* Josie becomes involved in the investigation of a murder in a year-round Christmas store. Roseann Marlett, writing for *Romantic Times,* felt that "Viets brings a sense of humor to a variety of difficult family situations in this fun novel."

If you enjoy the works of Elaine Viets, you may also want to check out the following books:

Bones, 1999, and other crime novels by Jan Burke.
Harley Jane Kozak's "Wollie Shelley" mysteries, including *Dating Dead Men,* 2004.
The "Stephanie Plum" novels by Janet Evanovich, including *Lean Mean Thirteen,* 2007.

In an online interview with Jennifer Vido for the *Harford County Public Library Readers Place,* Viets noted that her skills as a writer have grown over the years. "There is nothing quite like the passion of a first book," she remarked. "I don't think that can ever be duplicated. But along the way, I've learned about pacing, plotting and developing characters." Indeed, characterization is vital to the success of her novels, as Viets remarked to Vido. "If my readers don't care about the characters, they won't follow them through 300 pages. I try hard to make my characters believable, but also true to their environment. I can get by with much wackier characters in Florida, where my 'Dead-End Job' series is set, because it's a lawless, rootless place. In my 'Josie Marcus' series, which is set in St. Louis, I have to have different kinds of people. They need to be part of a community."

■ Biographical and Critical Sources

PERIODICALS

Albany Times Union (Albany, NY), June 24, 2007, Donna Gehrke-White, review of *Murder with Reservations,* p. J4.

Dallas Morning News, June 18, 2008, Jane Sumner, "Mystery Writer Elaine Viets Doesn't Let '07 Stroke Keep Her from Book Tour."

Kirkus Reviews, March 15, 2006, review of *Murder Unleashed,* p. 266; March 15, 2007, review of *Murder with Reservations.*

Library Journal, June 15, 1997, Elizabeth Caulfield Felt, review of *How to Commit Monogamy: A Lighthearted Look at Long-term Love,* p. 87; September 15, 1997, Ravonne A. Green, review of *How to Commit Monogamy,* p. 120; May 1, 2008, review of *Clubbed to Death,* p. 45.

MBR Bookwatch, February, 2005, Harriet Klausner, review of *Drop Dead Blonde;* April, 2005, review of *Just Murdered.*

Miami Herald, May 23, 2007, Donna Gehrke-White, review of *Murder with Reservations.*

Orlando Sentinel, January 28, 2004, Nancy Pate, review of *Murder between the Covers.*

Publishers Weekly, June 2, 1997, review of *How to Commit Monogamy,* p. 63; June 12, 2000, review of *Doc in the Box,* p. 58; March 6, 2006, review of *Murder Unleashed,* p. 49; March 17, 2008, review of *Clubbed to Death,* p. 53.

St. Louis Journalism Review, February, 1996, Staci D. Kramer, "Viets-*Post* Marriage on the Rocks? Editor Woo Takes over Negotiations," p. 1; September, 1996, Burt St. John, "Viets's Future with the *Post* Uncertain," p. 18; June, 2008, Eileen P. Duggan, "Elaine Viets: Murders She Wrote," p. 22.

St. Louis Post-Dispatch, October 23, 2005, Deb Peterson, "Elaine Viets Returns to Collect Key to City of Maplewood," p. C3; May 21, 2006, Sarah Casey Newman, "Animals Will Benefit from Mystery Set in Pet Boutique," p. 33.

St. Petersburg Times, June 8, 2008, Piper Jones Castillo, review of *Shop till You Drop,* p. 4D.

Sarasota Herald Tribune, May 21, 2006, Susan L. Rife, "Finding Humor in Dead-End Work," p. G6.

ONLINE

Aunt Agatha's Web site, http://www.auntagathas.com/ (January 13, 2009), interview with Viets.

Crescent Blues Web site, http://www.crescentblues.com/ (January 13, 2009), Teri Dohmen, "Tall Order: Elaine Viets."

Elaine Viets Home Page, http://www.elaineviets.com (April 1, 2009).

Harriet Klausner's Review Archive, http://harrietklausner.wwwi.com/ (January 13, 2009), Harriet Klausner, reviews of *Dying in Style, High Heels Are Murder, Accessory to Murder,* and *Murder with All the Trimmings.*

Harford County Public Library Readers Place, http://www.hcplonline.info/ (January 1, 2007), Jennifer Vido, interview with Viets.

Mystery File Web site, http://www.mysteryfile.com/ (February, 2005), Pamela James, interview with Viets.

Reviewing the Evidence Web site, http://www.reviewingtheevidence.com/ (April 1, 2006), P.J. Coldren, review of *Dying in Style;* (January 1, 2007) Carroll Johnson, review of *High Heels Are Murder;* (September 1, 2007) Linnea Dodson, review of *Accessory to Murder.*

Romantic Times Web site, http://www.romantictimes.com/ (October, 2005), Jo Peters, review of *Dying in Style;* (November, 2006) Pat Cooper, review of *High Heels Are Murder;* (May, 2007) Stephanie Schneider, review of *Murder with Reservations;* (November, 2007) Tara Gelsomino, review of *Accessory to Murder;* (November, 2008) Roseann Marlett, review of *Murder with All the Trimmings.*

Southern Scribe Web site, http://www.southernscribe.com/ (January 13, 2009), Elaine S. August, "A Journalist Is a Natural Sleuth."

Writerspace Web site, http://www.writerspace.com/ (February 1, 2005), Leena Hyat, interview with Viets.*

Lynd Ward

■ Personal

Born June 26, 1905, in Chicago, IL; died of complications from Alzheimer's disease, June 28, 1985, in Reston, VA; son of Harry F. (a minister and professor) and Daisy Ward; married May McNeer (a writer), June 11, 1926; children: Nanda Weedon, Robin Kendall. *Education:* Teachers College, Columbia University, B.S., 1926; attended National Academy for Graphic Arts (Leipzig, Germany), 1926-27. *Religion:* Methodist. *Hobbies and other interests:* Playing the accordion, building stone fireplaces, walks.

■ Career

Illustrator, graphic artist, and author, 1927-80. Federal Art Projects, New York, NY, director, graphic arts division, 1937-39. *Exhibitions:* Work included in exhibits at Art Center of Northern New Jersey, 1974; National Academy of Art; and Society of American Graphic Artists; exhibited wood engravings in most national print shows.

■ Member

Society of Illustrators, Society of American Graphic Artists (president, 1953-59), National Academy of Design, PEN.

■ Awards, Honors

Cateret Book Club Award, 1942; Zella de Milhau Prize, 1947; Library of Congress award for wood engraving, 1948; National Academy of Design award, 1949; Caldecott Medal, 1953, for *The Biggest Bear;* Silver Medal, Limited Editions Club, 1954; John Taylor Arms Memorial Award, 1962; Samuel F.B. Morse Medal, 1966; Rutgers University Award, 1970; Silver Medallion, University of Southern Mississippi, 1973; Distinguished Service Award for Outstanding Contributions to Children's Literature, Central Missouri State University, 1973; Regina Medal for Continued Distinguished Contributions to Children's Literature (corecipient with wife, May McNeer), 1975.

■ Writings

SELF-ILLUSTRATED

God's Man: A Novel in Woodcuts, Cape & Smith (New York, NY), 1929, reprinted, Dover Publications (Mineola, NY), 2004.

Madman's Drum: A Novel in Woodcuts, Cape & Smith (New York, NY), 1930, reprinted, Dover Publications (Mineola, NY), 2005.

Wild Pilgrimage: A Novel in Woodcuts, Smith & Haas (New York, NY), 1932, reprinted, Dover Publications (Mineola, NY), 2008.

Prelude to a Million Years (limited edition), Equinox Press (New York, NY), 1933.

Song without Words (limited edition), Random House (New York, NY), 1936.

Vertigo, Random House (New York, NY), 1937, reprinted, Dover Publications (Mineola, NY), 2009.

Storyteller without Words: The Wood Engravings of Lynd Ward, Harry F. Abrams (New York, NY), 1974.

Lynd Ward's Last, Unfinished, Wordless Novel, introduction by Michael McCurdy, essay by Michael Joseph, Rutgers University Libraries (New Brunswick, NJ), 2001.

(With Frans Masereel, Giacomo Patri, and Laurence Hyde) George A. Walker, editor, *Graphic Witness: Four Wordless Graphic Novels,* Firefly Books (Buffalo, NY), 2007.

FOR CHILDREN; SELF-ILLUSTRATED

The Biggest Bear, Houghton Mifflin (Boston, MA), 1953, reprinted, 1988.

Nic of the Woods, Houghton Mifflin (Boston, MA), 1965.

The Silver Pony: A Story in Pictures, Houghton Mifflin (Boston, MA), 1973.

Inner Room, Post Press (Newark, DE), 1988.

ILLUSTRATOR

Henry Milner Rideout, *Lola the Bear,* Duffield (New York, NY), 1928.

Dorothy Rowe, *The Begging Deer, and Other Stories of Japanese Children,* Macmillan (New York, NY), 1928.

Oscar Wilde, *The Ballad of Reading Gaol,* Macy-Masius (New York, NY), 1928.

May McNeer, *Prince Bantam,* Macmillan (New York, NY), 1929.

Dorothy Rowe, *Traveling Shops: Stories of Chinese Children,* Macmillan (New York, NY), 1929.

Hildegarde Hoyt Swift, *Little Blacknose: The Story of a Pioneer,* Harcourt, Brace (New York, NY), 1929.

Mary Elizabeth Barry and P.R. Hanna, *Wonder Flights of Long Ago,* Appleton (New York, NY), 1930.

Salvadore Madariaga, *Sir Bob,* Harcourt, Brace (New York, NY), 1930.

Carl Wilhelmson, *Midsummer Night,* Farrar & Rinehart (New York, NY), 1930.

May McNeer, *Waif Maid,* Macmillan (New York, NY), 1930.

Johann W. von Goethe, *Faust* (limited edition), R.O. Ballou, 1930, translated by Alice Raphael, Cape & Smith (New York, NY), 1930.

Frederick Marryat, *Children of the New Forest,* Macmillan (New York, NY), 1930.

Winfield Scott O'Connor, *Jockeys, Crooks, and Kings,* Cape & Smith (New York, NY), 1930.

Agnes D. Hewes, *Spice and the Devil's Cave,* Knopf (New York, NY), 1930.

May McNeer, *Stop Tim! The Tale of a Car,* Farrar & Rinehart (New York, NY), 1930.

Elizabeth Jane Coatsworth, *The Cat Who Went to Heaven,* Macmillan (New York, NY), 1930, reprinted, Aladdin Books (New York, NY), 1990.

Alec Waugh, *Hot Countries,* Farrar & Rinehart (New York, NY), 1930.

Alice W. Howard, *Ching Li and the Dragons,* Macmillan (New York, NY), 1931.

Richard Wagner, *The Story of Siegfried,* music arranged by Angela Diller, Cape & Smith (New York, NY), 1931.

Alec Waugh, *"Most Women . . .",* Farrar & Rinehart (New York, NY), 1931.

Lleyelyn Powys, *Impassioned Clay,* Longmans, Green (New York, NY), 1931.

Llewelyn Powys, *Now That the Gods Are Dead,* Equinox Press (New York, NY), 1932.

Charles Reade, *The Cloister and the Hearth,* two volumes, Limited Editions (New York, NY), 1932.

Thomas Mann, *A Christmas Poem,* Equinox (New York, NY), 1932.

Padraic Colum, *The White Sparrow,* Macmillan (New York, NY), 1933.

Antoine de Saint Exupery, *Southern Mail,* translated by Stuart Gilbert, Smith & Haas (New York, NY), 1933.

Harry F. Ward, *In Place of Profit: Social Incentive in the Soviet Union,* Scribner (New York, NY), 1933.

Myron Brinig, *The Flutter of an Eyelid,* Farrar & Rinehart (New York, NY), 1933.

Mary Wollstonecraft Shelley, *Frankenstein,* Smith & Haas (New York, NY), 1934, reprinted, Gramercy Books (New York, NY), 1994, published as *Frankenstein: The Lynd Ward Illustrated Edition,* Dover Publications (Mineola, NY), 2009.

Thomas Mann, *Nocturnes* (limited signed edition), translated by H.T. Love-Porter, Equinox Press (New York, NY), 1934, reprinted, Books for Libraries Press (Freeport, NY), 1970.

William J. Cowen, *The Man with Four Lives,* Farrar & Rinehart (New York, NY), 1934.

Donald Culross Peattie, *An Almanac for Moderns,* Putnam (New York, NY), 1935.

Marjorie Medary, *Topgallant: A Herring Gull,* Smith & Haas (New York, NY), 1935.

Granville Hicks, *One of Us: The Story of John Reed,* Equinox Press (New York, NY), 1935.

Alexander Kinnan Laing, editor, *The Haunted Omnibus,* Farrar & Rinehart (New York, NY), 1936, published as *Great Ghost Stories of the World,* Garden City (New York, NY), 1939.

Mabel L. Robinson, *Bright Island,* Random House (New York, NY), 1937.

Donald Culross Peattie, *A Book of Hours,* Putnam (New York, NY), 1937.

Story of Odysseus, translated by W.H.D. Rouse, Modern Age Books (New York, NY), 1937.

Louis J. Halle, *Birds against Men,* Viking (New York, NY), 1938.

F. Martin Howard, *Porpoise of Pirate Bay,* Random House (New York, NY), 1938.

Hildegarde Hoyt Swift, *House by the Sea,* Harcourt, Brace (New York, NY), 1938.

Victor Hugo, *Les Miserables,* five volumes, translated by Lascelles Wraxall, Limited Editions (New York, NY), 1938, published in two volumes, Heritage Press (New York, NY), 1960.

Mabel L. Robinson, *Runner of the Mountain Tops: The Life of Louis Agassiz,* Random House (New York, NY), 1939.

William Ellery Leonard, adapter, *Beowulf,* Heritage Press (New York, NY), 1939.

Maurice Genevoix, *Last Hunt,* Random House (New York, NY), 1940.

Alexandre Dumas, *Le comte de Monte-Cristo,* Limited Editions, 1941.

Stuart Chase, *Primer of Economics,* Random House (New York, NY), 1941.

Ernest Hemingway, *For Whom the Bell Tolls,* Princeton University Press (Princeton, NJ), 1942.

Hildegarde Hoyt Swift, *The Little Red Lighthouse and the Great Gray Bridge,* Harcourt, Brace (New York, NY), 1942, reprinted, Harcourt (San Diego, CA), 2003.

Edgar Lee Masters, *The Sangamon,* Farrar & Rinehart (New York, NY), 1942.

François Rabelais, *Gargantua and Pantagruel,* Heritage Press (New York, NY), 1942.

Julia L. Sauer, *Fog Magic,* Viking (New York, NY), 1943.

Esther Forbes, *Johnny Tremain: A Novel for Old and Young,* Houghton Mifflin (Boston, MA), 1943, student edition, 1954.

Donald Culross Peattie, *Journey into America,* Houghton Mifflin (Boston, MA), 1943.

Desiderius Erasmus, *Moriae Encomium; or, In Praise of Folly,* Limited Editions (New York, NY), 1943.

Richard Arthur Warren Hughes *The Innocent Voyage,* Limited Editions (New York, NY), 1944.

May McNeer, *The Gold Rush,* Grosset & Dunlap (New York, NY), 1944.

May McNeer, *The Covered Wagon,* Grosset & Dunlap (New York, NY), 1944.

Jean Karsavina, *Reunion in Poland,* International Publishers (New York, NY), 1945.

Esther Forbes, *America's Paul Revere,* Houghton Mifflin (Boston, MA), 1946.

Jessie Mae Orton Jones, *Many Mansions, from the Bible,* Viking (New York, NY), 1947.

May McNeer, *The Golden Flash,* Viking (New York, NY), 1947.

Hildegarde Hoyt Swift, *North Star Shining: A Pictorial History of the American Negro,* Morrow (New York, NY), 1947.

Robert Louis Stevenson, *Kidnapped,* Grosset & Dunlap (New York, NY), 1948.

Daniel Defoe, *The Life and Strange Surprising Adventures of Robinson Crusoe,* Grosset & Dunlap (New York, NY), 1948.

(With Lee Gregori) Johann David Wyss, *Swiss Family Robinson,* Grosset & Dunlap (New York, NY), 1949.

Stewart Hall Holbrook, *America's Ethan Allen,* Houghton Mifflin (Boston, MA), 1949.

May McNeer, *The California Gold Rush,* Random House (New York, NY), 1950.

Henry Steele Commager, *America's Robert E. Lee,* Houghton Mifflin (Boston, MA), 1951.

Mabel L. Robinson, *Strong Wings,* Random House (New York, NY), 1951.

May McNeer, *John Wesley,* Abingdon (New York, NY), 1951.

May McNeer, *Up a Crooked River,* Viking (New York, NY), 1952.

Carley Dawson, *Mrs. Wicker's Window,* Houghton Mifflin (Boston, MA), 1952.

Jeannette Covert Nolan, *The Story of Ulysses S. Grant,* Grosset & Dunlap (New York, NY), 1952.

Russel Owen, *Conquest of the North and South Poles,* Random House (New York, NY), 1952.

Nanda Weedon Ward, *The Black Sombrero,* Pellegrina & Cudahy, 1952.

Alfred Tennyson, *Idylls of the King,* Limited Editions (New York, NY), 1952.

May McNeer, *The Mexican Story,* Farrar, Straus (New York, NY), 1953.

Padraic Colum, editor, *Arabian Nights,* Macmillan (New York, NY), 1953.

May McNeer, *Martin Luther,* Abingdon (New York, NY), 1953.

God's Story Book: A First Book of Bible Stories for Little Catholics, Catechetical Guild Educational Society (St. Paul, MN), 1953.

May McNeer, *War Chief of the Seminoles,* Random House (New York, NY), 1954, published as *Osceola and the Seminole War,* E.M. Hale (Eau Claire, WI).

Arthur Hudson Parsons, *The Horn That Stopped the Band*, F. Watts (New York, NY), 1954.

May McNeer, *Little Baptiste*, Houghton Mifflin (Boston, MA), 1954.

Carley Dawson, *Sign of the Seven Seas*, Houghton Mifflin (Boston, MA), 1954.

Ann N. Clark, *Santiago*, Viking (New York, NY), 1955.

Carley Dawson, *Dragon Run*, Houghton Mifflin (Boston, MA), 1955.

Leonard F. Clark, *Explorer's Digest*, Houghton Mifflin (Boston, MA), 1955.

Nanda Weedon Ward, *High Flying Hat*, Farrar, Straus (New York, NY), 1956.

May McNeer, *America's Abraham Lincoln*, Houghton Mifflin (Boston, MA), 1957.

May McNeer, *Armed with Courage*, Abingdon (New York, NY), 1957.

Hildegarde Hoyt Swift, *The Edge of April: A Biography of John Burroughs*, Morrow (New York, NY), 1957.

May McNeer, *The Canadian Story*, Farrar, Straus (New York, NY), 1958.

Bible Readings for Boys and Girls, T. Nelson (Nashville, TN), 1959.

Marguerite Henry, *Gaudenzia: Pride of the Palio*, Rand McNally (Chicago, IL), 1960.

Jean Fritz, *Brady*, Coward (New York, NY), 1960, reprinted, Puffin Books (New York, NY), 1987.

May McNeer, *The Alaska Gold Rush*, Landmark Books, 1960.

May McNeer, *My Friend Mac: The Story of Little Baptiste and the Moose*, Houghton Mifflin (Boston, MA), 1960.

Marguerite Henry, *The Wildest Horse Race in the World*, Rand McNally, 1960.

Joseph Conrad, *Lord Jim: A Tale*, Heritage Press (New York, NY), 1960.

Thomas Paine, *The Rights of Man*, Heritage Press (New York, NY), 1961.

Nanda Weedon Ward, *Hi Tom*, Hastings House (New York, NY), 1962.

Hildegarde Hoyt Swift, *From the Eagle's Wing: A Biography of John Muir*, Morrow (New York, NY), 1962.

May McNeer, *America's Mark Twain*, Houghton Mifflin (Boston, MA), 1962.

May McNeer, *The American Indian Story*, Farrar, Straus (New York, NY), 1963.

May McNeer, *Give Me Freedom*, Abingdon (New York, NY), 1964.

William Shakespeare, *Five Plays from Shakespeare*, edited by Katherine Miller, Houghton Mifflin (Boston, MA), 1964.

May McNeer, *Profile of American History*, Hammond (Maplewood, NJ), 1964.

Annabel Johnson and Edgar Johnson, *A Peculiar Magic*, Houghton Mifflin (Boston, MA), 1965.

Robert Louis Stevenson, *The Master of Ballantrae*, Heritage Press (New York, NY), 1965.

Victor Barnouw, *Dream of the Blue Heron*, Delacorte (New York, NY), 1966.

May McNeer, *The Wolf of Lamb's Lane*, Houghton Mifflin (Boston, MA), 1967.

The Writings of Thomas Jefferson, Limited Editions (New York, NY), 1967.

Jean Fritz, *Early Thunder*, Coward (New York, NY), 1967.

May McNeer, *Go, Tim, Go!*, L.W. Singer (New York, NY), 1967.

Lee Kingman, *The Secret Journey of the Silver Reindeer*, Doubleday (Garden City, NY), 1968.

Robert Louis Stevenson, *Treasure Island*, American Education Publications (Middletown, CT), 1970.

May McNeer, *Stranger in the Pines*, Houghton Mifflin (Boston, MA), 1971.

Alvin Presselt, editor, *Stories from the Bible*, Coward (New York, NY), 1971.

Scott O'Dell, *The Treasure of Topo-el-Bampo*, Houghton Mifflin (Boston, MA), 1972.

May McNeer, *The Story of George Washington*, Abingdon (Nashville, TN), 1973.

May McNeer, *Bloomsday for Maggie*, Houghton Mifflin (Boston, MA), 1976.

Henry Hart, *A Relevant Memoir: The Story of the Equinox Cooperative Press*, Three Mountains Press (New York, NY), 1977.

François Marie Arouet de Voltaire, *Poem upon the Lisbon Disaster*, Penmaen Press (New York, NY), 1977.

Illustrator of frontispieces for books, including Llewelyn Powys's *Impassioned Clay*, Longmans, Green (New York, NY) 1931; Evelyn Waugh's *Thirteen Such Years*, Farrar & Rinehart (New York, NY), 1932; Robert Gessner's *Upsurge*, Farrar & Rinehart, 1933; Alexander Laing's *The Cadaver of Gideon Wyck*, Farrar & Rinehart, 1934; and Thomas Painter and Laing's *The Motives of Nicholas Holtz*, Farrar & Rinehart, 1936.

OTHER

Contributor to *American Artist* and *Horn Book*.

Ward's prints are housed in the permanent collections of the Library of Congress, Smithsonian Institution, Newark Museum, Metropolitan Museum, Victoria and Albert Museum, and others.

■ Adaptations

The Biggest Bear was adapted as a filmstrip, Weston Woods, 1958; *The Silver Pony* was adapted as a film produced by Bosustow.

■ Sidelights

Lynd Ward, a celebrated artist and author, was best known for his wood engraving, although he was skilled in many other media, including watercolor, oils, brush and ink, and lithography. Best known for his "woodcut novels"—engraved pictorial narratives first created during the 1930s to depict issues of the Great Depression—Ward contributed his art to more than two hundred works for children and adults. He was also the first person to create an entire adult novel solely from woodcuts. Ward crafted several such novels, using woodcuts (no words were included) to artistically express issues that surfaced as a result of the economic downturn of the 1930s. According to Christopher Capozzola, a contributor for *In These Times*, Ward continues to be "recognized as one of the founders of the American graphic novel," adding that his "contributions to the visual arts deliberately repudiated words."

Ward was born June 26, 1905, in Chicago, Illinois, to Harry F. Ward, a minister and professor, and Daisy Kendall Ward. He was frequently ill as a child, and there was some doubt that he would even survive infancy. The remedy his parents attempted was somewhat unusual: the Wards took their young son and his older sister to live in the woods of Lonely Lake, north of Sault Ste. Marie. After spending a summer in isolation, Ward regained his health and traveled back to Chicago with his family. The Wards spent each following summer at Lonely Lake, instilling a love of the wilderness in their son.

Develops a Love for Story and Art

During Ward's childhood, his family's religious temperament meant that playing games or enjoying other activities was forbidden on Sunday afternoons. Instead, Ward spent those times reading and examining pictures in the few books he had at his disposal. Among those books was a volume of Bible stories, illustrated with the vivid and sometimes grotesque artwork of Gustave Doré, as well as a children's story in which toys came to life. Ward later said that he likely absorbed these books in visual terms, and that his keen interest in their visual elements led to his interest in ways in which pictures can communicate without words.

Illustration by Lynd Ward from an edition of Robert Louis Stevenson's classic novel *Kidnapped*.

Ward first decided to become an artist "when, in the first grade, he made the astonishing discovery that the name Ward was really Draw turned backwards," explained his wife, May McNeer, in an essay for *Horn Book*. At the age of nine, Ward had his first encounter with commercialism: "At that time he was given an order book from some store," continued McNeer. "On his way to school he used to pass a shop with a sign saying, 'John Morris, Shoes Repaired While You Wait.' So, one morning, Lynd wrote on the order book a sign which read, 'Lynd Ward, Artist, Pictures Painted While You Wait,' and set it up on his desk. When he received no orders he went back to art for art's sake."

Ward attended college at the Teachers College of Columbia University during the mid-1920s, graduating with a bachelor's degree in fine arts. It was at Columbia that he met McNeer; they were married the week after graduation in 1926 and immediately departed for Europe. Ward enrolled as a special student at the National Academy for Graphic Arts in Leipzig, Germany, where he studied from 1926 to 1927, despite his lack of knowledge of the German language.

It was while he was "browsing through a bookstore in Leipzig" that "Ward discovered a small book by the early twentieth-century Belgian engraver and publisher Franz Masereel that told a story in woodcuts," related Ophelia Gilbert in the *Dictionary of Literary Biography*. "The pictures in the book triggered a flood of ideas for an original book with woodcuts telling a story. From then on the direction of his work as an artist lay in the slow, difficult medium of wood engraving, which had been the primary process for illustration in the eighteenth and nineteenth centuries."

When Ward returned to the United States in the spring of 1927, his newfound interest in woodcuts

The Swiss Family Robinson **is one of several books featuring Ward's detailed artwork.** (Copyright © 1949 by Grosset & Dunlap, Inc.; renewed 1977 by Lynd Ward. All rights reserved. Used by permission of Penguin Group (USA), Inc.)

led him to believe that there was a need for book illustration to revisit the basic technical processes that artists used before photographic reproduction became widespread. From the spring until fall of 1927, he worked at assembling a portfolio of his work, part of which included a series of woodcut illustrations that told a complete story without the use of words. This story became *God's Man*, the first novel ever produced in woodcuts. *God's Man* was first published in a limited edition by the Plimpton Press and as a trade edition in 1929. The work expresses Ward's views about the role of the artist in the Great Depression. According to Capozzola, "The book's subject matter—an allegorical fable about an artist who sells his soul for worldly success—was timeless. But its artistic innovations were unprecedented; its visual structure and pacing owed as much to silent film and mass-circulation comic pages as they did to artistic predecessors like [Käthe] Kollwitz or Honoré Daumier."

God's Man was followed in the 1930s by five similar works, including *Wild Pilgrimage: A Novel in Woodcuts*, which follows a dissatisfied young factory worker who leaves his gritty industrial town and ventures into the countryside, encountering a host of unusual characters. In *Wild Pilgrimage*, Ward adopted an innovative pictorial strategy: illustrations printed in black describe the narrative; in red, the protagonist's thoughts and dreams. According to a contributor in *Time*, the work "tells so straightforward a story that no clues are needed."

A Celebrated Career in Illustration

During the 1940s Ward continued to illustrate the works of others and do some work of his own. In 1953 he received the Caldecott Medal for *The Biggest Bear*, a self-illustrated children's book. "Humor, anxiety, pathos, and strength are expressed in Ward's opaque watercolors of black-and-white shadings and create an understated story of a boy and a bear, one of whom grows physically and one of whom grows emotionally," remarked Gilbert. In his acceptance speech for the award, published in *Caldecott Medal Books: 1938-1957*, Ward stated: "A moment like this is something for which an artist's day-to-day life ill prepares him. In spite of the embarrassment that results from being suddenly pushed into so bright a spotlight, there is this salutary result—you become very much aware of how little a person is by himself, and how much of what he is comes from others."

In 1957, Ward illustrated a biography of Abraham Lincoln that was written by his wife. He undertook five years of research before completing this task,

Ward's graphic images bring to life his original story in his award-winning 1953 picture book *The Biggest Bear.* (Copyright © 1952 by Lynd Ward. Copyright © renewed 1980 by Lynd Ward. Reproduced by permission of Houghton Mifflin Company.)

later reflecting in *American Artist:* "The completion of a historical subject is at best a slow and complicated process. There are innumerable factors that must be considered simultaneously—accuracy of costume and background, movement of figures, disposition of crowds, identifying characterizations of individuals who play subsidiary roles to the main character, and the characterization of the central figure himself. All these require mulling over and working out gradually."

Nic of the Woods, published in 1965, was the second children's book Ward both wrote and illustrated. It is the story of a boy and his spaniel, Nic, who have both been transplanted from the city to the northern wilderness. It is a simply told story which "contrasts the smallness and the vastness of nature and expresses the weakness and strength, happiness and sadness of persons coping with the wilderness," noted Gilbert.

In 1973, Ward's third self-illustrated work for children was published. *The Silver Pony* is a story in pictures about a boy who sees a pony, which is invisible to his father, and rides off with it to discover the necessity of cooperation among men for the survival of the earth. "The book is filled with adventure," wrote Gilbert. "The freedom felt by the boy and the pony, the dangers they encounter and overcome, and the changing universe are masterfully conveyed by the pictures."

Ward continued to work until 1980, when he became too ill to continue. He died June 28, 1985, of complications from Alzheimer's disease. Among Ward's "strongest assets," wrote Henry C. Pitz in *American Artist*, "is his sense of pulsing and dramatic composition. His imagination rejoices in any subject that gives this ample scope. He likes turbulent skies, networks of dramatic light and shade, forms that he can shape at will, like trees, water, rocks, and clouds. His human figures, too, feel the compulsion of urge," Pitz continued. "They bend, twist, and stiffen according to the exigencies of the design."

If you enjoy the works of Lynd Ward, you may also want to check out the following:

The art of Frans Masereel (1889-1972), a Flemish painter and woodcut artist.
White Collar: A Novel in Linocuts, 1938, and other works by Giacomo Patri.
The works of Eric Drooker (1958—), an American painter, graphic novelist, and illustrator who cites Ward as an influence.

Ward was "a craftsman of the highest order," concluded Gilbert. "His attention to detail and authenticity, his ability to express honest feelings common to mankind, and his expertise in dramatizing a text through the right illustrations . . . brought him the respect and admiration of the book world. . . . His talents have broadened understanding and appreciation of graphic arts as a medium of communication and have helped elevate the level of illustration in children's books."

■ Biographical and Critical Sources

BOOKS

Burke, W.J., and Will D. Howe, *American Authors and Books,* revised by Irving Weiss and Anne Weiss, Crown (New York, NY), 1972.
Contemporary Illustrators of Children's Books, Bookshop for Boys and Girls (Boston, MA), 1930, reprinted, Gale (Detroit, MI), 1978.
Dictionary of Literary Biography, Volume 22: *American Writers for Children, 1900-1960,* Gale (Detroit, MI), 1983.
Hoffman, Miriam, and Eva Samuels, *Authors and Illustrators of Children's Books: Writings on Their Lives and Works,* Bowker (New York, NY), 1972.

Ward's book-illustration projects for children include *The Cat Who Went to Heaven* **by Elizabeth Coatsworth.** (Copyright © 1930 by The Macmillan Company.)

Hopkins, Lee Bennett, *Books Are by People,* Citation Press (New York, NY), 1969.

Hopkins, Lee Bennett, *More Books by More People,* Citation Press (New York, NY), 1974.

Huber, Miriam Blanton, *Story and Verse for Children,* Macmillan (New York, NY), 1965.

Kingman, Lee, Joanna Foster, and Ruth Giles Lontoft, compilers, *Illustrators of Children's Books, 1957-1966,* Horn Book (Boston, MA), 1968.

Kingman, Lee, compiler, *Illustrators of Children's Books, 1967-1976,* Horn Book (Boston, MA), 1978.

Klenin, Diana, *The Art of Art for Children's Books,* Potter (New York, NY), 1966.

Miller, Bertha M., and Elinor Whitney Field, *Caldecott Medal Books: 1938-1957,* Horn Book (Boston, MA), 1957.

Reed, Walt, and Roger Reed, *The Illustrator in America, 1880-1980,* Madison Square Press (New York, NY), 1984.

Silvey, Anita, *Children's Books and Their Creators,* Houghton Mifflin (Boston, MA), 1995.

Ward, Martha E., and Dorothy A. Marquardt, *Illustrators of Books for Young People,* 2nd edition, Scarecrow Press (Metuchen, NY), 1975.

Ward, Martha E., and others, *Authors of Books for Young People,* 3rd edition, Scarecrow Press (Metuchen, NJ), 1990.

PERIODICALS

American Artist, March, 1955, Henry C. Pitz, "The Illustrations of Lynd Ward"; February, 1959, Lynd Ward, "Building a Lincoln Book"; November, 2004, review of *Gods' Man: A Novel in Woodcuts,* p. 75.

Bibliognost: The Book Collector's Little Magazine, May, 1976, special Lynd Ward Issue.

Columbia Literary Columns, November, 1977, D.B. Jones, "Lynd Ward: A Half-Century Association with the Limited Editions Club," pp. 20-31.

Elementary English, November, 1962, Helen W. Painter, "Lynd Ward: Artist, Writer, and Scholar."

Horn Book, August, 1953, May McNeer, "Lynd Ward," pp. 249-253.

In These Times, October 14, 2005, Christopher Capozzola, "Silent Beauty."

Time, January 2, 1933, review of *Wild Pilgrimage: A Novel in Woodcuts.*

■ Obituaries

PERIODICALS

Chicago Tribune, July 5, 1985.
Publishers Weekly, July 19, 1985.
Washington Post, June 30, 1985.*

Scott Westerfeld

■ Personal

Born May 5, 1963, in Dallas, TX; son of Lloyd (a computer programmer) and Pamela Westerfeld; married Justine Larbalestier (a researcher and writer), 2001. *Education:* Vassar College, B.A., 1985; graduate study in performance studies, New York University, 1987-88.

■ Addresses

Home—New York, NY; Sydney, New South Wales, Australia. *Agent*—Jill Grinberg, Jill Grinberg Literary Management, 244 5th Ave., 11th Fl., New York, NY 10001. *E-mail*—scott@scottwesterfeld.com.

■ Career

Writer, composer, and media designer. Has also worked as a factory worker, substitute teacher, and textbook editor.

■ Awards, Honors

Philip K. Dick Award special citation, 2000, for *Evolution's Darling;* Aurealis Award for Best Young-Adult Novel (Australia), 2004, for *The Secret Hour;* Victoria Premier's Award shortlist, 2005, for *So Yesterday;* New York Public Library Books for the Teen Age selection, 2005, for *The Secret Hour,* 2006, for both *Uglies, Pretties,* and *Peeps,* and 2007, for *Blue Noon;* Best Books for Young Adults citations, American Library Association, 2005, for *So Yesterday,* and 2006, for both *Peeps* and *Uglies.*

■ Writings

"MIDNIGHTERS" SERIES

The Secret Hour, Eos (New York, NY), 2004.
Touching Darkness, Eos (New York, NY), 2005.
Blue Noon, Eos (New York, NY), 2006.

"UGLIES" SERIES

Uglies, Simon Pulse (New York, NY), 2005.
Pretties, Simon Pulse (New York, NY), 2005.
Specials, Simon Pulse (New York, NY), 2006.
Extras, Simon Pulse (New York, NY), 2007.
Bogus to Bubbly: An Insider's Guide to the World of Uglies, Simon Pulse (New York, NY), 2008.

YOUNG-ADULT SCIENCE-FICTION NOVELS

So Yesterday, Razorbill (New York, NY), 2004.
Peeps, Razorbill (New York, NY), 2005.

The Last Days (sequel to *Peeps*), Razorbill (New York, NY), 2006.

Leviathan, illustrated by Keith Thompson, Simon Pulse (New York, NY), 2009.

ADULT SCIENCE-FICTION NOVELS

Polymorph, Penguin (New York, NY), 1997.

Fine Prey, Penguin (New York, NY), 1998.

Evolution's Darling, Four Walls Eight Windows (New York, NY), 1999.

The Risen Empire ("Succession" series), Tor (New York, NY), 2003.

The Killing of Worlds ("Succession" series), Tor (New York, NY), 2003.

FOR CHILDREN

The Berlin Airlift, Silver Burdett (Englewood Cliffs, NJ), 1989.

Watergate, Silver Burdett (Englewood Cliffs, NJ), 1991.

Blossom vs. the Blasteroid, Scholastic (New York, NY), 2002.

Diamonds Are for Princess, Scholastic (New York, NY), 2002.

Rainy Day Professor, Scholastic (New York, NY), 2002.

OTHER

(Editor) *The World of The Golden Compass: The Otherworldly Ride Continues,* Borders Group (Ann Arbor, MI), 2007.

Contributor to science-fiction anthologies, including *The Starry Rift: Tales of New Tomorrows,* Viking, 2008, and *Love Is Hell,* HarperTeen, 2009.

■ Adaptations

Twentieth Century-Fox purchased film rights to the first three "Uglies" books; *So Yesterday* was optioned for film; the WB television network optioned rights to the "Midnighters" series.

■ Sidelights

Although Scott Westerfeld has become known for his young-adult science fiction, he wrote several books for adults before hitting the bestseller lists with works such as his "Uglies" series. He also worked as a textbook editor, software designer, ghost writer, and composer of dance music. Reviewers have characterized Westerfeld's science-fiction novels as "space opera," which Gerald Jonas, writing in the *New York Times Book Review,* defines as "far-future narratives that encompass entire galaxies and move confidently among competing planets and cultures, both human and otherwise." In an interview on the Penguin Group Web site, Westerfeld defined science fiction as "a way of writing (and of reading) which utilizes the power of extrapolation. It expands both the real world . . . and the literary. In regular fiction, you might be alienated. In [science fiction], you're an alien."

Stories were an important part of growing up, Westerfeld told *SF Site* online interviewer Kevin Stone: "I come from a big family in Texas, in which story telling was very valued. And I've always written, as far back as I can remember." Moving around as a child also fed his creative spirit, Westerfeld told an interviewer for *Locus:* "I moved all over the country as a kid because my father was a computer programmer when computers were big as a house and came with guys in suits to make them work. Every time we went to a new place, I was reinventing myself." He completed high school in Texas, got a degree in philosophy at Vassar, and moved to New York City.

Westerfeld's first science-fiction novels were written for adults. Published in 1997, *Polymorph* explores identity and sexual issues with a title character who is able to change both gender and appearance. In his Penguin Group interview, Westerfeld explained how his move to New York City inspired the idea for the story. "When I first moved to New York in the 1980s, I was amazed that it was such a richly textured city: layers of graffiti, legacies of immigrant influences, overlapping strata of big money and extreme poverty. To explore it all, you'd have to be a polymorph." Praising *Polymorph, Booklist* contributor John Mort called Westerfeld "a writer to watch."

Westerfeld's other adult novels include *Evolution's Darling,* which earned its author a Philip K. Dick Award special citation. The novel tells the story of Darling, an artificial intelligence that evolves into a sentient being through a relationship with a teenage girl. The reader follows Darling as the character becomes a galactic art dealer and develops a relationship with Mira, a high-tech killer. Trevor Dodge, writing in the *Review of Contemporary Fiction,* stated that in *Evolution's Darling* Westerfeld challenges the reader to "ponder if a machine can be made human, and if so, what purpose humanity would serve." In the "Succession" series, which includes *The Risen Empire* and *The Killing of Worlds,* the author tells the story of a space empire at war with itself, complete with space battles, machine-enhanced humans, a kidnapped princess, and a heroic spaceship captain. Comparing *The Risen Empire* to sci-fi classics like *Dune* and *Star Wars*, *Kliatt* contributor Cara Chancellor dubbed the novel "a must-read that is sure to find an honored place in science fiction lore."

New Audience for His Works

Westerfeld had not planned to begin writing for young adults, but then he had the idea for the "Midnighters" series, about a group of teens who can see time freeze every night at midnight. "That was inspired by memories of sneaking out at night in Texas and walking around in the emptiness and stillness of the wee hours," Westerfeld told Rob Bed-

Cover of Scott Westerfeld's novel *The Secret Hour*, a "Midnighters" novel featuring cover art by Kamil Vojnar. (EOS, a HarperCollins Publishers imprint, 2004. Used by permission of HarperCollins Children's Books, a division of HarperCollins Publishers.)

ford for *SFF World.com*. "As a teenage memory, the idea only made sense as YA." The first volume, *The Secret Hour,* opens as teenager Jessica Day moves to Bixby, Oklahoma. She soon learns that she is a Midnighter, a person born at the hour of midnight who has the ability to move about during the twenty-fifth hour of the day, a blue-tinted hour in which all other life is immobile. She meets other Midnighters at Bixby High School, including Rex, Dess, and Melissa, and finds out that they possess a range of other special abilities, too: one teen can read minds, while another can float nearly weightless in the air. These powers help them avoid the unpleasant and dangerous creatures that also dwell in the twenty-fifth hour, including darklings and slithers. When Jessica arrives in Bixby, the darklings and other creatures suddenly increase in number and ferocity, and the Midnighters have to rely on steel weapons and thirteen-letter-words to fight them. Westerfeld "concocts a unique and fresh fantasy setting just beyond the edge of our consciousness," commented Michele Winship in *Kliatt*. "The story is exciting and the writing compelling," noted *School Library Journal* contributor Sharon Grover.

"Once I started writing YA, I found myself enjoying it too much to stop," Westerfeld told Lawrence Schimel in an interview for the Cynsations Web site. He continues the "Midnighters" saga in *Touching Darkness,* in which Jessica is stalked during the daytime by someone who may be related to the midnight hour's darkling monsters. "Westerfeld keeps the story going at a good pace and has deepened not only the mythology of the series, but also the characters," Charles de Lint wrote in the *Magazine of Fantasy and Science Fiction*. "I really like the way the individuals and group dynamics continue to evolve and change, the characters reacting the way real people do, showing petty traits as well as selfless heroics." In *Blue Noon,* the third volume of the series, the horrific creatures of the Midnight Hour can now appear in the daytime, and the Midnighters must prevent them from ripping the boundary between worlds and destroying their city. "Westerfeld has once again crafted a plot that keeps readers on the edges of their seats, not knowing what might be around the next corner," Winship noted. A *Kirkus Reviews* writer called *Blue Noon* a "thrilling conclusion to the trilogy" and added: "A powerful climax smoothly ties together the complexities of this original and well-drawn world."

In the standalone novel *So Yesterday,* seventeen-year-old Hunter spends his time working for a well-known sports show company, seeking out the newest fads, trends, and things that are "cool" on the streets of New York City. When he notices a girl named Jen, Hunter realizes that her unique shoe-lacing technique makes her an Innovator, a person who originates trends, whereas he is a Trendsetter, who adopts the trends and makes them cool. Hunter

Cover of Westerfeld's novel *So Yesterday*, his first work of science fiction written specifically for a teen readership. (Cover copyright © 2004 by Lauren Monchik and John Son, photographs. Reproduced by permission of Razorbill, a division of Penguin Putnam Books for Young Readers.)

takes a photo of the laces, and when his boss, Mandy, sees them, she invites Hunter and Jen to a brainstorming session. However, when the two teens arrive at the large warehouse where the meeting is scheduled to occur, Mandy is not there; they find only her cell phone, ominously ringing in the absence of its owner. The danger becomes more real when they realize that a radical group, with the apparent mission of dealing grassroots damage to large corporations, has kidnapped Mandy. Soon Hunter and Jen are on Mandy's trail, dodging the mounting danger and racing against time to save her. A *Kirkus Reviews* contributor called Hunter "a charming narrator with an original take on teen life." Westerfeld's "entertaining adventure doubles as a smart critique on marketing and our consumer culture," observed a *Publishers Weekly* critic.

Dystopian Novels

Westerfeld's *Uglies* is the first book in a series that explores a future world in which physical imperfection has been banished, and citizens receive operations on their sixteenth birthday that make them happy, carefree, and gorgeous. Fifteen-year-old Tally Youngblood, a resident of Uglyville, is herself an "ugly," and she eagerly anticipates her birthday and the procedure that will transform her into a blissful and lovely "pretty." Tally's best friend has already had the Pretty procedure, and she sneaks into town to see him. This act nearly gets her captured, but in the turmoil, she meets a new best friend, Shay. Shay tells Tally that she plans to run away to an outside settlement called The Smoke, outside the reach of the governmental powers that control the Uglies and the Pretties. Tally is forced into locating Shay and leading government agents to the rebel settlement; once there, however, she begins to realize that maybe the residents of the Smoke are rebelling for a very good reason. Her conscience keeps her from betraying the rebels, but her act of heroism leads her to consequences that will affect her forever. With its appealing storyline, this "ingenious series debut [will] cement Westerfeld's reputation for high-concept YA fiction that has wide appeal," noted *Booklist* reviewer Jennifer Mattson. *Uglies* "asks engaging questions about the meaning of beauty, individuality, and betrayal," observed Samantha Musher, writing in *Kliatt*.

The second book of the series, *Pretties,* opens with Tally enjoying the shallow, party-filled life of a Pretty. Only after opening a letter from herself does she remember that she is supposed to test a cure for the brain lesions given to those who undergo the Pretty procedure. When she splits the cure with her friend Zane, unforeseen consequences lead her to a hidden society once again. While *Horn Book* contributor Susan Dove Lempke did not think that *Pretties* is effective as a stand-alone novel, she added that "the pace moves quickly with twists; and Tally is a memorable, believable character." "*Pretties* continues to ask questions about friendship and betrayal, while building one of the most fascinating worlds in recent SF," Musher remarked, and *School Library Journal* contributor Tasha Saecker likewise noted of the novel that "Westerfeld has built a masterfully complex and vivid civilization."

In the third book, *Specials,* Tally has become part of an elite military force battling a neighboring city. "As the gripping plot progresses, Tally struggles with the underlying question of her identity," Lempke observed. Mattson wrote that "details of the cult like Specials . . . inventively combine with the premise's winning themes: free will, self-image, and teen-powered subversion of authority." Musher also offered praise for the work, noting that "Westerfeld is a master of grey areas" who offers readers big, world-shaking issues and small character problems. The result "is a thrilling, painful, and ultimately satisfying finale to the best YA SF in years."

In the 2008 sequel *Extras*, the author shows how the world of Uglies has changed now that beauty is no longer society's standard of success. In a nameless Japanese city, fifteen-year-old Aya aspires to gain "face rank," a measure of fame and celebrity. She pursues a story about a joyriding hoverboard group, hoping to become famous as a reporter, but she discovers a threat to her city instead. Eventually, Tally and her friend come to assist Aya in uncovering the plot. "As usual, Westerfeld excels at creating a futuristic pop culture that feels thrillingly plausible," Mattson noted in *Booklist*. In addition, Aya's numerous gadgets "keep the action popping, taking us on a thrilling joyride through Westerfeld's futuristic, technology-rich imagination," Anita L. Burkham remarked in *Horn Book*. "Teens will find themselves drawn to Aya," June H. Keuhn concluded in *School Library Journal*, the critic adding in her review that with *Extras* Westerfeld "delivers another page-turner."

Vampiric Tales

Peeps contains Westerfeld's unique take on the age-old vampire legend. Cal Thompson, a nineteen year old who has recently moved to New York for college. He has also recently lost his virginity, and this rite of passage has resulted in Cal becoming infected with the parasite that causes vampirism, turning him into a parasite-positive, or "peep." Cal does not become a full-fledged vampire; instead, he simply becomes a carrier of the parasite, and he acquires some of the heightened physical abilities of vampires. He lands a job with a shadowy organization called Night Watch, a group that identifies and hunts down other peeps. Cal begins searching for Morgan, the woman who infected him after a drunken one night stand, but during his search, he uncovers disturbing information about Night Watch that makes him question the motives of the organization he works for. Along with Cal's story, *Peeps* also offers information on parasitology and creepy details on how parasites find and interact with their hosts. "This is definitely a story to get the brain working," mused a *Publishers Weekly* writer. "A clever blend of adventure, horror, romance, and science text, *Peeps* holds great appeal for teen readers," commented Merri Lindgren in *Horn Book*. A *Kirkus Reviews* critic called the book "scary indeed, and a smashing page-turner offering supreme satisfac-

tion," while *School Library Journal* reviewer Karyn N. Silverman concluded that Westerfeld's "innovative and original vampire story, full of engaging characters and just enough horror without any gore, will appeal to a wide audience."

The Last Days is set in the same world as *Peeps* and focuses on five members of a rock band. "Having been in bands as a kid, I always wanted to set a novel inside that microcosm of clashing egos and crowd magic," the author told Bedford in *SFF World. com*. "Westerfeld continues his captivating, original vision, improving it in this tightly plotted sequel" to *Peeps*, Lynn Rutan observed in *Booklist*, and a *Kirkus Reviews* critic called *The Last Days* "a broader, lateral look at the same world [as *Peeps*], with suspense, touches of humor and eminently appealing characters." "Westerfeld knows how to create a narrative," Myrna Marler remarked in *Kliatt*. "His

Cover of Westerfeld's *The Killing of Worlds*, a "Succession" series novel featuring artwork by Stephan Martiniere. (TOR, a Tom Doherty Associates Book, 2003. Reproduced by permission.)

plots have action, vivid scenes, snappy dialog, and interesting characterizations." *School Library Journal* contributor Jack Forman likewise found the dialogue to be "crisp and clear and alternately funny and biting," and called *Peeps* "a real winner."

If you enjoy the works of Scott Westerfeld, you may also want to check out the following books:

Lois Lowry, *The Giver*, 1993.
Amelia Atwater-Rhodes, *Demon in My View*, 2000.
Robert J. Sawyer, *Rollback*, 2007.

Although he has other ideas for adult novels, Westerfeld plans to continue courting a young-adult audience. Not only has it brought him more fun and more success, he finds teens a good match for science fiction. "A lot of YA is about identity: 'Who am I?' 'How do I fit into this world?' There's that uncomfortableness in your skin," he explained in an interview with *Locus*. "And if you're a science fiction writer or reader that never goes away, because you're still looking at the world and challenging it, saying 'Does it have to be this way? Does it make any sense that we follow these rules?' Science fiction is about thought experiments. What does it mean to tell stories set in a different place than this one? How does that affect *our* world? It's a completely philosophical enterprise." As for his readers, Westerfeld told a *Publishers Weekly* contributor that he hopes they can see that "the world is a pretty weird and amazing place, especially when people look at it closely instead of trying to mystify it. A fascination with the world—the human world, the natural world, all of it—and a love of language are the two things I want to leave my readers with."

■ **Biographical and Critical Sources**

PERIODICALS

Booklist, December 1, 1997, John Mort, review of *Polymorph*, p. 612; February 15, 2003, Regina Schroeder, review of *The Risen Empire*, p. 1060; September 15, 2003, Regina Schroeder, review of *The Killing of Worlds*, p. 219; September 15, 2004, Gillian Engberg, review of *So Yesterday*, p. 235; March 15, 2005, Jennifer Mattson, review of *Uglies*, p. 1287; May 1, 2005, Gillian Engberg, review of *So Yesterday*, p. 1543; August, 2005, Jennifer Mattson, review of *Peeps*, p. 2019; September 15, 2005, Jennifer Hubert, review of *Pretties*, p. 60; May 15, 2006, Jennifer Mattson, "After the First Bite," review of *Peeps*, p. 56; May 15, 2006, Jennifer Mattson, review of *Specials*, p. 58; September 1, 2006, Lynn Rutan, review of *The Last Days*, p. 112; January 1, 2008, Jennifer Mattson, review of *Extras*, p. 58.

Horn Book, January-February, 2005, Roger Sutton, review of *So Yesterday*, p. 101; November-December, 2005, Susan Dove Lempke, review of *Pretties*, p. 727; January-February, 2006, Merri Lindgren review of *Peeps*, p. 91; September-October, 2006, Susan Dove Lempke, review of *Specials*, p. 599; November-December, 2007, Anita L. Burkam, review of *Extras*, p. 687.

Kirkus Reviews, January 15, 2003, review of *The Risen Empire*, p. 118; January 15, 2004, review of *The Secret Hour*, p. 90; August 1, 2004, review of *So Yesterday*, p. 750; February 1, 2005, review of *Touching Darkness*, p. 182; February 15, 2005, review of *Uglies*, p. 237; August 1, 2005, review of *Peeps*, p. 860; October 15, 2005, review of *Pretties*, p. 1148; January 1, 2006, review of *Blue Noon*, p. 46; May 1, 2006, review of *Specials*, p. 470; August 1, 2006, review of *The Last Days*, p. 798; September 15, 2007, review of *Extras*.

Kliatt, March, 2004, Michele Winship, review of *The Secret Hour*, p. 16; September, 2004, Michele Winship, review of *So Yesterday*, p. 17; March, 2005, Samantha Musher, review of *Uglies*, p. 29; September, 2005, Myrna Marler, review of *Peeps*, p. 16; January, 2006, Samantha Musher, review of *Pretties*, p. 22; March, 2006, Michele Winship, review of *Blue Noon*, p. 18; May, 2006, Samantha Musher, review of *Specials*, p. 17; September, 2006, Myrna Marler, review of *The Last Days*, p. 19; November, 2007, Samantha Musher, review of *Extras*, p. 15; November, 2008, Cara Chancellor, review of *The Risen Empire*, p. 19.

Library Journal, April 15, 2000, review of *Evolution's Darling*, p. 128; September 15, 2003, Jackie Cassada, review of *The Killing of Worlds*, p. 95.

Locus, May, 2006, "Scott Westerfeld: New Kid in Town," p. 6.

Magazine of Fantasy and Science Fiction, June, 2004, Charles de Lint, review of *The Secret Hour*, p. 32; June, 2006, Charles de Lint, reviews of *Touching Darkness* and *Blue Noon*, p. 29.

New York Times Book Review, June 18, 2000, Gerald Jonas, review of *Evolution's Darling*, p. 22; April 27, 2003, Gerald Jonas, review of *The Risen Empire*, p. 23.

Philadelphia Inquirer, September 13, 2006, David Hiltbrand, "Author Scott Westerfeld Found His Niche Writing for Teenagers."

Publishers Weekly, April 17, 2000, review of *Evolution's Darling*, p. 57; January 20, 2003, review of *The Risen Empire*, p. 61; September 15, 2003, review of *The Killing of Worlds*, p. 50; March 22, 2004, review of *The Secret Hour*, p. 87; October 4, 2004, review of *So Yesterday*, p. 89; March 21, 2005, review of *Uglies*, p. 52; October 3, 2005, review of *Peeps*, p. 71; October 17, 2005, review of *Pretties*, p. 70.

Review of Contemporary Fiction, fall, 2000, Trevor Dodge, review of *Evolution's Darling*, p. 151.

School Library Journal, December, 1989, Ann Welton, review of *The Berlin Airlift*, p. 127; June, 2004, Sharon Grover, review of *The Secret Hour*, p. 152; October, 2004, Kelly Czarnecki, review of *So Yesterday*, p. 182; March, 2005, Sharon Grover, review of *Touching Darkness*, p. 220; March, 2005, Susan W. Hunter, review of *Uglies*, p. 221; October, 2005, Karyn N. Silverman, review of *Peeps*, p. 178; December, 2005, Tasha Saecker, review of *Pretties*, p. 158; July, 2006, Karyn N. Silverman, review of *Peeps*, p. 37; July, 2006, Heather M. Campbell, review of *Blue Noon*, p. 114; July, 2006, Corinda J. Humphrey, review of *Specials*, p. 116; November, 2006, Jack Forman, review of *The Last Days*, p. 156; January, 2008, June H. Keuhn, review of *Extras*, p. 129.

Science Fiction Chronicle, February-March, 2003, Don D'Ammassa, review of *The Risen Empire*, p. 54.

ONLINE

Analog Science Fiction Online, http://www.analogsf.com/ (July 6, 2003), Tom Easton, review of *The Risen Empire*.

Baltimore City Paper Online, http://www.citypaper.com/ (July 12, 2000), Adrienne Martini, review of *Evolution's Darling*.

Cynsations Web log, http://cynthialeitichsmith.blogspot.com/ (February, 2006) Lawrence Schimel, "SCBWI Bologna 2006 Author Interview: Scott Westerfeld."

Penguin Group Web site, http://us.penguingroup.com/ (May 16, 2007), interview with Westerfeld.

Publishers Weekly Online, http://www.publishersweekly.com/ (March 23, 2006), Kate Pavao, interview with Westerfeld.

Sci-Fi.com, http://www.scifi.com/ (May 16, 2007), Thomas Myer, review of *Polymorph*; (May 16, 2007) Paul Witcover, review of *Evolution's Darling*; (May 16, 2007) Steven Sawicki, review of short story "Non-Disclosure Agreement"; (May 16, 2007) Donna McMahon, review of *Fine Prey*.

Scott Westerfeld Home Page, http://www.scottwesterfeld.com (April 1, 2009).

SF Crowsnest Web site, http://www.sfcrowsnest.com/ (January 4, 2005), interview with Westerfeld.

SF Site, http://www.sfsite.com/ (December, 2006), Kevin Stone, "A Conversation with Scott Westerfeld."

SFF World.com, http://www.sffworld.com/ (September 2, 2006), Rob Bedford, interview with Westerfeld.*

Author/Artist Index

The following index gives the number of the volume in
which an author/artist's biographical sketch appears:

Aaseng, Nathan 1953- 27
Abbey, Edward 1927-1989 75
Abbott, Berenice 1898-1991 40
Abelove, Joan 36
Abrams, J.J. 1966- 61
Achebe, Chinua 1930- 15
Adams, Ansel 1902-1984 14
Adams, Douglas 1952-2001 .... 4, 33
Adams, Neal 1941- 64
Adams, Richard 1920- 16
Adams, Scott 1957- 27
Adichie, Chimamanda Ngozi 1977- 80
Adler, C.S. 1932- 4, 41
Adoff, Arnold 1935- 3, 50
Agee, James 1909-1955 44
Aiken, Joan 1924-2004 .... 1, 25
Aird, Catherine 1930- 76
Albee, Edward 1928- 51
Albom, Mitch 1958- 38
Alcock, Vivien 1924-2003 .... 8, 57
Alcott, Louisa May 1832-1888 20
Aldiss, Brian W. 1925- 42
Alexander, Lloyd 1924-2007 .... 1, 27
Alexie, Sherman 1966- 28
Ali, Monica 1967- 67
Allen, Tim 1953- 24
Allen, Woody 1935- 10, 51
Allende, Isabel 1942- 18, 70
Allred, Michael 70
Allison, Dorothy 1949- 53
Almond, David 1951- 38
Alphin, Elaine Marie 1955- 76
Alvarez, Julia 1950- 25
Alvarez Bravo, Manuel 1902-2002 59
Ambrose, Stephen E. 1936-2002 44
Amend, Bill 1962- 52
Amis, Kingsley 1922-1995 77
Anaya, Rudolfo 1937- 20
Andersen, Hans Christian 1805-1875 57
Anderson, Ho Che 1970(?)- 55
Anderson, Kevin J. 1962- 34
Anderson, Laurie 1947- 72
Anderson, Laurie Halse 1961- 39
Anderson, M.T. 1968- 60
Anderson, Poul 1926-2001 .... 5, 34
Anderson, Sherwood 1876-1941 30
Andrews, Donna 73
Andrews, V.C. 1923(?)-1986 .... 4, 41
Angell, Judie 1937- 11, 71

Angelou, Maya 1928- 7, 20
Anouilh, Jean 1910-1987 67
Anthony, Piers 1934- 11, 48
Apatow, Judd 1968- 49
Appel, Allen 1945- 33
Applegate, K.A. 1956- 37
Aragones, Sergio 1937- 56
Archer, Jeffrey 1940- 16
Archie Comics 9
Armstrong, Gillian 1950- 74
Armstrong, Jennifer 1961- 28
Armstrong, William H. 1914-1999 18
Aronson, Marc 1948- 67
Asaro, Catherine 1955- 47
Ashabranner, Brent 1921- 6, 46
Asher, Sandy 1942- 17
Asimov, Isaac 1920-1992 13
Asprin, Robert L. 1946- 33
Attanasio, A.A. 1951- 45
Atwater-Rhodes, Amelia 1984- 40
Atwood, Margaret 1939- 12, 47
Auden, W.H. 1907-1973 18
Audubon, John James 1785-1851 76
Auel, Jean M. 1936- 7, 51
Austen, Jane 1775-1817 19
Avery, Tex 1908-1980 73
Avi 1937- 10, 37
Babbitt, Natalie 1932- 51
Bagdasarian, Adam 58
Bagnold, Enid 1889-1981 75
Baillie, Allan 1943- 25
Baldacci, David 1960- 60
Baldwin, James 1924-1987 .... 4, 34
Ballard, J.G. 1930-2009 .... 3, 52
Bambara, Toni Cade 1939-1995 .... 5, 49
Banks, Russell 1940- 45
Bantock, Nick 1949- 43
Baraka, Amiri 1934- 63
Barclay, Paris 1957- 55
Barker, Clive 1952- 10, 54
Barks, Carl 1901-2000 55
Barr, Nevada 1952(?)- 33
Barron, T.A. 1952- 30
Barry, Dave 1947- 14
Barry, Lynda 1956- 9, 54
Bartholdi, Frederic-Auguste 1834-1904 75
Bartoletti, Susan Campbell 1958- 44
Bat-Ami, Miriam 1950- 38
Bauer, Joan 34

Bauer, Marion Dane 1938- 19
Baum, L. Frank 1856-1919 46
Baxter, Stephen 1957- 67
Beagle, Peter S. 1939- 47
Bear, Greg 1951- 24
Bearden, Romare 1914-1988 67
Beatty, Patricia 1922-1991 16
Beckwith, James Carroll 1852-1917 78
Bedard, Michael 1949- 22
Bell, Hilari 1958- 78
Bell, William 1945- 75
Benchley, Peter 1940-2006 14
Bennett, Cherie 1960- 29
Bennett, James W. 1942- 26
Bennett, Jay 1912- 10, 73
Bergman, Ingmar 1918-2007 61
Berry, James 1925- 30
Bester, Alfred 1913-1987 71
Bethancourt, T. Ernesto 1932- 20
Bierce, Ambrose 1842-1914(?) 55
Billingsley, Franny 1954- 41
Bisson, Terry 1942- 43
Blackwood, Algernon 1869-1951 78
Blackwood, Gary L. 1945- 40
Blake, William 1757-1827 47
Blaylock, James 1950- 64
Bloch, Robert 1917-1994 29
Block, Francesca Lia 1962- 13, 34
Bloor, Edward 1950- 43
Blume, Judy 1938- 3, 26
Bober, Natalie S. 1930- 46
Bochco, Steven 1943- 11, 71
Bodanis, David 70
Bode, Janet 1943-1999 21
Bolden, Tonya 1959- 74
Bond, Edward 1934- 50
Bonham, Frank 1914-1989 .... 1, 70
Boorman, John 1933- 3
Borges, Jorges Luis 1899-1986 26
Borglum, Gutzon 1867-1941 80
Borgman, Jim 1954- 70
Bosch, Hieronymus 1450(?)-1516 65
Bosse, Malcolm 1933-2002 16
Bourke-White, Margaret 1904-1971 51
Bova, Ben 1932- 16
Boyle, T. Coraghessan 1948- 47
Bradbury, Ray 1920- 15
Bradley, Kimberly Brubaker 1967- 59
Bradley, Marion Zimmer 1930-1999 .... 9, 40
Brady, Mathew B. 1823-1896 75
Braff, Zach 1975- 70
Branagh, Kenneth 1960- 20, 59
Brancato, Robin F. 1936- 9, 68
Brâncuşi, Constantin 1876-1957 62
Branscum, Robbie 1937-1997 19
Brashares, Ann 52
Braun, Lilian Jackson 1916(?)- 29
Breashars, David 1955- 73

Breathed, Berke 1957- 5, 61
Breslin, Theresa 54
Brian, Kate 1974- 74
Bridgers, Sue Ellen 1942- 8, 49
Brin, David 1950- 21
Brite, Poppy Z. 1967- 44
Brontë, Charlotte 1816-1855 17
Brontë, Emily 1818-1848 17
Brooks, Bruce 1950- 8, 36
Brooks, Gwendolyn 1917-2000 20
Brooks, James L. 1940- 17
Brooks, Martha 1944- 37
Brooks, Mel 1926- 13, 48
Brooks, Terry 1944- 18
Brown, Chester 1960- 72
Brown, Claude 1937-2002 7
Brown, Dan 1964- 55
Brown, Dee 1908-2002 30
Brown, Fredric 1906-1972 77
Browning, Elizabeth Barrett 1806-1861 63
Brubaker, Ed 79
Bruchac, Joseph 1942- 19
Bruegel, Pieter, the Elder 1525(?)-1569 71
Brust, Steven K. 1955- 36
Bryan, Ashley F. 1923- 68
Buck, Pearl S. 1892-1973 42
Buffie, Margaret 1945- 23
Bujold, Lois McMaster 1949- 19, 54
Bulgakov, Mikhail 1891-1940 74
Bull, Emma 1954- 31
Bunting, Eve 1928- 5, 61
Burgess, Anthony 1917-1993 25
Burgess, Melvin 1954- 28
Burns, Ken 1953- 42
Burns, Olive Ann 1924-1990 32
Burns, Robert 1759-1796 51
Burroughs, Augusten 1965- 73
Burroughs, Edgar Rice 1875-1950 11
Burroughs, William S. 1914-1997 60
Burton, Tim 1958- 14, 65
Busiek, Kurt 1960- 53
Butler, Octavia E. 1947- 18, 48
Byars, Betsy 1928- 19
Byrne, John 1950- 66
Byron, Lord 1788-1824 64
Cabot, Meg 1967- 50
Cadigan, Pat 1953- 53
Cadnum, Michael 1949- 23
Cahill, Tim 1944- 25
Calatrava, Santiago 1951- 78
Caldecott, Randolph 1846-1886 .... 53, 64
Calder, Alexander 1898-1976 25
Caletti, Deb 75
Calhoun, Dia 1959- 44
Calvert, Patricia 1931- 18
Calvino, Italo 1923-1985 58
Cameron, Ann 1943- 59
Cameron, James 1954- 9, 27

Campbell, Bebe Moore 1950- 26
Campbell, Joseph 1904-1987 .... 3, 66
Campbell, Ramsey 1946- 51
Campion, Jane 1954- 33
Camus, Albert 1913-1960 36
Caniff, Milton 1907-1988 55
Cannell, Stephen J. 1941- 9, 68
Capa, Robert 1913-1954 66
Capote, Truman 1924-1984 61
Capra, Frank 1897-1991 52
Caputo, Philip 1941- 60
Carbone, Elisa 1954- 67
Card, Orson Scott 1951- 11, 42
Carey, Jacqueline 1964- 68
Carmack, John 1971- 59
Carpenter, John 1948- 2, 73
Carroll, Jim 1951- 17
Carroll, Jonathan 1949- 74
Carroll, Lewis 1832-1898 39
Carson, Rachel 1907-1964 49
Carter, Alden R. 1947- 17, 54
Carter, Chris 1956- 23
Cartier-Bresson, Henri 1908-2004 63
Carver, Raymond 1938-1988 44
Cash, Johnny 1932-2003 63
Cassatt, Mary 1844-1926 22
Castillo, Ana 1953- 42
Cather, Willa 1873-1947 24
Catlin, George 1796-1872 78
Cervantes, Miguel de 1547-1616 56
Cezanne, Paul 1839-1906 54
Chabon, Michael 1963- 45
Chadwick, Paul 1957- 35
Chagall, Marc 1887-1985 24
Chambers, Aidan 1934- 27
Chambers, Veronica 1970(?)- 54
Chandler, Raymond 1888-1959 25
Chaplin, Charlie 1889-1977 61
Charbonneau, Eileen 1951- 35
Charnas, Suzy McKee 1939- 43
Chatwin, Bruce 1940-1989 4
Cheever, John 1912-1982 65
Chekhov, Anton 1860-1904 68
Cherryh, C.J. 1942- 24
Chesterton, G.K. 1874-1936 57
Chevalier, Tracy 46
Chiang, Ted 1967- 66
Chicago, Judy 1939- 46
Chihuly, Dale 1941- 46
Child, Lincoln 1957- 32
Childress, Alice 1920-1994 8
Cho, Frank 1971- 68
Choi, Sook Nyul 1937- 38
Choldenko, Gennifer 1957- 73
Chopin, Kate 1851-1904 33
Christie, Agatha 1890-1976 9
Christo 1935- 53
Christopher, John 1922- 22

Cisneros, Sandra 1954- 9, 53
Clancy, Tom 1947- 9, 51
Clark, Catherine 76
Clark, Mary Higgins 1929- 10, 55
Clark Bekederemo, J.P. 1935- 79
Clarke, Arthur C. 1917-2008 .... 4, 33
Clarke, Judith 1943- 34
Cleary, Beverly 1916- 6, 62
Cleaver, Vera 1919-1993 12
Close, Chuck 1940- 28
Clowes, Dan 1961- 42
Clugston, Chynna 1975- 76
Cocteau, Jean 1889-1963 74
Coen, Ethan 1958- 54
Coen, Joel 1955- 54
Coetzee, J.M. 1940- 37
Cofer, Judith Ortiz 1952- 30
Cohen, Barbara 1932-1992 24
Cohn, Rachel 1968- 65
Cohen, Daniel 1936- 7
Cole, Brock 1938- 15, 45
Cole, Thomas 1801-1848 77
Coleridge, Samuel Taylor 1772-1834 66
Colfer, Eoin 1965- 48
Collier, Christopher 1930- 13
Collier, James Lincoln 1928- 13
Collins, Billy 1941- 64
Collins, Max Allan 1948- 51
Colman, Hila 1, 69
Colman, Penny 1944- 42
Coman, Carolyn 41
Conford, Ellen 1942- 10, 70
Conly, Jane Leslie 1948- 32
Connell, Evan S. 1924- 7
Conrad, Joseph 1857-1924 26
Conrad, Pam 1947-1996 18
Conroy, Pat 1945- 8, 52
Cook, Monte 63
Cook, Robin 1940- 32
Cooney, Caroline B. 1947- 5, 32
Cooper, James Fenimore 1789-1851 22
Cooper, J. California 12
Cooper, Susan 1935- 13, 41
Coppola, Francis Ford 1939- 39
Coppola, Sofia 1971- 69
Corcoran, Barbara 1911- 14
Cormier, Robert 1925-2000 .... 3, 19
Cornell, Joseph 1903-1972 56
Cornwell, Bernard 1944- 47
Cornwell, Patricia D. 1956- 16, 56
Coupland, Douglas 1961- 34
Coville, Bruce 1950- 40
Cox, Lynne 1957- 69
Crane, Stephen 1871-1900 21
Craven, Wes 1939- 6, 25
Creech, Sharon 1945- 21, 52
Cresswell, Helen 1934- 25
Crew, Gary 1947- 17

Crew, Linda 1951- 21
Crichton, Michael 1942- 10, 49
Crider, Bill 1941- 32
Crilley, Mark 1966- 50
Crispin, A.C. 1950- 33
Crombie, Deborah 1952- 45
Cross, Gillian 1945- 24
Crossley-Holland, Kevin 1941- 57
Crowe, Cameron 1957- 23, 59
Crowley, John 1942- 57
Crutcher, Chris 1946- 9, 39
Cullen, Countee 1903-1946 78
Cummings, E.E. 1894-1962 41
Cunningham, Imogen 1883-1976 54
Curtis, Christopher Paul 1954(?)- 37
Cushman, Karen 1941- 22, 60
Cusick, Richie Tankersley 1952- 14
Cussler, Clive 1931- 19
Daguerre, Louis 1787-1851 70
Dahl, Roald 1916-1990 15
Dali, Salvador 1904-1989 23
Dalkey, Kara 1953- 43
Daly, Maureen 1921-1983 .... 5, 58
Dante 1265-1321 53
Danticat, Edwidge 1969- 29
Danziger, Paula 1944-2004 .... 4, 36
Darabont, Frank 1959- 46
Dash, Julie 1952- 62
David, Larry 1947- 71
David, Peter 1956-
da Vinci, Leonardo .... See Leonardo da Vinci
Davis, Jack 1924- 69
Davis, Jenny 1953- 21
Davis, Jim 1945- 8, 72
Davis, Ossie 1917-2005 17
Davis, Stuart 1892-1964 71
Davis, Terry 1947- 50
Day, Dianne 1938- 43
Deans, Sis Boulos 1955- 59
Deaver, Jeffery 1950- 41
Deaver, Julie Reece 1953- 52
DeCarava, Roy 1919- 66
DeFelice, Cynthia 1951- 36
Defoe, Daniel 1660(?)-1731 27
Deford, Frank 1938- 14, 76
Degas, Edgar 1834-1917 56
Deighton, Len 1929- 6, 57
de Jenkins, Lyll Becerra 1925-1997 33
de Kooning, Willem 1904-1997 61
Delany, Samuel R. 1942- 24
de Lint, Charles 1951- 33
Delton, Judy 1931-2001 6
Demme, Jonathan 1944- 66
Desai Hidier, Tanuja 56
Dessen, Sarah 1970- 39
Deuker, Carl 1950- 26
Dexter, Colin 1930- 80
Dhondy, Farrukh 1944- 24

DiCamillo, Kate 1964- 47
Dick, Philip K. 1928-1982 24
Dickens, Charles 1812-1870 23
Dickey, James 1923-1997 50
Dickinson, Emily 1830-1886 22
Dickinson, Peter 1927- 9, 49
Dillard, Annie 1945- 6, 43
Disch, Thomas M. 1940-2008 17
Disney, Walt 1901-1966 22
Ditko, Steve 1927- 51
Doctorow, E.L. 1931- 22
Doherty, Berlie 1943- 18, 75
Doisneau, Robert 1912-1994 60
Donaldson, Stephen R. 1947- 36
Donne, John 1572-1631 67
Donnelly, Jennifer 1963- 72
Donner, Richard 1930- 34
Donovan, John 1928-1992 20
Doolittle, Hilda 1886-1961 66
Doran, Colleen 1963- 57
Dorris, Michael 1945-1997 20
Dostoevsky, Fedor 1821-1881 40
Douglas, Carole Nelson 1944- 17
Douglass, Frederick 1818-1895 48
Dove, Rita 1952- 46
Doyle, Arthur Conan 1859-1930 14
Doyle, Brian 1935- 16
Doyle, Roddy 1958(?)- 14
Drake, David 1945- 38
Draper, Sharon M. 1952- 28
Dr. Suess 1904-1991 48
Druett, Joan 1939- 77
Duane, Diane 1952- 30
Du Bois, W.E.B. 1868-1963 40
Duchamp, Marcel 1887-1968 47
Dumas, Alexandre 1802-1870 22
du Maurier, Daphne 1907-1989 37
Dunbar, Paul Laurence 1872-1906 75
Duncan, Lois 1934- 4, 34
Durbin, William 1951- 79
Dürer, Albrecht 1471-1528 58
Dygard, Thomas J. 1931-1996 .... 7, 69
Eastwood, Clint 1930- 18, 59
Eckert, Allan W. 1931- 18
Eddings, David 1931- 17
Edgerton, Clyde 1944- 17
Eggers, Dave 1970- 56
Egoyan, Atom 1960- 63
Eiseley, Loren 1907-1977 5
Eisenstaedt, Alfred 1898-1995 45
Eisner, Will 1917-2005 52
Elfman, Danny 1953- 14
Eliot, T.S. 1888-1914 28
Ellerbee, Linda 1944- 16
Elliott, Ted 1961- 80
Ellis, Bret Easton 1964- 2, 43
Ellis, Deborah 1960- 48
Ellis, Sarah 1952- 57

Ellison, Harlan 1934- 29
Ellison, Ralph 1914-1994 19
Elrod, P.N. 60
Emecheta, Buchi 1944- 67
Emerson, Ralph Waldo 1803-1882 60
Emmerich, Roland 1955- 53
Emmert, Jack 1969(?)- 76
Emshwiller, Carol 1921- 67
Engdahl, Sylvia Louise 1933- 36
Ephron, Nora 1941- 35
Erdrich, Louise 1954- 10, 47
Ernst, Kathleen 1959- 77
Escher, M.C. 1898-1972 16
Esquivel, Laura 1951(?)- 29
Estes, Richard 1932- 80
Estleman, Loren D. 1952- 27
Eugenides, Jeffrey 1960(?)- 51
Evanier, Mark 1952- 58
Evanovich, Janet 1943- 52
Evans, Greg 1947- 23
Evans, Walker 1903-1975 44
Ewing, Lynne 78
Falk, Lee 1911-1999 74
Farland, David .... See Wolverton, Dave
Farley, Walter 1915-1989 58
Farmer, Nancy 1941- 26, 53
Farmer, Philip José 1918- 28
Farrelly, Bobby 1957- 29
Farrelly, Peter 1956- 29
Fast, Howard 1914-2003 16
Faulkner, William 1897-1962 7
Feelings, Tom 1933-2003 25
Feiffer, Jules 1929- 3, 62
Feinstein, John 1956- 31
Feist, Raymond E. 1945- 72
Fellini, Federico 1920-1993 62
Ferlinghetti, Lawrence 1919- 74
Fernandez, Peter 1927- 67
Ferris, Jean 1939- 38
Ferry, Charles 1927- 29
Fey, Tina 1970- 72
Fielding, Helen 1958- 65
Fincher, David 1963- 36
Fine, Anne 1947- 20
Finney, Jack 1911-1995 30
Fisher, Terence 1904-1980 80
Fitzgerald, F. Scott 1896-1940 24
Fitzhugh, Louise 1928-1974 18
Flake, Sharon G. 76
Flanagan, John 1944- 78
Fleischman, Paul 1952- 11, 35
Fleming, Ian 1908-1964 26
Fleming, Victor 1889-1949 78
Fletcher, Susan 1951- 37
Flinn, Alex 1966- 50
Foer, Jonathan Safran 1977- 57
Fogelin, Adrian 1951- 67
Follett, Ken 1949- 6, 50
Foote, Shelby 1916-2005 40
Forbes, Esther 1891-1967 17
Ford, Jeffrey 1955- 57
Ford, John 1895-1973 75
Forman, James Douglas 1932- 17
Forman, Milos 1932- 63
Forster, E.M. 1879-1970 .... 2, 37
Foster, Alan Dean 1946- 16
Foster, Hal 1892-1982 51
Foster, Jodie 1962- 24
Fowler, Karen Joy 1950- 64
Fox, Paula 1923- 3, 37
Foxworthy, Jeff 1958- 80
Fradin, Dennis Brindell 1945- 49
Francis, Dick 1920- 5, 21
Frank, Anne 1929-1945 12
Frank, E.R. 1967- 60
Frank, Robert 1924- 67
Frankenthaler, Helen 1928- 62
Franzen, Jonathan 1959- 65
Frasconi, Antonio 1919- 58
Fraser, Antonia 1932- 57
Fraser, George MacDonald 1925- 48
Frayn, Michael 1933- 69
Frazetta, Frank 1928- 14
Frazier, Charles 1950- 34
Freedman, Russell 1929- 4, 24
Freymann-Wehr, Garret 1965- 52
Friedman, Thomas L. 1953- 72
Friesner, Esther M. 1951- 10
Frost, Robert 1874-1963 21
Fuentes, Carlos 1928- 4, 45
Fugard, Athol 1932- 17
Funke, Cornelia 1958- 68
Furlong, Monica 1930-2003 45
Gaiman, Neil 1960- 19, 42
Gaines, Ernest J. 1933- 18
Gallagher, Fred 1968- 67
Gallo, Donald R. 1938- 39
Gantos, Jack 1951- 40
Ganz, Lowell 1948- 69
García Lorca, Frederico 1898-1936 46
García Márquez, Gabriel 1928- 3, 33
Garden, Nancy 1938- 18, 55
Gardner, Erle Stanley 1889-1970 77
Gardner, John 1933-1982 45
Garfield, Leon 1921-1996 .... 8, 69
Garner, Alan 1934- 18
Gaskell, Elizabeth 1810-1865 80
Gaudí, Antonio 1852-1926 68
Gauguin, Paul 1848-1903 52
Gee, Maurice 1931- 42
Gehry, Frank 1929- 48
Gemmell, David 1948-2006 79
Gentileschi, Artemisia 1593-1652 68
George, Elizabeth 1949- 80
George, Jean Craighead 1919- 8, 69
Geras, Adèle 1944- 48

Gerritsen, Tess 1953- 42
Gershwin, George 1898-1937 62
Gerstein, Mordicai 1935- 69
Gibbons, Kaye 1960- 34
Giblin, James Cross 1933- 39
Gibson, Mel 1956- 80
Gibson, William 1948- 12, 59
Giff, Patricia Reilly 1935- 54
Gilliam, Terry 1940- 19, 59
Gilman, Charlotte Perkins 1860-1935 75
Gilstrap, John 1957- 67
Ginsberg, Allen 1926-1997 33
Giovanni, Nikki 1943- 22
Glenn, Mel 1943- 25
Godden, Rumer 1907-1998 6
Golding, William 1911-1993 .... 5, 44
Goldsworth, Andy 1956- 79
Gonzalez, Genaro 1949- 15
Gonzalez, Maya Christina 1964- 72
Goodkind, Terry 1948- 27, 74
Gordimer, Nadine 1923- 39
Gorey, Edward 1925-2000 40
Goudge, Eileen 1950- 6
Gould, Chester 1900-1985 7
Gould, Stephen Jay 1941-2002 26
Goya, Francisco 1746-1828 55
Grafton, Sue 1940- 11, 49
Graham, Heather 50
Graham, Jorie 1950- 67
Grant, Cynthia D. 1950- 23
Gray, Spalding 1941-2004 62
El Greco 1541-1614 64
Green, Jane 1968- 74
Greenaway, Kate 1846-1901 56
Greenberg, Joanne 1932- 12, 67
Greene, Bette 1934- 7, 69
Greene, Constance C. 1924- 7
Greene, Graham 1904-1991 61
Greenlaw, Linda 1962- 47
Greenwood, Ed 1959- 78
Griffin, Adele 1970- 37
Griffith, D.W. 1875-1948 78
Grimes, Nikki 1950- 53
Grisham, John 1955- 14, 47
Groening, Matt 1954- 8, 34
Gropius, Walter 1883-1969 79
Grove, Vicki 38
Guest, Judith 1936- 7, 66
Guisewite, Cathy 1950- 2, 45
Gutman, Dan 1955- 47
Guy, Rosa 1925- 4, 37
Guyton, Tyree 1955- 80
Gygax, E. Gary 1938- 65
Haddix, Margaret Peterson 1964- 42
Hague, Michael 1948- 18
Hahn, Mary Downing 1937- 23, 77
Haldeman, Joe 1943- 38
Hale, Shannon 75

Haley, Alex 1921-1992 26
Hall, Barbara 1960- 21
Hall, Donald 1928- 63
Hall, Lynn 1937- 4, 49
Hambly, Barbara 1951- 28
Hamilton, Steve 1961- 76
Hamilton, Virginia 1936-2002 .... 2, 21
Hamilton, Laurell K. 1963(?)- 46
Hammerstein, Oscar II 1895-1960 52
Hammett, Dashiell 1894-1961 59
Hampton, Brenda 1951- 62
Hamsun, Knut 1859-1952 79
Hand, Elizabeth 1957- 67
Hansberry, Lorraine 1930-1965 25
Hansen, Joyce 1942- 41
Hanson, Curtis 1945- 52
Hanson, Duane 1925-1996 39
Hardy, Thomas 1840-1928 69
Haring, Keith 1958-1990 21
Harris, Thomas 1940(?)- 34
Hart, Carolyn 1936- 69
Hartley, Marsden 1877-1943 63
Hartman, Rachel 1972- 68
Hartnett, Sonya 1968- 35
Haruf, Kent 1943- 44
Haskins, James S. 1941- 14
Hathorn, Libby 1943- 37
Haugaard, Erik Christian 1923- 36
Hautman, Pete 1952- 49
Hawke, Ethan 1970- 64
Hawking, Stephen 1942- 13
Hawks, Howard 1896-1977 67
Hawthorne, Nathaniel 1804-1864 18
Haydon, Elizabeth 46
Hayes, Daniel 1952- 29
Heaney, Seamus 1939- 61
Hearn, Lafcadio 1850-1904 79
Heat-Moon, William Least 1939- 9, 66
Heckerling, Amy 1954- 22, 74
Heinlein, Robert 1907-1988 17
Heitzmann, Kristen 78
Heller, Joseph 1923-1999 24
Hellman, Lillian 1906-1984 47
Hemingway, Ernest 1899-1961 19
Heneghan, James 1930- 54
Henkes, Kevin 1960- 59
Henley, Beth 1952- 70
Henry, O. 1862-1910 41
Hentoff, Nat 1925- 4, 42
Herbert, Frank 1920-1986 21
Hergé 1907-1983 55
Hermes, Patricia 1936- 15, 60
Hernandez, Lea 57
Herrera, Juan Felipe 1948- 44
Herriman, George 1880-1944 43
Herriot, James 1916-1995 .... 1, 54
Hersey, John 1914-1993 29
Hesse, Hermann 1877-1962 43

Hesse, Karen 1952- 27, 52
Hickman, Janet 1940- 62
Highsmith, Patricia 1921-1995 48
Highwater, Jamake 1942(?)-2001 .... 7, 69
Hijuelos, Oscar 1951- 25
Hildebrandt, Greg 1939- 12, 73
Hildebrandt, Tim 1939- 12, 73
Hillenburg, Stephen 1962- 53
Hillerman, Tony 1925- 6, 40
Hilton, James 1900-1954 76
Hinton, S.E. 1950- 2, 33
Hitchcock, Alfred 1899-1980 22
Hite, Sid 1954- 72
Ho, Minfong 1951- 29
Hobbs, Valerie 1941- 28, 78
Hobbs, Will 1947- 14, 39
Hockenberry, John 1957- 48
Hockney, David 1937- 17
Hoffman, Alice 1952- 37
Hoffman, Mary 1945- 59
Hoffman, Nina Kiriki 1955- 52
Hogarth, William 1697-1764 56
Holland, Isabelle 1920-2002 .... 11, 64
Holman, Felice 1919- 17
Holt, Kimberly Willis 1960- 38
Holzer, Jenny 1950- 50
Hoover, H.M. 1935- 11, 69
Hopkins, Ellen 1955- 80
Hopkins, Lee Bennett 1938- 18
Hopkinson, Nalo 1960- 40
Hopper, Edward 1882-1967 33
Hornby, Nick 1958- 74
Hornschemeier, Paul 1977- 77
Housman, A.E. 1859-1936 66
Houston, James 1921-2005 18
Houston, Jeanne Wakatsuki 1934- 49
Howard, Robert E. 1906-1936 80
Howard, Ron 1954- 8, 48
Howarth, Lesley 1952- 29
Howe, Norma 1930- 41
Howker, Janni 1957- 9, 68
Hoyt, Erich 1950- 58
Hubbard, L. Ron 1911-1986 64
Hudson, Jan 1954-1990 22
Huff, Tanya 1957- 38
Hughes, Albert 1972- 51
Hughes, Allen 1972- 51
Hughes, Dean 1943- 53
Hughes, John 1950(?)- 7
Hughes, Langston 1902-1967 12
Hughes, Monica 1925-2003 19
Hugo, Victor 1802-1885 28
Hunt, Helen 1963- 70
Hunt, Irene 1907-2001 18
Hunter, Kristin 1931- 21
Hunter, Mollie 1922- 13, 71
Huntington, Anna Hyatt 1876-1973 79
Hurd, Gale Anne 1955- 17

Hurmence, Belinda 1921- 17
Hurston, Zora Neale 1891-1960 .... 15, 71
Huxley, Aldous 1894-1963 11
Ibbotson, Eva 1925- 53
Ibsen, Henrik 1828-1906 46
Ingold, Jeanette 43
Irving, John 1942- 8, 62
Irving, Washington 1783-1859 56
Irwin, Hadley 13
Ishiguro, Kazuo 1954- 58
Ishinomori, Shotaro 1938-1998 70
Jackson, Peter 1961- 49
Jackson, Shirley 1919-1965 9
Jacques, Brian 1939- 20
Jakes, John 1932- 32
Janeczko, Paul B. 1945- 9, 28
Jeanne-Claude 1935- 53
Jefferson, Thomas 1743-1826 54
Jelinek, Elfriede 1946- 68
Jenkins, Jerry B. 1949- 39
Jennings, Paul 1943- 28
Jeunet, Jean-Pierre 1955- 56
Jewett, Sarah Orne 1849-1909 76
Jiang, Ji-li 1954- 42
Jiménez, Francisco 1943- 32
Jinks, Catherine 1963- 75
Johansen, Iris 38
Johns, Jasper 1930- 63
Johnson, Angela 1961- 32
Johnson, James Weldon 1871-1938 73
Johnson, Magic 1959- 17
Johnson, Maureen 77
Johnson, Philip 1906-2005 80
Johnston, Julie 1941- 27
Johnston, Lynn 1947- 12, 63
Johnston, Norma 12, 57
Jones, Chuck 1912-2002 2
Jones, Diana Wynne 1934- 12
Jones, Edward P. 1950- 71
Jones, Gwyneth A. 1952- 80
Jonze, Spike 1969(?)- 47
Jordan, June 1936-2002 .... 2, 66
Jordan, Robert 1948- 26
Jordan, Sherryl 1949- 45
Joyce, James 1882-1941 42
Joyce, William 1957- 38
Judge, Mike 1963(?)- 20
Junger, Sebastian 1962- 28
Kadohata, Cynthia 1956- 71
Kafka, Franz 1883-1924 31
Kahlo, Frida 1907-1954 47
Kandinsky, Wassily 1866-1944 64
Kane, Bob 1916-1998 .... 8, 70
Karr, Kathleen 1946- 44
Kassem, Lou 1931- 58
Katchor, Ben 1951- 54
Katz, Jon 43
Katz, Welwyn Wilton 1948- 19

Kaufman, Bel 1911- 4, 65
Kaufman, Charlie 1953- 68
Kay, Guy Gavriel 1954- 36
Kaysen, Susanna 1948- 42
Keaton, Buster 1895-1966 79
Keats, John 1795-1821 58
Keeping, Charles 1924-1988 26
Kehret, Peg 1936- 40
Keillor, Garrison 1942- 2, 62
Kelleher, Victor 1939- 31
Kellerman, Jonathan 1949- 35
Kelley, David E. 1956- 41
Kelly, Brigit Pegeen 1951- 71
Kelly, Walt 1913-1973 56
Kelton, Elmer 1926- 78
Kennedy, William 1928- 1, 73
Kenyon, Jane 1947-1995 63
Kerouac, Jack 1922-1969 25
Kerr, M.E. 1927- 2, 23
Kertesz, Imre 1929- 73
Kesel, Barbara 1960- 63
Kesey, Ken 1935-2001 25
Ketchum, Jack 1946- 61
Keyes, Daniel 1927- 23
Kherdian, David 1931- 42
Kidd, Chip 1964- 62
Kidd, Sue Monk 72
Kidder, Tracy 1945- 35
Kiernan, Caitlin R. 1964- 58
Kimmel, Haven 1965- 63
Kincaid, Jamaica 1949- 13, 56
Kindl, Patrice 1951- 55
King, Laurie R. 1952- 29
King, Stephen 1947- 1, 17
Kingsolver, Barbara 1955- 15
Kingston, Maxine Hong 1940- 8, 55
Kinkade, Thomas 1958- 64
Kinsella, W.P. 1935- 7, 60
Kipling, Rudyard 1865-1936 32
Kirby, Jack 1917-1994 49
Kirkpatrick, Katherine 1964- 75
Kiyama, Henry Yoshitaka 1885-1951 66
Klass, David 1960- 26
Klass, Sheila Solomon 1927- 34
Klause, Annette Curtis 1953- 27
Klee, Paul 1879-1940 31
Klein, Norma 1938-1989 .... 2, 35
Klein, Robin 1936- 21
Klimt, Gustav 1862-1918 61
Knowles, John 1926-2001 .... 10, 72
Knox, Elizabeth 1959- 80
Knudson, R.R. 1932- 20
Koertge, Ron 1940- 12, 43
Kogawa, Joy 1935- 47
Koja, Kathe 1960- 59
Koller, Jackie French 1948- 28
Kollwitz, Kathe 1867-1945 62
Konigsburg, E.L. 1930- 3, 41

Koontz, Dean R. 1945- 9, 31
Kooser, Ted 1939- 69
Korman, Gordon 1963- 10, 44
Koss, Amy Goldman 1954- 45
Kozol, Jonathan 1936- 46
Krakauer, Jon 1954- 24
Kramer, Stanley 1913-2001 68
Kress, Nancy 1948- 28, 75
Krisher, Trudy 1946- 32
Krueger, William Kent 1950- 79
Kubert, Joe 1926- 58
Kubrick, Stanley 1928-1999 30
Kuklin, Susan 1941- 27
Kundera, Milan 1929- 2, 62
Kuper, Peter 1958- 67
Kurosawa, Akira 1910-1998 .... 11, 64
Kurtz, Katherine 1944- 21
Kushner, Tony 1956- 61
Lackey, Mercedes 1950- 13
LaFaye, A. 1970- 44
LaHaye, Tim 1926- 39
Lahiri, Jhumpa 1967 56
Laird, Christa 1944- 30
Laird, Elizabeth 1943- 63
L'Amour, Louis 1908-1988 16
Lang, Fritz 1890-1976 65
Lange, Dorothea 1895-1965 14
Lansdale, Joe R. 1951- 50
Lantz, Francess 1952- 37
Lapham, David 1970- 72
Larson, Erik 65
Larson, Gary 1950- 1, 62
Larson, Jonathan 1960-1996 28
Lasky, Kathryn 1944- 19
Lasseter, John 1957- 65
Lawhead, Stephen R. 1950- 29
Lawrence, Iain 1955- 51
Lawrence, Jacob 1917-2000 30
Lawrence, Martha C. 1956- 61
Lean, David 1908-1991 65
Lear, Edward 1812-1888 48
Lebling, Dave 1950- 64
le Carré, John 1931- 42
Le Corbusier 1887-1965 66
Lee, Ang 1954- 44
Lee, Harper 1926- 13
Lee, Marie G. 1964- 27
Lee, Spike 1957- 4, 29
Lee, Stan 1922- 5, 49
Lee, Tanith 1947- 15
Legrow, M. Alice 79
Le Guin, Ursula K. 1929- 9, 27
Leguizamo, John 1965- 64
Lehane, Dennis 1965- 56
Lehman, Barbara 1963- 72
Leiber, Fritz 1910-1992 65
Leibovitz, Annie 1949- 11, 61
Leigh, Mike 1943- 72

Lem, Stanislaw 1921-2006 75
LeMieux, A.C. 1954- 40
L'Engle, Madeleine 1918-2007 .... 1, 28
Leonard, Elmore 1925- 22, 59
Leonardo da Vinci 1452-1519 40
Lessing, Doris 1919- 57
Lester, Julius 1939- 12, 51
Lethem, Jonathan 1964- 43
Letterman, David 1947- 10, 61
Levin, Betty 1927- 23
Levine, Gail Carson 1947- 37
Levinson, Barry 1942- 25
Levitin, Sonia 1934- 13, 48
Levoy, Myron 19
Lewis, E.B. 1956- 71
Lewis, C.S. 1898-1963 .... 3, 39
Lewis, Wyndham 1882-1957 77
Lichtenstein, Roy 1923-1997 55
Lin, Maya 1959- 20
Lindskold, Jane 1962- 55
Lingard, Joan 1932- 38
Link, Kelly 1969- 53
Linklater, Richard 1962- 28
Lipsyte, Robert 1938- 7, 45
Lisle, Janet Taylor 1947- 60
Littke, Lael J. 1929- 76
Little, Jean 1932- 43
Lloyd Webber, Andrew 1948- 1, 38
Llywelyn, Morgan 1937- 29
Lobel, Anita 1934- 70
Loeb, Jeph 1958- 73
London, Jack 1876-1916 .... 13, 75
Loos, Anita 1893-1981 77
Lopez, Barry 1945- 9, 63
Lovecraft, H.P. 1890-1937 14
Lovesey, Peter 1936- 79
Lowell, Amy 1874-1925 57
Lowry, Lois 1937- 5, 32
Lubar, David 1954- 52
Lucas, George 1944- 1, 23
Ludlum, Robert 1927-2001 .... 10, 59
Luhrmann, Baz 1962- 74
Lunn, Janet 1928- 38
Lupica, Mike 1952- 77
Lustig, Arnost 1926- 3
Lutes, Jason 1967- 54
Lynch, Chris 1962- 19, 44
Lynch, David 1946- 55
Lyons, Mary E. 1947- 26
Macaulay, David 1946- 21
MacDonald, George 1824-1905 57
MacGregor, Rob 75
Machiavelli, Niccolò 1469-1527 58
MacKay-Lyons, Brian 1954- 77
Mackler, Carolyn 1973- 56
MacLachlan, Patricia 1938- 18
MAD Magazine 13
Magorian, Michelle 1947- 49

Magritte, René 1898-1967 41
Maguire, Gregory 1954- 22
Maher, Bill 1956- 56
Mahfouz, Naguib 1911-2006 49
Mahy, Margaret 1936- 8, 46
Mailer, Norman 1923-2007 31
Major, Kevin 1949- 16
Malamud, Bernard 1914-1986 16
Mamet, David 1947- 3, 60
Mandel, Babaloo 1949(?)- 69
Manet, Édouard 1832-1883 58
Manship, Paul 1885-1966 78
Mantello, Joe 1962- 73
Marchetta, Melina 1965- 69
Marcus, Greil 1945- 58
Margulies, Donald 1954- 57
Marillier, Juliet 1948- 50
Marino, Jan 1936- 39
Mark, Mary Ellen 1940- 52
Marrin, Albert 1936- 35
Marsden, John 1950- 20
Marsh, Dave 1950- 52
Marshall, Garry 1934- 3
Marshall, Penny 1943- 10, 62
Martel, Yann 1963- 67
Martin, Ann M. 1955- 6, 42
Martin, George R.R. 1948- 35
Martin, Steve 1945- 53
Mason, Bobbie Ann 1940- 5, 42
Massey, Sujata 1964- 76
Masson, Sophie 1959- 43
Matas, Carol 1949- 22
Mathabane, Mark 1960- 4, 39
Matheson, Richard 1926- 31
Mathis, Sharon Bell 1937- 12
Matisse, Henri 1869-1954 34
Matthiessen, Peter 1927- 6, 40
Maugham, W. Somerset 1874-1965 55
May, Julian 1931- 17
Mayne, William 1928- 20
Mazer, Harry 1925- 5, 36
Mazer, Norma Fox 1931- 5, 36
McBain, Ed 1926-2005 39
McCafferty, Megan 59
McCaffrey, Anne 1926- 6, 34
McCall, Nathan 1955(?)- 59
McCammon, Robert 1952- 17
McCarthy, Cormac 1933- 41
McCaughrean, Geraldine 1951- 23
McCay, Winsor 1869(?)-1934 44
McCourt, Frank 1930- 61
McCrumb, Sharyn 1948- 27
McCullers, Carson 1917-1967 21
McCullough, Colleen 1938(?)- 36
McCullough, David 1933- 71
McDaniel, Lurlene 1944- 15, 38
McDonagh, Martin 1970- 71
McDonald, Joyce 1946- 47

McFarlane, Todd 1961- 34
McGraw, Eloise Jarvis 1915-2000 41
McGruder, Aaron 1974- 68
McHugh, Maureen F. 1959- 56
McInerney, Jay 1955- 18
McInerney, Ralph 1929- 78
McKenzie, Nancy 1948- 78
McKillip, Patricia 1948- 14
McKinley, Robin 1952- 4, 33
McKissack, Patricia C. 1944- 38
McMillan, Terry 1951- 21
McMurtry, Larry 1936- 15
McNally, Terrence 1939- 62
McPhee, John 1931- 61
McPherson, James M. 1936- 57
Mead, Alice 1952- 59
Meltzer, Milton 1915- 8, 45
Melville, Herman 1819-1891 25
Mendes, Sam 1965- 63
Meretzky, Steve 1957- 65
Merton, Thomas 1915-1968 61
Mertz, Barbara 1927- 24, 74
Meyer, Carolyn 1935- 16, 48
Meyer, Stephenie 1973- 77
Meyers, Nancy 1949- 44
Michaels, Lorne 1944- 12, 62
Michelangelo 1475-1564 43
Michener, James A. 1907(?)-1997 27
Miéville, China 1972- 52
Mies van der Rohe, Ludwig 1886-1969 54
Mignola, Mike 1960(?)- 54
Mikaelsen, Ben 1952- 37
Miklowitz, Gloria D. 1927- 6, 64
Miller, Arthur 1915-2005 15
Miller, Frank 1957- 45
Millhauser, Steven 1943- 76
Millidge, Gary Spencer 1961- 74
Milosz, Czeslaw 1911-2004 62
Milton, John 1608-1674 65
Miró, Joan 1893-1983 30
Mishima, Yukio 1925-1970 50
Mitchard, Jacquelyn 1952- 34
Mitchell, Margaret 1900-1949 23
Miyamoto, Shigeru 1952- 58
Miyazaki, Hayao 1941- 37
Modesitt, L.E., Jr. 1943- 33
Modotti, Tina 1896-1942 53
Moeri, Louise 1924- 33
Mohr, Nicholasa 1938- 8, 46
Momaday, N. Scott 1934- 11, 64
Mondrian, Piet 1872-1944 63
Monet, Claude 1840-1926 25
Monette, Sarah 77
Montgomery, L.M. 1874-1942 12
Monty Python 7
Moon, Elizabeth 1945- 73
Moorcock, Michael 1939- 26
Moore, Alan 1953- 51
Moore, Henry 1898-1986 73
Moore, Michael 1954- 53
Moore, Terry 1954- 73
Morales, Yuyi 1968- 71
Mori, Kyoko 1957- 25
Moriarty, Jaclyn 80
Morpugo, Michael 1943- 37
Morris, Gerald 1963- 44
Morrison, Toni 1931- 1, 22, 61
Mosley, Walter 1952- 17, 57
Moss, Thylias 1954- 37
Mowat, Farley 1921- 1, 50
Mowry, Jess 1960- 29
Mukherjee, Bharati 1940- 46
Muller, Marcia 1944- 25
Munch, Edvard 1863-1944 29
Munro, H.H. 1870-1916 56
Murphy, Jim 1947- 20
Murphy, Shirley Rousseau 1928- 45
Myers, Mike 1963- 34
Myers, Walter Dean 1937- 4, 23
Na, An 1972- 53
Nabokov, Vladimir 1899-1977 45
Naidoo, Beverley 1943- 23
Naka, Yuji 1966(?)- 59
Namioka, Lensey 1929- 27
Napoli, Donna Jo 1948- 25
Nast, Thomas 1840-1902 56
Naylor, Gloria 1950- 6, 39
Naylor, Phyllis Reynolds 1933- 4, 29
Needle, Jan 1943- 23
Neiderman, Andrew 1940- 70
Nelson, Theresa 1948- 25
Neufeld, John 1938- 11
Nevelson, Louise 1900-1988 77
Newman, Sharan 1949- 40
Newth, Mette 1942- 48
Nicholson, William 1948- 47
Niven, Larry 1938- 27
Nix, Garth 1963- 27
Nixon, Joan Lowery 1927-2003 .... 12, 54
Nodelman, Perry 1942- 30
Noguchi, Isamu 1904-1988 52
Nolan, Han 1956- 28
Norris, Frank 1870-1902 57
Norton, Andre 1912-2005 14
Novik, Naomi 1973- 80
Nye, Naomi Shihab 1952- 27
Oates, Joyce Carol 1938- 15, 52
O'Brian, Patrick 1914-2000 55
O'Brien, Robert 1918-1973 6
O'Brien, Tim 1946- 16
O'Brien, Willis 1886-1962 77
O'Connor, Flannery 1925-1964 7
O'Dell, Scott 1898-1989 .... 3, 44
Oke, Janette 1935- 30
O'Keefe, Susan Heyboer 72
O'Keeffe, Georgia 1887-1986 20

Okimoto, Jean Davies 1942- 31
Olmsted, Frederick Law 1822-1903 56
Olsen, Tillie 1912-2007 51
Ondaatje, Michael 1943- 66
Oneal, Zibby 1934- 5, 41
O'Neill, Eugene 1888-1953 54
Oppel, Kenneth 1967- 53
Orlean, Susan 1955- 64
Orlev, Uri 1931- 20
Orwell, George 1903-1950 15
Otomo, Katsuhiro 1954- 74
Oughton, Jerrie 1937- 44
Outcault, R.F. 1863-1928- 79
Paik, Nam June 1932-2006 75
Palahniuk, Chuck 1962- 59
Paolini, Christopher 1983- 71
Paretsky, Sara 1947- 30
Park, Linda Sue 1960- 49
Park, Nick 1958- 32
Park, Paul 1954- 78
Parker, Robert B. 1932- 28
Parker, Trey 1969- 27
Parks, Gordon 1912-2006 36
Parks, Suzan-Lori 1964- 55
Parrish, Maxfield 1870-1966 59
Pascal, Francine 1938- 1, 40
Pastis, Stephan 1968- 76
Patchett, Ann 1963- 69
Paterson, Katherine 1932- 1, 31
Paton, Alan 1903-1988 26
Paton Walsh, Jill 1937- 11, 47
Patterson, James 1947- 25
Paulsen, Gary 1939- 2, 17
Payne, Alexander 1961- 77
Payne, C.D. 1949- 43
Paz, Octavio 1914-1998 50
Pearson, Kit 1947- 19
Pearson, Ridley 1953- 44
Peck, Richard 1934- 1, 24
Peck, Robert Newton 1928- 3, 43
Pei, I.M. 1917- 39
Penman, Sharon Kay 43
Perelman, S.J. 1904-1979 79
Peretti, Frank E. 1951- 48
Perez, Amada Irma 1951- 74
Peters, Ellis 1913-1995 31
Peters, Julie Anne 1952- 44
Pevsner, Stella 15
Peyton, K.M. 1929- 20
Pfaff, Judy 1946- 69
Pfeffer, Susan Beth 1948- 12, 55
Philbrick, Rodman 1951- 31
Phillips, Arthur 1969- 65
Phillips, Jayne Anne 1952- 57
Phipson, Joan 1912-2003 14
Picasso, Pablo 1881-1973 10
Picoult, Jodi 1966- 71
Pierce, Meredith Ann 1958- 13, 60

Pierce, Tamora 1954- 26
Pike, Christopher 13
Pini, Richard 1950- 12
Pini, Wendy 1951- 12
Pinkwater, Daniel 1941- 1, 46
Pipher, Mary 1947- 39
Plath, Sylvia 1932-1963 13
Platt, Kin 1911-2003 11
Platt, Randall Beth 1948- 44
Plummer, Louise 73
Plum-Ucci, Carol 1957- 60
Poe, Edgar Allan 1809-1849 14
Pohl, Frederik 1919- 24
Poitier, Sidney 1927- 60
Pollock, Jackson 1912-1956 32
Porter, Connie Rose 1959- 65
Porter, Katherine Anne 1890-1980 42
Potok, Chaim 1929-2002 .... 15, 50
Pound, Ezra 1885-1972 47
Powell, Randy 1956- 35
Powers, Tim 1952- 49
Poyer, David 1949- 80
Pratchett, Terry 1948- 19, 54
Pratt, Jane 1963(?)- 9, 61
Pressfield, Steven 1943- 77
Preston, Douglas 1956- 32
Preston, Richard 1954- 60
Price, Susan 1955- 42
Prince, Hal 1928- 58
Prince, Mary 1788(?)-1833(?) 71
Proust, Marcel 1871-1922 58
Pullman, Philip 1946- 15, 41
Puryear, Martin 1941- 70
Pyle, Howard 1853-1911 57
Qualey, Marsha 1953- 39
Quindlen, Anna 1953- 35
Quin-Harkin, Janet 1941- 6, 48
Rackham, Arthur 1867-1939 31
Raimi, Sam 1959- 67
Ramis, Harold 1944- 14
Rand, Ayn 1905-1982 10
Randall, Alice 1959- 64
Randle, Kristen D. 1952- 34
Raphael 1483-1520 65
Rapp, Adam 1968(?)- 41
Rawlings, Marjorie Kinnan 1896-1953 20
Rawls, Wilson 1913-1984 21
Ray, Man 1890-1976 35
Raymond, Alex 1909-1956 67
Reaver, Chap 1935-1993 31
Redford, Robert 1937- 15
Reed, Kit 1932- 68
Reeder, Carolyn 1937- 32
Rees, Celia 1949- 51
Reid Banks, Lynne 1929- 6, 49
Reilly, Rick 1958- 40
Reiner, Rob 1945- 13
Remarque, Erich Maria 1898-1970 27

Rembrandt 1606-1669 50
Rennison, Louise 1951- 52
Renoir, Pierre-Auguste 1841-1919 60
Resnick, Mike 1942- 38
Reza, Yasmina 1959- 69
Rice, Anne 1941- 9, 53
Rice, Christopher 1978- 61
Rich, Adrienne 1929- 69
Richter, Conrad 1890-1968 21
Rinaldi, Ann 1934- 15
Ringgold, Faith 1930- 19
Riordan, Rick 1964- 80
Rios, Alberto 1952- 66
Ritter, John H. 1951- 43
Rivera, Diego 1886-1957 38
Roach, Hal 1892-1992 74
Roach, Jay 1957- 42
Robbins, Tom 1936- 32
Robbins, Trina 1938- 61
Roberson, Jennifer 1953- 80
Roberts, Nora 1950- 35
Roberts, Willo Davis 1928-2004 13
Robeson, Paul 1898-1976 63
Robinet, Harriet Gillem 1931- 50
Robinson, Edwin Arlington 1869-1935 72
Robinson, Kim Stanley 1952- 26
Robinson, Marilynne 1943- 69
Robinson, Spider 1948- 35
Rockwell, Norman 1894-1978 54
Roddenberry, Gene 1921-1991 5
Rodgers, Richard 1902-1979 52
Rodin, Auguste 1840-1917 48
Rodowsky, Colby 1932- 23
Rodriguez, Luis J. 1954- 40
Rogers, Bruce Holland 70
Rohmer, Sax 1883-1959 80
Rolvaag, O.E. 1876-1931 75
Rosoff, Meg 1956- 70
Ross, Alex 1970- 53
Rossetti, Christina 1830-1894 51
Rossetti, Dante Gabriel 1828-1882 51
Rostkowski, Margaret I. 1945- 22
Roth, Philip 1933- 67
Rottman, S.L. 1970- 55
Rowland, Laura Joh 1953- 78
Rowling, J.K. 1965- 34
Rozan, S.J. 66
Rubens, Peter Paul 1577-1640 72
Rubin, Jason 1970(?)- 55
Rubinstein, Gillian 1942- 22
Rumi, Jalal al-Din 1207-1273 64
Rusch, Kristine Kathryn 1960- 59
Rushdie, Salmon 1947- 65
Russell, Charles Marion 1865-1926 77
Russell, P. Craig 1951- 58
Ryan, Pam Muñoz 47
Ryder, Albert Pinkham 1847-1917 78
Rylant, Cynthia 1954- 10, 45

Saarinen, Eero 1910-1961 65
Sacco, Joe 1960- 57
Sachar, Louis 1954- 35
Sachs, Marilyn 1927- 2
Sackville-West, V. 1892-1962 79
Sagan, Carl 1934-1996 .... 2, 62
Saint-Exupery, Antoine de 1900-1944 63
St. George, Judith 1931- 7, 72
Sakai, Stan 1953- 64
Sala, Richard 1956- 75
Salgado, Sebastião 1944- 49
Salinger, J.D. 1919- 2, 36
Salisbury, Graham 1944- 26
Salsitz, Rhondi Vilott 67
Salvatore, R.A. 1959- 31
Sanchez, Alex 1957- 51
Sandburg, Carl 1878-1967 24
Santiago, Esmeralda 1948- 43
Sargent, Pamela 1948- 18
Saroyan, William 1908-1981 66
Sartre, Jean-Paul 1905-1980 62
Satrapi, Marjane 1969- 55
Saul, John 1942- 10, 62
Savage, Augusta 1892-1962 45
Savage, Candace 1949- 60
Savitz, Harriet May 1933- 57
Sawyer, Robert J. 1960- 73
Scarborough, Elizabeth Ann 1947- 28
Scarrow, Simon 1962- 75
Schlosser, Eric 1960(?)- 60
Schmidt, Gary D. 1957- 73
Schroeder, Karl 1962- 75
Schulz, Charles M. 1922-2000 39
Schwarzenegger, Arnold 1947- 19, 59
Scieszka, Jon 1954- 21
Scoppettone, Sandra 1936- 11, 65
Scorsese, Martin 1942- 38
Scott, Jerry 1955- 70
Scott, Melissa 1960- 37
Scott, Ridley 1937- 13, 43
Scott, Sir Walter 1771-1832 22
Scottoline, Lisa 1956(?)- 30
Sebestyen, Ouida 1924- 8
Sebold, Alice 1963- 56
Sedaris, David 1957- 47
Seidelman, Susan 1952- 68
Seinfeld, Jerry 1954- 11, 68
Serling, Rod 1924-1975 14
Service, Pamela F. 1945- 20
Shaara, Jeff 1952- 70
Shaara, Michael 1929-1988 71
Shadyac, Tom 1959- 36
Shakespeare, William 1564-1616 35
Shan, Darren 1972- 48
Shange, Ntozake 1948- 9, 66
Shanley, John Patrick 1950- 74
Shaw, George Bernard 1856-1950 61
Shear, Claudia 1963- 70

Sheffield, Charles 1935-2002 38
Sheldon, Sidney 1917-2007 65
Shelley, Mary 1797-1851 20
Shelley, Percy Bysshe 1792-1822 61
Shepard, Jim 1956- 73
Shepard, Sam 1943- 1, 58
Shepherd, Jean 1921-1999 69
Sherburne, Zoa 1912-1995 13
Sherman, Cindy 1954- 41
Shilts, Randy 1951-1994 19
Shinn, Sharon 1957- 79
Shirow, Masamune 1961- 61
Shuster, Joe 1914-1992 50
Shusterman, Neal 1962- 21
Shteyngart, Gary 1972- 68
Shyamalan, M. Night 1970- 41
Siegal, Aranka 1930- 5
Siegel, Jerry 1914-1996 50
Silko, Leslie Marmon 1948- 14
Silverberg, Robert 1935- 24
Silverstein, Shel 1930-1999 40
Simic, Charles 1938- 78
Simmons, Dan 1948- 16, 54
Simon, Neil 1927 32
Sinclair, Upton 1878-1968 63
Singer, Bryan 1965- 44
Singer, Isaac Bashevis 1904-1991 32
Singleton, John 1968- 50
Skurzynski, Gloria 1930- 38
Sleator, William 1945- 5, 39
Slepian, Jan 1921- 20
Smiley, Jane 1949- 66
Smith, Clark Ashton 1893-1961 76
Smith, Cynthia Leitich 1967- 51
Smith, Dodie 1896-1990 68
Smith, Jeff 1960- 38
Smith, Kevin 1970- 37
Smith, Lane 1959- 21
Smith, L.J. 1964(?)- 53
Smith, Patrick 1972- 70
Smith, Sharon 1943- 72
Smith, Zadie 1976- 50
Smithson, Robert 1938-1973 76
Snicket, Lemony 1970- 46
Snyder, Gary 1930- 72
Snyder, Zilpha Keatley 1927- 15
Soderbergh, Steven 1963- 43
Solzhenitsyn, Alexander 1918-2008 49
Sondheim, Stephen 1930- 11, 66
Sones, Sonya 1953(?)- 51
Sonnenblick, Jordan 78
Sonnenfeld, Barry 1953- 26
Sorkin, Aaron 1961- 55
Soto, Gary 1952- 10, 37
Southall, Ivan 1921- 22
Southgate, Martha 1960(?)- 56
Sparks, Michael 1965- 71
Speare, Elizabeth George 1908-1994 76
Spencer-Fleming, Julia 68
Spenser, Edmund 1552(?)-1599 60
Spheeris, Penelope 1945- 46
Spiegelman, Art 1948- 10, 46
Spielberg, Steven 1947- 8, 24
Spinelli, Jerry 1941- 11, 41
Springer, Nancy 1948- 32
Stabenow, Dana 1952- 31
Stackpole, Michael A. 1957- 77
Stanton, Mary 1947- 75
Staples, Suzanne Fisher 1945 26
Staub, Wendy Corsi 1964- 79
Steadman, Ralph 1936- 45
Steel, Danielle 1947- 23
Stein, Gertrude 1874-1946 64
Steinbeck, John 1902-1968 12
Steinhauer, Olen 77
Stella, Frank 1936- 76
Stephenson, Neal 1959- 38
Sterling, Bruce 1954- 78
Stevenson, Robert Louis 1850-1894 24
Stevermer, Caroline 1955- 76
Stewart, Jon 1962- 57
Stewart, Mary 1916- 29, 73
Stieglitz, Alfred 1864-1946 59
Stine, R.L. 1943- 13
Stockton, Frank R. 1834-1902 68
Stoehr, Shelley 27
Stoker, Bram 1847-1912 23
Stoll, Clifford 1950- 68
Stolz, Mary 1920-2006 ..... 8, 73
Stoppard, Tom 1937- 63
Stone, Matt 1971- 27
Stone, Oliver 1946- 15
Story, Tim 1970- 68
Stout, Rex 1886-1975 79
Stowe, Harriet Beecher 1811-1896 53
Straczynski, J. Michael 1954- 30
Strasser, Todd 1950- 2, 35
Stratton, Allan 1951- 73
Strohmeyer, Sarah 72
Stroman, Susan 1954- 46, 74
Sturgeon, Theodore 1918-1985 51
Sutcliff, Rosemary 1920-1992 10
Swanwick, Michael 1950- 60
Swarthout, Glendon 1918-1992 55
Sweeney, Joyce 1955- 26
Swift, Jonathan 1667-1745 41
Swindells, Robert 1939- 20
Szymborska, Wislawa 1923- 76
Takahashi, Rumiko 1957- 62
Talbert, Marc 1953- 25
Talbot, Bryan 1952- 77
Tamar, Erika 30
Tan, Amy 1952- 9, 48
Tanner, Henry Ossawa 1859-1937 49
Tarantino, Quentin 1963- 58
Tartt, Donna 1963- 56

Tate, Eleanora E. 1948- 25
Taylor, G.P. 1958- 79
Taylor, Mildred D. 1943- 10, 47
Taylor, Theodore 1921-2006 .... 2, 19, 76
Taymor, Julie 1952- 42, 74
Temple, Frances 1945-1995 19
Tennyson, Alfred Lord 1809-1892 50
Tepper, Sheri S. 1929- 32
Terkel, Studs 1912-2008 32
Tezuka, Osamu 1926-1989 56
Theroux, Paul 1941- 28
Thesman, Jean 16
Thomas, Dylan 1914-1953 45
Thomas, Joyce Carol 1938- 12, 54
Thomas, Rob 1965- 25
Thompson, Craig 1975- 55
Thompson, Hunter S. 1939-2005 45
Thompson, Jill 1966- 52
Thompson, Julian F. 1927- 9, 70
Thoreau, Henry David 1817-1862 42
Thurber, James 1894-1961 56
Tiernan, Cate 1961- 49
Tiffany, Louis Comfort 1848-1933 78
Timm, Bruce 1961- 66
Titian 1488(?)-1576 70
Tolan, Stephanie S. 1942- 45
Tolkien, J.R.R. 1892-1973 10
Tolstoy, Leo 1828-1910 56
Tomine, Adrian 1974- 71
Toulouse-Lautrec, Henri de 1864-1901 ... 53
Townsend, John Rowe 1922-1973 11
Townsend, Robert 1957- 24
Townsend, Sue 1946- 28
Trottier, Chris 63
Trudeau, Garry 1948- 10, 60
Trueman, Terry 1947- 46
Tuck, Lily 1938- 74
Tune, Tommy 1939- 68
Turgenev, Ivan 1818-1883 58
Turner, J.M.W. 1775-1851 57
Turner, Megan Whalen 1965- 31
Turnley, David 1955- 72
Turow, Scott 1949- 53
Turtledove, Harry 1949- 33
Tutuola, Amos 1920-1997 76
Twain, Mark 1835-1910 20
Tyler, Anne 1941- 18, 60
Uchida, Yoshiko 1921-1992 16
Undset, Sigrid 1882-1949 77
Updike, John 1932- 36
Ure, Jean 1943- 33
Utzon, Jørn 1918- 55
Vail, Rachel 1966- 33
Vallejo, Boris 1941- 13
Van Allsburg, Chris 1949- 69
Van Draanen, Wendelin 36
van Gogh, Vincent 1853-1890 29
Van Sant, Gus 1952- 17

Vande Velde, Vivian 1951- 32
Vasarely, Victor 1908-1997 62
Veitch, Rick 1951- 75
Velázquez, Dieggo 1599-1660 65
Vermeer, Jan 1632-1675 46
Verne, Jules 1828-1905 16
Vidal, Gore 1925- 64
Viets, Elaine 1950- 80
Vinge, Joan D. 1948- 32
Vinge, Vernor 1944- 49
Voigt, Cynthia 1942- 3, 30
Vonnegut, Kurt 1922-2007 .... 6, 44
von Ziegesar, Cecily 1970- 56
Wachowski, Andy 1967- 58
Wachowski, Larry 1965- 58
Waddell, Martin 1941- 23
Waid, Mark 1962- 77
Walker, Alice 1944- 3, 33
Wallace, David Foster 1962- 50
Wallace, Rich 1957- 34
Ward, Lynd 1905-1985 80
Ware, Chris 1967- 47
Warhol, Andy 1928(?)-1987 12
Warner, Gertrude Chandler 1890-1979 ... 71
Wasserstein, Wendy 1950-2006 73
Waters, John 1946- 16
Watson, Ian 1943- 56
Watterson, Bill 1958- 9, 63
Watts, Leander 1956- 79
Waugh, Evelyn 1903-1966 78
Wayans, Keenan Ivory 1958- 11, 66
Weaver, Will 1950- 30
Weber, David 1952- 52
Weeks, Sarah 74
Wegman, William 1943- 15
Weis, Margaret 1948- 33
Welles, Orson 1915-1985 40
Wells, H.G. 1866-1946 18
Wells, Rosemary 1943- 13
Welty, Eudora 1909-2001 48
Werlin, Nancy 1961- 35
Wersba, Barbara 1932- 2, 30
West, Nathanael 1903-1940 77
Westall, Robert 1929-1993 12
Westerfeld, Scott 1963- 80
Westmore, Michael 1938- 74
Whale, James 1889-1957 75
Wharton, Edith 1862-1937 25
Whedon, Joss 1964- 50
Whelan, Gloria 1923- 42
Whelan, Michael 1950- 28
White, E.B. 1899-1985 62
White, Edmund 1940- 7
White, Minor 1908-1976 60
White, Robb 1909-1990 29
White, Ruth 1942- 41
White, T.H. 1906-1964 22
Whitman, Walt 1819-1892 42

Whitney, Gertrude Vanderbilt 1875-1942 57
Whitney, Phyllis A. 1903-2008 36
Whyte, Jack 1941- 45
Wieler, Diana 1961- 36
Wiesel, Elie 1928- 7, 54
Wiesenthal, Simon 1908-2005 36
Wiggins, Marianne 1947- 70
Wilbur, Richard 1921- 72
Wilde, Oscar 1854-1900 49
Wilder, Billy 1906-2002 66
Wilder, Laura Ingalls 1867-1957 26
Wilder, Thornton 1897-1975 29
Wilhelm, Kate 1928- 20
Willems, Mo 71
Willey, Margaret 1950- 27
Williams, Carol Lynch 1959- 39
Williams, Lori Aurelia 52
Williams, Tad 1957- 31
Williams, Tennessee 1911-1983 31
Williams, Walter Jon 1953- 48
Williams, William Carlos 1883-1963 46
Williams-Garcia, Rita 22
Williamson, Jack 1908-2006 76
Williamson, Kevin 1965- 30
Willis, Connie 1945- 30, 74
Wilson, Claggett 1887-1952- 79
Wilson, August 1945-2005 16
Wilson, Gahan 1930- 55
Winchester, Simon 1944- 66
Windling, Terry 1958- 59
Windsor, Patricia 1938- 23
Windsor-Smith, Barry 1949- 58
Winfrey, Oprah 1954- 32
Winick, Judd 1970- 41
Winspear, Jacqueline 1955- 71
Winston, Stan 1946- 45
Winton, Tim 1960- 34
Wise, Robert 1914 2005 76
Wittlinger, Ellen 1948- 36
Wodehouse, P.G. 1881-1975 65
Wojciechowska, Maia 1927-2002 .... 8, 46

Wolfe, Gene 1931- 35
Wolfe, Tom 1931- 8, 67
Wolff, Tobias 1945- 16
Wolff, Virginia Euwer 1937- 26
Wolfram, Stephen 1959- 51
Wolitzer, Meg 1959- 6, 63
Wolverton, Dave 1957- 55
Woo, John 1946- 35
Wood, Grant 1891-1942 72
Wood, June Rae 1946- 39
Wood, Wally 1927-1981 73
Woodson, Jacqueline 1964- 21, 54
Woolf, Virginia 1882-1941 44
Woolfolk, William 64
Wordsworth, William 1770-1850 70
Wormser, Richard 1933- 38
Wrede, Patricia C. 1953- 8, 53
Wright, Frank Lloyd 1867-1959 33
Wright, Richard 1908-1960 .... 5, 42
Wright, Will 1960- 60
Wrightson, Patricia 1921- 5, 58
Wyeth, Andrew 1917- 35
Wyler, William 1902-1981- 79
Wynne-Jones, Tim 1948- 31
Yamanaka, Lois-Ann 1961- 40
Yarbro, Chelsea Quinn 1942- 40
Yeats, William Butler 1865-1939 48
Yee, Paul 1956- 24
Yep, Laurence 1948- 5, 31
Yolen, Jane 1939- 4, 22
Yoshimoto, Banana 1964- 50
Zach, Cheryl 1947- 21
Zahn, Timothy 1951- 14, 56
Zelazny, Roger 1937-1995 .... 7, 68
Zemeckis, Robert 1952- 16
Zettel, Sarah 1966- 46
Zindel, Paul 1936-2003 .... 2, 37
Ziolkowski, Korczak 1908-1982 57
Zuiker, Anthony 1968- 64
Zusak, Markus 79